LINCOLN CHRISTIAN UNIVERSITY

WITHDRAWN
University of
Illinois Library
at Urbana-Champaign

THE COLLEGE PRESS NIV COMMENTARY

GENESIS
VOLUME 1

THE COLLEGE PRESS NIV COMMENTARY

GENESIS
VOLUME 1

PAUL KISSLING

Old Testament Series Co-Editors:

Terry Briley, Ph.D.
Lipscomb University

Paul Kissling, Ph.D.
TCMI Institute

 COLLEGE PRESS PUBLISHING COMPANY
Joplin, Missouri

Copyright © 2004 College Press Publishing Co.
All Rights Reserved
Printed and Bound in the United States of America

All Scripture quotations, unless indicated, are taken from
THE HOLY BIBLE: NEW INTERNATIONAL VERSION®.
Copyright © 1973, 1978, 1984 by International Bible Society.
Used by permission of Zondervan Publishing House.
All rights reserved.

Library of Congress Cataloging-in-Publication Data

Kissling, Paul J.
   Genesis/ by Paul Kissling.
     p.   cm. — (College Press NIV commentary. Old
  Testament series)
   Includes bibliographical references.
   ISBN 0-89900-875-5 (hardcover)
   1. Bible. O.T. Genesis—Commentaries.   I. Title.
II. Series.
BS1235.53.K57 2004
222'.11077—dc22

                                                   2004022577

A WORD FROM THE PUBLISHER

Years ago a movement was begun with the dream of uniting all Christians on the basis of a common purpose (world evangelism) under a common authority (the Word of God). The College Press NIV Commentary Series is a serious effort to join the scholarship of two branches of this unity movement so as to speak with one voice concerning the Word of God. Our desire is to provide a resource for your study of the Old Testament that will benefit you whether you are preparing a Bible School lesson, a sermon, a college course, or your own personal devotions. Today as we survey the wreckage of a broken world, we must turn again to the Lord and his Word, unite under his banner and communicate the life-giving message to those who are in desperate need. This is our purpose.

ABBREVIATIONS

AB ......*Anchor Bible*
ABD .....*Anchor Bible Dictionary*
ANET ....*Ancient Near Eastern Texts*
AOAT ....*Alter Orient und Altes Testament*
AUSS ....*Andrews University Seminary Studies*
BBC .....*IVP Bible Background Commentary*
BibSac ...*Bibliotheca Sacra*
BRev .....*Bible Review*
BTB .....*Biblical Theology Bulletin*
CBQ .....*Catholic Biblical Quartery*
COS .....*The Context of Scripture*, Edited by W.W. Hallo. 3 vols. Leiden, 1997–2002
EDOB ....*Eerdman's Dictionary of the Bible*
GKC .....*Gesenius' Hebrew Grammar*, ed. by E. Kautzsch, trans. by A.E. Cowley
HALOT ..*Hebrew and Aramaic Lexicon of the Old Testament*
HBT .....*Horizons in Biblical Theology*
HTR .....*Harvard Theological Review*
ICC ......*International Critical Commentary*
JAOS .....*Journal of the American Oriental Society*
JBL ......*Journal of Biblical Literature*
JBLMS ..*Journal of Biblical Literature Monograph Series*
JETS .....*Journal of the Evangelical Theological Society*
JJS ......*Journal of Jewish Studies*
JNES .....*Journal of Near Eastern Studies*
JPS ......*Jewish Publication Society*
JSOT .....*Journal for the Study of the Old Testament*
JSOTSup ..*Journal for the Study of the Old Testament Supplement Series*
JSS ......*Journal of Semitic Studies*

KJV . . . . . .King James Version
LXX . . . . . .Septuagint
MT . . . . . . .Masoretic Text
NASB . . . .New American Standard Bible
NICOT . . .New International Commentary on the Old Testament
NIDOTTE .New International Dictionary of Old Testament Theology and Exegesis
NIV . . . . . .New International Version
NRSV . . . .New Revised Standard Version
OTL . . . . . .Old Testament Library
POTT . . . .Peoples of Old Testament Times
SCJ . . . . . .Stone-Campbell Journal
SP . . . . . . .Samaritan Pentateuch
TBT . . . . . .The Bible Today
TDOT . . . .Theological Dictionary of the Old Testament, ed. by G.J. Botterweck and H. Ringgren
TynBul . . .Tyndale Bulletin
VT . . . . . . .Vetus Testamentum
VTSup . . .Vetus Testamentum Supplements
WBC . . . . .Word Bible Commentary
WTJ . . . . .Westminster Theological Journal
ZAW . . . . .Zeitschrift für die alttestamentliche Wissenschaft

Simplified Guide to Hebrew Writing

Heb. letter	Translit.	Pronunciation guide
א	ʾ	Has no sound of its own; like smooth breathing mark in Greek
ב	b	Pronounced like English B *or* V
ג	g	Pronounced like English G
ד	d	Pronounced like English D
ה	h	Pronounced like English H, silent at the end of words in the combination āh
ו	w	As a consonant, pronounced like English V or German W
וּ	û	Represents a vowel sound, pronounced like English long OO
וֹ	ô	Represents a vowel sound, pronounced like English long O
ז	z	Pronounced like English Z
ח	ḥ	Pronounced like German and Scottish CH and Greek χ (chi)
ט	ṭ	Pronounced like English T
י	y	Pronounced like English Y
כ/ך	k	Pronounced like English K
ל	l	Pronounced like English L
מ/ם	m	Pronounced like English M
נ/ן	n	Pronounced like English N
ס	s	Pronounced like English S
ע	ʿ	Stop in breath deep in throat before pronouncing the vowel
פ/ף	p/ph	Pronounced like English P *or* F
צ/ץ	ṣ	Pronounced like English TS/TZ
ק	q	Pronounced very much like כ (k)
ר	r	Pronounced like English R
שׂ	ś	Pronounced like English S, much the same as ס
שׁ	š	Pronounced like English SH
ת	t/th	Pronounced like English T *or* TH

Note that different forms of some letters appear at the end of the word (written right to left), as in כָּפַף (*kāphaph*, "bend") and מֶלֶךְ (*melek*, "king").

Vowels in Hebrew (except where the ו is used to represent a vowel sound), are represented by "vowel points" added to the consonant. For example: הַ (*ha*, "the"). The letter *yod* (י, *y*) also becomes a *part of* certain vowel sounds, as in the conjunction כִּי (*kî*, "that"). Originally, Hebrew was written as "unpointed" text, with just the consonants. For convenience, the different vowel points are shown below on the letter Aleph (א).

אָ	ā	Pronounced not like long A in English, but like the broad A or AH sound
אַ	a	The Hebrew short A sound, but more closely resembles the broad A (pronounced for a shorter period of time) than the English short A
אֶ	e	Pronounced like English short E

אֵ	ē	Pronounced like English long A, or Greek η (eta)
אִ	i	Pronounced like English short I
אִ	î	The same vowel point is sometimes pronounced like אִי (see below)
אָ	o	This vowel point sometimes represents the short O sound
אֹ	ō	Pronounced like English long O
אֻ	u	The vowel point ֻ sometimes represents a shorter U sound and
אוּ	ū	is sometimes pronounced like the וּ (û, see above)
אֵי	ê	Pronounced much the same as אֵ
אֶי	ê	Pronounced much the same as אֶ
אִי	î	Pronounced like long I in many languages, or English long E
אְ	ə	An unstressed vowel sound, like the first E in the word "severe"
אֳ, אֲ, אֱ	ŏ, ă, ĕ	Shortened, unstressed forms of the vowels אָ, אַ, and אֶ, pronounced very similarly to אְ

ACKNOWLEDGMENTS

This commentary has been written during the stolen moments of a busy life of teaching around the world and mentoring students. It began with a Sabbatical Semester generously granted by Great Lakes Christian College and largely spent at Calvin College's fine library. A three-year hiatus while I served as Vice President of Academic Affairs has delayed its completion. I am grateful for the patience and encouragement of successive editors at College Press, John Hunter and Dru Ashwell. The book of Genesis has been an almost lifelong source of stimulation and personal growth for me. It began when I memorized the King James Version of the text as a new Christian for Bible Bowl. I have benefited greatly from my teachers of Genesis, John Sailhamer and Gordon Wenham. Every biblical commentator stands on the shoulders of those who have taught him and preceded him, and I have learned much from the numerous fine commentaries currently available. My doctoral supervisor at Sheffield, David Clines, taught me much about reading biblical narrative. I am grateful. My friend from those halcyon days at Sheffield, Laurence Turner, has had an important impact on my approach. John Nugent, a former student and now a valued colleague, gave helpful feedback on the introduction and first three chapters. The feedback from papers on Genesis 1–11 delivered at various conferences over the years has sharpened my thinking. I am only too conscious of the fact that weaknesses remain despite the counsel of such a company of friends.

The primary audience of this commentary is, however, not the isolated scholar but the church. I am thankful for a father who loved the Bible and his children. I am equally grateful for supportive Christian communities in Toledo; Chicago; Niles, Michigan; Ancona, Illinois; Chester, England; and for the last dozen years our church family at Meridian Christian Church in Okemos, Michigan. I am aware that these good Christian people will probably not agree with every idea expressed in this commentary, but I hope they will see my own passion for Genesis as Scripture for the church and catch a glimpse of its power to speak to us through the centuries.

I would not have been able to complete this work without the support of my family on both the Lantzer and Kissling sides. My sons, Joshua and Jeremiah, have made life full and rich. But my wife Cathy is owed debts of gratitude which I will never be able to repay. No one could have been a better or more supportive partner in ministry, in life, and in service to the church. I am still a little in awe of her Christian graciousness and servant's heart. Inadequate though the gift be, I dedicate this work to her.

INTRODUCTION

Genesis is the first book of the Bible, the first book of the Christian Old Testament, and the first book of the Pentateuch. As such it provides the foundation upon which the rest of Scripture builds both historically and theologically. The interpretation of Genesis has been the subject of heated debate in the church throughout its history and for the last two centuries or so in particular. The questions of authorship, unity, and the authenticity of its depiction of creation and the early history of humanity are vexing questions that continue to divide Christians. While these questions are important to us, they were not the questions which Genesis was designed to answer. The author (or authors) does not identify himself. He tells us very little about how God created and never attempts to date creation. The author of Genesis, writing under the inspiration of the Holy Spirit, was not addressing the question of the theory of evolution in twenty-first-century Western culture. If Genesis is to speak to us, we must learn to put our questions on the sidelines and attempt to understand it on its own terms. If I have anything new to say about Genesis (it has been well served by commentators), it is based on a fundamental conviction that this wonderful book's message is best understood on its own terms. The recent history of the interpretation of Genesis has been noteworthy for the obviousness with which interpreters come to the text with their own contemporary agendas. I am not exempt from having agendas. I will, however, attempt to be forthright about them at the beginning of this commentary.

I write as a Christian Old Testament scholar, minister, and elder. For me Genesis is Scripture for the church. While the tools of critical scholarship are helpful and are used throughout this commentary, I deliberately choose to interpret the final, canonical form of the text. It is that canonical form which was accepted by God's people as Scripture and as therefore useful for teaching, rebuking, correcting and training in righteousness (2 Tim 3:16). The acceptance of Genesis as Scripture probably took place no earlier than the time of Ezra c. 458 B.C.[1] While much[2] of the Pentateuch was undoubtedly written much earlier, its widespread acceptance as Scripture for God's people evidently occurred only after the partial return from Babylonian exile.

The implied audience for the Pentateuch,[3] Israel newly in the promised land, was in remarkably parallel circumstances to the "original canonical audience," Israel recently returned to the promised land after exile. The Israel which publicly accepted the Pentateuch as Scripture in the time of Ezra had experienced the dispersion and exile of most of its people. Relatively speaking a small number had returned. Israel was a fledgling nation yet again. Israel was once again without a king. The priestly mediated worship at the sanctuary was vital to the unity and spiritual health of its people just as worship at the tabernacle had been for the nation at its beginnings. The danger of assimilating with those around them and thus compromising their loyalty to the one and only God was an ever-present danger.[4] The law, originally given to Israel at Mt. Sinai, was being reestablished as the norm for Israel's corporate life. By reading from the point of view of the original canonical audience it is as though we look over the shoulder of a postexilic Jew who is reading

---

[1]While the Pentateuch had been available for some time, the fact that it (or at least a substantial part of it) had been lost prior to the time of Josiah (2 Kings 22:3-13) indicates that it did not at that time yet enjoy canonical status for most of the nation.

[2]For the evidence of updating in the Pentateuch see below.

[3]I am not suggesting that the Pentateuch in its final form is that early. See the discussion of date and authorship below.

[4]Notice how the problem of mixed marriages in Ezra 9 is described in terms which recall early Israel's temptation to intermarry with the original inhabitants of the land and thus adopt their gods: "The people of Israel, the priests, and the Levites have not separated themselves from the peoples of the lands with their abominations, from the Canaanites, the Hittites, the Perizzites, the Jebusites, the Ammonites, the Moabites, the Egyptians, and the Amorites. For they have taken some of their daughters as wives for themselves and for their sons. Thus the holy seed has mixed itself with the peoples of the lands and in this faithlessness the officials and leaders have led the way." (Ezra 9:1b,2, NRSV).

the Pentateuch. He or she hears the narrative of Genesis and imagines himself or herself as a member of Israel just after entering the land. In a sense we are reading over the shoulder of someone (a postexilic Jew) who is reading over the shoulder of someone else (a Jew recently come into the land under Joshua). We ask, "What would the Pentateuch mean for the postexilic Jew who is looking back on the original, founding events of the nation of Israel?" It is this "double reading over the shoulder" which I attempt in this commentary.

But I also read as a Christian who has "read the last chapter of the book." As a Christian I know how the story "turns out," and I cannot help but eventually read with the totality of Scripture in mind. In this commentary I will attempt to put this last stage of reading off until the text has been understood on its own terms in its final canonical form. I am also aware that I write as a white, American male and that sometimes my background, education, social class, gender, and race inevitably affect my reading. My only defense is that I have honestly tried to be aware of my own tendencies and not allow them to influence my interpretations.

My biggest agenda is my lifelong concern that the Old Testament actually speak to the Church today. While Christians of all sorts affirm the inspiration and authority of the Old Testament, in practice, most Christians ignore the Old Testament. My hope is that, as you read this commentary along with Scripture, you will catch some of the vitality and relevance that has been such a source of spiritual nourishment for me.

THE PURPOSES OF GENESIS

Genesis functions as the introduction to the Pentateuch. As such it explains how it came about that the people of Israel arose and were called to be God's people. The nation to which the Pentateuch is addressed is about to enter the promised land. There they will face the culture and religion of the inhabitants of Canaan. The polytheistic nature religion of the Canaanites is a great temptation to Israel. The long stay in Egypt had had its impact on Israel. At the first sight of trouble they revert to polytheism. The plaster on the tablets of the Ten Commandments had not yet dried before Israel had broken several of them. The laws which Yahweh reveals to Israel and which are recorded in the Pentateuch are designed to prevent Israel from falling into the destructive patterns of life present in Canaan. While Genesis certainly explains in historical terms how it came about that Israel arose and ended up in Egypt, it tells this story in a way that has particular relevance to its intended audience which is about to face the pressure of Canaan. For example, Genesis 1–11 functions to explain why the God who created the world ultimately began to work primarily through a single nation beginning with Abram. Moreover the way in which Genesis 1–11 describes creation, the Fall, and the Flood makes it obvious that the author has the needs of Israel in mind.

In ways that would have been obvious to the original audience, Genesis 1–11 tells its story of creation and flood as arguments against the creation and flood stories of the polytheistic world in which Israel lived. For example, the worship of the sun and moon as major deities in the ancient Near East and Egypt is well attested from the earliest times. The Hebrew words for "sun" (*šemeš*) and moon (*yārēaḥ*) were often understood as the sun god and the moon god or goddess. Genesis, not wanting to suggest that God created the Sun god and the Moon god, used instead "the greater light" and "the lesser light" to refer to them. They are merely inanimate objects. They are not subordinate gods. In narrating the creation of the stars, which were widely believed to control the destiny of humankind, the author of Genesis 1 treats them as almost an afterthought. Unlike the myths with which Israel was familiar, creation is not portrayed as some sort of conflict between the high god and the natural world. There is no battle with the Sea. The "expanse" is not constructed from one half of the arched corpse of the goddess Tiamat. It merely separates the water in the clouds from the water in seas, lakes, and rivers. God has no resistance when creating. He merely speaks and it happens. Humankind is not created to provide the gods with food but to rule over creation as God's vice-regent. The Flood is sent as a judgment on the violence and sexual immorality of the world, not because the noise of an overpopulating humanity disturbs the sleep of the gods! In Genesis matter is not eternal but is created "in the beginning." It therefore has no power to rival the creator. The ancient myths envisioned creation as a battle with the forces of chaos. As a result, gradually, as chaos was defeated, things got better. An imperfect creation improved over time. In Genesis the opposite is the case. A perfect ("very good") creation is ruined by human sin and its consequences. Sin and its consequences get successively worse ultimately culminating in the universal judgment of the Flood. In all these ways (and in many others dealt with in the commentary) Genesis is critiquing the creation myths which were so much a part of the polytheistic worldview of the ancient Near East.

But Genesis also speaks to the situation of its implied audience by showing that the laws which the LORD gave Israel at Sinai were founded in creation and were operative in one form or another from the earliest times. Jacob and Abraham tithe even though they had not received the commandment to tithe, as Israel had. God ceases from creation and rests in chapter 2 and in so doing sanctifies the Sabbath. The law of the Sabbath originated in creation and is based on principles which are built into the nature of creation. The description of the garden of Eden reminds the intended audience of the recently constructed tabernacle, or to be more precise, vice versa. The offerings of Cain and Abel are described in terms reminiscent of the laws of sacrifice. The fact that Abel gave the firstborn while Cain merely gave some of his crops (and not the firstfruits) explains for the intended audience why Abel's sacrifice is accepted and Cain's is not. There is no record in Genesis of sacrifice being commanded or expected but Cain and Abel's narrative seems to suggest that the laws of sacrifice are a natural response of humanity to God. Joseph has not received the commandment, "Thou shall not commit adultery," and yet he knows it is a grievous sin against God. All of these examples (and there are numerous others) reassure the implied audience that God's laws are based on universal principles.

While the specific laws given to Israel fit Israel's situation in the promised land, Genesis reassures them that they are not the arbitrary imposition of a despotic deity. From the earliest times humanity at its best was obedient to their underlying principles. A form of what theologians sometimes refer to as "natural law" is operative. Genesis 26:5 says that "Abraham obeyed my voice and kept my charge, my commandments, my statutes, and my laws." The promise is extended to Isaac because of Abraham's obedience to God's law. The words for law here are the specific words (מִשְׁמַרְתִּי מִצְוֹתַי חֻקּוֹתַי וְתוֹרֹתָי, *mišmartî mişôthay ḥuqqōthay wᵉthôrōthāy*). While the specific regulations of the law were not revealed until Sinai, Abraham obeys even some of the specifics of the law as later revealed. This seems most naturally explicable in terms that the laws of Sinai are based on fundamental and earlier principles which were available to people like Abraham without specific revelation from God. Noah even knows the difference between clean and unclean animals. The duty of levirate marriage is presumed in the story of Judah's sons in Genesis 38.

HOW TO READ GENESIS

The approach that I have adopted to reading Genesis in this commentary is discussed in detail below.

READING GENESIS CANONICALLY

Genesis is read in this commentary as part of the canon of Holy Scripture. As a result it should be read both inter- and intratextually. In practice this means that the reader should be sensitive to the repeated echoes of earlier parts of the canon. This inter- and intratextual echoing is so pervasive that it is hard to imagine that it is accidental. It begins within Genesis itself. For example, the Flood story is echoed in many ways in the Sodom and Gomorrah narrative. What God did on a worldwide basis in the Flood he also did at Sodom. It is no accident that the chief character in each narrative is a righteous person in the midst of a violent and sexually exploitative time. In each case there is cataclysmic judgment. Each cataclysm is followed by the fall of the righteous person into a drunken state during which he is sexually abused by one of his children. The upshot of that abuse is a people who ultimately fall under God's curse. The narratives of the Flood and Sodom and Gomorrah are constructed in such a way as to invite the reader to notice the commonality and differences between these parallel narratives.

This intertextual echoing also happens between Genesis and the rest of the Pentateuch. For example the use of the words, "image" and "likeness" in the creation of humanity as God's representative ruler over creation would probably be read as one part of the anti-idolatry polemic of the Pentateuch. God already has an "image"; he does not need for humanity to misrepresent him by making one of inert wood or ivory or gold. Israel is not to make an image of God because he already has an image. This intertextual reading spares the interpreter from many anachronistic speculations about just what the image of God in humanity really consists of.

Intertextual reading does not stop with the Pentateuch but carries over into the rest of the Old Testament. The turning point of the book of Genesis is the decision by God to cease working with all nations and focus his efforts on a single family and its descendants. That theme is the theological center of the Pentateuch. But the theme does not stop at the end of Deuteronomy with Israel outside of the promised land. The story is continued in the former prophets and forms the theological backdrop to the rest of the Old Testament. In the time of Solomon the promise seems on the verge of fulfillment, only for the foolish decisions of Solomon later in life to result in the loss of each aspect of the promise. The kingdom of twelve tribes splits; the Assyrians and then the Babylonians conquer the resulting halves of the kingdom; the land is lost, the people are scattered; the idea that the descendants of Abraham will be the channel of blessing to the world is a fading hope. The prophets are sent initially to try to turn the nation back to faithfulness to Yahweh. When they are unsuccessful, they are sent to announce judgment: dispersion and exile. But they also give pictures to Israel of a hopeful future. The poetic and wisdom literature helps Israel to live "in the meantime" as they face the challenges of Diaspora living. Genesis is read as Scripture by the Diaspora nation. They quite naturally would see a parallel between their own exile and the exile of Adam and Eve, for example.

The book of Genesis, for Christians, should also be read as part of the entire Bible including the New Testament. I include this last because the tendency is for Christians to project the New Testament's ideas back into the Old Testament without concern for its original context. But a Christian does and should read the Bible as a whole. We know, for example, from the book of Revelation and elsewhere that the serpent is a manifestation of the devil. We should not lose track of the fact that in Genesis the serpent is a creature who has gone against God's will. He sets off a conflict between the human family and the animal kingdom that will only be ultimately resolved when the "lion lies down with the lamb" and animals no longer run in fear of humans (Gen 9:2). But we should also use the fuller and clearer revelation about Satan in the New Testament to inform our reading of Genesis 3. This sort of reading backwards into the Old Testament from the New flows from the conviction of the dual authorship of Scripture. Holy men of God spoke as they were moved by the Holy Spirit. The Bible thus is authored both by the men and women of God and by God himself. It therefore takes on a fuller sense when read in light of the end.

Reading the book of Genesis within its canonical context involves a constant interplay between the narrow and successively wider contexts. In this commentary I attempt to keep the entire book of Genesis, the Pentateuch, the Old Testament, and the New Testament in view without suppressing any of the meanings derived from the preceding contexts.

READING GENESIS HISTORICALLY

While this is not intended to be a historically oriented commentary, it is irresponsible in my judgment to pretend that the Bible can or should be read without an understanding of its historical contexts. Information gained from Ancient Near Eastern history and literature, Semitic languages related to Hebrew, archaeology, anthropology and sociology, and even the history of the transmission of the Massoretic text is essential if Genesis is to be understood well. The creation and flood stories of the polytheistic cultures which surround Israel teach us much about the questions and concerns of the original audience. Anthropological studies of genealogies in contemporary "primitive" societies help us not to misread the "genealogical" materials in Genesis 4, 5, 10 and 11. Comparative Semitic philology helps us to make "best guesses" on the meaning of rare words in Hebrew, and knowledge of Hebrew syntax is necessary for any careful study. While the focus of this commentary is not on these issues, they provide essential information which protects us from the tendency to project our own culture and experience onto the text rather than reading the text on its own terms.

READING GENESIS SENSITIVELY

Genesis is a surprisingly subtle text and can only be read well with a sensitivity to that subtlety. This shows up, for example, in the many wordplays in the Hebrew text (e.g., the "craftiness" of the serpent and the "nakedness" of the man and the woman [i.e., naïveté] are linked by a rhyme in the Hebrew words) and the careful intertextual echoing of earlier or later parts of the narrative. My biggest concern with the traditional historical-critical methods is that they are often based on a rather blunt-fisted handling of a text which requires a scalpel. The seeming tensions in the text that we have often stumbled over require a more subtle reading. Brichto comments:

> All the problems of pointless repetition, inconsistency and discrepancy fall away when we pay close attention to the subtle resources of biblical Hebrew (in regard to diction and syntax) and the author's masterful deployment of these resources in his poetic repertory of narrative and dialogue: direct and indirect discourse, actual and implied, strict and free; shifts in point of view and perspective; depiction of events in a seemingly direct time flow, and the ambiguation of both events and their chronological order in episodic techniques such as the synoptic-conclusive/resumptive-expansive.[5]

The three episodes in which the Patriarch lies about his wife being his sister serve very different functions in the narrative. Traditional scholarship has assumed that one original (oral?) story has been filtered through the conflicting sources to yield an implausible text in which the Patriarchs repeat the same mistakes. But a careful and sensitive reading of these texts in their narrative contexts makes it clear that it is precisely the repetition of mistakes that is at the center of the point the narrator is making. While the biblical narrators rarely give explicit moral evaluations, they often expect the reader to do so in a way that is consistent with the ideology (theology) of the text. The seeming tensions in the narrative are often better explained as subtle indicators of a different point than they are evidence of the use of sources which have been so poorly edited

---

[5]Herbert C. Brichto, *The Names of God* (Oxford: Oxford University Press, 1998), p. 204.

that the rough edges still show. These chapters are full of perplexing texts. Why did Noah curse Canaan for what Ham did? Where did Cain's wife come from? Does Genesis approve of polygamy?

In some cases modern translations such as the NIV attempt to harmonize texts which seem to be in tension by translating them in ways that are unusual and beg the question. In Genesis 2:8 the NIV translates, "Now the LORD God *had* planted a garden in the east, in Eden; and there he put the man he had formed." This avoids the seeming difficulty of God creating plants first before humanity in Genesis 1 while the man is created first and then the garden is formed followed by the creation of the woman in Genesis 2. The verb translated "had planted"[6] is ordinarily translated as a simple past with the connotation of narrative sequence. The NIV adopts a forced translation for the verb in order to smooth over what seems to be a rough spot in the two creation accounts in Genesis 1 and 2 respectively. A more sensitive reading looks for another explanation rather than retranslating a well-understood Hebrew construction. Perhaps this text is an indication that strict chronological sequence is not always the goal of the creation accounts. Perhaps our questions about how and when and in what sequence creation happened are of little interest to the author. Or perhaps there is some other explanation. A reading which grants the possibility of more subtlety to the author often bears interpretive fruit, as I hope to show in the body of this commentary.

READING GENESIS POETICALLY

Genesis is written almost entirely[7] in prose, not poetry. But at times that prose is so highly structured that it takes on some of the characteristics of Hebrew poetry. Herder called it "narrative poetic." For example the Flood narrative has a palistrophic[8] structure where the events leading up to the center point of the narrative are paralleled with corresponding events in reverse order after the center point. The chart below demonstrates this.

---

[6]*Waw*-consecutive with the imperfect.

[7]Genesis 49 (Jacob's Blessing) and 4:23,24 (Lamech's speech) are examples of poetic inserts into a prose account.

[8]"Palistrophe" is another term for chiasm.

The Flood Narrative has 7 stages:

1) 6:11,12 — Divine speech — the decision to send the Flood and rescue Noah;
2) 6:13-22 — the command to build the ark;
3) 7:1-5 — the command to enter the ark
4) 7:6-24 — the floods come;
5) 8:1-14 — the floods abate;
6) 8:15-19 — the command to exit the ark
7) 8:20–9:17 — the building of the altar and the covenant

The Flood Narrative as a Palistrophe

1] 6:1-12   2'] 9:1-17
   2] 6:13-22   1'] 8:20-22
      3] 7:1-10   3'] 8:15-19
         4] 7:11-16   4'] 8:6-14
            5] 7:17-24 5'] 8:1-5
               6] 8:1

The center of the palistrophe is found in 8:1 where God remembers Noah and begins the process of reversing the Flood. Poetry-like structures such as chiasm, palistrophe, parallelism, etc. are common in the prose narrative sections of the Hebrew Bible and have often been documented by scholars, especially in the last 20 years.[9] Brichto comments helpfully:

> The poetical approach exposes the similarity in the imaginative patterns of narrative and structure deployed by artists in different times and places; it reveals how parallelism in narrative and parataxis in syntax, how narrative in the frame of the prescriptive and the prescriptive imbedded in narrative, enrich or deepen the author's message; so, also, how apparently pointless repetition, inconsistencies, and contradictions are actually significant elements in a single coherent design.[10]

I am not saying that Genesis 1–11 is poetry. It is not. But the

---

[9]See my *Reliable Characters in the Primary History: Profiles of Moses, Elijah and Elisha*, JSOTSup 224 (Sheffield: Sheffield Academic Press, 1996), pp. 155-167, for a discussion of chiastic structure in the Elijah-Elisha narratives.
[10]Brichto, *Names*, p. x.

narrative style of the Hebrew authors uses poetry-like conventions to which modern authors must be sensitive. It is historical narrative, but it does not share the interests of modern historians.

READING GENESIS THEOLOGICALLY

The dominant concerns of Genesis 1–11 are theological (or ideological), not historical or scientific. It is written to provide guidance to God's people about how to conduct their lives as they face the pressures of conformity to the culture and religion of Canaan. Its center of interest seems to be God's creational intentions for humanity and what he does in response to humanity's refusal to submit to those intentions and go his or her own way. Genesis 1–11 prepares the reader for the promise to Abraham, making clear why it became necessary for the God of all the peoples of the earth to choose one man and his descendants as the channel through which he would bring humanity back to their created purpose and relationship with him. Genesis is designed to be read theologically and I have attempted to keep the focus there in this commentary.

THE THEOLOGY OF GENESIS

Genesis, as the first book of the Pentateuch, shares the latter's theme which has been summarized by David Clines as "the partial fulfillment — which implies also the partial non-fulfillment — of the promise to or blessing of the Patriarchs. The promise or blessing is both the divine initiative in a world where human initiatives always lead to disaster, and a re-affirmation of the primal divine intentions for man."[11] In other words, God's initial intentions in creation were frustrated by sinful human attempts to make life work without God. In Genesis 12 the divine strategy moves from dealing with the world at large to dealing with a single, chosen individual, Abraham, and his descendants. The promise which God makes to Abraham (12:1-3) includes a great nation of descendants, a land stretching from the

---

[11]David J.A. Clines, *The Theme of the Pentateuch*, JSOTSup 10 (Sheffield: JSOT Press, 1978), p. 29.

Euphrates to the river of Egypt (Genesis 15:18), a promise to protect Abraham and his descendants through blessing and cursing others based on their treatment of his descendants, and (most theologically significant) the assurance that all nations will receive God's blessing through their relationship with the people of Abraham. Genesis 1–11 fits in with this theme by explaining why it became necessary for God to shift strategy from the entire world to a single man and his descendants. Genesis 12–50 explains the promise and the early threats to its fulfillment brought about by human choices (initiatives) which invariably put the promise in jeopardy.

The rest of the Pentateuch explains how the descendants of Abraham became a great nation, how they were protected by God despite threats, both external and internal, and how they came to the verge of taking possession of the promised land. The actual possession of that land and the use of the nation to begin channeling God's blessing to all other nations is narrated in the ensuing biblical books, Joshua through 1 Kings 11.[12] The rest of the narrative in Kings explains how Israel successively lost each of the elements of the promise which seemed so near to fulfillment in 1 Kings 11. The nation is split into two parts beginning in 1 Kings 12. The ten northern tribes survive little more than 200 years, and their land is conquered and their people scattered. The two remaining tribes last only another century or so when their land is also conquered and many of their people exiled to Babylon. After the exile the vast majority of Abraham's descendants remain dispersed. Except for one brief period the land is never really under their complete control, and they are certainly not the channel of God's blessing to the world. The Old Testament ends with the promise unfulfilled and its readers looking forward to some fulfillment which only God can bring about. The nation has proven itself to lack the faithful perseverance necessary for God's mission to be fulfilled except through some extraordinary set of circumstances. As Christians we realize that it would take God becoming human in Christ (extraordinary circumstances indeed) for the fulfillment to begin.

Genesis 3–11 is thus a prologue to the story of the promise of God to Abraham. God chooses one family out of all humanity as the

---

[12]See the discussion in my *A Sketch of Old Testament Theology* (Lansing, MI: GLCC Publication, 1999), ch. 3.

channel of his blessing to the world. This is necessitated by the three "Falls" in these chapters: in the garden, in the time leading up to the Flood, and in the Babel episode. In each case God responds with judgment: expulsion from the garden, destruction of all humanity in the Flood, and the dispersal of all humanity into people with different languages and cultures following Babel. Genesis 1–2 describes creation, humanity's role in creation, and God's purposes for humankind within that creation. As such it functions as the introduction to the entire Bible. The promise to Abraham is God's strategy to regain his purposes in creation which were lost in the Fall.

GOD IN GENESIS 1–11

God is portrayed in Genesis 1–11 as the all-powerful creator. He speaks the world into existence, and there is not a hint of resistance by the creation. This point which seems so obvious to us was strikingly original in the ancient world where the forces of what we call nature were actually manifestations of various gods who were in tension with each other. The God of Genesis is also a God of order. His creation follows a sort of logic in which the environment is created before it is filled with those things which inhabit it. The creation is designed to work in harmony, and it is only the destructive results of human sin which cause the disorder that Israel experiences. The world God creates is good and, with humanity at its head, very good. He is a God of goodness. He is a God who desires fellowship with his creatures. He is also a God who gives responsibility and freedom to humanity, making genuine fellowship possible. Humanity is responsible to rule over the world God created as his representatives. They are also responsible to obey God's boundaries. When they do not, God shows his unimaginable holiness by bringing judgment upon his perfect creation, focused particularly on humanity and the serpent, those creatures who violated his boundaries. While God is a God of grace and forgiveness, his holiness will not be disregarded. God is also portrayed as a God who cares. The sexual perversion and violence of humanity prior to the Flood hurts God deeply to the extent that he grieved ever having made humanity and his heart was full of pain (6:5). The blood of violence cries out to God from the ground (4:10). God is also a God who loves life and graciously gives it. The command to procreate is a blessing from God (1:28). Violence which destroys the gift of life is not something which God will tolerate. This is evident in his interactions with Cain, his decision to judge the world because of its violence prior to the Flood, and his warning about violence to Noah after the Flood (9:4-6). God is thus a God who has particular concern for the vulnerable who may be victimized by others.

But above all God is a God who persists in his purposes, and he will accomplish them — the sinful choices of humanity notwithstanding. While we perhaps see this most easily when we take into account the "metanarrative" of the entire Bible, its roots are in these early chapters of Genesis. God's blessing on humanity to be fruitful and multiply and thus be able to rule over the earth as God's representatives is *temporarily* frustrated by the choices of humanity to live in ways contrary to his intended purposes. This purpose will be accomplished with or without the cooperation of the majority of humanity. Humanity will end up in a new creation, in a new Eden as the book of Revelation makes clear. Even if God is forced to start over with creation and with a new Adam as he does in the time of Noah, God will find a way to accomplish his purposes. Most of the Bible deals with the plan God designed because of these inevitable failings of humanity. Because humanity as a whole persists in resisting God's purposes, there is what might be called a "shift in strategy" in the time of Abraham. From then on God works primarily through the descendants of Abraham (Israel) as a means of bringing his blessing to all the world. That blessing is directly related to God's creational blessings referred to in Genesis 1!

HUMANITY IN GENESIS 1–11

The portrayal of humankind in Genesis 1–11 is supremely realistic and honest on the one hand and hopeful on the other. Humankind, male and female, is created to serve as God's representative (his image) in ruling over creation on his behalf. To accomplish this they must be fruitful and multiply and fill the earth. Humanity is the pinnacle of creation, and it is only after having created humankind that God's evaluation elevates from "good" to "very good." As the image of God, humanity is endowed with the capacities needed to fulfill their intended function in creation. They have the responsibility to guard and serve the creation (2:15) and the privilege to live in harmonious fellowship with the LORD and with the rest of creation, both animate and inanimate. The mental, physical, and spiritual capacities needed to live out their created purposes are graciously provided them by a good and gracious God. Among those gifts is the freedom to choose to respect or transgress God's boundaries.

But with the choice to stop trusting in the LORD's boundaries and to trespass those boundaries comes the destruction of the created harmony. Humanity now struggles with the terror of intimate fellowship with God. The unity of the original pair is turned to mutual blame. The first child of that marriage brutally and cynically murders the second child. Humanity's relationship with the physical creation changes from grateful and pleasant enjoyment to frustrating and difficult toil in order to eke out a living. The animal world is now in conflict with the world of man. While there is an attempt at restoring the relationship with the LORD (4:26) the general picture of humanity "east of Eden" is one of degenerating relationships with God, fellow humans, and creation. Murder is followed by polygamy and violence without consequences.[13] The escalating violence and sexual misconduct of humanity ultimately results in God's decision to send the Flood for "The LORD saw how great man's wickedness on the earth had become, and that every inclination of the thoughts of his heart was only evil all the time" (Gen 6:5). Ironically while the Flood is designed to purge creation of the evil so bound up in the human heart, Genesis makes clear that nothing has fundamentally changed in humanity after the Flood: "Never again will I curse the ground because of man, even though every inclination of his heart is evil from childhood. And never again will I destroy all living creatures, as I have done" (Gen 8:21b). Genesis views evil as bound up in the hearts of human beings. The problem of human sin and rebellion is so serious that not even a universal flood will stop it. Even after starting over with blameless Noah, there is another fall. Furthermore humanity, after being recommissioned at the end of the Flood, refuses to "fill the earth" in order to be able to represent God in ruling over the creation. Instead they gather to build the city

---

[13]Cf. Lamech's distorted misuse of God's grace to Cain in Gen 4:24.

of Babel so as not to be scattered over the face of the ground in direct rebellion to God's expressed will. Humanity still bears the image of God (Gen 5:1-3) and has the same purpose (Gen 9:1,7). These chapters make clear that if God's ultimate intentions for humanity are to be realized, the strategy of commanding them and expecting obedience on a widespread scale will not work. Instead God's purposes will only be accomplished through chosen, faithful people who put their hope in God's Son.

CREATION IN GENESIS 1-11

Genesis is positive about the material universe. It is "good" in God's estimation and with the addition of humanity to rule over it, "very good." Fruits and plants are readily available to feed animals and humans. Free access to sources of food which are both pleasing to the eye and good for food makes the process of "making a living" an enjoyable and pleasant one. In God's creation there is, prior to the Fall, no conflict between the human and animal kingdoms. Humanity's food and the food of animals are vegetarian in nature. There is no fear of wild beasts by humanity, nor are wild beasts afraid of humankind because they are not a food source. But ironically it is out of the animal kingdom itself (the serpent) that the decisions to rebel against God's boundaries come and with those decisions the consequent disruption of the created harmony. The decision of the original human pair to follow the serpent in direct disobedience to the Lord's expressed command and in cynical distrust of his motives results in distorted relationships of every sort. Humanity's relationship to the material universe is distorted. Instead of ruling over creation as God's representative and by God's standards, humanity will now only with great difficulty eke out a living. A weed is a useful plant in the wrong place, and the process of carefully managing plants in order to live will be complicated by many such useful plants in many wrong places. The original harmony of the human and animal kingdoms will be replaced by ongoing enmity between the descendants of the woman and the serpent. After the flood the animal kingdom is given as a potential regular[14] food source as a sort

---

[14]The argument that humanity was entirely vegetarian (and not merely

of divine concession. But there is a compensating factor which prevents animals from being eaten into extinction; fish and animals will now fear humanity and respond by fleeing from or attacking them. The good creation of God, made to function harmoniously with humanity at its head, becomes the scene of great conflict and struggle. Serpent-inspired human rebellion against God and his standards results in a creation in which all of its parts are in conflict with the others, whether that be the physical creation, the animal kingdom, or humanity. The material creation itself is ultimately brought under God's judgment in the flood. The good gift of God is turned into the backdrop for conflict between God, the physical world, the animals, and man.

THE STRUCTURE OF GENESIS

While modern scholars can and have speculated about the structure of Genesis, it is perhaps safest to use the structural markers given explicitly by the author. The phrase, "[these are] the generations of" (תּוֹלְדוֹת, *tôlᵉdôth*), is the most obvious structural marker in the book and (with the possible exception of 2:4a) is used as an introductory formula. Generally speaking there is alternation between narrative material and name list or genealogical material. This yields the following structure for the book:

1:1–2:4	Prologue (Narrative)
2:4–4:26	History of the Heavens and the Earth (Narrative with Genealogy)
5:1–6:8	Family History of Adam (Genealogy)
6:9–9:29	Family History of Noah (Narrative)
10:1–11:9	Family History of Noah's Sons (Genealogy with Narrative)
11:10-26	Family History of Shem (Genealogy)
11:27–25:11	Family History of Terah (Narrative)
25:12-18	Family History of Ishmael (Genealogy)
25:19–35:29	Family History of Isaac (Narrative)
36:1–37:1	Family History of Esau (Genealogy)
37:2–50:26	Family History of Jacob (Narrative)

---

primarily so) prior to the flood is based on silence and disregards the fact that the first recorded descendants of humankind brought animal sacrifices.

Notice the following:

1) This is an introductory formula and only the dogmatic assertion of the Documentary Hypothesis would lead to fudging this in the single case of 2:4a. Further, having 2:4a refer exclusively back to 1:1–2:3 leaves 2:4b–4:26 without any introductory formula when the rest of the book is divided by the formula. Perhaps the safest conclusion is to regard 2:4 as a bridge backwards forming an inclusio with 1:1 to end the first major section *and* the introductory formula to the next section. While the documentary theory has traditionally regarded this formula as a characteristic of the putative Pentateuchal source P, it seems more likely that the author has used this formula intentionally to arrange his material.

2) Terah's family history is dominated by Abraham; Isaac's by Jacob; and Jacob's by Joseph. Why? Terah sets out for the land of Promise but never gets there, so the significant role that he could have played in the outworking of God's promise was given to his son who did have the faith to go to the promised land. Perhaps Isaac's role is taken by Jacob because he too is resistant to the promise to a degree (e.g., the attempt to bless Esau when he knew God had other plans). Perhaps Jacob's part is taken by Joseph because he was already the focus of the previous section and because the narrative is not just about Joseph, but about Jacob's sons and therefore it would be inappropriate to call it the family history of Joseph.

3) Notice that offshoots of the promise are written out by "mere" genealogies rather than narratives (Ishmael, Esau, Noah's sons).

4) Shem's genealogy also includes the narrative of **Babel** and is perhaps redundantly included because of the theme of the name [שֵׁם, *shēm*] in the Babel narrative and in the ensuing promise to Abraham.

5) Notice the alternation between genealogy with a few narrative comments and straight narrative with occasional genealogical information. Why? Certainly the "major" characters in the story are given narratives and the relatively speaking "minor" ones are given genealogies, but is there more? Perhaps the genealogies catch the narrative up, so to speak? They also by contrast give emphasis to the nonchosen sons of the Patriarchs (Ishmael, Esau) and Noah (Ham).

6) Genesis 36:1,9 repeats the phrase, "these are the generations of" for some reason which will be investigated later.
7) The genealogies are obviously crucial to the structuring of the book and we should expect to find good reasons for their existence other than an antiquarian interest on the part of the author of Genesis.
8) Cain's line doesn't even receive a genealogy that is a part of the structuring of the book and this fact may be an indication of the author's negative evaluation of Cain and his line.
9) The genealogies are obviously written in light of the circumstances of Israel within the promised land. The origins of their neighbors and their enemies are explained, and this points forward to the later discussion in Numbers and Deuteronomy about "banned" and nonbanned peoples.

THE STRUCTURE OF GENESIS 1–11

While the *tōlᵊdōth* formula is the most obvious structural marker for the entire book of Genesis there is evidence that Genesis 1–11 has a sort of dual structure. Hess comments:

> [T]he intent of the writer was to weave together an account of the creation of the world and of humanity using as a major technique doublets of repetitive patterns which serve to focus on a particular theme of the narratives and to provide the major means of moving the events forward into the history of a world known to the early readers of the text. Such a technique suggests a distinct literary form to the first eleven chapters of Genesis.[15]

The Flood, for example, is portrayed as a sort of de-creation followed by a re-creation. Noah is recommissioned as a sort of "new Adam." After each creation story there is a story of a fall. Gary Rendsburg in his book *The Redaction of Genesis*[16] suggests the following structure for Genesis 1–11:

---

[15]Richard S. Hess, "Genesis 1–2 in its Literary Context," *TynBul* 41.4 (1990): 143-152.
[16]Gary A. Rendsburg (*The Redaction of Genesis* [Winona Lake, IN: Eisen-

A Creation, God's Words to Adam (1:1–3:24)	A' Flood, God's Words to Noah (6:9–9:17)
B Adam's Sons (4:1-16)	B' Noah's Sons (9:18-29)
C Technological Development of Mankind (4:17-26)	C' Ethnic Development of Mankind (10:1-32)
D Ten Generations from Adam to Noah (5:1-32)	E' Downfall: Tower of Babel (11:1-9)
E Downfall: The Nephilim (6:1-8)	D' Ten Generations from Noah to Terah (11:10-32)

He assembles an impressive list of intertextual echoes between the corresponding parts of the outline. His list of parallels between A and A' is summarized below. While some of his observations could be questioned and others are based on particular interpretations (e.g., the meaning of the "sons of God"), his case is solid. I would only add that Genesis 1–11 is structured to describe the two hopes of God for humanity — both of which did not come to fruition due to mankind's sinful choices. The Garden Strategy was to allow humanity maximum freedom and access to the presence of God. It came to an end through human choices to stop trusting and obeying the LORD. The Flood Strategy did not drive evil from the heart of humanity (Gen. 6:5; 8:21) and resulted in the Babel episode where humanity tries to build its own life in direct rebellion against the LORD. These two strategies make sense of the LORD's choice to elect a faithful individual (Abram) and his descendants (Israel) as the channel for the LORD to accomplish his purposes with humankind.

Rendberg's Parallels between Sections A and A':

1. *Ruach Elohim*, "Spirit of God" or "Wind from God" in 1:2 and *ruach* in 8:1 with *Elohim* as the immediately preceding word
2. *Tehom* "the deep" in 1:2 and 7:11; 8:2
3. In 1:9 God gathers the waters together and dry land becomes visible; in 8:13 the waters recede and dry land again becomes visible
4. God says "be fruitful and multiply" to humans in 1:28 and in 9:1 and to animals in 1:22 and 8:17

---

brauns, 1986]) drawing on J.M. Sasson, "The 'Tower of Babel' as a Clue to the Redactional Structuring of the Primeval History (Gen. 1–11:9)," in *The Bible World: Essays in Honor of Cyrus H. Gordon,* ed. by G. Rendsburg (New York: KTAV, 1980), pp. 211-219.

5. Humans are given mastery over animals in 1:28 and 9:2
6. The root *shabat* = "rest, cease" closes one creation account (2:2-3), and the same root occurs at the end of the Flood in 8:22
7. "Every living thing which creeps . . . according to its kind" in 1:21; "every creeper of the earth according to its kind" are brought on board the ark in 6:20 (7:14)
8. "Every winged fowl according to its kind" created on the fifth day in 1:21, and "the fowl according to its kind" are brought onto the ark in 6:20; 7:14
9. "The beasts of the earth according to its kind" are created in 1:25 and board in 7:14
10. The last group of animals created on the sixth day and to board the ark are "the cattle according to its kind" in 1:25 and 6:20; 7:14
11. "In the image of God he created/made man" in 1:27 and 9:6
12. "Male and female" in 1:27 and 6:19; 7:3,9,16
13. "God blessed them and said to them" in 1:28 and 9:1
14. After 1:28 and 9:1 descriptions of food are given in 1:29 and 9:3
15. "Make" and "complete" are collocated in both 2:1-2 and 6:16
16. The seventh day climaxes creation in 2:2-3 and "seven day" periods punctuate the Flood in 7:10; 8:10,12
17. In 2:5 Yahweh had not yet brought rain upon the earth; in 7:4 God will bring rain upon the earth
18. "In his nostrils the breath of life" in 2:7 and "the breath of the spirit of life in its nostrils" in 8:21
19. *Yaṣar* "form" in 2:7-8 and cognate noun in 8:21
20. "He closed off" man's flesh in 2:21 and identical verb of closing of ark in 7:16
21. *mithhallek*, "moving" and *hithallek*, "moving, walking" in 3:8 and 6:9
22. A weapon ends the creation story (cherub's sword in 3:24) and the Flood (bow in 9:13-16)

GENESIS 1–11 AND MODERN SCIENCE

Genesis is not a treatise on science. It was not primarily written to answer questions about the origin of the physical universe. Throughout history many well-meaning Christians have read the Bible, and Genesis in particular, as though it was intended to give scientific information about the how and when of creation. Whatever the reigning cosmology of the day, Genesis has been read to support it (or contest it!) — from the flat earth and geocentric universe to the earth, air, wind, and fire of Greek cosmology to the Big Bang and evolution of contemporary scientific theory. In general these readings have been unsuccessful and problematic and have sometimes brought disrepute on the Bible and the church. Genesis is concerned with the who and why of creation.

Further, Genesis itself shows little interest in the date of creation. The first time the Bible adds up time periods to date an event chronologically is in 1 Kings 6:1 where Solomon is said to have begun building the temple 480 years after Israel came out of Egypt. The genealogies of Genesis should not be used to date creation or the Flood within the Bible. The story of the attempt to date creation from the Bible up to and including the time of Bishop Ussher is a classic example of trying to get answers from texts not designed to give them.[1]

It is, of course, natural for us to be curious about the when and how of creation. In approaching Scripture with such questions, however, several cautions are necessary. First we should be careful about reading the statements of Genesis about creation as though they were written by a contemporary who has our interests in mind. It is all too easy to twist the words of Genesis into scientific statements which support a theory that we are convinced is accurate. Hugh Ross's reading of Genesis 1 as an account of the Big Bang is one of several examples discussed below. Another example is the vapor canopy theory which reads Genesis 2:5 as though it actually said that there was no rain prior to the Flood. We should be cautious of reading scientific information "between the lines of" Genesis.

The history of the attempts at reconciling Genesis with current cosmology should also give us pause. Every generation is tempted to think that its cosmological theories are the final word. Every generation so far in human history has evidently been wrong about that! It borders on hubris to assume that our generation is any different.

---

[17]For a sympathetic but realistic account of Ussher see, E.H. Merrill, "Chronology," *Dictionary of the Old Testament: Pentateuch*, ed. by T. Desmond Alexander and David W. Baker (Downers Grove, IL: InterVarsity, 2003), pp. 113-122 (especially p. 118).

Science is provisional. Like all human attempts at understanding any extremely complex system, it is prone to make mistakes. Since the famous work of Thomas Kuhn on the history of science and paradigm shifts, it has been obvious that scientists, like all other humans, tend to be swayed by currently popular theories and do not merely "weigh the facts." The church should be careful of wedding itself too closely to any scientific theory about cosmology. Those theories keep changing. It should be even more careful of "finding" confirmation of such theories in the Bible.

We should also be careful of turning our own preferred harmonizations between science and Scripture into dogma or doctrine. Since Genesis does not give us dates for creation or detailed discussions of exactly how God created, those matters must remain in the realm of opinion and not be used to judge the Christian character or intelligence of those with whom we disagree. They certainly should not cause division in the church.

Perhaps most important of all, our interest in the questions of the when and how of creation must not prevent us from hearing the central concerns of the early chapters of Genesis. Discussions of, e.g., creation vs. evolution and the reliability of dating methods are not the concern of Genesis. Genesis is concerned with who God is and who we are as his creations.

There are several currently popular attempts to reconcile scientific knowledge with the account in the early chapters of Genesis. Some of these are somewhat forced, and I would conclude that ultimately none of them is without its problems. We must be careful not to allow our desire to have answers to our questions drown out the questions which this key portion of Scripture wants to ask and answer. At the end of the day it is perhaps preferable to say that Genesis does not address questions such as the exact "how" of creation nor the "when" of creation in scientific terms. In any case, we should, given the complexity of the issues, hold our opinions humbly.

THE GAP THEORY

This theory, made famous in its popular version by the Schofield Reference Bible, argues that Genesis 1:2 ought to be translated, "The earth *became* formless and void." The idea is that some unexplained event resulted in the earth, although created in perfection in verse 1, becoming empty (void) and without organization (formless). The speculation then follows that the implied event was the rebellion of Satan and his angels and the subsequent judgment of God against the creation because of that rebellion. This theory is convenient in that it allows for the fossil record. There was a world that lasted for untold ages prior to this one which the fossil record reflects. But this theory fails on several accounts. To begin with the Hebrew word *hāyāh* almost always is some form of the verb "to be." The translation "to become" is rare at best with clear examples difficult to find, and none of the possible examples really parallels Genesis 1:2. Second, this requires one to read quite a lot into this passage. There is no mention of the fall of Satan and his angels or the resulting judgment of God upon creation. All of this is based on pure supposition. Third, interpretations which seem to be motivated by the desire to avoid conflict with contemporary views not addressed by the original author(s) are inherently suspect. The original audience had no concerns regarding the reconciling of the fossil record with the account of creation in Genesis 1. They knew nothing of the fossil record, of radiometric and other forms of dating, of Darwin and neo-Darwinian theories, etc. Fourth, this is not the natural way to understand the text, which makes perfect sense when translated in the traditional way.

SAILHAMER ON THE CREATION OF THE SUN AND MOON[18]

One of the seeming anomalies which contemporary readers see in Genesis 1 is the fact that light is created before the sun and moon. Since strong scientific evidence leads contemporary readers to assume that light on earth only comes from the sun (the moon reflects the sun's light) and other stars, we wonder how there could be light on day 1 and not hear of the creation of the sun or moon until day 4. Sailhamer has suggested a way around this difficulty. He argues that Genesis 1:14 be translated, "Let the lights in the expanse of the heavens be to separate day from night, and let them be for

---

[18]John H. Sailhamer, *Genesis*, Expositor's Bible Commentary, vol. 2 (Grand Rapids: Zondervan, 1990), pp. 33-34.

signs and for seasons and for days and for years." His suggestion is that the sun, moon, and stars were created on day 1 but only given their designated function within the created order on day 4. This purportedly resolves the anomaly. While this translation is possible syntactically in Hebrew, I see little reason to adopt it. The ordinary way to read the construction in Hebrew is in the traditional way. Unless there are compelling internal reasons for translating this construction in this unusual way, there is little to commend the suggestion. Once again this reading seems to be motivated by a desire to harmonize Genesis 1 with modern science. This desire, understandable though it be, results in readings that may be a little forced.

THE DAY-AGE THEORY

This theory suggests that the days of Genesis 1 are not literal days but correspond to great epochs of time. While Genesis presents the acts of creation as occurring within a single week, in fact the word "day" is not to be taken literally. Thus the evidence for the great age of the universe is not in conflict with the biblical creation account. One potential problem with this view is that the scientific data for the age of the universe does not suggest uniform periods of time over which the physical universe develops whereas Genesis would seem to suggest six periods of equal time. But a bigger issue is the strained exegesis which must take place and the assumption, once again, that Genesis is even designed to answer questions about how the universe was created. The six days of creation along with the Sabbath rest are given to Israel to show them how to live their lives in the promised land. The recently released slaves of Egypt must learn to work and rest and to provide rest to those who depend upon them — animals, servants, hired workers, etc. The pattern of creation described in Genesis 1 is not designed to answer questions about how and when.

THEISTIC EVOLUTION

Often related to the day-age theory is the concept of theistic evolution. This hypothesis suggests that God used the Big Bang and evolution to produce the world and that process is described in layman's terms in Genesis 1. Zimmer provides the following account of how he thinks the Evolutionary Periods correspond to the days of creation.[19]

Day	Corresponding Evolutionary Period
One	Formation of solar system and ignition of sun
Two	Accretion of planet earth
Three	Appearance of continents and the earliest life which was photosynthetic and propagated through DNA
Four	Reduction of greenhouse effect by weathering of continental rock and the transformation of the atmosphere by photosynthesis from anoxic to oxidative
Five	The beginning of the eukaryotes to the end of the age of dinosaurs
Six	The age of mammals

Zimmer further describes the correspondence between the account of the creation of humanity in Genesis 1 with the current account of human evolution:[20]

Verse	Action	Resemblance
26	declaration of intention	*Homo habilis* and *erectus*
	declaration of dominion	Oldowan and Acheulean stone tools used for scavenging
27	creation	Appearance of *Homo sapiens sapiens* and *neandertalis* in fossil record: single source evolution predicted by molecular biology
28	blessing and declaration of dominion	Late Paleolithic
29	plants given to humans	Epipaleolithic/Archaic Neolithic
30	fodder to the animals	Developed Neolithic: "Neolithic Agricultural Revolution"

But once again, we must be skeptical of such approaches. For example, day four is hardly a description of the reduction of the greenhouse effect and the transformation of the atmosphere from anoxic to oxidative. One arrives at such conclusions only by forced exegesis

---

[19]J. Raymond Zimmer, "The Creation of Man and the Evolutionary Record," *Perspectives of Science and the Christian Faith* (1996): 18.
[20]Ibid., p. 24.

which already has the desired results in mind. Genesis is turned into a science textbook instead of Scripture for God's people Israel.

YOUNG EARTH CREATION

According to this view the Bible asserts that creation happened in a six-day period of time some four to ten thousand years ago. The genealogical materials in Genesis 5 and 11 can be used to reconstruct the age of the universe chronologically. While God created the world with the appearance of age,[21] in fact it is of very recent origin. Dating methods which suggest otherwise are fundamentally flawed by uniformitarian assumptions about physical processes and in other ways.

The primary strength of this view is that it seems to many readers (believers and nonbelievers) the natural way to read the text. If a text like this about creation were written today, it would certainly seem to imply a very young earth and a literal six-day creation. According to this view the doctrine of the Bible's infallibility must override any current scientific theory. Since history has taught us that such theories tend to be discarded over time, the church should listen to Scripture and not the current cosmological speculation. Those who have constructed such theories today were and are often suspicious of the miraculous and have allowed their antisupernatural biases to affect their interpretations of the physical data.

A concern that I have with this view is not with the theory itself, but the fact that some forms of it are based on strained interpretations of the biblical text.[22] For example, the theory that the first rainbow that ever occurred happened only after the Flood is based on a questionable reading of the Genesis account. The vapor canopy which is supposed to have covered the earth prior to the Flood and affected the seeming ages of the physical universe is the product of what I believe to be a questionable exegesis of the Genesis account.[23]

---

[21]For example, trees were full-grown, not seedlings. Adam was a grown man, not an embryo or infant.

[22]For a more thorough discussion of the concerns that Dr. Kissling has with this position, please feel free to request his contact information through the publisher's offices (1-800-289-3300).

[23]See my "The Rainbow in Genesis 9:12-17: A Triple Entendre?" *SCJ* 4 (2001): 249-261.

Is Genesis interested in scientific questions and descriptions? We must keep in mind that Genesis was primarily written to instruct Israel as they faced the challenges of living in faithfulness to Yahweh in the midst of the polytheistic temptations of Canaan. It was the creation myths of the Canaanites which it attacks, not contemporary theories about the origin of the universe.

INTELLIGENT DESIGN

The most recent attempt to reconcile Christian faith and modern science is the intelligent design movement. While writers and thinkers with a variety of viewpoints have aligned themselves with "Intelligent Design Theory," there are certain characteristic ideas. One key theme is that there is no attempt by most proponents to read Genesis as a science textbook, although the work of Hugh Ross would be an exception.[24] Buoyed by the Hubble Telescope confirmation that the Oscillating Universe theory is finally dead, intelligent design theorists contest the cogency of the current "scientific" creation story, the Big Bang followed by evolution. Instead, intelligent design thinkers challenge contemporary science at the level of its underlying naturalistic presuppositions. Accepting the typical 13-14-billion-year age for the universe, intelligent design thinkers argue that there is simply not enough time for the universe to have evolved by chance and mere naturalistic processes given the complexity of life and the mathematical odds of so many factors necessary for the emergence of life as we know it actually coming together to produce

---

[24]Hugh Ross (*The Creator and the Cosmos*, 2nd ed. [Colorado Springs: Navpress, 1993], p. 15) tells of his own experience of reading Genesis 1 in an attempt to prove it to be myth, only to come to the opposite conclusion: "Instead of another bizarre creation myth, here was a journal-like record of the earth's initial conditions — correctly described from the standpoint of astrophysics and geophysics — followed by a summary of the sequence of changes through which Earth came to be inhabited by living things and ultimately by humans. The account was simple, elegant and scientifically accurate. From what I understood to be the stated viewpoint of an observer on Earth's surface, both the order and the description of creation events perfectly matched the established record of nature. I was amazed." I don't see how someone could be "on Earth's surface" observing the Big Bang when there would be no earth to stand on at that time.

it. I am no scientist and therefore have no expertise to evaluate the many arguments for intelligent design in the material universe. Certainly a Christian does not easily recognize a God who winds the universe up and leaves it to evolve in and of itself. Chance, time, genetic mutations, etc. are not, in my judgment, adequate explanations by themselves for the universe we currently inhabit. If intelligent design leads thoughtful people to consider the reasonableness of faith, I am in favor of it. When, however, there is an attempt (as in Ross's case) to find the story of the Big Bang followed by evolution in Genesis 1, I must object. It hardly seems plausible that the original audience would have read the words in the way that Ross does. Genesis 1 made sense to the original audience. That sense was not a disguised description of the Big Bang followed by evolution.

CONCLUSION ON GENESIS AND SCIENCE

Genesis is not a scientific treatise and does not attempt to describe how or when the universe was created. The narrative of creation was designed to contest the polytheistic creation (and flood) stories of Israel's neighbors. To read the words as some sort of disguised scientific account is to read in a forced and perhaps question-begging way. Worse, it is a reading that brings our questions to the forefront before it has humbly asked of this marvelous text what questions are important! The answers to those questions is the purpose of Genesis. We miss its teaching when our questions drown out the questions and answers of the text in its original setting.

THE AUTHORSHIP OF GENESIS

Traditionally Jews and Christians have regarded the Pentateuch as authored by Moses. It was certainly called the "Torah (or Law) of Moses" or even just "Moses" within the time of the Old Testament itself (Mal 4:4; Neh 8:1) as well as in the New Testament (Luke 24:44; John 7:19). Jesus even explicitly says that Moses (the person) wrote about him (John 5:46). But nowhere does the Pentateuch nor other Scripture identify Moses as its author. Certainly Moses would have been capable of writing and is said to have actually written significant sections of the Pentateuch (Exod 34:27; 17:14; 24:4; Deut 31:9,24; Num 33:2; Exod 25:16,21-22). But there are a series of texts within the Pentateuch itself which makes Mosaic authorship of the entire Pentateuch problematic. These passages have been discussed throughout the history of the church and can be categorized as *post-Mosaica* (things written after the time of Moses) and *a-Mosaica* (things which may or may not be contemporary with Moses but could not have been written by him).

POST-MOSAICA

To begin with, the death and burial of Moses are recorded at the end of Deuteronomy. While it is theoretically possible that God could inspire Moses to write prophetically of his death, there seems to be no reason to suppose this other than the desire to support a theory of authorship which Scripture never explicitly affirms. Furthermore the evaluation of Moses' life immediately after the record of his death and burial seems to reflect a time long after the death of Moses: "No prophet like Moses ever arose in Israel whom the LORD knew face to face" (Deut 34:10). This text seems to come from a period long after the death of Moses and perhaps even after the end of the era of prophecy. It seems to assume that prophets have come (and are no longer coming?), but none of them was like Moses. Moses in Deuteronomy 18:15-18 prophesied that a prophet like him would arise. Deuteronomy 34:10 says that no such prophet ever arose in Israel. This seems to suggest a period after the cessation of prophecy in the postexilic period and calls upon the reader to look to the future messianic era when prophecy would return and Moses' prophecy of a prophet like him would be fulfilled.[25] Even if we do not assume a setting after the cessation of prophecy for this text, it clearly indicates a time long after the death of Moses and after the sending of at least some prophets. Clearly Moses did not write at least this section of the Pentateuch.

Another example of *post-Mosaica* is found in Genesis 14:14 which describes Abram's pursuit of the northern coalition of armies

---

[25]Cf. 1 Macc. 9:27. I am aware that not all Jews accepted the idea of the cessation of prophecy.

which had taken Lot, his nephew, as a captive. Abram is said to have pursued them "as far as Dan." Dan is one of Jacob's sons, the great-grandson of Abram. The Danites have no place in the promised land until after the time of the conquest under Joshua. Furthermore the northern location of Dan does not come about until long after the conquest. The tribe of Dan was initially given an allotment in the southern portion of Israel near the Philistine coastal strip (Josh 19:40-46). Unable to control that allotment they moved to the extreme northern boundary of the land and conquered a northern city called Laish and renamed it Dan (Josh 19:47; Judg 18). It is to this northern city that Abram pursued Lot's captors. This could only be written by someone well after the time of Moses since he died before the initial conquest of the land when the Danites had neither received an initial inheritance nor moved to a northern location.

In Genesis 36:31 we read, "These are the kings who reigned in Edom before any Israelite king reigned." Since Israel had no kings until at least 200 years[26] after the death of Moses this passage is post-Moses. Genesis 11:28,31 refer to the city of Ur as "of the Chaldeans." A Chaldean dynasty came to power over Babylonia in 626 B.C. and the Chaldeans did not even begin to penetrate Babylonia until c. 1000 B.C. Clearly this is post-Moses. In fact this comment was probably added at a later time to clarify to postexilic readers that the Ur in southern Mesopotamia was meant, not the possible northern Ur.[27]

A-MOSAICA

The evaluation of Moses' life in Deuteronomy 34 is not only post-Moses; it is also not something Moses would have written about himself, thus the term *a-Mosaica*. The most famous example of a-Mosaica is Numbers 12:3, "Now Moses was a very humble man, more humble than anyone else on the face of the earth." Humble men do not brag about their humility! This does not seem to be something which Moses would have written, although a contemporary could have.

---

[26]Or 400 years if one subscribes to the early date for the Exodus and Conquest. See J.J. Bimson, *Redating the Exodus and Conquest*, JSOTSup 5 (Sheffield: JSOT Press, 1978).

[27]K.A. Kitchen, *On the Reliability of the Old Testament* (Grand Rapids: Eerdmans, 2003), p. 316.

Three times in the opening chapters of Deuteronomy Moses lays responsibility for God's refusal to allow him into the promised land at the feet of Israel. "Because of [Israel] the LORD became angry with [Moses] and said, You shall not enter it, either" (1:37). Although Moses pleaded with the LORD (3:23) "because of [Israel] the Lord was angry with [Moses] and would not listen to him" (3:26). "The LORD was angry with [Moses] because of [Israel], and he solemnly swore that [Moses] would not cross the Jordan" (4:21). The author/final editor of Deuteronomy sees it differently:

> On that same day the LORD told Moses, "Go up into the Abarim Range to Mount Nebo in Moab across from Jericho and view Canaan. . . . There on the mountain that you have climbed you will die and be gathered to your people . . . This is because you broke faith with me in the presence of the Israelites at the waters of Meribah Kadesh in the Desert of Zin and because you did not uphold my holiness among the Israelites. Therefore you will see the land only from a distance; you will not enter the land I am giving to the people of Israel" (Deut 32:48-52).

This does not seem to have been written by Moses who blames the nation for his own personal destiny.

It seems clear that, at least in its final form, Moses did not write the entire Pentateuch. This, however, does not mean that the bulk of the Pentateuch comes from later editors. Certainly there was updating of place names and a few explanatory comments similar to the updating of contemporary Bible translations.[28] But that is very different from suggesting that the bulk of Genesis is written more than a millennium after the events which it records.

THE HISTORICAL CONTEXT OF GENESIS

If Moses did not write all of the Pentateuch, does that mean that it does not reflect accurately upon the times it writes about? Is the Pentateuch a retrojection of very late traditions onto the past which

---

[28]The revision in 1995 of the New American Standard Bible comes to mind as a parallel.

cannot be trusted to give us reliable information about that past? For a variety of reasons I would argue that the answer to this question is "no." While the Pentateuch (Genesis included) was certainly updated, there is evidence that it relies on very ancient sources which do reflect the time period described.

Sarna, for example, has assembled a long list of details from Genesis which ill fit later times in the history of Israel and argue strongly for the authenticity of at least the traditions lying behind the text of Genesis. If Genesis is a *de novo* creation of a much later time period, the author has a remarkable ability to present the past in a way that seems authentic. For example, after the revelation of God's name, Yahweh, during the call of Moses, the people of Israel begin to give names to their children which have Yahweh's name as a part of them (Yahu names). Sarna: "Of 38 names for the Patriarchs and family members, 27 are never found elsewhere in the Bible and most are compounds of El; there are no Yahu names, consistent with Exod 6:2-3."[29] Prior to Exodus 3:6 Israel's deity is referred to as the "God of your (singular) or his father." After this time "he is God of your (plural) or their fathers" consistent with the fact that God is making explicit his covenant with the nation as a whole. Genesis has several unique or rare names for God prior to the revelation of Yahweh's name in the time of Moses — El Elyon, El Shaddai, El-Roi, El Olam, El Bethel, El-elohe-Israel, Elohe-ha-shamayim, etc. Since El is the short form of the more generic (and not specifically Israelite) word for God, this is what one would expect in an era prior to the revelation of Yahweh's name.

There are also a series of practices in which the Patriarchs of Genesis participate which are later prohibited by the law. One wonders why a late author of Genesis would not try to cover up these rather embarrassing facts. Sarna (p. xv) notes,

> The matsevah [sacred stone] is sternly forbidden in Lev 26:1 and Deut 16:21-22, yet the Genesis narratives do not hesitate to ascribe its use to Jacob. Similarly Abraham planted a tamarisk tree and worshiped there (Gen 21:33). It seems odd that this would not be altered in a later age. The Patriarchs never do so

---

[29]Nahum Sarna, *Genesis*, JPS Torah Commentary (Jerusalem: Jewish Publication Society, 1989), p. xvi.

at Jerusalem, which is odd if the authors/sources of Genesis come from the time of the monarchy. . . . Jacob was married to two sisters even though this is outlawed in Lev 18:18. The illicit union of Judah and Tamar leads directly to David; again something one would assume would be covered up by later authors. Intermarriage by Judah, Simeon, and Joseph brings no approbation as in Deut 7:3; Exod 34:16.[30]

Further, using a concubine when the legitimate wife was barren and the passing over of the firstborn is illegal according to Deuteronomy 21:15-17, but these actions are recorded as done by the Patriarchs.

Genesis also has unique features which are hard to explain on a late date. Oath-taking symbolized by placing a hand under the thigh (Gen 24:2,3,9; 47:29) is unique to Genesis. Only in Genesis is Hebron called Mamre, and Paddan Aram rather than Aram used. In fact the Arameans were later enemies of Israel, but are friends and family in Genesis. Writing is altogether absent even in the purchase of the cave of Machpelah (Genesis 23), unlike later practice (Jer 32:10-14). Genesis 15:19-21 lists ten nations in Canaan which are to be displaced, but the Philistines are left out. This may well reflect the fact that the later Philistines had not yet migrated from Caphtor (Amos 9:7) in the thirteenth century B.C. By the time of the conquest the Kenites and Kennizites are not conquered but are friends and are absorbed into Israel even though they were initially listed. Caleb was a Kennizite. Esau (also called Edom) as the brother of Jacob (also called Israel) seems odd if invented at a later time in light of the long hostility between the two nations during the exile and after (cf. Obad). The story of Simeon's participation with Levi in deceiving the Shechemites (Genesis 34) and their consequent curse by Jacob (Gen 49:5-7) precede Simeon's absorption into Judah soon after the conquest (Josh 19:9). And why would later authors invent Reuben and Manasseh, the firstborn sons of Jacob and Joseph, who nevertheless serve a more marginal role in the history of the nation? Sarna's conclusion is persuasive:

> The cumulative effect of all this internal evidence leads to the decisive conclusion that the patriarchal traditions in the Book of Genesis are of great antiquity. This assertion is quite inde-

---

[30]Ibid., p. xv.

pendent of the external material culled from thousands of documents uncovered in the towns of Mari, Nuzi, Alalakh, and Ugarit, as well as in other ancient sites in the Near East. These texts issue from the second millennium B.C.E. and provide numerous parallels with patriarchal traditions. . . . The many different kinds of internal biblical evidence cited above reinforce the case viewing Genesis as an authentic mirror of early historical tradition and weaken a claim of later inventiveness.[31]

Kenneth Kitchen's recent work, *On the Reliability of the Old Testament*, gives even more evidence for the plausibility of the setting of Genesis. While most of this is of more direct relevance for the next volume of this commentary, what he notes for Genesis 12–50 applies to the book as a whole. He notes that such facts as long-distance marriages (Genesis 24), east delta residences of Pharaohs, eastern alliances of kings and Elamite intervention west of the Euphrates (Genesis 14), and the price of male slaves being 20 shekels all occurred specifically in the early second millennium, during the time of the Patriarchs and not in other periods.[32] He concludes:

> It should be clear . . . that the main features of the patriarchal narratives either fit specifically into the first half of the second millennium [2000–1500 BC] or are consistent with such a dating; some features common to that epoch and to later periods clearly must be taken with the early-second-millennium horizon. In contrast to this, data in these narratives that do clearly originate from well after circa 1600 are relatively few and are merely late updates.[33]

Genesis is no attempt to write a history book in anything like a modern sense. This does not mean that it has no interest in what actually happened. Like all pieces of literature it must be evaluated on its own terms with its own purposes in mind, not in ours. Merrill helpfully comments (p. 9):

> It is therefore appropriate to describe Genesis as "sacred history" or an account of history with a preeminently theological slant and agenda. This by no means undercuts its reliability as "real"

---

[31]Ibid., xvii.
[32]Kitchen, *Reliability*, Ch. 7.
[33]Ibid., p. 372.

history but it does necessitate a sensitive hermeneutic, one that takes account of the human author's own special objectives and perspectives as he, led by the Holy Spirit, addressed his own generation about the meaning of their current situation and the historical events that brought them to where they are.[34]

THE DOCUMENTARY HYPOTHESIS[35]

Since the time of French court physician Jean Astruc, western critical biblical scholarship has been engaged in an ongoing debate regarding the unity and authorship of the Pentateuch. Astruc noticed that Genesis seemed to begin with two creation accounts. The first (Genesis 1:1-24a) used the Hebrew word Elohim (God) for deity and described how the transcendent creator spoke the world into existence in an orderly fashion. The second account (Genesis 2:4b-24) referred to deity as Yahweh Elohim (LORD God) and spoke in anthropomorphic terms of God creating the male from the dust of the ground and breathing into his nostrils the breath of life. He then realizes that the male is lonely and creates the woman from the side of the man. Astruc argued that these differences indicated that Moses used sources in the composition of the book of Genesis.

Eichhorn, however, built upon Astruc's work to argue against the unity of Genesis suggesting that it was composed of multiple conflicting sources which were pasted together late in Israel's history. The first of these sources (later known as 'P' for priestly) was found in the first creation account and particularly in the book of Leviticus. The second source (known as 'J' for Jahwist) was famous for using the special covenant name for Israel's God prior to its revelation to Moses in Exodus 6. J was believed to have come from the southern kingdom of Judah. The third source (later known as 'E') used Elohim to refer to deity prior to the Exodus and derived from the northern kingdom of Israel. The fourth source ('D') was found mainly in the book of Deuteronomy.

---

[34]Eugene H. Merrill, "The Peoples of the Old Testament according to Genesis 10," *BibSac* 154 (Jan–Mar 1997): 9.
[35]See the fuller account in Ronald E. Clements, *One Hundred Years of Old Testament Interpretation* (Guildford, UK: Lutterworth, 1976).

DeWette helped supply a chronological framework for the authorship of the putative sources by noticing that the book of the law found in Josiah's day seemed remarkably like the book of Deuteronomy and not like Exodus, Leviticus, or Numbers. DeWette suggested that Deuteronomy was not just discovered in 622 B.C. but was actually written as a sort of pious fraud to support the revival of Josiah. With the source 'D' now having a secure date, critical scholars began the business of hypothesizing about the possible dates for the other three sources of the Pentateuch.

At first it was suggested that the four sources be arranged PJED. But the work of Graf and Wellhausen moved P to the end of the sequence yielding JEDP. Adopting the evolutionary thought of the last half of the nineteenth century with an almost anti-Semitic[36] distaste for anything priestly and ritualistic and a rather naïve acceptance of the theory of the golden age, Wellhausen portrayed the growth of the Pentateuch as mirroring the experiences of the nation throughout its history. Beginning with polytheism Israel's religion evolved through henotheism (the worship of one god without denying the existence of others) to monotheism, reaching its spiritual and intellectual peak in the time of David and Solomon. This golden era was represented in the Pentateuch by the source J. After the split of the kingdom the northern source E followed in the 8/9th century B.C. D, which was authored to support Josiah's reform, followed in the late 7th century. D, with its theology of blessings for obedience and curses for disobedience, is the first indication of a sort of spiritual degeneration from the grace-oriented traditions of J and E. But it was in the postexilic period, when the priests were in control, that the legalism of late Judaism began to develop. The source P purportedly comes from this time and represents a serious decline from the golden age. This view of Pentateuchal origins was the consensus view of critical scholarship until the 1970s and is still dominant in many scholarly circles.

More recent Pentateuch scholarship has attacked this consensus on a number of fronts. To begin with, recent scholarship has asked, So what? Even if the documentary hypothesis or something

---

[36]I am not suggesting that Wellhausen himself was anti-Semitic or that he would have supported the development in Germany of Nazism. But he, like all of us, was a child of his times and his background.

like it were proven to be true, the text which was accepted as Scripture is the text we have. Certainly sources were used but that does not preclude inspiration nor even historical reliability. Secondly, recent scholarship has questioned the certainty with which earlier scholarship has argued for the documentary hypothesis. For example, how can one be so certain about a theory which presumes simplistic evolutionary progress? Such confidence in smooth progress is understandable in the late nineteenth century when evolution as an idea was at its heyday, but today evolution, if it takes place at all, is known to occur in a very irregular fashion. Also, the Lutheran dichotomy between grace and works and gospel and law which so influenced Wellhausen in the late nineteenth century is no longer regarded as tenable.

From within the critical consensus such works as Whybray's *The Making of the Pentateuch* have questioned the criteria for distinguishing between sources. While his work is limited to the narrative portions of the Pentateuch and not the legal materials, Whybray demonstrates the inconsistencies, inaccuracies and other errors of logic in the criteria used to distinguish sources by the classical documentary hypothesis. Detailed studies such as McConville's work, *Law and Theology in Deuteronomy*, and Sprinkle's *'The Book of the Covenant': A Literary Approach* suggest that the criteria as typically applied fare no better when applied to the legal materials. Recent approaches drawing on insights from the study of literature more generally have argued that many of the supposed contradictions between the sources are actually better explained by assuming a more sophisticated literary technique by the authors of biblical narratives. While the author of the Pentateuch undoubtedly used sources, what we have is a carefully crafted literary unity. Attempts to uncover the supposed sources and then date them have proven to be ultimately unsuccessful in sustaining a scholarly consensus. Even if we could identify the sources with confidence, they would only be of historical interest. They would not be considered authoritative outside of their canonical context. In this commentary I will focus on the final form of the text and not on speculation about the possible underlying sources.

INTERPRETIVE OUTLINE OF GENESIS 1–11

GOD'S ATTEMPT TO SUSTAIN A RELATIONSHIP WITH ALL HUMANKIND

I. THE CREATOR AND HIS CREATION — 1:1–2:25
  A. The Creation Viewed Cosmically — 1:1–2:4a
    1. The First Act of Creation — 1:1

Excursus on the Translation of Genesis 1:1-3

    2. The State of the Unfinished Earth at Its Creation: Unformed and Unfilled — 1:2
    3. The Forming of the Earth — The First Three Days — 1:3-13
        a. Day One: The Forming of Day and Night — 1:3-5
        b. Day Two: The Forming of the Atmosphere and Seas — 1:6-8
        c. Day Three: The Forming of the Land — 1:9-13
    4. The Filling of the Earth — Days Four to Six — 1:14-25
        a. Day Four: The Filling of Day and Night — 1:14-19
        b. Day Five: The Filling of the Atmosphere and Seas — 1:20-23
        c. Day Six: The Filling of the Land — 1:24-25
    5. Man: The Goal and Crown of Creation — 1:26-30

Excursus on the Interpretation of Humanity as "The Image and Likeness of God"

    6. The Creator's Evaluation of His Work — 1:31
    7. The Creator's Cessation of His Work — 2:1-3
    8. Summary Inclusio — 2:4a
  B. The Creation Viewed in Terms of Personal Relationships — 2:4-25
    1. The Pre-Fall Male — 2:4-7
    2. The Environment of the Pre-Fall Male — 2:8-14

Excursus: Parallels between the Garden of Eden and the Tabernacle

    3. The Pre-Fall Work of Man and the Limitations on His Freedom — 2:15-17

4. The Completion of the Pre-Fall Male — 2:18-25
II. **THE RELATIONSHIP BETWEEN GOD AND HUMANITY BROKEN** — 3:1-24
   A. **The First Disobedience** — 3:1-7
   Excursus on the Lord God's Words and Their Distortion in the Temptation Scene
   B. **The Discovery and Punishment of the Disobedience** — 3:8-19
      1. The Discovery of the Disobedience — 3:8-13
      2. The Punishment of the Disobedience — 3:14-19
         a. The Punishment of the Serpent — 3:14-15
         b. The Punishment of the Woman — 3:16
         c. The Punishment of the Man — 3:17-19
   C. **Grace in the Midst of Judgment** — 3:20-24
III. **HUMAN SOCIETY WITHOUT THE DIVINE-HUMAN RELATIONSHIP** — 4:1-26
   A. **The Sacrifices of Cain and Abel** — 4:1-7
      1. The Birth of Cain and Abel — 4:1-2a
      2. The First Offerings to the LORD — 4:2b-4a
      3. The LORD's Evaluation of the Offerings — 4:4b-5a
      4. Cain's Reaction to the Rejection of His Offering — 4:5b
      5. The LORD Warns Cain about His Reaction — 4:6-7
   B. **The Onset and Punishment of Violence** — 4:8-12
      1. Cain Becomes the First Murderer — 4:8
      2. The LORD Confronts Cain for His Violence — 4:9
      3. The LORD's Punishment of Cain for His Violence — 4:10-12
   C. **The Mitigation of the Punishment** — 4:13-16
      1. Cain's Plea to the LORD — 4:13-14
      2. The Protective Sign for Cain — 4:15
      3. Cain Settles East of Eden — 4:16
   D. **The Family History from Cain to Lamech** — 4:17-24
      1. The Line from Cain to Lamech — 4:17-18
      2. The Polygamous Family Line of Lamech — 4:19
      3. Civilization Begins — 4:20-22
      4. Lamech's Cynical Boast — 4:23-24
   E. **Partial Rehabilitation of Divine-Human Relationships** — 4:25-26
      1. The Birth of Seth to Replace Abel — 4:25
      2. Humanity Begins to Call on the Name of the LORD — 4:26
IV. **THE DESTRUCTION AND RESTORATION OF CREATION** — 5:1–9:17

A. The Family Line from Seth to Noah — 5:1-32
Special Study: Concrete Evidence That Biblical Genealogies Are Not Modern
1. Resumptive Repetition of Creation — 5:1-2
2. Ten "Generations" from Adam to Noah — 5:3-31
3. The Sons of Noah — 5:32

B. The Two Lines Intermarry — 6:1-4
1. The Sons of God and the Daughters of Men — 6:1-2
2. The Decision to Reduce the Life Span of Humanity — 6:3
3. The Nephilim — 6:4a
4. The Warrior Children Born from the Illicit Unions — 6:4b

C. The Decision to Send the Flood — 6:5-13
1. The LORD Recognizes the Extent of the Evil — 6:5
2. The LORD's Regret at Having Made Humankind — 6:6
3. Decision to Destroy Creation — 6:7
4. The Exception of Noah — 6:8

Introduction to the Flood Narrative
5. Noah Introduced — 6:9-10
6. Reiteration of the Corruption and God's Recognition of It — 6:11-12
7. Announcement to Noah of Decision to Judge Humanity — 6:13

D. The Directive to Build the Ark — 6:14-22
1. Command to Build the Ark with Detailed Instructions — 6:14-16
2. Warning of the Flood — 6:17
3. God's Promise of a Covenant with Noah and Family — 6:18
4. Command to Preserve Animals — 6:19-20
5. Food for Noah's Family and the Animals — 6:21
6. Noah's Obedience — 6:22

E. The Command to Enter the Ark — 7:1-10
1. The Command to Enter — 7:1
2. Provision for Clean and Unclean Animals — 7:2-3
3. God's Pronouncement of Imminent Destruction — 7:4
4. Noah's Obedience — 7:5
5. Noah's Family and the Animals Actually Enter the Ark — 7:6-9
6. Seven-Day Waiting Period for the Flood — 7:10

F. The Floodwaters Rise — 7:11-24
1. The Underground and Aboveground Waters Begin — 7:11-12
2. Noah's Family and Creatures Safe in the Ark — 7:13-16

3. The Rising of the Floodwaters to Their Peak — 7:17-24
G. **The Turning Point of the Flood: God Remembers Noah** — 8:1a
H. **The Floodwaters Abate** — 8:1b-14
   1. The Rain Stops and the Flood Begins to Abate — 8:1b-3
   2. The Floodwaters Dry Up and the Dry Land Reappears — 8:4-14
I. **Exiting the Ark** — 8:15-19
   1. The Command to Exit the Ark — 8:15-17
   2. The Exiting of the Ark — 8:18-19
J. **Yahweh's Gracious Response to Noah's Altar** — 8:20-22
   1. The Altar and Sacrifice of Noah — 8:20
   2. Yahweh's Response — 8:21-22
K. **The Preservation of Noah's Line** — 9:1-7
   1. The Recommissioning of Humanity — 9:1
   2. The Conditions under Which Animals May Now Be Eaten — 9:2-5a
   3. Prohibition of Killing Other Humans — 9:5b-6
   4. Reminder of the Recommissioning — 9:7
L. **The Covenant and Its Sign** — 9:8-17
   1. The Covenant with the New Creation — 9:8-11
   2. The Sign of the Covenant: The Bow — 9:12-17

Excursus: The Bow in Genesis 9:12-17

V. **THE FALL OF THE POST-FLOOD GENERATIONS** — 9:18–11:32
   A. **The Fall of Noah** — 9:18-29
      1. Introduction — 9:18-19
      2. The Sin of Ham — 9:20-22
      3. The Contrasting Respectfulness of Shem and Japheth — 9:23
      4. The Curse of Ham's Son Canaan — 9:24-25
      5. The Blessing of Shem and Japheth — 9:26-27
      6. The Remainder of Noah's Life and His Death — 9:28-29
   B. **The Families of the Sons of Noah** — 10:1-32
      1. Introduction — 10:1
      2. The Descendants of Japheth — 10:2-5
      3. The Descendants of Ham — 10:6-20
         a. The Descendants of Ham — 10:6
         b. The Descendants of Cush (Ethiopia) — 10:7-12
         c. The Descendants of Mizraim (Egypt) — 10:13-14
         d. The Descendants of Canaan — 10:15-19
         e. Summary Statement — 10:20
      4. The Descendants of Shem — 10:21-31

         a. Introduction — 10:21
         b. The Descendants of Shem — 10:22
         c. The Descendants of Aram (Syria) — 10:23
         d. The Descendants of Arphaxad — 10:24
         e. The Descendants of Eber — 10:25-29
         f. Summary Statement — 10:30-31
      5. Overall Summary Statement — 10:32
   C. The Babel Episode — 11:1-9
      1. The Setting for the Episode — 11:1-2
      2. The Goals of Babel — 11:3-4
      3. The LORD's Judgment on Babel — 11:5-9
   D. The Family History from Shem to Abraham's Father Terah — 11:10-26
      1. Introduction — 11:10a
      2. Ten "Generations" between Shem and Abram — 11:10b-26

BIBLIOGRAPHY OF SOURCES FOR GENESIS

Alexander, P.S. "The Targumim and Early Exegesis of 'Sons of God' in Gen 6." *Journal of Jewish Studies* 23 (1972): 60-71.

Alexander, T. Desmond. *From Paradise to the Promised Land.* Grand Rapids: Baker Books, 1995.

Alexander, T. Desmond, and David W. Baker, eds. *Dictionary of the Old Testament: Pentateuch.* Downers Grove, IL: InterVarsity Press, 2003.

Alter, Robert. *The Art of Biblical Narrative.* New York: Harper Collins, 1981.

_____. *The Art of Biblical Poetry.* New York: Harper Collins, 1985.

_____. *Genesis.* New York: W.W. Norton, 1996.

Andersen, Francis I. *The Hebrew Verbless Clause in the Pentateuch.* Journal of Biblical Literature Monograph Series XIV. Edited by Robert A. Kraft. Nashville: Abingdon Press, 1970.

_____. "On Reading Genesis 1-3." In *Backgrounds for the Bible.* Edited by Michael Patrick O'Connor and David Noel Freedman, 137-150. Winona Lake, IN: Eisenbrauns, 1987.

_____. *The Sentence in Biblical Hebrew.* Janua Linguaoum Series Practica, 231. The Hague: Mouton Publishers, 1974.

Anderson, Bernard W., and Walter Harrelson, eds. *Israel's Prophetic Heritage.* New York: Harper & Brothers, 1962.

Anderson, Gary. "Celibacy or Consummation in the Garden? Reflections on Early Jewish and Christian Interpretations of the Garden of Eden." *Harvard Theological Review* 82:2 (1989): 121-148.

_____. *The Genesis of Perfection.* Louisville, KY: Westminster John Knox Press, 2001.

Arnold, Bill T. *Encountering the Book of Genesis.* Grand Rapids: Baker Books, 1998.

Atkinson, David. *The Message of Genesis 1–11.* Leicester, England: Inter-Varsity Press, 1990.

Auld, A. Graeme. "Sabbath, Work and Creation: Reconsidered." *HENOCH* VIII (1986):273-280.

Baker, D.W., J.K. Hoffmeier, and A.R. Millard, eds. *Faith, Tradition, & History.* Winona Lake, IN: Eisenbrauns, 1994.

Baldwin, Joyce G. *The Message of Genesis 12–50.* Leicester, England: Inter-Varsity Press, 1986.

Bane, Gordon. *Geocentric Bible #2.* Cleveland, OH: The Biblical Astronomer, 2003.

Bar-Efrat, Shimon. *Narrative Art in the Bible.* Sheffield: The Almond Press, 1989.

Barr, James. *Biblical Faith and Natural Theology.* Oxford: Clarendon, 1993.

_____. *The Garden of Eden and the Hope of Immortality.* Minneapolis: Fortress Press, 1992.

_____. "The Image of God in the Book of Genesis – A Study of Terminology." *Bulletin of the John Rylands Library* 51 (1968–69): 11-26.

Bassett, F.W. "Noah's Nakedness and the Curse of Canaan: A Case of Incest?" *Vetus Testamentum* 21 (1971): 232-237.

Benjamin, Don C. "Israel's God: Mother and Midwife." *Biblical Theology Bulletin* 19 (1989): 115-120.

Bergant, Dianne. "Is the Biblical Worldview Anthropocentric?" *New Theology Review* 4 (1991): 5-14.

Berlin, Adele. *Poetics and Interpretation of Biblical Narrative.* Sheffield: The Almond Press, 1983.

Betto, Frei. *Fidel and Religion.* Sydney: Pathfinder, 1986.

Bimson, J.J. *Redating the Exodus and Conquest.* Journal for the Study of the Old Testament Supplement Series 5. Sheffield: JSOT Press, 1978.

Bird, Phyllis A. "'Male and Female He Created Them': Gen 1:27b in the Context of the Priestly Account of Creation." *Harvard Theological Review* 74:2 (1981): 129-159.

Bledstein, Adrien Janis. "Was Eve Cursed?" *Bible Review* 9 (1993/1): 42-45.

Blenkinsopp, Joseph. *Prophecy and Canon.* Notre Dame, IN: University of Notre Dame Press, 1977.

Blocher, Henri. *In the Beginning. The Opening Chapters of Genesis.* Translated by David G. Preston. Downers Grove, IL: InterVarsity, 1984.

Boadt, Lawrence. "Chronicles and Genealogies." *The Bible Today* 26 (1988): 203-208.

Borgman, Paul. *Genesis: The Story We Haven't Heard.* Downers Grove, IL: InterVarsity Press, 2001.

Bouw, Gerardus D. *Geocentricity Primer.* Cleveland, OH: The Biblical Astronomer, 1999.

Brichto, Herbert Chanan. *The Names of God.* Oxford: Oxford University Press, 1998.

_____. *Toward a Grammar of Biblical Poetics.* Oxford: Oxford University Press, 1992.

Brodie, Thomas L. *Genesis as Dialogue.* Oxford: Oxford University Press, 2001.

Bruckner, James K. *Implied Law in the Abraham Narrative.* Journal for the Study of the Old Testament Supplement Series 335. Sheffield: Sheffield Academic Press, 2001.

Brueggemann, Walter. *Genesis.* Interpretation. Atlanta: John Knox Press, 1982.

Brunner, Emil. *Man in Revolt: A Christian Anthropology.* Trans. by Olive Wyon. Philadelphia: Westminster, 1939.

Bryant, David T. "A Reevaluation of Gen 4 and 5 in Light of Recent Studies in Genealogical Fluidity." *Zeitschrift für die Alttestamentliche Wissenschaft* 99 (1987): 180-188.

Bultmann, Christoph. "Creation at the Beginning of History: Johann Gottfried Herder's Interpretation of Genesis 1." *Journal for the Study of the Old Testament* 68 (1995): 23-32.

Burke, Derek, ed. *Creation and Evolution*. When Christians Disagree. Downers Grove, IL: InterVarsity, 1985.

Burns, Dan E. "Dream Form in Genesis 2:4b–3:24: Asleep in the Garden." *Journal for the Study of the Old Testament* 37 (1987): 3-14.

Buth, Randall. "Methodological Collision between Source Criticism and Discourse Analysis." In *Biblical Hebrew and Discourse Linguistics*. Edited by Robert D. Bergen. Dallas: Summer Institute of Linguistics, 1994.

Calvin, John. *Commentaries on the First Book of Moses, Called Genesis*. Translated by John King. Grand Rapids: Eerdmans, 1948.

Campbell, Gordon. "Milton's Eden." In *A Walk in the Garden: Biblical, Iconographical and Literary Images of Eden*. Edited by Paul Morris and Deborah Sawyer, 220-228. Journal for the Study of the Old Testament Supplement Series 136 (1992).

Carlson, Richard F., ed. *Science & Christianity: Four Views*. Downers Grove, IL: InterVarsity, 2000.

Carr, David M. "The Politics of Sexual Subversion: A Diachronic Perspective on the Garden of Eden Story." *Journal of Biblical Literature* 112/4 (1993): 577-595.

_____ . *Reading the Fractures of Genesis*. Louisville, KY: Westminster John Knox Press, 1996.

Cassuto, Umberto. *A Commentary on the Book of Genesis. Part One: From Adam to Noah. Part Two: From Noah to Abraham*. Jerusalem: Magnes Press, 1961, 1964.

Castellino, G. "The Origins of Civilization according to Biblical and Cuneiform Texts." In *I Studied Inscriptions from before the Flood: Ancient Near Eastern, Literary, and Linguistic Approaches to Genesis 1–11*. Edited by Richard S. Hess and David Tsumura, 75-95.

Translated by David W. Baker. Winona Lake, IN: Eisenbrauns, 1994.

Charlesworth, James H., ed. *The Old Testament Pseudepigrapha.* Garden City, NY: Doubleday, 1983–1985.

Clark, W.M. "The Animal Series in the Primeval History." *Vetus Testamentum* 18 (1968): 433-449.

Clements, Ronald E. *One Hundred Years of Old Testament Interpretation.* Guildford, UK: Lutterworth, 1976.

Clines, David J.A. "The Image of God in Man." *Tyndale Bulletin* 19 (1968): 53-103.

_____. *The Theme of the Pentateuch.* Journal for the Study of the Old Testament Supplement Series 10. Sheffield: JSOT Press, 1978.

_____. *What Does Eve Do to Help? And Other Readerly Questions to the Old Testament.* Journal for the Study of the Old Testament Supplement Series 94. Sheffield: JSOT Press, 1990.

Clines, David J.A., and Philip R. Davies, eds. *The World of Genesis.* Journal for the Study of the Old Testament Supplement Series 257. Sheffield: Sheffield Academic Press, 1998.

Clines David J.A., Stephen E. Fowl, & Stanley E. Porter, eds. *The Bible in Three Dimensions.* Journal for the Study of the Old Testament Supplement Series 87. Sheffield: Sheffield Academic Press, 1990.

Clines, David J.A., and Stephen D. Moore, eds. *Auguries.* Journal for the Study of the Old Testament Supplement Series 269. Sheffield: Sheffield Academic Press, 1998.

Coats, George W. *Genesis with an Introduction to Narrative Literature.* Grand Rapids: Eerdmans, 1983.

Cole, Timothy J. "Enoch, a Man Who Walked with God." *Bibliotheca Sacra* 148 (1991): 288-297.

Collins, C. John. "The *Wayyiqtol* as 'Pluperfect': When and Why." *Tyndale Bulletin* 46.1 (1995): 117-140.

Cotter, David W. *Genesis.* Berit Olam. Studies in Hebrew Narrative & Poetry. Collegeville, MN: Liturgical Press, 2003.

Cottrell, Jack. *Gender Roles and the Bible: Creation, the Fall, and Redemption.* Joplin, MO: College Press, 1994.

Dahood, M.J. *Psalms II.* Anchor Bible. Garden City, NY: Doubleday, 1966.

Davidson, Richard M. "The Theology of Sexuality in the Beginning: Genesis 1–2." *Andrews University Seminary Studies* 26/1 (1988): 5-24.

Davies, Philip R. "Sons of Cain." In *A Word in Season: Essays in Honor of William McKane.* Edited by James D. Martin and Philip R. Davies. Journal for the Study of the Old Testament Supplement Series 42. Sheffield: JSOT Press, 1986.

Davila, James R. "The Flood Hero as King and Priest." *Journal of Near Eastern Studies* 54 (1995): 199-214.

Dawson, David Allen. *Text-Linguistics and Biblical Hebrew.* Journal for the Study of the Old Testament Supplement Series 177. Sheffield: Sheffield Academic Press, 1994.

Delitzsch, F. *A New Commentary on Genesis.* Vol. 1. Trans by S. Taylor. Edinburgh: T & T Clark, 1888.

Dembski, William A., ed. *Mere Creation: Science, Faith & Intelligent Design.* Downers Grove, IL: InterVarsity, 1998.

Dembski, William A., and James M. Kushner, eds. *Signs of Intelligence: Understanding Intelligent Design.* Grand Rapids: Brazos Press, 2001.

Dines, Jennifer. "Imaging Creation: The Septuagint Translation of Genesis 1:2." *Heythrop Journal* 36 (1995): 439-450.

Eichler, Barry L. "On Reading Genesis 12:10-20." *Tehillah le-Moshe: Biblical and Judaic Studies in Honor of Moshe Greenberg.* Edited by Mordechai Cogan, Barry L. Eichler, and Jeffrey H. Tigay. Winona Lake, IN: Eisenbrauns, 1997.

Etheridge, J.W. *The Targums of Onkelos and Jonathon Ben Uzziel on the Pentateuch with the Fragments of the Jerusalem Targum.* New York: KTAV Publishing, 1968.

Evans, A. *The Palace of Minoa at Knossos.* London: Mcmillan, 1921–1936.

Fields, Calvin. *Things You Never Heard.* Pheonix: ACW Press, 2001.

Fields, Weston W. *Sodom and Gomorrah.* Journal for the Study of the Old Testament Supplement Series 231. Sheffield: Sheffield Academic Press, 1997.

Fishbane, Michael. *Text and Texture.* New York: Schocken Books, 1979.

Foh, Susan T. "What Is the Woman's Desire?" *Westminster Theological Journal* 37 (1974/75): 376-383.

Forrest, Robert W.E. "Paradise Lost Again: Violence and Obedience in the Flood Narrative." *Journal for the Study of the Old Testament* 62 (1994): 3-18.

Fox, Everett. *The Five Books of Moses.* Schocken Bible, Volume I. New York: Schocken Books, 1995.

Fretheim, Terence E. *Genesis.* New Interpreter's Bible. Volume 1. Nashville: Abingdon, 1994.

_____. *The Pentateuch.* Nashville: Abingdon Press, 1996.

Friedman, Richard Elliot. "Torah (Pentateuch)" *Anchor Bible Dictionary* 6 (1992): 605-622.

Frishman, Judith, and Lucas Van Rompay, eds. *The Book of Genesis in Jewish and Oriental Christian Interpretation.* Traditio Exegetica Graeca 5. Louvain: Peeters, 1997.

Futato, Mark D. "Because It Had Rained: A Study of Gen 2:5-7 with Implications for Gen 2:4-25 and Gen 1:1–2:3." *Westminster Theological Journal* 60 (1998): 1-21.

Galambush, Julie. "'ADAM FROM 'ADAMA, 'SSA FROM 'IS: Derivation and Subordination in Genesis 2.4b–3.24." In *History and Interpretation: Essays in Honour of John H. Hayes.* Edited by M. Patrick Graham, William P. Brown, and Jeffrey K. Kuan, 33-46. Journal for the Study of the Old Testament Supplement Series. 173. Sheffield: Sheffield Academic Press, 1993.

Gelander, Shamai. *The Good Creator.* Atlanta, GA: Scholars Press, 1997.

Gibson, John L. *Genesis*. Volumes 1 and 2. Daily Study Bible. Philadelphia: Westminster Press, 1981, 1982.

Gispen, W.H. *Genesis I.* Commentar op het Oude Testament. Kampen: Kok, 1974.

Gitay, Yehoshua. "Geography and Theology in the Biblical Narrative: The Question of Genesis 2–12." In *Prophets and Paradigms. Essays in Honor of Gene M. Tucker.* Edited by Stephen Breck Reid, 205-216. Journal for the Study of the Old Testament Supplement Series 229. Sheffield: Sheffield Academic Press, 1996.

Good, Edwin M. *Irony in the Old Testament.* Philadelphia: The Westminster Press, 1950.

Greenspahn, Frederick E. "A Mesopotamian Proverb and Its Biblical Reverberations." *Journal of the American Oriental Society* 114 (1994): 33-38.

Hamilton, Victor P. *The Book of Genesis, Chapters 1–17.* New International Commentary on the Old Testament. Grand Rapids: Eerdmans, 1990.

_____. *The Book of Genesis, Chapters 18–50.* New International Commentary on the Old Testament. Grand Rapids: Eerdmans, 1995.

Harland, P.J. "Vertical or Horizontal: The Sin of Babel." *Vetus Testamentum* XLVIII/4 (1998): 515-533.

Hart, Ian. "Genesis 1:1–2:3 as a Prologue to the Book of Genesis." *Tyndale Bulletin* 46.2 (1995): 315-336.

Hauser, Alan J. "Linguistic and Thematic Links between Genesis 4:1-16 and Genesis 2–3." *Journal of the Evangelical Theological Society* 23 (1980): 297-305.

Heidel, Alexander. *The Babylonian Genesis.* Chicago: The University of Chicago Press, 1942.

Hendel, Ronald S. "4Q252 and the Flood Chronology of Genesis 7–8: A Text Critical Solution." *Dead Sea Discoveries* 2 (1995): 72-79.

_____. "Of Demigods and the Deluge: Toward an Interpretation of Genesis 6:1-4." *Journal of Biblical Literature* 106/1 (1987): 13-26.

_____. *The Text of Genesis 1–11*. New York: Oxford University Press, 1998.

Hertz, J.H., ed. *The Pentateuch and Haftorahs*. London: Soncino Press, 1956.

Hess, Richard S. "Eden — A Well-watered Place." *Bible Review* 7 (1991/6): 28-33.

_____. "The Genealogies of Genesis 1–11 and Comparative Literature." *Biblica* 70 (1989): 241-254.

_____. "Genesis 1–2 in Its Literary Context." *Tyndale Bulletin* 41.4 (1990): 143-152.

_____. *Studies in the Personal Names of Genesis 1–11*. Alter Orient und Altes Testament. Neukirchen-Vluyn: Neukirchen Verlag, 1993.

Hess, Richard S., and David Toshio Tsumura, eds. *I Studied Inscriptions from before the Flood: Ancient Near Eastern, Literary, and Linguistic Approaches to Genesis 1–11*. Sources for Biblical and Theological Study 4. Winona Lake, IN: Eisenbrauns, 1994.

Hess, Richard S., Gordon J. Wenham, and Philip E. Satterthwaite, eds. *He Swore an Oath: Biblical Themes from Genesis 12–50*. Grand Rapids: Baker, 1994.

Hobbs, Herschel H. *The Origin of All Things*. Waco, TX: Word Books, 1975.

Holloway, Steven W. "What Ship Goes There: The Flood Narratives in the Gilgamesh Epic and Genesis Considered in Light of Ancient Near Eastern Temple Ideology." *Zeitschrift für die Alttestamentliche Wissenschaft* 103 (1991): 328-355.

House, Colin L. "Some Notes on Translating in Genesis 1:16." *Andrews University Seminary Studies* 25 (1987): 241-248.

Jacob, B. *Der Erste Buch der Tora*. New York: KTAV, 1974 reprint.

Jaki, Stanley L. *Bible and Science*. Front Royal, VA: Christendom Press, 1996.

―――――. *Genesis 1 through the Ages*. London: Thomas More Press, 1992.

―――――. *The Savior of Science*. Grand Rapids: Eerdmans, 2000.

―――――. *Science & Creation*. Lanham, NY: University Press of America, 1990.

Joüon, Paul. *A Grammar of Biblical Hebrew*. Translated and revised by T. Muraoka. Subsidia Biblica 14. Two Volumes. Rome: Editrice Pontificio Istituto Biblio, 1993.

Kaiser, Walter C. *Toward an Old Testament Theology*. Grand Rapids: Zondervan, 1978.

Kashner, Menachem M. *Encyclopedia of Biblical Interpretation*. New York, NY: American Biblical Encyclopedia Society Inc., 1953.

Keil, C.F., and Delitzsch, F. *Commentary on the Old Testament: The Pentateuch*. Grand Rapids: Eerdmans, 1978.

Kempf, Stephen. "Introducing the Garden of Eden: The Structure and Function of Genesis 2:4b-7." *Journal of Translations and Text Linguistics*. Vol. 7, no. 4. Pp. 33-55.

Kidner, Derek. *Genesis*. Tyndale Old Testament Commentary. Downers Grove, IL: InterVarsity, 1967.

Kikawada, Isaac, and Arthur Quinn. *Before Abraham Was: The Unity of Genesis 1–11*. Nashville: Abingdon, 1985.

Kio, Stephen Hre. "The Problem of Cultural Adjustment: Understanding and Translating Genesis 2:24." *The Bible Translator* 42/2 (1991): 210-217.

Kissling, Paul J. "The Rainbow in Genesis 9:12-17: A Triple Entendre?" *Stone-Campbell Journal* 4 (2001): 249-261.

―――――. *Reliable Characters in the Primary History: Profiles of Moses, Joshua, Elijah, and Elisha*. Journal for the Study of the Old Testament Supplement Series 224. Sheffield: Sheffield Academic Press, 1996.

_____. *A Sketch of Old Testament Theology.* Lansing, MI: GLCC Publication, 1999.

Kitchen, K.A. *On the Reliability of the Old Testament.* Grand Rapids: Eerdmans, 2003.

Klein, R.W. "Archaic Chronologies and the Textual History of the Old Testament." *Harvard Theological Review* 67 (): 255-263.

Kugel, James L. *The Bible as It Was.* Cambridge, MA: The Belknap Press of Harvard University Press, 1997.

Labuschagne, C.J. "The Life Spans of the Patriarchs." *Oudtestamentum Studien* 25 (1989): 121-127.

Laffey, Alice. *The Pentateuch.* Minneapolis: Fortress Press, 1998.

Lambden, Stephen N. "From Fig Leaves to Fingernails: Some Notes on the Garments of Adam and Eve in the Hebrew Bible and Select Early Postbiblical Jewish Writings." In *A Walk in the Garden: Biblical, Iconographical and Literary Images of Eden.* Edited by Paul Morris and Deborah Sawyer, 74-90. Journal for the Study of the Old Testament Supplement Series 136 (1992).

Landy, Francis. *Paradoxes of Paradise: Identity and Difference in the Song of Songs.* Bible and Literature Series 7. Sheffield: JSOT, 1983.

Lanser, Susan S. "(Feminist) Criticism in the Garden: Inferring Genesis 2-3." *Semeia* 44 (1988): 67-84.

Lapide, Pinchas. "Touching the Forbidden Fruit." *Bible Review* 4 (1988): 42-43.

Leupold, H.C. *Exposition of Genesis.* Two Volumes. Grand Rapids: Baker, 1942. Standard evangelical Lutheran exposition of a previous generation.

Levinson, Jon D. *Creation and the Persistence of Evil.* Princeton, NJ: Princeton University Press, 1994.

_____. *Sinai & Zion.* New Voices in Biblical Studies. New York: Winston Press, 1985.

Lewis, Jack P. *A Study of the Interpretation of Noah and the Flood in Jewish and Christian Literature.* Leiden, Netherlands: Brill, 1968.

Long, V. Philips. *The Art of Biblical History*. Foundations of Contemporary Interpretation 5. Grand Rapids: Zondervan, 1994.

Loughlin, Thomas O. "Adam's Rib and the Equality of the Sexes: Some Medieval Exegesis of Gen 2:21-22." *Irish Theological Quarterly* 59 (1993): 44-54.

Manns, Frederic, ed. *The Sacrifice of Isaac*. Jerusalem: Franciscan Printing Press, 1995.

Martin, W.J. *"Dis-Chronologized" Narrative in the Old Testament*. Vetus Testamentum Supplements 17. Pp. 179-186. Leiden: E.J. Brill, 1968.

Matthews, Kenneth A. *Genesis 1–11:26*. New American Commentary. Nashville: Broadman & Holman, 1996.

McCarter, Kyle P. "A New Challenge to the Documentary Hypothesis." *Bible Review* 4 (1988/2): 34-39.

McEvenue, Sean E. *Narrative Style of the Priestly Writer*. Rome: Biblical Institute Press, 1971.

Meier, Samuel. "Linguistic Clues on the Date and Canaanite Origin of Genesis 2:23-24." *Catholic Biblical Quarterly* 53 (1991): 18-24.

Mendenhall, George E. *The Tenth Generation: The Origins of the Biblical Tradition*. Baltimore: Johns Hopkins University Press, 1973.

Merrill, Eugene H. "The Peoples of the Old Testament according to Genesis 10." *Bibliotheca Sacra* 154 (Jan–Mar 1997): 3-22.

Meyers, Carol. "Naamah 1." In *Women in Scripture*. Edited by Carol Meyers. Grand Rapids: Eerdmans, 2000.

Milgrom, Jacob. "Sex and Wisdom: What the Garden of Eden Story Is Saying." *Bible Review* 10 (1994/6): 21, 51.

Millard, Alan. "Ezekiel 27:19: The Wine Trade of Damascus," *Journal of Semitic Studies* 7 (1962): 201-203.

Millard, A.R., and D.J. Wiseman, eds. *Essays on the Patriarchal Narratives*. Downers Grove, IL: InterVarsity, 1980.

Miscall, Peter D. "Jacques Derrida in the Garden of Eden." *Union Seminary Quarterly Review* 44 (1990): 1-9.

Moberly, R.W.L. *Genesis 12–50*. Sheffield: Sheffield Academic Press, 1995.

Moor, Johannes C. de. "East of Eden." *Zeitschrift für die Alttestamentliche Wissenschaft* 100 (1988): 105-111.

Morris, Henry M. *The Genesis Record*. Grand Rapids: Baker Book House, 1976.

Naeh, Shlomo. "Freedom and Celibacy: A Talmudic Variation on Tales of Temptation and Fall in Genesis and Its Syrian Background." In *The Book of Genesis in Jewish and Oriental Christian Interpretation*. Edited by Judith Frishman and Lucas Van Rompay. Translated by Peretz A. Rodman, 73-89. Traditio Exegetica Graeca 5. Louvain: Peeters, 1997.

Niccacci, Alviero. *The Syntax of the Verb in Classical Hebrew Prose*. Translated by W.G.E. Watson. Journal for the Study of the Old Testament Supplement Series 86. Sheffield: Sheffield Academic Press, 1990.

Nicole, Roger. *Reformed Journal* 34/6 (June 1984): 6-7.

Niditch, Susan. *Chaos to Cosmos*. Atlanta: Scholars Press, 1985.

Niehaus, Jeffrey. "In the Wind of the Storm: Another Look at Genesis III 8." *Vetus Testamentum* XLIV (1994): 263-267.

Oded, B. "The Table of Nations (Genesis 10) — A Socio-Cultural Approach." *Zeitschrift für die Alttestamentliche Wissenschaft* 98 (1986): 14-31.

Park, William. "Why Eve?" *St. Vladimir's Theological Quarterly* 35 (1991): 127-135.

Patai, Raphael. *Man and Temple in Ancient Jewish Myth and Ritual*. London: Thomas Nelson, 1947.

Pawlikowski, John T. "Participation in Economic Life." *The Bible Today* 24 (1986): 363-369.

Pelikan, Jaraslav, ed. *Luther's Works*. St. Louis, MO: Concordia, 1958.

Pennock, Robert T. *Tower of Babel.* Cambridge, MA: The MIT Press, 1999.

Perry, T.A. "A Poetics of Absence: The Structure and Meaning of Genesis 1.2." *Journal for the Study of the Old Testament* 58 (1993): 3-11.

Peterson, Thomas Virgil. *Ham and Japheth: The Mythic World of Whites in the Antebellum South.* ATLA Monograph Series, no. 12. Metuchen, NJ: The Scarecrow Press, 1978.

Plaut, W. Gunther. "Genesis." In *The Torah: A Modern Commentary.* Edited by W. Gunther Plaut. New York: Union of American Hebrew Congregations, 1981.

Pope, Marvin W. *Job.* Anchor Bible. Volume 15. Garden City, NJ: Doubleday, 1965.

Ramsey, G.W. "Is Name-Giving an Act of Domination in Genesis 2:23 and Elsewhere?" *Catholic Bbiblical Quarterly* 50 (1988): 24-35.

Rashi. *Commentaries of the Pentateuch.* Translated by Chaim Pearl. New York: W.W. Norton, 1970.

Rendsburg, Gary A. "Gen 10:13-14: An Authentic Hebrew Tradition Concerning the Origin of the Philistines." *Journal of Northwest Semitic Languages* XIII (1983): 89-96.

_____. *The Redaction of Genesis.* Winona Lake, IN: Eisenbrauns, 1986.

Rendtorff, Rolf. "'Covenant' as a Structuring Concept in Genesis and Exodus." *Journal of Biblical Literature* 108/3 (1989): 385-393.

Robertson, O. Palmer. "Current Critical Questions Concerning the 'Curse of Ham' (Gen 9:20-27)." *Journal of the Evangelical Theological Society* 41/2 (1998): 177-188.

Robinson, Robert B. "Literary Functions of the Genealogies of Genesis." *Catholic Biblical Quarterly* 48 (1986): 595-608.

Rogerson, John W. *Genesis 1-11.* Sheffield: JSOT Press, 1991.

Rogerson, John W., R.W.L. Moberly, and William Johnstone. *Genesis and Exodus.* Sheffield: Sheffield Academic Press, 2001.

Rollston, Christopher A. "The Rise of Monotheism in Ancient Israel: Biblical and Epigraphic Evidence." *Stone-Campbell Journal* 2003 (6.1): 95-115.

Rooker, Mark F. "Genesis 1:1-3: Creation or Re-creation?" *Bibliotheca Sacra* 149 (1992): 411-427.

Rosenberg, Roy A. "*Besaggam* and *Shiloh*." *Zeitschrift für die Alttestamentliche Wissenschaft* 105 (1993): 258-261.

Ross, Allen P. *Creation and Blessing*. Grand Rapids: Baker, 1988.

Ross, Hugh. *Beyond the Cosmos*. Colorado Springs: Navpress, 1996.

_____. *The Creator and the Cosmos*. Second Edition. Colorado Springs: Navpress, 1993.

_____. *The Genesis Question: Scientific Advances and the Accuracy of Genesis*. Colorado Springs: Navpress, 1998.

Ryan, William, and Walter Pitman. *Noah's Flood*. New York: Simon and Schuster, 1998.

Sailhamer, John H. *Genesis*. Expositor's Bible Commentary. Volume 2. Grand Rapids: Zondervan, 1990.

_____. *Genesis Unbound*. Sisters, OR: Multnomah Books, 1996.

_____. *The Pentateuch as Narrative*. Library of Biblical Interpretation. Grand Rapids: Zondervan, 1992.

Sarna, Nahum M. *Genesis*. JPS Torah Commentary. Jerusalem: Jewish Publication Society, 1989.

_____. *Studies in Biblical Interpretation*. Philadelphia: The Jewish Publication Society, 2000.

_____. *Understanding Genesis*. New York: Schocken Books, 1966.

Sasson, J.M. "The 'Tower of Babel' as a Clue to the Redactional Structuring of the Primeval History (Gen. 1–11:9)." In *The Bible World: Essays in Honor of Cyrus H. Gordon*. Edited by G. Rendsburg, 211-219. New York: KTAV, 1980.

Schaeffer, Francis A. *Genesis in Space and Time.* Downers Grove, IL: InterVarsity, 1972.

Schmitt, John J. "Like Eve, Like Adam: *mšl* in Gen 3,16." *Biblica* 72 (1991): 1-22.

Shanks, Herschel, ed. *Ancient Israel.* Washington, DC: Biblical Archaeology Society, 1988.

Sherwin, Byron L. "The Tower of Babel." *The Bible Today* 33 (1995): 104-109.

Skinner, John. *A Critical and Exegetical Commentary on Genesis.* Second Edition. International Critical Commentary. Edinburgh: T & T Clark, 1910.

The Soul of the Text: An Anthology of Jewish Literature. Chicago: The Great Books Foundation, 2000.

Speiser, E.A. *Genesis.* Anchor Bible 1. New York: Doubleday, 1964.

_____. *Oriental and Biblical Studies.* Collected Writings of E.A. Speiser. Edited by J.J. Finkelstein and Moshe Greenberg. Philadelphia: University of Pennsylvania, 1967.

_____. "The Rivers of Paradise." In *Oriental and Biblical Studies.* Collected Writings of E.A. Speiser. Edited by J.J. Finkelstein and Moshe Greenberg, 23-34. Philadelphia: University of Pennsylvania, 1967.

Spina, F.A. "The 'Ground' for Cain's Rejection (Gen 4): *'adamah* in the Context of Gen 1-11." *Zeitschrift für die Alttestamentliche Wissenschaft* 104 (1992): 319-332.

Steck, O.H. *Der Schopfüngsbericht der Priesterschrift.* Göttingen: Vandenhoeck und Ruprecht, 1975.

Steinmetz, Devora. "Vineyard, Farm, and Garden: The Drunkenness of Noah in the Context of Primeval History." *Journal of Biblical Literature* 113/2 (1994): 193-207.

Sternberg, Meir. *Hebrews between Cultures.* Bloomington, IN: Indiana University Press, 1998.

Stordalen, L. "Genesis 2,4: Restudying a *locus classicus.*" *Zeitschrift für die Alttestamentliche Wissenschaft* 104 (1992): 163-177.

Stratton, Beverly J. *Out of Eden: Reading, Rhetoric, and Ideology in Genesis 2–3.* Journal for the Study of the Old Testament Supplement Series 208. Sheffield: Sheffield Academic, 1995.

Stroes, H.R. "Does the Day Begin in the Evening or the Morning?" *Vetus Testamentum* 16 (1966): 460-475.

Thompson, J.A. "Samaritan Evidence for 'All of Them in the Land of Shinar' (Gen 10:10)," *Journal of Biblical Literature* 90 (1971): 99-102.

Timmer, David. *Reformed Journal* 34/4 (April 1984): 2-3.

Toorn, K. van der, and P.W. van der Horst. "Nimrod before and after the Bible." *Harvard Theological Review* 83 (1990):1-29.

Tosato, Angelo. "On Genesis 2:24." *Catholic Biblical Quarterly* 52 (1990): 389-409.

Trible, Phyllis. *God and the Rhetoric of Sexuality.* Overtures to Biblical Theology. Philadelphia: Fortress, 1978.

_____. "Not a Jot, Not a Tittle: Genesis 2–3 after Twenty Years." In *Eve and Adam: Jewish, Christian and Muslim Readings on Genesis and Gender.* Edited by Kristen E. Kvam, Linda S. Shearing, and Valarie H. Ziegler. Bloomington, IN: Indiana University Press, 1995.

Tsevat, M. "The Basic Meaning of the Biblical Sabbath." *Zeitschrift für die Alttestamentliche Wissenschaft* 84 (1973): 447-457.

Tsumura, David T. *The Earth and the Waters in Genesis 1 and 2: A Linguistic Evaluation.* Journal for the Study of the Old Testament Supplement Series 83. Sheffield: JSOT Press, 1989.

Tucker, Gene. "Creation and the Limits of the World: Nature and History in the Old Testament." *Horizons in Biblical Theology* 15 (1993): 105-118.

Turner, Laurence A. *Announcements of Plot in Genesis.* Journal for the Study of the Old Testament Supplement Series 96. Sheffield: Sheffield Academic Press, 1990.

_____. *Genesis.* Sheffield: Sheffield Academic Press, 2000.

_____. "The Rainbow as the Sign of the Covenant in Genesis IX 11-13." *Vetus Testamentum* XLIII (1993): 119-124.

Vanderkam, James C. "Genesis 1 in Jubilees 2." *Dead Sea Discoveries* 1 (1994): 300-321.

Van Seters, John. *The Pentateuch*. Sheffield: Sheffield Academic Press, 1991.

Vogels, Walter. "The Power Struggle between Man and Woman." *Biblica* 77 (1996): 197-209.

von Rad, Gerhard. *Genesis*. Revised Edition. Old Testament Library. Philadelphia: Westminster, 1972.

Von Soden, Wolfrom. *The Ancient Orient*. Trans. by Donald G. Schley. Grand Rapids: Eerdmans, 1994.

Wallace, Howard N. "Genesis 2:1-3 — Creation and Sabbath." *Pacifica* 1 (1988): 235-250.

Waltke, Bruce K. "Cain and His Offering." *Westminster Theological Journal* 48 (1986): 363-372.

_____. *Genesis*. Grand Rapids: Zondervan, 2001.

Walton, John H. *Genesis*. The NIV Application Commentary. Grand Rapids: Zondervan, 2001.

Walton, John H., Victor H. Matthews, and Mark W. Chavalis. *The IVP Bible Background Commentary: Old Testament*. Downers Grove, IL: InterVarsity, 2000.

Watts, James W. *Reading Law*. Sheffield: Sheffield Academic Press, 1999.

Wenham, Gordon J. *Genesis 1-15*. Word Biblical Commentary 1. Waco, TX: Word, 1987.

_____. *Genesis 16-50*. Word Biblical Commentary 2. Waco, TX: Word, 1994.

_____. "Sanctuary Symbolism in the Garden of Eden Story." In *I Studied Inscriptions from before the Flood: Ancient Near Eastern, Literary, and Linguistic Approaches to Genesis 1-11*. Edited by Richard S. Hess and David Toshio Tsumura, 399-404. Winona Lake, IN: Eisenbrauns, 1994.

_____. *Torah as Story: Reading Old Testament Narrative Ethically*. London: T & T Clark, 2000.

Westermann, Claus. *Creation*. Philadelphia: Fortress Press, 1974.

_____. *Genesis*. Three volumes. Translated by John J. Scullion. Minneapolis: Augsburg, 1984, 1985, 1986.

White, Hugh C. *Narration and Discourse in the Book of Genesis*. Cambridge: Cambridge University Press, 1991.

White, Lynn Jr. "The Historical Roots of Our Ecological Crisis." *Science* 155 (1967):1204-1207.

Whybray, R.N. *The Making of the Pentateuch: A Methodological Study*. Journal for the Study of the Old Testament Supplement Series 53. Sheffield: JSOT Press, 1987.

Williams, Michael E., ed. *The Storyteller's Companion to the Bible: Genesis*. Nashville: Abingdon, 1991.

Willis, John T., ed. *Genesis*. Austin: Sweet Publishing, 1979.

Wilson, Robert R. *Genealogy and History in the Biblical World*. New Haven, CT: Yale University Press, 1977.

_____. "The Old Testament Genealogies in Recent Research." In *I Studied Inscriptions from before the Flood: Ancient Near Eastern, Literary, and Linguistic Approaches to Genesis 1–11*. Edited by Richard S. Hess and David Tsumura, 200-223. Winona Lake, IN: Eisenbrauns, 1994.

Wolde, Ellen van. "A Text-Semantic Study of the Hebrew Bible, Illustrated with Noah and Job." *Journal of Biblical Literature* 113/1 (1994): 19-35.

_____. *Words Become Worlds: Semantic Studies of Genesis 1–11*. Biblical Interpretation Series 6. Leiden: Brill, 1994.

Wright, David P. "Holiness, Sex and Death in the Garden of Eden." *Biblica* 77 (1996): 305-329.

Yoder, John Howard. *The Jewish-Christian Schism Revisited*. Edited by Michael G. Cartwright and Peter Ochs. Grand Rapids: Eerdmans, 2003

Young, Davis A. *The Biblical Flood*. Grand Rapids: Eerdmans, 1995.

Zimmer, J. Raymond. "The Creation of Man and the Evolutionary Record." *Perspectives on Science and the Christian Faith* (1996): 16-26.

Zimmerli, Walther. *Ezekiel 2*. Hermeneia. Philadelphia: Fortress, 1983.

Zornberg, Avivah Gottlieb. *Genesis: The Beginning of Desire*. Philadelphia, Jerusalem: The Jewish Publication Society, 1995.

GENESIS 1

I. THE CREATOR AND HIS CREATION (1:1–2:25)

A. THE CREATION VIEWED COSMICALLY (1:1–2:4a)

This majestic chapter, along with its sister narrative in Genesis 2:4-25, is the foundation for the rest of the Bible both in terms of its story and its theology. Its account of creation seems so simple and so obvious to modern readers that we have difficulty imagining how revolutionary it was when it was first written. There is no mythological speculation about rival gods here. In fact the center of interest is not on what happens in heaven with God but on the earth.[1] God, the one true God, creates the heavens and earth and then fashions the earth into a place where humanity and the rest of creation can live. The chapter is noteworthy for its simple logic as the different parts of creation necessary for life are systematically fashioned. In its original context this text was an assault on the polytheistic myths and worldviews so common in the ancient world. Here the forces of nature are not divinized or worshiped. The God who creates does so alone with no rivals. He speaks worlds into existence with a simple, "Let there be." The stars are almost an afterthought. The greater and lesser lights (not the sun and moon) are mere objects spoken into existence by the all-powerful God. The physical universe here portrayed is one that can be trusted and need not be feared. The

---

[1] Sarna, *Genesis*, p. 3: "The story of Creation, or cosmology, that opens the Book of Genesis differs from all other such accounts that were current among the peoples of the ancient world. Its lack of interest in the realm of heaven and its economy of words in depicting primeval chaos are highly uncharacteristic of this genre of literature. The descriptions in Genesis deal solely with what lies beneath the celestial realm, and still the narration is marked by compactness, solemnity, and dignity."

highly structured organization of the narrative speaks of an orderly God who can be relied upon to act consistently in the physical world. There is no one before him, beside him, or in opposition to him. There is only God.

This God is also perfectly moral. He does not create because he needs to. His creation is good, yes, even very good. Any evil that arises in creation comes not from God but from the choices of creatures to rebel against him. Israel was very familiar with polytheistic versions of creation, whether they be Egyptian or Mesopotamian.[2] In those stories the chaos deities, usually depicted as violent and unstable monsters, had to be subdued by some god or gods. The threat that they might return to wreak havoc on creation was ever present and not far from the surface. In this account there is no evil, personal or otherwise, with which God has to contend. He is in control, and he creates an orderly world.

The account begins and ends in a similar way. This structuring device known as an *inclusio* reinforces the orderliness of creation portrayed throughout the passage. Every word here counts and the author has evidently counted every word.[3] Creation is divided into two sets of three days which parallel each other, with days 1 and 4,

---

[2]Ibid. "There is abundant evidence that other cosmologies once existed in Israel. Scattered allusions to be found in the prophetic, poetic, and wisdom literature of the Bible testify to a popular belief that prior to the onset of the creative process the powers of watery chaos had to be subdued by God. These mythical beings are variously designated Yam (Sea), Nahar (River), Leviathan (Coiled One), Rahab (Arrogant One), and Tannin (Dragon) [Isa 27:1; 51:9-10; Job 26:12-13; Ps 104:9; Prov 8:27; Job 26:10; 38:8-11]. There is no consensus in these fragments regarding the ultimate fate of these creatures. One version has them utterly destroyed by God; in another, the chaotic forces, personalized as monsters, are put under restraint by His power." My insertions.

[3]Gordon J. Wenham, *Genesis 1–15*, WBC 1 (Waco, TX: Word, 1987), p. 6: "The correspondence of the first paragraph, 1:1-2, with 2:1-3 is underlined by the number of Hebrew words in both being multiples of 7. 1:1 consists of seven words, 1:2 of fourteen (7 x 2) words, 2:1-3 of 35 (7 x 5) words. The number seven dominates this opening chapter in a strange way, not only in the number of words in a particular section but in the number of times a specific word or phrase recurs. For example, 'God' is mentioned 35 times, 'earth' 21 times, 'Heaven/firmament' 21 times, while the phrases 'and it was so' and 'God saw that it was good' occur 7 times."

2 and 5, and 3 and 6 corresponding to each other. Nearly every creative act follows a pattern which is consistent but with minor variations for specific purposes. Each command is introduced with, "Then God said."[4] Next there is the actual command with "Let there be" or its equivalent.[5] The fulfillment of the command, "And it was so," is mentioned seven times (vv. 3,7,9,11,15,24,30). Seven times we are told, "And God made" (vv. 4,7,12,16,21,25,27), and seven times God's approval is recorded (vv. 4,10,12,18,21,25,31 [very good]). Seven times there is a subsequent word from God of either blessing or commission (vv. 5[2×],8,10[2×],22,28). Wenham comments on the numerical and other patterning in this chapter:

> It is worth noting that although there are ten announcements of the divine words and eight commandments actually cited, all the formulae are grouped in sevens. Indeed, the fulfillment formula is omitted in v 20, the description of the act in v 9, and the approval formula in vv 6-8. In each case the LXX adds the appropriate formula, but it is characteristic of P to indulge in "dissymmetric symmetry" (McEvenue, *Narrative Style*, 113-115), and these additions obscure the sevenfold patterning of this section.[6]

The account begins with "heaven and earth" (1:1) and ends with "earth and heaven" (2:4). The narrative focuses more and more on things that happen on earth, rather than in the skies or heavens. Days 1, 2, and 4 concern events in the heavens, while days 3, 5, and 6 concern the earth. This yields a parallelistic pattern[7] in which focus is directed more and more toward the earth, where humanity is eventually created.

Day 1	Heaven	
Day 2	Heaven	
Day 3		Earth
Day 4	Heaven	
Day 5		Earth
Day 6		Earth

---

[4]This occurs 10 times (vv. 3,6,9,11,14,20,24,26,28,29).
[5]This occurs 8 times (vv. 3,6,9,11,14,20,24,26).
[6]Wenham, *Genesis 1–15*, p. 6.
[7]Ibid., p. 7.

The way in which God creates is designed to provide a pattern for Israel's life. He works for six days and then rests on the seventh, not because he was exhausted by the onerous work of creation, but in order to provide a pattern of life for Israel, who did need to work and rest. The orderliness of his creative acts helps Israel to make the distinctions necessary for her life in the promised land. The account explains and exemplifies holiness. The ordinary and the special, the common and the holy are to be kept as distinct as the kinds of animals are kept distinct in the creation account. The tabernacle's worship was patterned after creation. The descriptions of the eternal state in the book of Revelation are also patterned after creation.

In Genesis 1 we witness the creation from a cosmic point of view. The reader is transported to somewhere "outside of" the physical universe to see it come into existence before his or her very eyes. As the account continues the reader is brought closer and closer to events on earth. This account is not as personal as the following narrative of the garden. Here only God speaks and creation responds with perfect obedience. But the focus narrows as the account moves on to focus on the final creation, humanity male and female. The transcendent God who speaks worlds into existence is concerned about humanity and our destiny in the world. The rest of the Bible explains how God has begun to and will eventually finish the job of restoring humanity to our original place and purpose in creation. This chapter begins the story in a majestic, cosmic view of creation.

1. The First Act of Creation (1:1)

¹**In the beginning God created the heavens and the earth.**

1:1 In the beginning God

The Bible begins with God the creator. There is no attempt to explain the existence of God. The Bible assumes his existence. What the Bible does explain is just what sort of God he is. He is already there "in the beginning." Nothing precedes him and everything in the cosmos finds its origin in him. While there is disagreement on the translation of this verse (see excursus), the traditional translation "In the beginning" is, in my view, the only one which does justice to the original intention of the author and the wider "canonical context." The implications of that translation are enormous. God is "before" and "outside of" the time and space universe as we know it. There is no "preexistent" matter. There is no impersonal force and no person to rival God. The gods of the ancient world were limited in power and in morality. The God of Genesis one is the only God, and he is unlimited in power and unimaginably holy. He always and only acts morally. In fact, his character defines what "moral" is. He is separate from the material universe and not in conflict with it. There is no battle with the preexisting forces of chaos here. There is only God.

Unlike pagan creation myths Genesis 1 shows no interest in the question of God's origin. His existence is assumed and needs no defense. The word used for "God" here and throughout Genesis 1:1–2:4 is the Hebrew word אֱלֹהִים (*'ĕlōhîm*). This is not a personal name like Yahweh, but the generic Hebrew word for God. Although the form appears to be plural (masculine nouns in Hebrew normally form their plurals by adding *îm*) it is usually used with a singular verb or adjective (as throughout this chapter). The plural is probably a plural of majesty or intensification. The use of *'ĕlōhîm* here, rather than the sacred divine name Yahweh, may be for theological reasons. Of the two, *'ĕlōhîm* connotes the universal God and not the particular God of Israel. It also connotes God's transcendence rather than his particular redemptive acts on behalf of one nation. While the second chapter of Genesis makes clear that the one and only God is Yahweh, this chapter wants to emphasize God's universality as creator and his transcendent power over all things.

Often in the history of Christian interpretation of the noun *'ĕlōhîm* there has been an attempt by those not thoroughly conversant with Hebrew to argue that the plural form of this word implies a plurality in the godhead. Later revelation and theological discussion then relates this plurality as a subtle hint of the doctrine of the Trinity. Unfortunately the grammatical form of a word in Hebrew does not necessarily tell us anything about whether the word should be understood in English as a singular or a plural. For example, the word translated "heaven" in verse 1 is grammatically plural (שָׁמַיִם, *šāmayim*), but is quite properly translated as a singular in English. Calvin warns against reading too much into this:

Moses has it *Elohim*, a noun of the plural number. Whence the inference is drawn, that the three Persons of the Godhead are here noted; but since, as a proof of so great a matter, it appears to me to have little solidity, I will not insist upon the word; but rather caution readers to beware of violent glosses of this kind.[8]

created

The Hebrew verb בָּרָא (*bārā'*)[9] is found 46 times in the Old Testament. In every case in the Qal or Niphal[10] God is the one who does the creating, and there is never any material substance which he uses to create. While this verb in and of itself does not tell us that God created *ex nihilo* (out of nothing), the implication may be there. When one considers that Genesis 1 is a polemic against pagan cosmologies which place great importance on preexisting matter, the intimation is even clearer. The doctrine of Creation out of nothing is first *explicitly* articulated in 2 Maccabees 7:28, "Look up to heaven and earth and see all that is therein, and know that God made them out of things that did not exist." Hebrews 11:3 informs us that "By faith we understand that the worlds were prepared by the word of God, so that what is seen was made from things that are not visible." In Romans 4:17 God is described as the one who "calls into existence the things that do not exist." Second Enoch 24:2 also teaches this doctrine explicitly.

the heavens and the earth

Often this phrase is seen as a merism, a figure of speech where two words are linked together to mean something more than the

---

[8]John Calvin, *Commentaries on the First Book of Moses, Called Genesis*, trans. by John King (Grand Rapids: Eerdmans, 1948), pp. 70-71.

[9]The word *bara'* begins with the same three letters in Hebrew as the phrase בְּרֵאשִׁית (*bᵉrē'šîth*) which is the first of the Hebrew Bible's many wordplays. These wordplays do not necessarily imply that we are reading poetry as they are common in Hebrew narrative texts, not just poetic texts.

[10]Stanley L. Jaki notes (*Genesis 1 through the Ages* [London: Thomas Moore Press, 1992], p. 9) that *bārā'* occurs 40 or so times in the OT, and it is only in the Qal and Niphal that God is the subject. Three certain cases in the Piel (Josh 17:15,18, hacking down trees; Ezek 23:47, hacking the adulterous partners of Oholah and Oholibah) and two uncertain cases (1 Sam 2:23; Ezek 21:24) are of purely human actions. Most lexicons regard the Piel instances as deriving from a homonymous root with a different meaning and so are not really exceptions.

sum of the individual parts. In this case, "heavens and earth" is viewed as a merism for "the totality of all things that exist." According to this view, Genesis 1:1 is a sort of summary heading which summarizes the entire process of creation which is then described in detail beginning in verse 2. The main strength of this argument is that elsewhere the phrase, "heavens and earth" refers to the perfect creation and not some intermediate stage of creation.

I am not so sure. One problem with this view is that, if Genesis 1:1 acts as a summary statement, Genesis 1:2 is the beginning of the account and the unformed and unfilled earth is already there as pre-existent matter without any explanation of the origin of that matter. As we have attempted to demonstrate in the excursus, this is not consistent with the polemic against idolatry which fills this chapter.

If the words did not sound so fairytale like in English, I would suggest translating "heavens and earth" as "sky and land." What God created was the basic stuff of the physical universe, both "terrestrial" and "celestial." Genesis chapter 1 then tells us how God took that basic stuff and fashioned and formed it into the physical universe in its "perfect" state. God clearly differentiates between the sky and the land by creating the "expanse," something similar to our word atmosphere, or at least the thing that makes the atmosphere possible. He then proceeds to form them into day and night for the sky and into dry land and water for the earth. After forming them, he proceeds to fill them. The earth is "filled" with vegetation and then creatures which inhabit the expanse (birds), the water (fish, etc.), and dry land (land animals and humankind) respectively. The sky is "filled" with the greater light (inhabiting the day) and lesser light (inhabiting the night) and the stars.

EXCURSUS
ON THE TRANSLATION OF GENESIS 1:1-3

NIV	NASB[11]	NRSV Text	NRSV Footnote 1
1:1 In the beginning God created the heavens and the earth.	1:1 In the beginning God created the heavens and the earth.	1:1 In the beginning when God created the heavens and the earth,	1:1 When God began to create the heavens and the earth,
1:2 Now the earth was[12] formless and empty, darkness was over the surface of the deep, and the Spirit of God was hovering over the waters.	1:2 The earth was formless and void, and darkness was over the surface of the deep, and the Spirit of God was moving over the surface of the waters.	1:2 the earth was a formless void and darkness covered the face of the deep, while a wind from God swept over the face of the waters.	1:2 the earth was a formless void and darkness covered the face of the deep, while the spirit of God[13] swept over the face of the waters.
1:3 And God said, "Let there be light," and there was light.	1:3 Then God said, "Let there be light," and there was light.	1:3 Then God said, "Let there be light"; and there was light.	1:3 Then God said, "Let there be light"; and there was light.

Notice the following significant differences among these three translations.[14]

1. Both the NIV and NASB regard verse one as a complete sentence and punctuate with a period. Both the text and the first footnote in the NRSV regard verse one as the introduction to verse two and so punctuate with a comma.[15]

---

[11]NRSV footnote 2 for Gen 1:1 reads "In the beginning God created the heavens and the earth," — ending with a comma.

[12]The NIV footnote suggests "became" as a possible alternative translation to the word "was." This is a classic proof text of traditional dispensationalist thought. The translation is implausible at best. See the commentary on verse 2 for the details.

[13]The NRSV gives a third alternative to "a wind from God" and "the spirit of God": "a mighty wind." This takes the Hebrew word ʾĕlōhîm, which usually means God as an adjective meaning "mighty."

[14]Most of these differences will be addressed in the commentary. This excursus focuses on verse 1.

[15]I find it mystifying why NRSV's second footnote translation also ends

2. Both the NRSV text and the first footnote in NRSV introduce the word "when" into verse one. This word is not found in the Hebrew text. The result of this translation is/may be[16] to regard verse one as introducing the situation in which creation actually began in verse 3 and not to describe the initial act of creation. The earth is already in existence when God proceeds to create it.
3. The NIV, NASB, and NRSV text and footnote 2 all imply that the creation took place "In the beginning"; the NRSV footnote 1 does not refer to the beginning at all, only the time when God began to create.
4. The NIV and NASB use "Spirit of God" with a capital "S" to render the Hebrew phrase, *rûaḥ 'ĕlōhîm*. The NRSV footnote 1 suggests "spirit of God" with a lowercase "s."
5. The NRSV translates "a wind from God" for the same Hebrew phrase. This is because the Hebrew word רוּחַ (*rûaḥ*) can mean "Spirit," "spirit," or "wind."
6. The verb used to describe what the Spirit or wind of God was doing is "hovering" in NIV, "moving" in NASB, and "swept over" in NRSV and NRSV footnote.
7. NASB and NRSV in the text and in the footnotes begins verse 3 with the word "Then," while the NIV has merely "And." In Hebrew this is the first of the Bible's waw-consecutives which in narrative texts ordinarily means "then." In NIV and NASB God's decision to create light follows in sequence after the creation of the heavens and the earth in verse 1. In NRSV text and footnotes it follows logically from a description of the earth before God began to act on it in creation.

---

with a comma. It makes no grammatical sense to translate: In the beginning God created the heavens and the earth, the earth was a formless void. . . .

[16]It is possible to read the NRSV text as being ambiguous about this. "In the beginning when God created the heavens and the earth, the earth was a formless void . . ." could be read as saying that the result of the creation of the heavens and the earth was an earth that was a formless void. The more likely reading is suggested above and does not materially differ from the alternative proposed in footnote 1.

EXCURSUS   COLLEGE PRESS NIV COMMENTARY

THE TRANSLATION OF GENESIS 1:1

It may be surprising to learn that the translation of the first word of the Bible is a matter of considerable controversy. The Hebrew word בְּרֵאשִׁית (*bᵊrēʾšîth*), traditionally translated "In the beginning," does not actually have the word "the" (the definite article) in it. In Hebrew this does not necessarily mean that it is wrong to translate it in the traditional way; anyone who has learned another language knows that no two languages use the definite and indefinite articles in precisely the same way. In addition, the noun *rēʾšîth* (*bᵊ* is the Hebrew preposition meaning "in a" or "in the") is usually thought to be in the construct state, a special construction in Hebrew where the head noun is connected to the next noun by the word "of," i.e., "In [the] beginning of God's creating." It is thus potentially possible to translate the first phrase of Genesis "When God began to create" or "In the beginning when God" (NRSV). While the issue cannot be resolved by grammatical arguments[17] alone, a consideration of the grammatical details is the first step in considering the issue.

The Absence of the Article

The first word in the Hebrew Bible is actually a phrase with the noun *rēʾšîth* ("beginning") combined with the Hebrew inseparable preposition *bᵊ* (meaning "in a" or "in the"). The Hebrew definite article is not present. A key question is, "Is *bᵊrēʾšîth* in the construct

---

[17]Victor P. Hamilton (*The Book of Genesis, Chapters 1–17*, NICOT [Grand Rapids: Eerdmans, 1990], p. 103) comments on the possibilities from grammatical considerations alone: "A number of options are available here: (1) The first word, *berēʾshit*, is in the absolute state (i.e., it functions independently of any other word) and all of v. 1 is an independent clause and a complete sentence. (2) The first word is an indeterminate noun, used as a relative temporal designation: 'Initially (or first, to start with) God created. . . .' (3) The first word is in the construct state (i.e., it functions in close connection with another word, usually a noun) and the verse is a temporal clause subordinated to v. 2: 'When God began to create . . . the earth was without form and void.' (4) The first word is in the construct state and the verse is a temporal clause subordinated to v. 3, with v. 2 taken as a parenthesis: 'When God began to create the heavens and the earth — the earth being without form and void — God said. . . .'"

state because it does not have the Hebrew definite article?" One of the strongest arguments for this is the fact that, of the 50 uses of the word, only Isaiah 46:10 has *rē'šîth* in the simple, absolute state; the 49 other occurrences are in the construct state.[18] The spelling is exactly the same for the absolute and construct of a noun like *rē'šîth*, therefore only context can decide the issue.

The Vowel Pointing on the Hebrew Verb *bara'*

The Hebrew verb traditionally translated "created" in Genesis 1:1 is pointed as a Qal perfect third person masculine singular verb. Hebrew words are made up of consonants and markings placed above, under or beside the consonants called vowel points. The Hebrew text was for many centuries copied with the consonants only, without the vowel points. The vowels were supplied from memory and did not need to be written down. It was only about 500 A.D. that a group of Hebrew scribes known as the Masoretes began adding the vowel points because Hebrew was being lost as a living language and readers were beginning to forget the vowel pointing. By "repointing" (changing) the vowels a Hebrew word can mean something entirely different.

In order for the first phrase of Genesis to be translated "When God began to create . . ."[19] the Hebrew word for "created" (*bārā'*) has to be repointed (i.e., supplied with a new set of vowels) from a simple past tense verb (called a simple perfect in Hebrew), to an infini-

---

[18]Sarna, *Genesis*, p. 5, gives the following considerations: "In favor of the traditional English translation are the arguments that *be-re'shit* does not have to be in the construct state and that the analogies of 2:4 and 5:1, as well as of Enuma Elish are inexact. In each instance, the word translated 'when' is literally 'in the day,' which is not the case in this verse."

[19]Sarna (ibid.) supplies the main grammatical arguments for this translation, adopted in, e.g., NRSV footnote 1: "This rendering of the Hebrew looks to verse 3 for the completion of the sentence. It takes verse 2 to be parenthetical, describing the state of things at the time when God first spoke. Support for understanding the text in this way comes from 2:4 and 5:1, both of which refer to Creation and begin with 'When.' The Mesopotamian creation epic known as *Enuma Elish* also commences the same way. In fact, *enuma* means 'when.' Apparently, this was a conventional opening style for cosmological narratives. As to the peculiar syntax of the Hebrew sentence—

tive, *bᵊroʾ*, meaning "to create." While sometimes in attempting to reconstruct the meaning of an incomprehensible text scholars are forced to repoint a text, in this case the repointing is not necessary. The text makes sense as it stands, and the ancient translators also understood it in the traditional way.[20]

The Genre of Genesis 1 as Anti-Idolatry Polemic

One problem with the translations of NRSV, whether main text or footnote 1, is that these translations, while grammatically possible, fail to consider adequately the anti-idolatry polemic throughout this text. NRSV's translation (whether text or footnote 1) has Genesis 1, in common with polytheistic creation myths, begin with the presumption of primordial matter. The matter with which God works is already presumed to be present in these translations. But this is the very sort of notion which this chapter is critiquing. There is no initial chaos in Genesis 1. Everything, including matter, is under God's complete control. It seems inconsistent to argue that Genesis 1 critiques the polytheistic myths while implicitly accepting one of the key features of those myths, eternal matter. While this argument is less strong for Israel on the verge of entering the promised land, there seems to me to be little doubt that the original canonical audience, most of which was still living among polytheistic cultures, would have accepted such a reading. It is amazing how much ideological baggage can be loaded onto the lack of a definite article in the first word of the Hebrew Bible.

The Wider Canonical Context

Certainly when the entire Christian canon is taken into account, there seems to be little doubt that Christians are to read this text in

---

a noun in the construct state (*be-reʾshit*) with a finite verb (*baraʾ*) — analogies may be found in Leviticus 14:46, Isaiah 29:1, and Hosea 1:2."

[20]The LXX translators evidently had a text identical to the MT. They do not supply the definite article in the phrase "In the beginning" (ἐν ἀρχῇ) and translated the Hebrew "he created" by a simple aorist (ἐποίησεν). The Samaritan Pentateuch has the definite article ("In the beginning") and a simple past tense verb.

the traditional way, "In the beginning God created the heavens and the earth." The "earth" which is described in verse 2 as "formless and void" is not a foe of God's creation, but merely the incomplete state of the land in the initial stages of creation. The rest of Scripture[21] makes it clear that this verse speaks of the initial creation of all things. The further revelation which these Scriptures provide leads to the doctrine of creation *ex nihilo*, i.e., creation out of nothing.

The Theological Issue

In a world in which the boundaries between religions are under attack and people throughout the world are being invited to a sort of "New Age pot luck supper" in which differing, conflicting, and even contradictory religious ideas are chosen as personal preferences, it may be time that the church gives renewed attention to the boundaries. The NRSV text and footnote 1 would seem to imply that the book of Genesis is more syncretistic in its presentation of creation than it has been understood to be by Christians throughout the ages. NRSV seems to imply that Genesis 1:1-2 presumes the pre-existence of matter without explaining its origins. But while this is possible grammatically, it is no more plausible than the traditional translation, and it begs the question from a theological point of view.[22] If Genesis 1:1 does not describe an absolute beginning, where

---

[21]Hebrews 11:3 informs us that "by faith we understand that the worlds were prepared by the word of God, so that what is seen was made from things that are not visible." In Romans 4:17 God is described as the one who "calls into existence the things that do not exist." See also 2 Maccabees 7:28, "Look up to heaven and earth and see all that is therein, and know that God made them out of things that did not exist." Cf. Enoch 24:2.

[22]Sarna, *Genesis*, p. 5, addresses the theological issue: "The traditional English translation reads: 'In the beginning God created the heaven and the earth.' This rendering construes the verse as an independent sentence complete in itself, a solemn declaration that serves as an epitomizing caption to the entire narrative. It takes the initial word *be-re'shit* to mean 'at the beginning of time' and thus makes a momentous assertion about the nature of God: that He is wholly outside of time, just as He is outside of space, both of which He proceeds to create. In other words, for the first time in the religious history of the Near East, God is conceived as being entirely free of temporal and spatial dimensions."

in the Bible is that beginning described? Certainly other parts of Scripture read this text as speaking of an absolute beginning (John 1:1-3; Heb 11:3; Rom 4:17). Something can easily be grammatically possible and theologically suspect.

2. The State of the Unfinished Earth at Its Creation: Unformed and Unfilled (1:2)

²Now the earth was^a formless and empty, darkness was over the surface of the deep, and the Spirit of God was hovering over the waters.

^a2 Or possibly *became*

1:2 Now the earth was

This phrase describes the earth in its original state prior to it being formed and filled into the perfect world which God is about to create. While it is true that the Hebrew verb הָיָה (*hāyāh*), translated "was," can in some rare instances mean "became," there is no reason other than pure apologetics to translate it that way in this verse. The so-called "Gap Theory" posits that between the initial creation of the heavens and the earth in a perfect state (Gen 1:1), some cataclysmic event caused the earth to "become" formless and empty. It is even reasoned that the event can be inferred — the fall of Satan and his angels. This event helps to explain away the fossil record and the seemingly long history of geological time. Genesis 1 is then an account of the re-creation of the earth after its cataclysmic destruction as God's judgment on Satan's rebellion. Creation is based on an initial chaos which is brought under God's control. It seems to me that the primary motivation for this theory is the desire to avoid the perceived conflict between Western culture's current creation "story" (otherwise known as the scientific theory of evolution) and this chapter. There is no indication in this statement that the earth was in any sense flawed. It is incomplete at this stage, but there is no suggestion that this incomplete state is a defect.

There is also no good reason to imagine that the word "earth" in verse 2 is different from the earth that is created in verse 1. In verse 1 God created the heavens and the earth. Verse two begins with "and" in the Hebrew text. The phrase "and the earth" is brought into first position syntactically[23] in order to emphasize it. It seems to me this construction explains the state the earth/land[24] was in after the initial creation. Otherwise one must read the last word of verse 1 as meaning something entirely different from the same word used as the first word of verse 2! The land here is not the product of the primeval waters as was common in the creation myths of the ancient Near East.[25] Tsumura says of the earth:

> In Gen 1 the earth in v. 2 is simply a part of the created cosmos ("heaven and earth" in v. 1) and refers to everything under the heaven including the subterranean waters. However, the earth was totally covered by waters and the dry land was "not yet" formed (or seen) until v. 9 where God said: "Let the waters from under the heaven be gathered to one place and let the dry land appear."[26]

formless and empty,

The phrase translated "formless and empty" actually rhymes in Hebrew תֹהוּ וָבֹהוּ, (tōhû wᵊbōhû). It seems to describe the fact that the land has not yet been formed into something which can be inhabited (i.e., it is "formless"),[27] and it does not yet have anything inhabiting it (i.e., it is "empty"). In beginning Hebrew in college someone came up with "junk and gunk" as carrying the wordplay over into

---

[23]Ordinarily in Hebrew prose the order is verb, subject, object. When the subject is brought into first position as here, it is given emphasis.

[24]The Hebrew word אֶרֶץ ('ereṣ) is not the spinning globe which modern readers tend to read into the word "earth." The word can mean either the entire land or a specific land such as Egypt or especially the promised land.

[25]David T. Tsumura, *The Earth and the Waters in Genesis 1 and 2: A Linguistic Evaluation*, JSOTSup 83 (Sheffield: JSOT Press, 1989), p. 83, "Unlike the cosmology in Enuma Elish and other ancient myths, the land in Gen 1:9f. was not a product of the primeval water, hence a part of the water, but a product of the divine fiat by which God gathered the waters from under the heaven 'to one place', i.e. as 'seas', which is part of the earth."

[26]Ibid., p. 82.

[27]Tsumura (ibid., p. 19) argues for the etymology of tōhû, "In the light of the above, it is probable that Ugaritic *thw* is a cognate of Hebrew *tōhû* and that both have the common meaning of 'a desert.' If so, they are most probably <qutl-> pattern nouns (<*/tuhwu/) from the common (West) Semitic root *thw." But this does not account sufficiently for the wordplay and the parallelistic structure of days 1-3 and days 4-6.

English. Alter suggests "welter and waste."[28] But the unintended result of such suggestions is to give credence to the initial chaos reading of this verse. I would prefer the translation, "unformed and unfilled." This preserves the Hebrew wordplay[29] and points to the clear structure of the chapter. Genesis 1 describes the process of God first *forming* the basic stuff of heaven and earth into various environments in which creatures or inanimate created things could "live," and then *filling* those environments with living creatures (or created things) appropriate to them. Thus God first *forms* the day and night on day one and then *fills* the day and night with the greater and lesser lights on day four. On day two he *forms* the expanse (atmosphere) leaving the earth covered with water. On day 5 he *fills* the expanse with birds and the water with water creatures. Day 3 sees the *forming* of dry land and the vegetation on it while day 6 has the *filling* of that dry land with land animals and man who have the vegetation to eat. The creator first *forms* the environment in which the creature lives (exists), and then he forms the creatures which need that environment for their very existence (see the chart below).[30]

---

[28]Robert Alter, *Genesis* (New York: W.W. Norton, 1996), p. 3.

[29]The Septuagint attempted to bring the wordplay over into Greek by choosing two words which begin with an α privative (meaning "not") and ending in ος (*os*), ἀόρατος (*aoratos*) and ἀκατασκεύαστος (*akataskeuastos*). According to Dines (Jennifer Dines, "Imaging Creation: The Septuagint Translation of Genesis 1:2," *Heythrop Journal* 36 [1995]: 439-450.) the word *bōhû* was coined to rhyme with *tōhû*. There are two broad usages for *tōhû*, one where it represents the desert; the other, where it suggests 'futility,' 'deceptiveness.' The LXX uses *aoratos* and *akataskeuastos* to translate *tōhû wᵊbōhû*. The first word is rare before LXX and refers to what is "unseen" or "invisible." It has a background in Platonic philosophy which Philo uses. Josephus understands the original world to be "unseen" because it is covered in darkness (*Ant.* 1, 27). The latter word is found only in Theophrasus' *History of Plants*, 9, 16, 6, referring to what happens when the antidote to a poison has not been properly prepared. She suggests that LXX did not use *amorphos* because of its specific meaning in Middle Platonism. The Greek words are, according to Alexandre, an attempt to reproduce the alliteration, since both words begin with alpha privative and end in *os*. Since *bōhû* shares with *tōhû* consonants and vowels, the LXX use of *akataskeuastos* also carries the alliteration with yet another word beginning with alpha privative and ending in *os*. She suggests "unseen," "unsorted," and "unfathomable" as an attempt to carry the entire alliteration over into English.

[30]The structure can also be analyzed in terms of the environment neces-

The Structure of Genesis 1:2-31

Gen 1:2   the *earth* as **unformed** and **unfilled** (*tōhû webōhû*)

Forming of environments	Filling the environments
[DAY 1] light and darkness	[DAY 4] "greater light" and "lesser light"
[DAY 2] expanse separates two waters	[DAY 5] fish and birds
[DAY 3] *earth* and seas vegetation	[DAY 6] **animals** and **man** on the *earth*

darkness was over the surface of the deep,

The early land was covered in water, here referred to as the "deep." Since light had not yet been created at this point there is only darkness.³¹ The Hebrew word translated "deep," תְהוֹם (*tᵊhôm*), is seen by some as the Hebrew equivalent of the deity Tiamat in the Babylonian creation myth Enuma Elish.³² In the story the goddess Tiamat is the evil, warlike ocean goddess who leads in a battle against the supreme god Anu. Before she wins the battle, however, another god, Marduk kills her, then splits her corpse lengthwise "like a shell fish." From the two halves of her body Marduk forms heaven and earth. It is argued that the remnants of this story remain in the Genesis account where the expanse is created to separate the waters of the deep.

This view treats *tᵊhôm* as a proper name and not a material object. The gender of *tᵊhôm* is feminine, and it lacks the definite article "the," as do Hebrew proper nouns, in 33 of its 35 occurrences. Only in Isaiah 63:13 and Psalm 106:9, where the deep is the waters of the Red Sea which Israel crossed through, does *tᵊhôm* have the definite article. Furthermore, Isaiah 51:9-11 poetically pictures the Crossing of the Red Sea in terms of the mythological battle between the gods at creation. Clearly Israel was familiar with these myths if

---

sary for the things which move in that environment. This explains why vegetation is created on day 3 rather than day 6. Birds (and presumably fish) created on day 5 will need the vegetation to eat. The vegetation is also a prerequisite for the sustenance of the animate world of fish, birds, land animals, and mankind.

³¹There is no indication in this verse that the "darkness" is somehow suggestive of evil forces. God names the "darkness" just as he does the "light."

³²See Hamilton, *Genesis, 1-17*, p. 110.

they could be used in poetry to describe God's miraculous deliverance of his people. Hamilton comments:

> Further support for *tᵊhôm* as a hebraized form of Tiamat is found (a) in its association with verbs that can be applied only to human beings or animals; thus Gen. 49:25, "the deep that lies (couches or crouches) below," and Hab. 3:10, "the deep gave forth its voice," (b) in several uses of *tᵊhôm*, apart from Gen. 1:2, that occur in a paragraph dealing with Yahweh's obliteration of superhuman monsters. The best example is Isa. 51:9-11, where a list of Yahweh's conquests includes Rahab, the dragon, the sea, and the waters of the great "deep."[33]

But there are several problems with this view, even though it is a popular one in critical scholarship and is often asserted in university textbooks as though it is a fact. First, Genesis one is prose, not poetry, and there is not a single instance of the use of *tᵊhôm* as a mythological force in prose in the Hebrew Bible. Secondly, this view forgets that Genesis one is antimythological polemic, not myth. Why would a creation account so full of critiques of pagan cosmologies entertain the existence of a sea goddess in its second verse? Third, the supposed etymological relationship between *tᵊhôm* and Tiamat has been discredited.[34] That Israel knew of the creation stories of other cultures in the ancient Near East is indisputable. For most of their history those pagan gods were a temptation to the majority of Israelites! But Genesis one treats the material elements of the physical universe as mere objects without divine power. God has no struggle with subordinate deities in order to make creation work.

and the Spirit of God was hovering over the waters.

The Hebrew word translated Spirit (רוּחַ, *rûaḥ*) can also mean "wind" or even "breath," and some translations thus render the

---

[33]Ibid.

[34]Ibid., p. 111: "Strong negative arguments may be sounded regarding the linguistic relationship between Heb. *tehom* and Babylonian Tiamat. Much more likely is the correspondence between Heb. *tehom* and Ugar. *thm* (dual *thmtm*, plural *thmt*), "deep, depth(s),"or even earlier Eblaite *ti-á-matum*, "ocean abyss." M.J. Dahood (*Psalms II,* Anchor Bible [Garden City, NY: Doubleday, 1966], p. 231) wonders why scholars who know well the Ugaritic evidence continue to maintain an "unsustainable connection" between Babylonian Tiamat and *tehom* both mythologically and philologically.

phrase as, "and a wind from God swept over the waters." Very rarely, the word *'ĕlōhîm* (usually translated "God") can be translated "mighty" and thus NRSV margin suggests "a mighty wind." Here I think the translation "Spirit" (with a capital S) is to be preferred since winds do not "hover"; they blow. Alter's suggestion, "God's breath," runs into the same difficulty. Translations which adopt the translation "wind" for *rûaḥ* must change the meaning of the Hebrew verb רָחַף (*rāḥaph*) = "hovering."[35]

3. The Forming of the Earth — The First Three Days (1:3-13)

³And God said, "Let there be light," and there was light. ⁴God saw that the light was good, and he separated the light from the darkness. ⁵God called the light "day," and the darkness he called "night." And there was evening, and there was morning—the first day.

⁶And God said, "Let there be an expanse between the waters to separate water from water." ⁷So God made the expanse and separated the water under the expanse from the water above it. And it was so. ⁸God called the expanse "sky." And there was evening, and there was morning—the second day.

⁹And God said, "Let the water under the sky be gathered to one place, and let dry ground appear." And it was so. ¹⁰God called the dry ground "land," and the gathered waters he called "seas." And God saw that it was good.

¹¹Then God said, "Let the land produce vegetation: seed-bearing plants and trees on the land that bear fruit with seed in it, according to their various kinds." And it was so. ¹²The land produced vegetation: plants bearing seed according to their kinds and trees bearing fruit with seed in it according to their kinds. And God saw that it was good. ¹³And there was evening, and there was morning—the third day.

---

[35]The Hebrew verb *rāḥaph* only occurs elsewhere in Jeremiah 23:9 where it refers to the shaking of a terrified person's bones, and in Deuteronomy 32:11 where it describes what the eagle does above its nest. Hovering or fluttering thus seem to be the best translations. Dines ("Imaging Creation," pp. 439-450) notices that the Septuagint's translation of the word *epephereto* is also used of the ark being "borne along" upon the waters of the Flood in 7:18.

The first three days of creation narrate the preparing or forming of the heavens and earth to hold its inhabitants. On day one the day and night are formed so that on day four they can be filled with the greater and lesser lights and the stars.[36] The second day sees the creation of the firmament which separates the water in the clouds from the waters in rivers, lakes, and seas. The fifth day sees the filling of the living spaces created on the second day as birds and water creatures are created. The birds fly in the expanse and the fish swim in the waters. The third day sees the emergence of dry land and vegetation growing on it. This prepares for the sixth day when animals and humanity are created to live on the land and eat the vegetation.

The account is very formulaic using repetition with variation in a style characteristic of Hebrew narrative. The account of each day begins with a "let there be" statement or its equivalent in which God's intention to create is articulated. This happens twice on the third day. There follows an "and there was" statement or its equivalent. Again this happens twice on the third day, but does not occur in the account of the second day. Next there is the statement, "And God saw that it was good" which once again occurs twice on the third day and not at all on the second day. God next names his creations with the phrase "then God called." This occurs on all three days and twice on the third day. The account of each of the three days ends with the statement, "And there was evening and there was morning" followed by the naming of the specific day. Day one is set apart from the other days because it uses the cardinal number rather than the ordinal as on other days ("One" not "First"). The second and third days have a unique feature also. On the second day, which lacks the "and there was . . ." statement God is said to have specifically made the expanse. On the third day the land (and not specifically God himself) produced the vegetation almost as though it was self-generating. The possible significance of the variations from the clear pattern will be discussed in the commentary below. The narrator seems to be making some point about the second and third days through variation from the pattern.

---

[36]The Hebrew text is actually ambiguous as to when the stars were created although the fourth day is the natural candidate.

Day One: The Forming of Day and Night (1:3-5)

1:3 And God said, "Let there be light," and there was light.

This verse begins with a special Hebrew grammatical structure known as the waw-consecutive. In virtually all cases the waw-consecutive, when used in narrative texts like Genesis 1, indicates the *next* thing that happened in the narrative sequence. Here it perhaps should be translated, "*Then* God said." This is another strong argument in favor of viewing Genesis 1:1 as a description of the creation of the basic stuff of the universe, and not a summary statement of the entirety of Genesis 1:2-2:3. After God's initial act of creation[37] of the basic stuff of the universe, he *then* began the process of forming and filling it into the very good (1:31) creation that he intended.

The account in Genesis is very different from the accounts familiar in the ancient world. God has no battle on his hands. Creation is not personified as somehow a rival to God. He speaks and effortlessly his commands are obeyed. He creates by the power of his word with his Spirit or breath standing by, ready to act. The terseness of God's command ("Let there be light") and the equally terse and immediate response ("and there was light") demonstrates his sovereign power in a particularly memorable way.

The question of how there could be "light" before there was a sun (which is not created until the fourth day) would never have occurred to the original author or audience. This is a modern question because current science tells us that light from outer space only comes from stars which burn up hydrogen. Once again, it is the modern question which runs the interpretation of this chapter. This question has preoccupied Christian and Jewish interpretation for centuries. The history of groundless speculation should caution us against our own reading of contemporary scientific theories into the text.[38] Frankly, this chapter is not interested in such questions, and the attempt to get an answer from this text often results in distorting it. Light is created because there is only darkness prior to its creation.

---

[37]As noted above the verb "created" in 1:1 is in the perfect which usually means simple past tense, i.e., "he created."

[38]Michaelis, for example, speculated that the light was probably caused by the eruption of a sub-marine volcano (cited in Christoph Bultmann, "Creation at the Beginning of History: Johann Gottfried Herder's Interpretation of Genesis 1." *JSOT* 68 [1995]: 27).

Since both light and darkness serve God's purposes in creation, and since the alternating cycle of darkness and light is the way we as humans measure time, the account begins by segmenting time in order to show the orderly and even logical progress of creation.

Hamilton [*ad loc.*] notes that the Latin phrase for "let there be light" is *fiat lux*. Thus when we speak of creation by "divine fiat" we refer to God merely speaking something into existence. He also notes that only here in Genesis 1 does creation take place merely by words without subsequent action by God. Apparently the point being subtly made is that God, and God alone, is the source of light.

1:4 God saw that the light was good,

When verse 4 says that God "saw" that the light was good, it does not mean that like humans, he requires light in order to "see." God recognizes the goodness or even beauty (the word can mean either) of the light. This is the first of God's evaluations of his creative work in this chapter. With each repetition of the phrase the creation comes closer and closer to the final evaluation, "very good." In the ancient world with its polytheistic worldview, what we call creation was typically conceived of as a battle between the personal forces of chaos and the personal forces of order. The powers of chaos were dark and evil and always threatened to undo the powers of order. In Genesis there is nothing evil. The material universe is good, not evil; impersonal, not personal.

and he separated the light from the darkness.

Usually in Genesis 1 God's execution of the divine word precedes his evaluation of it as "good"; here it follows. But slight variations within an overall pattern of formulaic repetition is characteristic of the style of this section. The word "separated" (hiphil of בדל, *bdl*) is used of separating between upper and lower waters, and day and night elsewhere in this chapter. But the word is also used of Israel being set apart from the nations (Lev 20:24; 1 Kgs 8:53); of the Levites being set apart from the other tribes to serve at the tabernacle (Num 8:14; Deut 10:8); and of the cities of refuge being set apart for their special purpose of protecting accidental man-slaughterers (Deut 4:41). It should probably be understood here as separating things that do not belong together.[39] Throughout this chapter the

---

[39]Cornelius Van Dam ("*bādal*," *NIDOTTE*, p. 604): "Judging from the usage

elements of creation are carefully distinguished from each other and thus separated. This is the author's way of showing the orderliness of the world to an audience familiar with mythological stories of creation in which there was chaos and disorder.

1:5 God called the light "day," and the darkness he called "night."

The right to name something in biblical times often indicates ownership or authority over it. Here God shows his sovereign power by naming the light and the darkness. They are not independent entities, but mere creations. Literally the Hebrew says, "God called *to* the light, 'day' and *to* the darkness he called, 'night.'" Light and darkness are not rival gods nor is there any power or force behind them. Darkness is merely the absence of light. Darkness was already there before the creation of the light. It is no evil force.

And there was evening, and there was morning

This formula closes the account of God's work on each of the six days. Evening probably is mentioned before morning because of the Jewish custom of regarding the day as beginning at dusk, not at dawn.[40] The Hebrew verb translated "and there was" is actually a waw-consecutive, which usually indicates sequence (i.e., "Then there was evening . . ."). Here, however, its use with the verb "to be" should probably lead us not to translate it so strictly.[41]

—the first day.

Literally the Hebrew says, "day one." In listing the other days, however, the ordinal numbers second, third, etc. are used. While this can happen in Hebrew and Akkadian for no apparent reason,[42] here it stands out. For some reason "day one" is subtly differentiated from the other days. The word "day" undoubtedly refers to the

---

of *bdl* elsewhere, its usage in Gen should probably be understood in terms of separating what does not belong together and separating for a specific task. This separation can, therefore, indicate a transition from a state of mixture to a more ordered state of creation."

[40]H.R. Stroes, "Does the Day Begin in the Evening or the Morning?" *VT* 16 (1966): 460-475.

[41]If we did regard it as indicating narrative sequence, that would seem to indicate that the passing of the day happens after the events of creation associated with that day. In other words the creation of light did not happen on day one. Instead light was created and then day one occurred.

[42]E.A. Speiser, *Genesis*, AB 1 (New York: Doubleday, 1964), p. 6.

ordinary and most typical use of the word of one cycle of light and darkness.⁴³

Day Two: The Forming of the Atmosphere and Seas (1:6-8)

1:6 And God said, "Let there be an expanse between the waters to separate water from water."

The word translated "expanse" (רָקִיעַ, *rāqîa'*) comes from a Hebrew verb meaning "to stamp or spread," sometimes of beating out metal into thin sheets. The word is translated as "firmament" in the KJV because of the Latin Vulgate's *firmamentum* implying something firm or solid.⁴⁴ But the word only occurs eight times outside of this chapter and always elsewhere in poetic contexts. Ezekiel 1:22 and Daniel 12:3 describe it as shiny or sparkling. Perhaps this suggests that it was viewed as a glass dome covering the earth. But we must remember that these are poetic texts and the language is undoubtedly figurative. Elihu asks Job, "Can you join him in spreading out⁴⁵ the skies⁴⁶ hard as a mirror of cast bronze?" (Job 37:18). But again this is poetry and Elihu undoubtedly refers to the mysterious fact that the invisible skies are strong enough to support the clouds (37:16). And furthermore the meaning of a related verb in Hebrew cannot by itself tell us what a noun which is derived from it means. Here the firmament is a hyponym of the word "heaven" or "sky" (שָׁמַיִם, *šāmayim*), that is, it is a synonym for heaven (1:8 God called the expanse "sky"), but refers only to one part of the heavens (1:20 "the expanse of the sky"). The expanse is the space between the water on earth and the water carried in the clouds. In the expanse birds fly and the greater and lesser lights appear. There is no modern English word which is fully equivalent. Our word atmosphere works in part, but we do not refer to the sun and moon as being *in*

---

⁴³This passage is almost as interesting for what it leaves out as for what it includes. There is no account of the creation of angels or other spiritual beings. Jubilees asserts that God created seven things on the first day: heavens, earth, waters, spirits or angels, depths, darkness, and light. The types of angels are enumerated in great detail.

⁴⁴Many modern interpreters who take an essentially mythological approach to this passage use a word to describe the solid state of the expanse. The NRSV uses "dome." Alter suggests "vault."

⁴⁵The Hebrew verb here *rāqa'* is the root for the word "expanse" (*rāqîa'*).

⁴⁶The skies are שְׁחָקִים (*šᵉḥāqîm*) in Hebrew, not *rāqîa'*.

the atmosphere (1:14). We must constantly keep in mind that Genesis one is not a scientific treatise, and it uses ordinary language, not scientific language. We also speak of the sun rising in popular language even though we know that scientifically the sun does not rise at all; the earth turns to face it.

1:7 So God made the expanse and separated the water under the expanse from the water above it. And it was so.

This time God doesn't merely speak the expanse into existence, he "makes" it and then puts the expanse to work in accomplishing its stated purpose, to separate the waters above and below it. Perhaps this is an instance of the subtle polemic of Genesis 1 against idolatrous cosmogonies that seems everywhere just below the surface. The separation of the waters came only after a colossal struggle in the myths of the ancient Near East. In one of them, *Enuma Elish*, the firmament is formed by the victorious god Marduk by arching the flayed half of the defeated goddess Tiamat after a titanic struggle.[47] Here God indicates that the expanse should come into existence and then makes it in the most matter-of-fact fashion. There is not the slightest hint of a struggle.

1:8 God called the expanse "sky." And there was evening, and there was morning—the second day.

The NIV here uses the word "sky" to translate the Hebrew word *šāmayim*, usually translated "heaven." The connection with 1:1 is thus lost, although the translation is accurate. The expanse is necessary for all nonwater life to have an environment in which to live and is also the necessary preparation for day five when birds, which fly in the expanse, are created. Lacking here is the statement of divine approval, "and God saw that it was good." Perhaps the author viewed the creation of the expanse as merely a preliminary stage to

---

[47]In Enuma Elish after Marduk has killed Tiamat in a fierce battle we read:
    Then the lord [Marduk] paused to view her [Tiamat's] dead body,
    that he might divide the monster and do artful works
    He split her like a shellfish into two parts;
    Half of her he set up and ceiled it as sky,
    Pulled down the bar and posted guards,
    He bade them to allow not her waters to escape (*ANET*, p. 67).

How different Genesis! In the most matter-of-fact fashion, the creation of the rain clouds and what we might call the air are related.

the emergence of the dry land on day three. Another possibility is that, given the fear that ancient people had of the firmament falling, it was important to make it clear that God was in complete control of it. He himself made it and it is, therefore, not to be feared. Another reason the formula of divine approval was withheld may be for stylistic reasons. Since the formula was to be used twice on the third and sixth days giving seven in total, not using it here allowed the author to preserve the pattern of sevens.[48]

Once again the recording of the passing of evening and morning marking the day is given. Here the ordinal number "second" is used in contrast to day one. The rest of the days are also given ordinal numbers. This sets day one off from the others as somehow unique.

Day Three: The Forming of the Land (1:9-13)

1:9 And God said, "Let the water under the sky be gathered to one place, and let dry ground appear." And it was so.

This passage records the uncovering of the dry ground which up to this stage of creation has been covered with the deep water. It also records the creation of plants, many of which can be eaten by animals and humans as food. This section thus prepares the living space for the animals and humans who will inhabit it after their creation on the sixth day.

Wenham argues that while moderns tend to view the land masses of the world as islands floating in the seas, the biblical author depicts the world as land with oceans and seas within it. Perhaps this reflects the lack of experience with the great oceans of the world in the ancient world. Or perhaps this is another subtle hint of the polemic against idolatrous cosmologies in this chapter. The seas are not some frightening, other-worldly power. They are merely the gathering of the primordial ocean so that their underlying founda-

---

[48]Wenham, *Genesis 1-15*, p. 6: "The correspondence of the first paragraph, 1:1-2, with 2:1-3 is underlined by the number of Hebrew words in both being multiples of 7. 1:1 consists of seven words, 1:2 of fourteen (7 x 2) words, 2:1-3 of 35 (7 x 5) words. The number seven dominates this opening chapter in a strange way, not only in the number of words in a particular section but in the number of times a specific word or phrase recurs. For example, "God" is mentioned 35 times, 'earth' 21 times, 'Heaven/firmament' 21 times, while the phrases 'and it was so' and 'God saw that it was good' occur 7 times."

tion, dry land, can show itself. There is no battle with Apsu, the god of the oceans here. God spoke of his desire and it happened ("And it was so."). The great oceans and seas of the world can be cradled in the palm of one of God's hands (Isa 40:12). They came into existence by the mere desire of the Creator. Certainly even modern readers can relate to the raw power of the sea and be respectful of it. For the imagined audience about to enter the promised land the sea was terrifying. Israel was tempted to believe along with their neighbors that the Sea was in a constant battle with other forces in the world and could not be trusted. Genesis critiques that mythological view and assures Israel that the sea is under God's control. He had recently shown his control of the Red Sea and this account makes it clear that not even the oceans were to be feared.

1:10 God called the dry ground "land," and the gathered waters he called "seas." And God saw that it was good.

This is the last time in the creation account that God names anything. In the future that responsibility will be delegated to mankind. In naming the land and seas God shows his sovereign power over them. Once again we have in this verse God's evaluation. The seas were not hostile powers but something "good." Hamilton suggests the translation, "and God saw how beautiful it was." I think this captures the point and spirit of this passage which calls us as readers to wonder at the marvels of creation which we experience. But we should not lose sight of the original audience who feared the Sea and might think of it in personified or deified terms.[49]

1:11 Then God said, "Let the land produce vegetation: seed-bearing plants and trees on the land that bear fruit with seed in it, according to their various kinds." And it was so.

On the third day for the first time we have two distinctive acts of creation. This also happens on the climactic sixth day. On each of these days we twice hear "and God saw that it was good." Day three thus functions as the climax of the first half of creation in which the environments are formed so that those environments can be filled during the last half of creation week. Just as day three climaxes this

---

[49]Alter (*Genesis*, p. 4), by capitalizing the words Earth and Seas, hints at the mythological undertones such words may well have had for the original audience. But this fails to account for the antimythological polemic so prevalent in this chapter.

first phase of creation, so day six climaxes the second phase. Here we have the creation of vegetation which is further subdivided into plants and trees. It is possible to understand the Hebrew as meaning three types of vegetation: grass, plants, and trees.[50] But in verses 29-30 only two types (plants and trees) are mentioned as qualifying for food for both man and beast. Since grass was obviously eaten by many beasts, it seems odd that it is omitted. It seems better to translate the word grass (דֶּשֶׁא, *d^ešē'*) as a general word for vegetation as in the NIV.

These creations differ from previous ones in that they are self-reproducing. The word "kinds" (מִין, *mîn*) has been used to prove the genetic stability of animate creatures over against the claims of evolution that species change over time into entirely new species. It seems doubtful that it is the intent of this chapter to comment on such questions. The word is certainly not a technical term corresponding to our scientific words[51] family, genus, or species.

Instead this seems to be one of several narrative anticipations of the law in the book of Genesis. What God has created to be distinct, man should not mix. The problem of the mixing of kinds seems to be behind several prohibitions in the laws on holiness or "set-apartness" in the clean and unclean animal laws in Leviticus 11 and Deuteronomy 14.[52] It is as though Genesis were saying, "What God hath separated, let no man join together." The word "*mîn* is a key term used for articulating the theme of order through separation."[53] God has made a world of order with each plant and animal serving a particular role in that ordered creation.

---

[50]W.H. Gispen, *Genesis I*, Commentar op het Oude Testament (Kampen: Kok, 1974), 1:57.

[51]Mark D. Futato (*"mîn," NIDOTTE*, 2:934-935) notes: "This biblical taxonomy, of which *mîn* is a part, does not reflect a modern taxonomic perspective (Morris, 71), but uses the 'language of visual appearance' (Jordan, 12). While modern taxonomy separates birds from bees, the biblical perspective groups them together as 'winged creatures' (Gen 1:20-21). Both are legitimate perspectives. Modern Christians need not reject a modern taxonomy out of hand, nor should they dismiss the biblical classification, which will be used elsewhere in the Bible."

[52]Ibid., "In Lev 11:14-29 and Deut 14:14-18, presupposing the use in Gen 1, Moses articulates the theme of order through separation by using *mîn* to refer to groups of clean and unclean animals, which are part of a symbolic representation of holiness and unholiness (Poythress, 81-83)."

[53]Ibid.

1:12 The land produced vegetation: plants bearing seed according to their kinds and trees bearing fruit with seed in it according to their kinds. And God saw that it was good.

Here the creation itself becomes involved in God's creation. The land responds to God's command in exact obedience. Notice the nearly exact repetition between the command in verse 11 and its execution in verse 12. Perhaps we once again have a subtle polemic against idolatrous notions of creation. There is no struggle with matter in this creation story, unlike the myths so prevalent in the biblical world. Once again we have God's evaluation. He saw that it was good. Just as the emerging of the dry ground was necessary for land animals and humans to live, so also the emergence of food for them was necessary. Both of these things necessary for the life and well being of animals and humanity are "good" in God's eyes.

1:13 And there was evening, and there was morning—the third day.

Once again the author of Genesis repeats the refrain which structures the account of creation. The Hebrews apparently counted the evening first when referring to a 24-hour day. The environments and living spaces along with food sources have now been prepared. The first half of creation, the forming of the unformed earth has now been finished. The earth is a place where God's creatures can live!

4. The Filling of the Earth — Days Four to Six (1:14-25)

¹⁴And God said, "Let there be lights in the expanse of the sky to separate the day from the night, and let them serve as signs to mark seasons and days and years, ¹⁵and let them be lights in the expanse of the sky to give light on the earth." And it was so. ¹⁶God made two great lights—the greater light to govern the day and the lesser light to govern the night. He also made the stars. ¹⁷God set them in the expanse of the sky to give light on the earth, ¹⁸to govern the day and the night, and to separate light from darkness. And God saw that it was good. ¹⁹And there was evening, and there was morning—the fourth day.

²⁰And God said, "Let the water teem with living creatures, and let birds fly above the earth across the expanse of the sky." ²¹So God created the great creatures of the sea and every living and moving thing with which the water teems, according to their

kinds, and every winged bird according to its kind. And God saw that it was good. ²²God blessed them and said, "Be fruitful and increase in number and fill the water in the seas, and let the birds increase on the earth." ²³And there was evening, and there was morning—the fifth day.

²⁴And God said, "Let the land produce living creatures according to their kinds: livestock, creatures that move along the ground, and wild animals, each according to its kind." And it was so. ²⁵God made the wild animals according to their kinds, the livestock according to their kinds, and all the creatures that move along the ground according to their kinds. And God saw that it was good.

The account of the fourth, fifth, and sixth days of creation narrate the "filling" of the "void" in the initial creation. The previous section (vv. 3-13) described the forming of the formless heaven and earth. The environment or living space for the rest of creation has been provided. God now fills each of those environments with the creatures or created things which fill those environments. The fourth day sees the filling of day and night with the greater and lesser lights. Day and night were created on the first day. The fifth day sees the filling of the air and the water with birds and fish. The air and water were created on the second day when the expanse was formed to separate the water in rain clouds from its liquid form in rivers and seas. The sixth day sees the filling of that which was created on the third day. Dry land and vegetation provide living space and food for land animals and humans. The sixth day parallels the third in that on each of these days God declares his work of creation as good or very good. Also these two days share a sort of double creation: land and vegetation on the third day and animals and humans on the sixth day.

The anti-idolatry polemic in this chapter comes to the forefront in this section. In the ancient context the sun, moon, and stars were gods and to one degree or another were believed to control the destiny of humanity and the material world. Great sea creatures were believed to be horrifying semidivine creatures empowered by or embodying dark and dangerous forces. The fear which such a worldview must have engendered is remarkable. Israel lived, both in Egypt and later in exile, in societies controlled by that worldview and was heavily influenced by it. In Genesis the account of the creation of the heavenly bodies and the great sea creatures is designed to demonstrate their powerlessness.

As is the case with verses 3-13 this account is highly structured with minor variations. On each of the three days the account begins with God's statement, "Let there be," or its equivalent. Each contains the formula of accomplishment, "And it was so." The statement that "God made" (עָשָׂה, *'āśāh*) or "God created" (*bārā'*) then follows. The evaluation formula, "God saw that it was good," is found next, and "there was evening, and there was morning—the ___ day" closes the account. In parallel with the account of the third day, the narrative of the sixth day is longer and has a sort of double structure. Animals are "made" and humanity is "created" on the sixth day. There are two evaluation formulas, one after the making of the animals and one after the creation of humanity. There are also two formulas of God's decision to create, "Let there be" or its equivalent.

There are other examples of the careful structuring of the account. Two examples will illustrate. God's creative work is described with two different Hebrew verbs, the more generic "made" (*'āśāh*) and the specific "create" (*bārā'*). Notice the pattern created:

Verse	Hebrew word used	Thing Created
16a	"made" (*'āśāh*)	two great lights
21	(*bārā'*)	great creatures of the sea
25a	"made" (*'āśāh*)	animals
31a	(*bārā'*)	humans

The alternating between the Hebrew verbs for "made" and "created" forms a pattern which draws special attention to those things which are "created" rather than simply made.

A second example of the highly structured account with variations is the introduction of the word "bless." God blesses both the birds and fish (v. 22) and humanity (v. 28) with the commission to "be fruitful and increase in number and fill" the environment in which the creature is to live. The blessing of procreativity is explicitly given only to the first humans and the birds and fish. This reinforces the previous example where the special word "created" is used of these, and only these, special creations. Theologically speaking, the word "bless" will play a key role in the rest of the book of Genesis, in the Pentateuch, and in the remainder of Scripture. The creation blessing of procreation becomes the promise of God in building a people who will channel his blessing to the entire creation.

Day Four: The Filling of Day and Night (1:14-19)

One of the great questions which interpreters of Genesis 1 through the ages have discussed is how there could be light (created on the first day) before there was a sun, the source of light, apparently not created until the fourth day. Prior to the discovery of the rotation of the earth around the sun and the realization that sunlight and starlight are the only known sources of light great enough to produce daylight, this question was not so pressing. One possible resolution of this issue goes back to the technicalities of translation. Verse 14 could be translated, "Let the lights in the expanse of the sky be to separate the day from the night and let them serve as signs. . . ." In other words, the lights are already present, presumably being created on day one or "In the beginning," and now they are formally given their designated purpose. While this does resolve the question of how light could be created without the sun, this view creates its own set of difficulties. For one, verse 16, which describes the actual creation of the lights, begins with a waw-consecutive, the ordinary way to indicate sequence in Hebrew narrative. This would ordinarily imply that God's creation of the luminaries did not take place until he had resolved to do so on day four. Further, the sequential nature of this chapter would be thus disturbed. Also this view would require a translation of *yᵉhî*, "Let there be," which differs from its use elsewhere in the chapter.

Sailhamer, who advocates this view, attempts to answer all of these objections.[54] He notes quite rightly that the grammar of this verse differs from its closest parallel in verse 6. There the Hebrew reads literally, "*Let there be* an expanse in the midst of the waters; and *let it be dividing* between day and night. Here, in verse 14 the Hebrew reads, "*Let there be* lights in the expanse of the heavens *to divide between* the day and night." Sailhamer notes that when a form of the Hebrew verb "to be" (*hāyāh*) is followed by an infinitive clause with 'to' as here in verse 14, the idea of aiming at a purpose is empha-

---

[54]Sailhamer, *Genesis*, pp. 33-34.

sized. He further treats the phrase "lights in the expanse of the heavens" as the subject of the verb "to be" and not the object. Thus the lights, which were created previously, are now given their specific purpose. Sailhamer deals with verse 16 by suggesting that this verse is a comment to the reader. The author's report of what happened ended with "and it was so" in verse 15.

While Sailhamer's view cannot be excluded as a possibility, it seems to be motivated at least partially by the desire to avoid conflict with our current understanding of science in which it seems implausible, if not impossible, for daylight to occur without its only source, the sun. But this methodology is in danger of letting our modern questions about how to harmonize this chapter with contemporary science drive the process of interpretation. If we instead ask what questions were of concern to an ancient author, who did not know that the sun was a star which burns hydrogen to produce sunlight, very different answers arise.

First of all, it is noteworthy how detailed the description of the creation of the luminaries is. This undoubtedly indicates its importance to the original author. It is remarkable that in a cultural context in which the sun and moon were usually chief gods within ancient Near Eastern pantheons and stars were worshiped as divine beings who controlled human destiny to some degree, that the words for sun (שֶׁמֶשׁ, šemeš) and moon (יָרֵחַ, yārēaḥ) are not used; instead we read of "the greater light" and the "lesser light." This seems likely to be to avoid confusion with Shamash the sun god and Yarich the moon god. Here they are mere objects created by God Almighty to perform particular functions in his natural world. Their functions are limited to giving light, governing day and night, and separating light from darkness. The stars are given even less significance. Their creation is recorded by a single Hebrew word thrown onto the end of verse 16 "and the stars." They have no specific function and almost seem to be an afterthought.

Sarna suggests that the emergence of vegetation on day three prior to the creation of the sun on day four, serves to demonstrate how dispensable the heavenly bodies really were to God.[55] God didn't need the sun to make the plants grow or for that matter to give light to the creation. Instead of being above creation, the lumi-

---

[55]Sarna, *Genesis*, p. 9.

naries were creations themselves. Like all other created things, the luminaries serve God's purposes and had no independent existence or function. The subtle polemic of Genesis 1 against idolatry with its divinization of the processes of nature seems a far more likely explanation for the sun, moon, and stars being created after light and vegetation. The text does not seem the least bit interested in answering modern cosmological questions or harmonizing with modern creation theories.

The repetitiousness of the account often hides from modern readers a carefully structured palistrophe, common in Hebrew prose, especially the elevated prose of this chapter which at times approaches poetry. McEvenue notes the structure in this way:

> A to divide the day from the night (14a)
>   B for signs, for fixed times, for days and years (14b)
>   C to give light on the earth (15)
>   D to rule the day (16a)
>   D' to rule the night (16b)
>   C' to give light on the earth (17)
>   B' to rule the day and the night (18a)
> A' to divide the light from the darkness (18b)[56]

1:14 Let there be lights in the expanse of the sky

The word translated "lights" here is always used elsewhere in the Pentateuch to designate the sanctuary lamp in the tabernacle. This is one example of several in Genesis 1 in which the early chapters of Genesis point forward from the pristine creation to the tabernacle. The tabernacle is like the garden of Eden or the original creation in many ways. This is apparently designed to teach the original readers about the importance of the worship in which the nation, now freed from Egyptian slavery, could access the very presence of God. The foundations of that system of worship are to be found in the very creation itself. The original readers[57] would thus have understood the story of the creation of the lights both on a literal level and as a

---

[56]Sean E. McEvenue, *Narrative Style of the Priestly Writer* (Rome: Biblical Institute Press, 1971), pp. 157-158.

[57]The original "canonical readers," i.e., the readers when Genesis was first recognized as canonical Scripture would likely see a parallel between Israel's stay in Egypt and their own stay in exile. The lamp of the tabernacle would have its parallel in the recently rebuilt temple in Jerusalem.

subtle reminder of the light within the tabernacle (temple) that points to the Creator and the creation of that light.

and let them serve as signs to mark seasons and days and years,

Westermann and Steck argue that the word "signs" (אֹתֹת, *'ōthōth*) covers two subcategories: (a) seasons; and (b) days and years.[58] The NIV seems to follow this interpretation. Certainly "days and years" are likely to be a single category since the two nouns are governed by one preposition. The KJV followed by the NRSV sees four separate categories, "signs, seasons, days and years." Wenham mentions the possibility of three categories: celestial signs, festal seasons, and chronological periods.[59]

The word for seasons (מוֹעֲדִים, *mô'ădîm*) might better be translated as "festivals" or even "meetings." An exact homonym refers to the tabernacle as the tent of "meeting." The intent seems to be that the sun and moon[60] serve to measure time and especially to determine the timing of Israel's religious festivals. The worship of God commanded in the Pentateuch was carefully prepared for in the creation itself. The concept of holy time, where at intervals the people of God gather in joyous celebration of God's graciousness to them, is built into the warp and woof of the universe. What we experience now in Christian worship is but a foretaste of the everlasting party that God is planning for us now. For Israel there was the ever-present temptation to neglect the worship of the only true God and worship idols. The early Christians are warned about the importance of not forsaking the times of gathering with fellow believers (Heb 10:25). In either case the spiritual results would be devastating. The same is true for us.

1:15 and let them be lights in the expanse of the sky to give light on the earth." And it was so.

The formula "and it was so" which concludes verse 15 shows God's complete control over creation. He thinks the greater and lesser lights into existence with a specific purpose and it happened

---

[58]Claus Westermann, *Genesis*, trans. by John J. Scullion (Minneapolis: Augsburg, 1984), 1:130; and O.H. Steck, *Der Schöpfungsbericht der Priesterschrift* (Göttingen: Vanderhoeck und Ruprecht, 1975), *ad loc.*

[59]Wenham, *Genesis*, pp. 22-23.

[60]The book of Jubilees blatantly removes the moon from calendrical functions so as to tendentiously defend a 364-day solar calendar. Only the sun, not the moon, serves to mark time.

just as he imagined it. God's mastery over these awe inspiring phenomena of nature would have been even more striking to the imagined audience who are tempted to regard the sun and moon as gods.

1:16 God made two great lights—the greater light to govern the day and the lesser light to govern the night.

In the most matter-of-fact way this passage describes God's making of the two great lights and their created purposes. They have no role in determining human destiny. They do not have personalities, nor can they think or speak. They are mere objects which make day and night possible. The decision to not use the typical words for sun and moon seems deliberate. The author does not want his audience to infer that God made the sun god Shamash and the moon god Yirach. He did not make lesser gods. He merely made two great lights.

He also made the stars.

In Hebrew the creation of the stars is mentioned only in passing by the addition of the phrase, "and the stars."[61] The NIV supplies the words, "He also made." Given the significance of the stars as divine beings in the ancient world, the author of Genesis is subtly critiquing the common ancient idea that the stars control human destiny. They are almost an afterthought in Genesis, of little real significance. In any case, God created them.

1:17 God set them in the expanse of the sky to give light on the earth,
1:18 to govern the day and the night, and to separate light from darkness. And God saw that it was good.

Not only did God create the greater and lesser lights, he set them in the expanse of the heavens (NIV "sky") and gave them their cre-

---

[61]Colin L. House ("Some Notes on Translating וְאֵת הַכּוֹכָבִים in Genesis 1:16," *AUSS* 25 [1987]: 241-248) argues that וְאֵת (*wᵉēth*, with schewa [ᵉ] and tserey [*ē*]) in Gen 9:10 clearly means "with" and it could mean "with" here also. If so, the creation of the stars falls outside of the six-day time frame of the chapter. He gives 1:1 (God created the heavens *with* the earth); 3:24 (he placed the cherubim *with* the flaming sword); and 49:31 (There they buried Abraham *with* Sarah) as other examples. The famous crux in 4:1 is another possibility discussed. House also argues that an Akkadian loan word which came into Hebrew as a homonym of the sign of the direct object is behind these instances. They are possibilities, but there is no way to be certain in 1:16. The motivation may be to find a way to harmonize current science with Genesis 1, a dangerous exegetical procedure.

ational purpose. He is in total control. This is no account of the highest God creating lesser gods. This is the account of the one God creating physical objects which while wondrous in their power and beauty have no personality or power independent of him. God's evaluation of the creation of these objects as "good" would have been more noteworthy for the original audience than it is for contemporary readers. The sun and moon gods were powerful and could be capricious and dangerous to humanity. Genesis is telling its readers that even the most powerful physical forces in the universe are nothing more than that and are part of the all-powerful Creator's good creation.

1:19 And there was evening, and there was morning—the fourth day.

The pattern of a day passing after the account of God's creation on that day continues. The Hebrew way of counting the beginning of a day with the evening is displayed once again.

Day Five: The Filling of the Atmosphere and Seas (1:20-23)

1:20 And God said, "Let the water teem with living creatures, and let birds fly above the earth across the expanse of the sky."

The second day saw the separation by the expanse of the primeval ocean and the water in the clouds which produced rain. Here on the fifth day God creates living, moving creatures to fill the waters and the expanse. God desires that the waters "teem" with living creatures. They are not just to exist but to be abundant. This is perhaps part of the reason why God blesses them specifically in verse 22 with the command to be "fruitful and increase." Birds are to fly in the expanse which was created on day two. Here the expanse seems to be the lowest level of the "heavens" ("sky" in NIV).

1:21 So God created the great creatures of the sea and every living and moving thing with which the water teems, according to their kinds, and every winged bird according to its kind. And God saw that it was good.

After God's determination to create fish and birds, he does so. The special word בָּרָא (*bārā'*, translated "created" in NIV) appears for the second time in Genesis 1. The other two times are used of the initial creation of the heavens and the earth (1:1) and of the special creation of man (1:26-28). More perplexing is just why it is used here and not when vegetation is created or when land animals are created. One explanation is that for the first time animate creatures are made. Thus the special word *bārā'* is used of the initial creation of all things (1:1), the first creation of animate creatures (1:21), and finally at the creation of humankind, the apex of creation (1:26). Another possibility, and in my judgment the most likely, is that the word is used here because of exactly what God is said to have created, the "great creatures of the sea" (הַתַּנִּינִם, *hattannînim*). These creatures were often given divine status in the ancient Near East, and the author of Genesis 1 wants to make sure that they are seen as the special creations of the one and only God and not rival deities. Sarna says,

> The Hebrew word **tannin** appears in Canaanite myths from Ugarit, together with Leviathin, as the name of a primeval dragon-god who assisted Yam (Sea) in an elemental battle against Baal, the god of fertility.[62]

Such passages as Isaiah 27:1; 51:9; Psalm 74:13; and Job 7:12 use the language of Canaanite myth to describe God's victory over his foes. It seems likely that the special word for God's creation is used for the *tannînim* in order to insist that they are under God's sovereign power. They are not his rivals but his creatures, and therefore the myths about them are not to be believed. While such great creatures are still the cause of wonder, they are not to be feared or deified.

Once again we have God's evaluation of his work as "good." The fifth day was deemed "good" since the empty earth is reversed during this day in addition to the innate source of wonder fish and birds are.

1:22 God blessed them and said, "Be fruitful and increase in number and fill the water in the seas, and let the birds increase on the earth."

For the first time in this chapter we hear of God's blessing, and it is held until there are creatures who can obey the blessing of procreation. In its context, when fish and birds were few and far between, to procreate was a blessing. Sarna offers a twofold explanation for why it is only on the fifth day that God's blessing comes:

---

[62]Sarna, *Genesis*, p. 10.

Animate creation receives the gift of fertility. Plant life was not so blessed, both because it was thought to have been initially equipped with the capacity for self-reproduction by nonsexual means and because it is later to be cursed. The procreation of animate creatures, however, requires individual sexual activity, mating. This capacity for sexual reproduction is regarded as a divine blessing.[63]

The tendency of humanity to hunt birds and fish (along with other animals) to the brink of extinction receives its critique here. Those who believe that the world is God's world naturally want to preserve its beauty and fruitfulness. Regarding fish and birds merely as food sources or prizes for the trophy case may indicate a callous disregard for the wonder of God's creation. This is not to suggest that hunting and fishing are innately wrong, but a Christian sees God's blessing in the multiplication of God's creatures.

The word "blessing" is a theologically loaded word, and it is the key term which links the primeval history with the promise to Abraham. The blessings which God gave to his original creation and still wants that creation to experience are to be achieved through the descendants of one man, Abram (Gen 12:3).

1:23 And there was evening, and there was morning—the fifth day.

Again the author repeats the refrain in his highly structured, prose account. Once again the Hebrew custom of counting a 24-hour period as an evening and a morning occurs.

Day Six: The Filling of the Land (1:24-25)

1:24 And God said, "Let the land produce living creatures according to their kinds:

The sixth day parallels the third day in that the environment and food necessary for the survival of land animals and humankind are prepared on the third day, and those very creatures are placed within that environment and given that food on the sixth day. The sixth day forms the apex of the account of creation. As on the third day, twice on this day God evaluates his work positively, once after the creation of land animals, and once after the creation of humankind; only this last time the creation is complete, and it is not just "good" but "very good."

---

[63]Ibid., pp. 10-11.

It is remarkable that land animals are said to have been produced from the "land" or literally the "earth." Does this speak to the natural environment of these creatures? In Genesis 2:19 we are informed that prior to the creation of the woman the LORD God formed all the beasts of the field "out of the ground." Once again the creation itself is called upon to participate in the creative process.[64]

livestock, creatures that move along the ground, and wild animals, each according to its kind."

The NIV paraphrases the third type of land creatures as "wild animals." But the Hebrew reads literally, "animals of the earth." Why is this threefold division of land creatures given? W.M. Clark points out that this tripartite division of the animal kingdom can be found in Hosea 4:3; Psalm 8; and Zephaniah 1:3.[65] It may therefore be the traditional Hebrew way of dividing up the animal kingdom. Kikawada and Quinn suggest that the concern of the classifying system is primarily with locomotion.[66] The author's summary in 1:28 is "every living thing that *moves* on the earth." They argue that livestock walk on top of the ground, creatures that move along the ground slide on it, while the NIV's "wild animals" are animals which dig through it, i.e., "animals of the earth." They note that part of the punishment of the serpent has to do with its "manner of locomotion."

1:25 God made the wild animals according to their kinds, the livestock according to their kinds, and all the creatures that move along the ground according to their kinds. And God saw that it was good.

This verse relates how God follows his decision to create land animals. They are made "according to their kinds." The order of the

---

[64]The author of Jubilees is apparently (see James C. Vanderkam, "Genesis 1 in Jubilees 2," *Dead Sea Discoveries* 1 [1994]: 300-321) uncomfortable with the notion of creation being drawn into the process of creation because of the possibility of interpreters then deifying those parts of nature. But this is an overreaction to Greek mythology. Our text makes it crystal clear that the ground is an inanimate thing. The use of the jussive (third-person imperative "let it") rather than the imperative (second person command implying a person) suggests this.

[65]W.M. Clark, "The Animal Series in the Primeval History," *VT* 18 (1968): 433-449.

[66]Isaac Kikawada and Arthur Quinn, *Before Abraham Was: The Unity of Genesis 1–11* (Nashville: Abingdon, 1985), pp. 78-79.

report of the creation of land creatures (wild animals, livestock, and creatures moving on the ground) differs from the order in which God commissioned their creation in verse 24 (livestock, creatures moving on the ground, wild animals). Sarna speculates that this is to bring the word for ground (אֲדָמָה, *'ădāmāh*) nearer to the word for humankind (אָדָם, *'ādām*) so that the wordplay could be highlighted.[67]

The lack of a blessing on the land creatures is striking, especially in view of the fact that the birds and water creatures did receive one. It could be that the environment and means of procreation of birds and water creatures allows them to freely reproduce without endangering or encroaching upon the territory of humankind. Wild animals, on the other hand, could and did pose a threat to humankind (Exod 23:29; Lev 26:22). Their uncontrolled proliferation would not be desirable for humankind in its infancy. But the tension between wild animals and humanity is only explicitly mentioned after the Flood. That tension should not be projected back into the circumstances of creation. Another possibility is that the lack of blessing is a narrative anticipation that it is a land animal (the serpent) which receives the curse for deceiving the original human pair. Perhaps the blessing is omitted to offer the reader a hint of what is to ensue between land animals and humanity in the garden scene.

5. Man: The Goal and Crown of Creation (1:26-30)

²⁶Then God said, "Let us make man in our image, in our likeness, and let them rule over the fish of the sea and the birds of the air, over the livestock, over all the earth,ᵃ and over all the creatures that move along the ground."

²⁷So God created man in his own image, in the image of God he created him; male and female he created them.

²⁸God blessed them and said to them, "Be fruitful and increase in number; fill the earth and subdue it. Rule over the fish of the sea and the birds of the air and over every living creature that moves on the ground."

²⁹Then God said, "I give you every seed-bearing plant on the

---

[67]Sarna, *Genesis*, p. 11.

face of the whole earth and every tree that has fruit with seed in it. They will be yours for food. ³⁰And to all the beasts of the earth and all the birds of the air and all the creatures that move on the ground—everything that has the breath of life in it—I give every green plant for food." And it was so.

ᵃ*26* Hebrew; Syriac *all the wild animals*

The second part of the sixth day of creation recounts the creation of humanity, male and female, as the apex or crown of creation. Narrative time slows down as God carefully considers his final act of creation. He decides upon a ruling role for humanity over the rest of his creatures. This creature is to be his representative on earth and be like him. For the first time God has a conversation with one of his creatures. This creature is given a special blessing of fertility and commanded to increase in number and rule over creation as God's vice-regent. The humans are also informed of how their need and the animal's need for food are to be met.

Two questions of interpretation in this passage have a long (and fascinating) history. The first is, "Who is the 'us' referred to in the phrase, 'Let us make man in our image'?" Second, "How should the phrase, 'in our image, in our likeness' be translated, and what does it mean?" While the issues are complex and the details will be considered below, I think it is helpful to persist in asking how the imagined audience is likely to have heard this text. Since this text records the creation of human beings, human readers are particularly interested in discovering how this text speaks to the human search for meaning and identity in the world. There has been a tendency to force the text to address issues it was not designed to address and to project onto the text ideas that would have been foreign to both the original and earliest canonical audiences. This is natural and inevitable. After all, we do not read this text merely to satisfy our idle curiosity about what people in an entirely different situation 3,000 years ago thought of this text; we read as people of the twenty-first century A.D. But attention to the likely meaning for the earliest audience does serve as a check on our tendency to get out of the Bible what we bring to it without humbly allowing the text to set the agenda for our conversations about application.

1:26 Then God said, "Let us make man in our image, in our likeness,

When Genesis 1 finally comes to the creation of humankind, the goal toward which the chapter has been moving, creation by divine fiat is replaced by careful contemplation. Although it may be only a figure of speech, it is as though now others are brought into the process. This is just one of a number of indications of the exalted position of humankind in this text. When an especially important work is to be done, consultation is called for.

It has been argued by Christian interpreters for centuries that the plurals "us" and "our" in this passage refers to a conversation between the members of the Trinity. Calvin is representative of this view:

> [S]ince the Lord needs no other counselor, there can be no doubt that he consulted with himself. The Jews make themselves altogether ridiculous, in pretending that God held communication with the earth or with angels. The earth, forsooth, was a most excellent advisor! And to ascribe the least portion of a work so exquisite to angels, is a sacrilege to be held in abhorrence. Where, indeed, will we find that we were created after the image of the earth, or of angels? Does not Moses directly exclude all creatures in express terms, when he declares that Adam was created after the image of God? Others, who deem themselves more acute, but are doubly infatuated, say that God spoke of himself in the plural number, according to the custom of princes. As if, in truth, that barbarous style of speaking, which has grown into use within a few past centuries, had, even then, prevailed in the world.[68]

But this is far too dogmatic (not to mention acerbic in tone) and demonstrates a lack of understanding of the progressive nature of revelation. The idea that the author of Genesis understood the doctrine of the Trinity or even the plurality of persons within the one Godhead seems a stretch at best. While Calvin makes a good point when he reasons that man was not made in the image of angels and that therefore "let us make man in our image" could not be literally true of the angels, he fails to consider several other points. First of all, when the report of God actually making humankind is given, God acts alone. "Let us make man" is not an invitation to literal participation on the part of the angels in the act of creating humankind,

---

[68]John Calvin, *Commentaries on the First Book of Moses, Called Genesis*, trans. by John King (Grand Rapids: Eerdmans, 1948), p. 92.

but is instead an announcement to the heavenly court drawing attention to the *coup de grace* of his creation. Job 38:4,7 puts it: "When I [God] laid the foundation of the earth . . . all the sons of God shouted for joy." Second, the language had to be comprehensible to people who had not yet received revelation of the doctrine of the Trinity. It meant something to them. The imagined audience was struggling with the temptation to succumb to the polytheism of Egypt and the ancient Near East. A revelation of the doctrine of the Trinity at that time would have been taken in a polytheistic sense, not a monotheistic trinitarianism. Third, Calvin excludes other possible understandings of the words. Fourth, the polemic against polytheism which seems to be a major factor for the way in which creation is narrated in this text argues against a Trinitarian reading. Fifth, the rest of the Bible, including the New Testament never refers to this text as an intimation of the Trinity. This interpretation only arose after the time of the New Testament[69] during the controversies with "heretics" over the divine nature of Jesus Christ. The fuller revelation of Scripture does not explicitly authorize the reading of this text as a conversation with the preincarnate Logos or among the other members of the Trinity.

Wenham helpfully outlines five other interpretations of the plural in 1:26,27: (a) God is addressing his heavenly court of angels (cf. Isa 6:8); Jewish commentaries since Philo have taken this position as well: Skinner, von Rad, Zimmerli, Kline, Mettinger, Gispen, Day, and Wenham himself; (b) Gunkel suggested that this is a carryover from an originally polytheistic account — but this seems highly unlikely given Genesis one's antimythological thrust; (c) Keil, Dillmann and Driver suggested the "plural of majesty" but Joüon's observation (114e) that "we" as a plural of majesty is not used with verbs, has led to the rejection of this view by most scholars; (d) Joüon prefers the plural of self-deliberation. Cassuto and Westermann argue similarly; (e) Clines and Hasel argue for plurality within the Godhead because God is addressing his Spirit who was present and active at creation (1:2). This requires the translation of *rûaḥ* as "Spirit" and not "wind," "spirit," or "breath" in Genesis 1:2.[70]

---

[69]As far as I am aware, the first time the text was understood in this way was during the time of Justin Martyr (*c.* 100–165 A.D.) and the writing of the Epistle of Barnabas (*c.* 130–140).

[70]Wenham, *Genesis,* pp. 27-28.

Of these five views (a), (d), and (e) have the strongest arguments in their favor. The book of Genesis does not discuss the creation of angels or the cherubim or seraphim. But angels as well as cherubim appear in the book of Genesis and throughout the Pentateuch as though their existence could be taken for granted. When Isaiah has a vision of the exalted LORD seated upon a throne and surrounded by seraphim, he hears the LORD say, "Whom shall I send and who will go for us?" One way of reading this text is to suggest that the "us" is the LORD and the seraphim who surround him and declare his holiness. There is no reason to exclude the angel view out of hand. Only God does the actual creating in Genesis 1 just as only the LORD does the actual sending in Isaiah 6. But angels have a role to play in the working out of God's purposes just as the seraphim have a role to play in the preparation of Isaiah for his prophetic calling (Isa 6:6). The ministry of angels does not in any way diminish God's glory, nor does it threaten the doctrine of Christ's unique divine status.

The "plural of self-deliberation" (view (d) above) suggests that God is alone when he makes the decision to create humanity, but the use of "us" and "our" is a Hebrew way of describing the interior conversation between God and himself. While this view is impossible to prove or disprove, it does sound inherently plausible. The weightiness of the decision and the significance of what God is about to create is given emphasis by the plural of self-deliberation.

The view that God is here addressing his Spirit (view e) is also plausible. While Christian readers must be careful not to read the Old Testament revelation of the Spirit as though he was the third person of the Trinity, the Spirit does have a personality and can be spoken to within the revelation of the Old Testament. It is significant that the two men who worked on crafting the tabernacle furniture, Bezalel and Oholiab, do so by the power of the Spirit of God (Exod 31:2-3). The intimation would seem to be that God creates by the power of his Spirit, and in something as special as the tabernacle even the human craftsmen must be filled with God's Spirit if they are to do the work God has called them to with faithfulness.

In the final analysis any of these three views is plausible and makes sense for the imagined audience. Perhaps the three views are not mutually exclusive; the imagined audience might well have read this text in more than one way.

The phrases, "in our likeness" and "in our image" have produced an extensive amount of speculation and scholarly discussion.⁷¹ The words translated "image" (צֶלֶם, ṣelem) and "likeness" (דְּמוּת, dᵉmûth) are used elsewhere in the very concrete sense of statues or other physical representations of gods.⁷² The Aramaic equivalents of these words also refer to literal statues or idols.⁷³ The word translated "in" is an all-purpose Hebrew preposition which can be legitimately translated into English in a variety of ways. It is interesting that in verse 26 the phrase "in our image" seems to be glossed by the phrase "as our likeness." In this second phrase the Hebrew preposition is כְּ (kᵉ) which also has a broad semantic range but often means "like" or "as." Since in the account of God actually creating in verse 27 only "*in* his image" recurs, it seems to me that the phrase "as our likeness" is an interpretive gloss by the author⁷⁴ which is designed to help clarify the meaning of "in our image." Clines has argued, successfully in my view, that the image of God is not something external to mankind. Instead the *beth* should be read as a *beth essentiae*, i.e., humankind is not made in God's image, but created to be God's image.⁷⁵ Just as an idol is a physical representation of an

---

⁷¹See the discussion below of the varying interpretations of these words in the excursus.

⁷²Num 33:52; 1 Sam 6:5,11; 2 Kgs 11:18; 16:10; 2 Chr 4:3; 23:17; Isa 40:18; Ezek 7:20; 16:17; 23:14; Amos 5:26.

⁷³Hess ("Genesis 1–2") argues that since the Aramaic equivalents to these two words are translated by the same Akkadian word in the Tell Fakhariyah bilingual inscription, that the Akkadian word and the Aramaic words refer to the statue which holds the inscription.

⁷⁴Barr (James Barr, "The Image of God in the Book of Genesis – A Study of Terminology," *Bulletin of the John Rylands Library* 51 [1968–69]: 11-26) argues, incorrectly in my view, that ṣelem is the more important word but also the more general and ambiguous and dᵉmût was added in the postexilic period to clarify. By then ṣelem became a standard word for idol. He argues that the words are synonyms added for artistic reasons. More convincingly he contends that the words refer to something substantial, if not physical.

⁷⁵David J.A. Clines, "The Image of God in Man," *TynBul* 19 (1968): 81-83.

⁷⁶As Jeroboam I was apparently attempting to do when he made "golden calves" at the altars at Bethel and Dan (1 Kgs. 12:26-33). Yahweh, who brought Israel out of Egypt was apparently being represented by these calves.

invisible god, so humankind is to act as the representation of the one and only true God. To represent the true God with an idol[76] is to misrepresent him. Humankind as they exercise their God-given responsibility to rule over creation on behalf of God *is* his image. Humanity is not to represent God with an idol because he already has a much more adequate representation, a personal representative humanity.

In the ancient context kings sometimes claimed to be the image of specific gods. Certainly Israel had experienced the hard downside of a culture (Egypt) which exalted the king, and the king alone, to the status of divine representative. Part of the critique of polytheism in the book of Genesis is also a critique of the way in which polytheistic cultures justified tyrannical forms of hierarchical leadership by myths of the divine nature of kings. Pharaoh's ability to subjugate his people and terrorize the underclasses of his society was dependent on a mythological view of Pharaoh as representative of the gods. Genesis responds to this and later forms of tyranny by claiming that on the contrary all of humanity serve together as the one God's representatives.

EXCURSUS

THE INTERPRETATION OF HUMANITY AS "THE IMAGE AND LIKENESS OF GOD"

Wenham discusses five main suggestions for the meaning of "image" and "likeness":[77] a) "Image" and "likeness" are distinct aspects of man's nature, i.e., "image" means one thing and "likeness" means something else. Perhaps the distinction is between "natural" qualities such as reason or personality and "supernatural graces" such as ethical discernment. But this view falters on the fact that the words "image" and "likeness" seemed to be used interchangeably. b) A second and popular view is that the words "image" and "likeness" mean the mental and spiritual qualities which humanity has but animals lack. The difficulty with this view is pinning down exactly which qualities. Suggestions are: reason, personality, free will, self-con-

---

[77]Wenham, *Genesis 1–15*, pp. 29-30.

sciousness, intelligence. But this results in arbitrariness of interpretation. c) A third view is "image" is physical resemblance, i.e., man looks like God literally. But this seems too simplistic in light of passages in the Pentateuch such as Deuteronomy 4:15-16: "You saw no form of any kind the day the LORD spoke to you at Horeb out of the fire. Therefore watch yourselves very carefully, so that you do not become corrupt and make for yourselves an idol, an image of any shape, whether formed like a man or a woman. . . ." d) A fourth suggestion is that the "image" makes man God's representative on earth. This is argued from the immediate context "and let them rule over" all creation. It is also argued from the ancient Near Eastern background where the function and status of kings seems to be democratized here to apply to all mankind. Both Egyptian and Assyrian texts describe the king as the image of God.[78] Man's ruling of creation is a royal function and Psalm 8, the closest parallel to Genesis 1, speaks of man having been made a little lower than the angels, but crowned with glory and honor and made to rule over the works of God's hands. Man is clearly viewed in royal terms in Psalm 8. Further the very idea of an image is that of a representation of the deity. e) A final suggestion is that the "image" is the capacity to relate to God. Since humanity is made to be like God, humans uniquely have the capacity to relate to God. This is the once popular view of Barth and more recently of Westermann. The latter argues that "in our image" should be viewed as an adverbial modifier of "let us make" rather than an adjectival description of mankind. The process of how God made humanity is thus highlighted and not the result.

In my judgment views a) and c) can be dismissed. There is no reason to infer some great distinction between the words "image" and "likeness," and the God of the Bible does not have a body after which human bodies are constructed. View b) seems to be an invitation for speculation. Its strength is that regardless of what the words "image" and "likeness" mean, God obviously has given certain capacities to human beings which he has not given to animals and which enable humans to relate to him in unique ways. Certainly humankind cannot rule or even obey God's commands without the

---

[78]P.A. Bird, "Male and Female He Created Them," *HTR* 74 (1981): 129-159.

ability to reason or without an innate interest in spiritual things. Those gifts are to be appreciated even if we reject them as the intended meaning of the words. View e) is a variation of this view. I would support view d) both for linguistic reasons and because it fits best with the anti-idolatry polemic of these chapters. Statues of wood, stone or ivory cannot represent God. Neither can the representation of God be limited to human kings.

and let them rule over the fish of the sea and the birds of the air, over the livestock, over all the earth, and over all the creatures that move along the ground."

In creating humanity as his image, his representative on earth, God simultaneously decides on a ruling role for humanity in creation. Humanity is not created to take over mindless work or to provide the gods with food through sacrifice as the myths taught.[79] They are to rule[80] over all of the other creatures on God's behalf as his representative.

1:27 So God created man in his own image, in the image of God he created him; male and female he created them.

This verse narrates with almost poetic repetition the carrying out of God's decision to create humanity. Notice the synonymous parallelism[81] of the statement:

---

[79]By contrast the Jewish Rabbis having been influenced by Genesis are struck by the greatness of mankind. W. Gunther Plaut ("Genesis," in *The Torah: A Modern Commentary*, ed. by W. Gunther Plaut [New York: Union of American Hebrew Congregations, 1981], p. 22) notes: "In a midrash the angels at first mistook man for a divine person and sang hymns to him" (Genesis Rabbah 18:10).

[80]Alter (*Genesis*, p. 5) suggests that the verb typically translated "rule" be translated "hold sway" noting: "The verb *radah* is not the normal Hebrew word for 'rule' (the latter is reflected in "dominion" of verse 16), and in most of the contexts in which it occurs it seems to suggest an absolute or even fierce exercise of mastery." But this fails to account for the perfect ("very good") state of creation at this point. In such a creation humanity has no need to rule harshly over creation.

[81]Synonymous parallelism is the common repetitive structure found in Hebrew poetry where the second line repeats (and in subtle ways alters) the first line. For example, Psalm 19:1 reads:

A The heavens	declare	the glory of God
A' The earth	shows	his handiwork.

➤

A So God created man in his own image,
B in the image of God he created him;
C male and female he created them.

Notice the following: The special verb "create" (בָּרָא, *bārā'*) occurs in each line; God or the pronoun "he" referring to God occurs in each line; the word order in line B is the reverse of line A; the word "man" (הָאָדָם, *hā'ādām*) in line A is paralleled by the pronoun "him" in line B and by "them" with the explanatory "male and female" added in line C. "Man" is actually "male and female." By Hebrew convention the masculine word *'ādām* refers both to the male human and to humanity in general of both genders. The God of the Bible is neither male nor female, and if humanity is to serve as his representative, his image, they do so as male and female work[82] together to be that image. If the notion of humanity being created "as God's representative image" is taken seriously, then it is only men and women working together that are the image of God and not them separately. As individuals we only participate in what it means to be the image of God in cooperation with others, specifically cooperation that involves both genders. If humanity, male and female, is to rule over the creation, it will take both the male and female working together. This is obvious in the need for procreation. If men and

---

Notice how each element in line A is given a corresponding and synonymous element in line A'.

[82]While many of the Bible's metaphor's for God are masculine there are also many feminine metaphors for God. Unlike the petty gods of polytheism which display their gender in the most stereotypical ways, the God of the Bible is beyond gender. Don C. Benjamin ("Israel's God: Mother and Midwife," *BTB* 19 [1989]: 115-120) has helpfully catalogued the female images of God in the Bible and Apocrypha. God is portrayed as **mother** (*dea mater*): God labors to give birth to rain and sleet (Job 38:28-29), carries humanity in her womb (Deut 32:18; Num 11:12-13; Acts 17:26-28), labors to give birth to humanity (Deut. 32:18; Isa 42:14; John 1:12; Rom 8:22), teaches humanity to walk (Hos 11:3-4), wipes humanity's tears when it cries (Isa 66:13-14; Rev 21:4); **midwife** (*dea obstetrix*): God delivers the sea (Job 38:8), delivers Zion's child (Isa 66:9), bathes humanity (Ezek 36:25), clothes the sea (Job 38:8-9), clothes humanity (Gen 3:21; Job 10:10-12), places humanity in its mother's arms (Ps 22:9-10); and **wet nurse** (*dea nutrix*): God cradles humanity in her arms (Hos 11:3-4; Isa 46:3-4), nurses humanity (Isa 49:15; Ps 34:9; Hos 11:4; 2 Esdras 1:28-29; John 7:37-38; 1 Pet 2:2-3), weans humanity from breast milk to solid food (Wis 16:20-21; Ps 131:1-2).

women do not procreate, they will not be able to fill the earth and rule over it as God's representative. But humans, both male and female, must cooperate in other ways if they are to be good representatives of God.

In a world of male and female deities in conflict with one another this would have been read as a revolutionary statement. A God without gender creates gender in the humans who are to serve as his representatives over the rest of creation. This God does not fall in love romantically with the oversexed goddesses of the myths. Sexuality is created for humanity, and God does not participate in it. For the imagined audience this was truly revolutionary.[83] To us it seems so obvious; but to the imagined audience this text is striking in the way it portrays men and women as partners, and in the way that sexuality is given only to humans; it is not part of the nature of God.[84]

1:28 God blessed them and said to them, "Be fruitful and increase in number; fill the earth and subdue it. Rule over the fish of the sea and the birds of the air and over every living creature that moves on the ground."

For the first time in the Bible human beings are said to be blessed by God. The "blessing" is the command to procreate[85] so that humanity might rule over creation. Modern readers have a hard time with this mandate in light of the popular accounts of the world's population explosion. Further, it is often alleged that this

---

[83]Richard M. Davidson ("The Theology of Sexuality in the Beginning: Genesis 1–2," *AUSS* 26/1 [1988]: 7): "In contrast to the view of creation as divine procreation, the account of Gen 1, with its emphasis upon the transcendent God (Elohim) and a cosmic view of creation, posits a radical separation of sexuality and divinity. God stands 'absolutely beyond the polarity of sex.' The sexual distinctions are presented as a creation by God, not part of the divine order."

[84]Emil Brunner tersely comments (*Man in Revolt: A Christian Anthropology*, trans. by Olive Wyon [Philadelphia: Westminster], 1939, p. 60): "That is the immense double statement, of a lapidary simplicity, so simple indeed that we hardly realize that with it a vast world of myth and Gnostic speculation, of cynicism and asceticism, of the deification of sexuality and fear of sex completely disappears."

[85]While the form of the blessing is a command, God provided human beings with the capacity to obey the command in creation. The capacity to procreate, therefore, is not to be viewed as an obligation or burden, but as a blessing.

passage, with its call to "rule"[86] over creation, justifies the rape of the environment that has been occurring since the industrial revolution.[87] But the commission to multiply is given when procreation is absolutely essential for the survival of humankind. The commission to rule over the animate world of creatures cannot mean to dominate them and hunt them into extinction. They are not even given as a potential source of food in this narrative.

God's blessing on humankind parallels the blessing on water creatures and birds in verse 22, but here God addresses them directly in speech, showing the different status of humankind. The command to "be fruitful and multiply" is repeated to Noah after the Flood (Gen 9:1), who is there depicted as a sort of New Adam. The Patriarchs, whose role is to funnel God's blessing to all mankind are reminded of this blessing and the implicit promise accompanying it, that God will enable them to fulfill it (Gen 17:2,20; 28:3; 35:11). At the end of Genesis we are informed that it has begun to be fulfilled in the family of Jacob (47:27; 48:4).

Early interpreters, both rabbinic and Christian argued about whether Adam and Eve engaged in sexual activity before the Fall or only after it. Many of the early church fathers viewed sex as something subspiritual and therefore argued in the strongest terms against there being sex in the garden of Eden. This view ultimately led to the exaltation of celibacy and the prohibition of married people from the priesthood.[88] While this passage does not refer to the garden of Eden,

---

[86]John T. Pawlikowski, "Participation in Economic Life," *TBT* 24 (1986): p. 366, asserts: "The Hebrew word *radah* ("have dominion") is extremely forceful. It does not refer simply to a kind of benign maintenance over an essentially docile and pacific natural world. Its appearance in the Hebrew Scriptures is rather rare, and when it is employed it is nearly always in the context of kingship (see 1 Kgs 5:4; Ps 72:8; Ezek 34:4). This leads us to believe that it was part and parcel of the language of royal rule." But this is a long way from justifying the harming of the environment in the name of ruling over it.

[87]See the classic argument of Lynn White Jr., "The Historical Roots of Our Ecological Crisis," *Science* 155 (1967): 1204-1207.

[88]Gary Anderson, "Celibacy or Consummation in the Garden? Reflections on Early Jewish and Christian Interpretations of the Garden of Eden," *HTR* 82:2 (1989): 121-148. "The interpretation of Adam and Eve's sexual life was a matter of some concern for early Jewish and Christian exegetes. As Louis Ginsberg observed, several Jewish pseudepigraphical works as well as the

it seems clear that since sex was necessary for procreation to take place, and procreation was necessary for humankind to rule over God's creation. God intended that humanity would procreate without regard to whether or not there would ever be a Fall.

1:29 Then God said, "I give you every seed-bearing plant on the face of the whole earth and every tree that has fruit with seed in it. They will be yours for food.

Here God assigns every sort of vegetable life to humanity as food, both plants and the fruit of trees. The repetition of the word "every" emphasizes the generosity of God and the freedom which he entrusts to humanity. The words "you" and "yours" in this verse are plural in the Hebrew. To humanity, both male and female, God shows his generosity toward and trust in humanity. Humanity as male and female are given this gracious privilege. This text also implies that, at least in terms of God's ideal, humanity is not to use animals as a food source. The text does not explicitly prohibit the eating of animals, but neither does it authorize it at this stage of God's relationship with humanity. The prophets anticipate a time when the current cursed relationship with the animal world is reversed in a sort of return to paradise (Hos 2:18; Isa 11:69; 65:25).

---

writings of many of the early Church Fathers 'presuppose that not only the birth of the children of Adam and Eve took place after the expulsion from paradise (Gen 4:1ff), but that the first "human pair" lived in paradise without sexual intercourse.' The reasons for such an exegesis are not difficult to discern. The Garden of Eden was not simply a story about the primeval world; it could also function as a metaphor for the world-to-come [especially for early Syriac Christianity which did not include Revelation in its canon]. Hence the Garden was a paradigm for the ideal world of the eschaton, a world one should attempt to actualize or bring into existence now. Because Christians believed that the next world was devoid of marriage (Luke 20:27-40), it followed that the Garden was as well. In addition to this reason, Christians were also exhorted to abstain from marriage as a concession to the apocalyptic ferment of the present world (1 Corinthians 7).

"Rabbinic Judaism, on the other hand, did not have a high regard for the celibate condition. One midrashic text compares the celibate individual to one who impairs God's image and, even worse, to a murderer [Gen Rabbah 34:14]. The act of human procreation was not simply an acceptable act, it was a commanded act. It is the subject of the very first command God gives men and women: 'Be fruitful and multiply' (Gen 1:28)."

1:30 And to all the beasts of the earth and all the birds of the air and all the creatures that move on the ground—everything that has the breath of life in it—I give every green plant for food." And it was so.

The animals and birds also are assigned their food. They receive "every green plant." The difference between the food assigned to humans and that assigned to animals and birds is interesting. The more expansive diet of human beings is undoubtedly a reflection of their more exalted status (and more exalted responsibility) within the created order. What we might call the animal kingdom is divided into beasts, birds, and creatures which move along the surface of the ground (cf. KJV's "creeping things"). All three of these types of animals are said to have "the breath of life" in them. The Hebrew phrase for this expression is literally translated "a soul of life." This does not mean that animals have "souls" and will therefore be in heaven.[89] Instead the Hebrew word translated "soul" or "life" here (נֶפֶשׁ, *nepheš*) does not mean "soul" in the theological sense. In the Hebrew Old Testament humanity shares certain characteristics with animals and *nepheš* is one of those. They have a "life force" or an "animating principle" which plants do not have.

6. The Creator's Evaluation of His Work (1:31)

1:31 God saw all that he had made, and it was very good. And there was evening, and there was morning—the sixth day.

The evaluation "very good" is kept in reserve until the creation of humankind has topped off the creation account. It is only when God sees the creation with humanity, both male and female, at its head that it receives the highest evaluation. The creation account has reached its summit. In the ancient context, with its polytheistic myths of creation as a prolonged battle between the forces of evil and chaos on the one hand and the forces of order and good on the other, the declaration of creation as "very good" would have been striking.[90]

---

[89]I apologize in advance to any offense this may cause pet lovers.

[90]Gene Tucker comments ("Creation and the Limits of the World: Nature and History in the Old Testament," *HBT* 15 [1993]: 105): "With respect to nature and the world, the Old Testament treads a fine line. The world is good because it is God's. But it is not God."

The passing of the sixth day and the end of God's creative work comes after this declaration.

7. The Creator's Cessation of His Work (2:1-3)

2:1Thus the heavens and the earth were completed in all their vast array. 2By the seventh day God had finished the work he had been doing; so on the seventh day he rested^a from all his work. 3And God blessed the seventh day and made it holy, because on it he rested from all the work of creating that he had done.

^a2 Or *ceased*; also in verse 3

In this section the creation is completed. God marks its completion by setting aside the seventh day as a holy day. His pattern of work followed by rest is given to humanity as a blessing. The imagined audience, who had recently received the law including the foundational ten words[91] knows that one of the reasons given for the observance of the Sabbath by the recently freed Egyptian slaves is God's pattern of work in creation (Exod 20:11). The Sabbath with which Israel was blessed was founded not only on the LORD's acts in history in delivering Israel but also on the very pattern of creation. This is perhaps the most obvious example of how the law which Israel received when they came out of Egypt was anticipated in Genesis's account of the creation and early years of humanity's existence.

This account also anticipates the law in other more subtle ways. Levinson argues persuasively that the creation account is mirrored in the account of the building of the tabernacle. He argues that the tabernacle/temple is constructed to be the "form of the world" and as such should "mirror the creation of the world." He notes the following parallels between this section of Genesis and the account of the construction of the tabernacle:[92]

---

[91]What are popularly known as the ten commandments are never called that in the Old Testament. Instead the title is "the ten words" or "the ten covenant matters" (Deut 4:13 in Hebrew). See Kissling, *Sketch*, p. 33.

[92]Jon D. Levinson, *Sinai and Zion*, New Voices in Biblical Studies (New York: Winston Press, 1985), pp. 142-143: "If the Temple is the form of the world, then the construction of the Temple, and of its predecessor, the

A1 The heaven and the earth were *finished*, and all their array. On the seventh day God finished the work which he had been doing, and he rested on the seventh day from all the work he had done (Gen 2:1-2).	A2 All the work of the tabernacle, the Tent of Encounter, was *finished*. The Israelites had done everything exactly as YHWH had commanded Moses: Thus had they done it (Exod 39:32).
B1 And God *saw* all that he had made and found it very good. And there was evening and there was morning, a sixth day (Gen 1:31).	B2 And Moses *saw* all the work and found that they had made it as YHWH had commanded: Thus had they made it. And Moses *blessed* them. (Exod 39:43)
C1 And God *blessed* the seventh day and *made it sacred*, for on it God had ceased from all the work of creation which he had done (Gen 2:3).	C2 same as B2
D1 same as C1	D2 You shall take the anointing oil and anoint the tabernacle and all that is in it, and you shall *make it sacred*, along with all its furnishings. It shall be sacred. (Exod 40:9)[93]

Notice that both accounts refer to the *finishing* of the project; that both accounts have the principal character *see* the finished work and then give a blessing which makes the created thing "holy" (*sacred*). Levinson also notes that the account of the building of the temple echoes these two texts.[94] I have discussed the parallels between the

---

Tabernacle, should mirror the creation of the world. In fact, exactly such a parallelism can be seen from a comparison of the language describing the two building programs."

[93]Levinson's translation.

[94]Ibid, pp. 143-144: "In the case of Solomon's Temple, the presence of the cosmic symbolism that we discussed in the previous section compensates for the absence of precise verbal correspondences of the sort demonstrated above. There are, however, several features of Solomon's building program that recall its protological archetype. For example, it takes him seven years to complete the work (I Kgs 6:38), just as it takes the divine king seven days to complete creation (Gen 2:2). That the correspondence is more than coincidence can be seen from the fact that Israelite agricultural law included a cycle of seven years, six of work and one of rest, which is called 'Sabbath' (Lev 25:3-7). The cycles of seven days and seven years share a common vocabulary and are of the same order. Furthermore, Solomon dedicates his

garden of Eden narrative and the tabernacle/temple in more detail in the commentary below. The imagined audience would undoubtedly see the interechoing of the two accounts. They would undoubtedly conclude that what they were allowed to experience of God's presence and blessing in the tabernacle worship was a reminder of what humanity originally experienced at creation in a fuller and unhindered way.[95] The tabernacle was the world, theologically speaking, as it was intended to be.

2:1 Thus the heavens and the earth were completed in all their vast array.

This verse serves as a sort of summary statement of creation's completion. The NIV regards the waw-consecutive which begins this verse as indicating logical sequence ("thus") rather than temporal sequence ("then"). This is certainly plausible although the more common temporal sequence should not be dismissed out of hand. If the verse is read as indicating temporal sequence the point would seem to be that God put the finishing touches on creation. The NIV's "all their vast array" is literally "and all their host." The Hebrew word (צָבָא, ṣābā') usually refers to an army whether angelic or human, although it can be a way of referring to the stars (Deut

---

Temple during the feast of Tabernacles, a seven-day feast (Deut 16:13) that occurs in the seventh month (I Kgs 8:2). His speech on that occasion includes a carefully constructed list of seven specific petitions (vv 31-53)."

[95]Levinson relies heavily here on Joseph Blenkinsopp's discussion of the purported source P in *Prophecy and Canon* (Notre Dame, IN: University of Notre Dame Press, 1977). Blenkinsopp draws a further parallel between the accounts of creation and the distribution of the land in the time of Joshua.

Creation of the World	Distribution of the Land
Be fruitful and multiply, and fill the earth (*'ereṣ*) and subdue it (*kibsuha*) (Gen. 1:28)	And the land (*'ereṣ*) was subdued (*nikbesah*) before them (Jos. 18:1)
God completed his work which he had done (Gen. 2:2)	So they finished dividing the land (*'ereṣ*) (Jos. 19:51)

Blenkinsopp adds (p. 68): "Use of the same verb (*kbs*) suggests that with the allotment of land the command given at creation to fill the earth and subdue it has now been fulfilled. It is also noteworthy that in P the word *'ereṣ* stands for both the creation world and the land of promise, the usage strongly suggesting symbolic association between the two meanings. It is also possible that there is a conscious parallelism between the work of dividing in creation and the dividing of the land, even though different verbs are employed."

4:19) or the large number of something.⁹⁶ Here it probably refers to either the multitude of things created or is a way of showing the marvelous diversity of the many things which God created.

2:2 By the seventh day God had finished the work he had been doing; so on the seventh day he rested from all his work.

This verse describes the completion of God's work in creation and his cessation from that work.⁹⁷ The NIV is a little misleading here; the Hebrew says, "Then God completed his work which he did in (or on) the seventh day." The NIV uses a pluperfect "had finished" for a waw-consecutive. Westermann also uses this approach, although he translates "on the seventh day" rather than "by" the seventh day.⁹⁸ The NIV attempts to avoid the impression that God worked on the seventh day. The LXX and SP saw this problem and read "sixth" day. But surely this is legalism influencing translation. The fact that the finishing of God's work occurs on the seventh day causes no problems unless one assumes that the pattern of God's work must be in some legalistic conformity to the prohibition of work by God's creatures, whether human or animal.⁹⁹

In 2:2,3 the phrase "the seventh day" occurs three times, each in a sentence of seven Hebrew words. This and the fact that the pattern of creation on the six days is not followed in describing the seventh day gives it a special significance.¹⁰⁰ In a sense the seventh day is the

---

⁹⁶*HALOT* II:995. See also Ringgren's article in *TDOT*, XII:211-215, esp. p. 213.

⁹⁷Graeme Auld ("Sabbath, Work and Creation: מְלַאכְתּוֹ Reconsidered." *Henoch* VIII [1986]: 273-280) has argued that מְלַאכְתּוֹ in 2:2,3 should not be translated "work" but something like "commission/task/charge."

⁹⁸Westermann, *Genesis*, 1:78.

⁹⁹M. Tsevat ("The Basic Meaning of the Biblical Sabbath," *ZAW* 84 (1973): 447-457) argues that in the entire OT rest is never mentioned as an aspect of the Sabbath for Israelites, but only for God (Exod 31:17) and for animals, slaves, and foreigners (Exod 23:12); rest is therefore unlikely to have been the basic character of the Sabbath for Israel. While this is an argument from silence and one could as easily presume that rest for Israel is presumed rather than explicitly articulated, he does make a significant point. What the Sabbath came to be and what it was originally intended to be may be overlapping but distinct things.

¹⁰⁰Wenham, *Genesis 1–15*, p. 7, "However, 2:1-3, the account of the seventh day, stands apart from the standard framework of each of the other six days. The terms 'heaven and earth,' 'God,' 'create' reappear in the reverse order to

crowning of the creation account. It is of interest to note that the word "Sabbath" does not occur in this description of the seventh day. Hamilton notes that the word "Sabbath" does not occur here.[101] Instead "the seventh day" is used. The Hebrew noun šabbāth (= Sabbath) is, according to Hamilton, etymologically related to the Akkadian word šapattu, the day of the full moon when the heart was to be quieted by rituals of appeasement. The deliberate omission of the word "Sabbath" may be to avoid any connection with the pagan festival. If so, this would be another example of the anti-idolatry polemic that seems so pervasive in Genesis 1–11.

2:3 And God blessed the seventh day and made it holy, because on it he rested from all the work of creating that he had done.

After resting from all his work of creation God blessed the seventh day and set it apart ("made it holy") for special purposes in creation. The word "bless" at its most basic means to "speak well of." When the all-powerful creator of the universe "blesses," however, something much more significant happens. His word does not return to him void without accomplishing the purpose for which it was sent out (Isa 55:11). His word has the power to enact itself. In blessing the seventh day God made it special, set apart for his particular purposes. The Sabbath principle is then built into a whole set of laws which Israel was to enjoy and obey; the Sabbath day, the Sabbatical Year, and the year of Jubilee.[102]

For the imagined audience, Israel perched on the edge of the promised land, this text makes it clear that the laws they had so recently received from the LORD were not newly invented ad hoc. Instead those laws were particular exemplifications of the most ancient principles. The law of the Sabbath and those based upon the Sabbath principle (e.g., the Sabbatical Year and the Year of Jubilee) were built into the very nature of creation itself. Prior to the Fall and unaffected by it

---

that of 1:1, and this inverted echo of the opening verse rounds off the section. The threefold mention of the seventh day, each time in a sentence of seven Hebrew words, draws attention to the special character of the Sabbath."

[101]Hamilton, *Genesis 1–17,* pp. 142-143.

[102]Ian Hart ("Genesis 1:1–2:3 as a Prologue to the Book of Genesis," *TynBul* 46.2 [1995]: 315-336) argues from the Sabbatical year to the idea that the festival of the Sabbath recognizes God's sovereignty over the rest of the week, just as the Sabbatical year acknowledges his sovereignty over the other six years when the land is worked.

the Sabbath was something that God gave to humanity by his choice to create in the pattern with which he did. He did not rest because he was tired out by the strenuous labor of creation.

8. Summary Inclusio (2:4a)

2:4a This is the account of the heavens and the earth when they were created.

This is the first instance of the introductory formula which the author of Genesis uses to start new sections of the book. In every other instance the Hebrew phrase translated here as "This is the account of" introduces the ensuing narrative or genealogical material.[103] But in this particular case it seems to serve a double function. It introduces the account of the creation in the garden and the Fall (2:4–3:24), and it closes off the creation account in Genesis 1:1–2:3. In regard to the latter, notice how Genesis 2:4a seems to echo Genesis 1:1:

1:1: "In the beginning God created the heavens and the earth."
2:4a: "This is the account of the heavens and the earth when they were created."

Notice that the words "created," "heavens," and "earth" appear in both texts, whether Hebrew or English. The special word for "create" is used in both texts, and the latter concludes the account of God's creation. This text also introduces the next section of Genesis. Notice how the two halves of Genesis 2:4[104] complement each other:

This is the account of the heavens and the earth when they were created,
on the day the LORD God made the earth and the heavens.

In the second half of the verse the phrase "LORD God" is found for the first time in contrast to merely "God" in Genesis 1. The special Hebrew verb "create" (*bārā'*) is replaced by the more common and generic word "made" (עָשָׂה, *'āśāh*). Turner[105] notices the following pattern of vocabulary repetition with variation:

---

[103]See "The Structure of Genesis" in the Introduction to this commentary.
[104]My translation.
[105]Laurence A. Turner, *Genesis* (Sheffield: Sheffield Academic Press, 2000), pp. 25-26.

v. 4a	heavens	earth	created
	(šāmayim)	('ereṣ)	(bārā')
v. 4b	made	earth	heavens
	('āśāh)	('ereṣ)	(šāmayim)

The reversal of the words "heaven" and "earth" in verse 4b along with the repetition with variation indicates a chiastic structure which binds the two halves of the verse together. Thus the verse serves the double function of closing off the creation account in Genesis 1:1–2:3 and introduces the Garden and Fall account of Genesis 2:4b–3:24.

It is only the dogmatism and lack of literary feel so characteristic of the traditional documentary analysis that prevents many scholars from seeing the double function of this unique formula. On the other hand, insisting that it must introduce the next section because it always does so elsewhere in Genesis fails to account for the unique situation of the creation with two ways of viewing it put before the reader.

GENESIS 2

B. THE CREATION VIEWED IN TERMS OF PERSONAL RELATIONSHIPS (2:4-25)

After the majestic cosmic view of creation in Genesis 1:1–2:4a here we have another account of creation[1] which focuses on the personal relationships between the LORD God, the original man, and his partner. The reader is transported to a specific spot on earth to witness the creation of the first man, his environment, and his partner. Gone is the structured orderliness of chapter 1. The deity is no longer the transcendent creator who speaks things into existence. Here he is the LORD God, the God who brought Israel out of Egypt and provided the promised land for them to live in. He is the covenant-making God who "gets his hands dirty" in creation and who has a personal relationship with those whom he creates.

But this text is part of a larger whole with chapter 3 and in various ways anticipates the Fall narrated there (see the outline above). The trees of the garden are pleasing to the eye and good for food as was the tree of the knowledge of good and evil. Humanity is about to fall and chapter 2 makes the fact of that fall all the more poignant. There is no reason for the man and the woman to rebel against the LORD God. He has provided everything they could possibly want or need. They are not predetermined to fall.

Attempts have been made to (mis)read this wider narrative as though it did not refer to a fall at all. Certainly the notion that humanity outside of the garden inherits a sinful nature from birth does not come from this nor any other biblical text properly under-

---

[1]Walter Brueggemann, *Genesis*, Interpretation (Atlanta: John Knox Press, 1982), p. 40: "We should not speak of a second, parallel story of creation. Rather, this is a more intense reflection upon the implications of creation for the destiny of humanity."

stood.² But it seems impossible to imagine that humanity's existence outside of the Garden of Eden is in any sense as good as their existence in the garden. This text prepares the reader to see the Fall for what it is. The original human pair do not grow into maturity by eating of the tree of the knowledge of good and evil.³ This text sets the scene for the Fall narrative which follows. It includes the creation of the characters involved in the Fall, the place where it occurs, the trees whose fruit determine the outcome, and the single prohibition which is later violated and the violation punished.

This text is not concerned with the order of creation or with the totality of creation as chapter 1 is. Details provided here either are essential for what unfolds in the larger narrative or have special significance for the intended audience. A surface reading of the text would suggest that, unlike chapter 1, after the initial creation of the heavens and earth, the male is created first followed by the garden⁴ with its plants and trees. These are followed by the animals⁵ and finally the woman. While this has been used in traditional source criticism as proof of the use of conflicting sources in Genesis 1 (P) and 2 (J), it seems more likely that the author of Genesis is not concerned with such matters.⁶ The author's concerns are with teaching Israel (and

---

²Brueggemann (ibid.) notes that Deuteronomy 30:11 clearly implies Israel's ability to obey: "Now what I am commanding you today is not too difficult for you or beyond your reach. . . . No, the word is very near you; it is in your mouth and in your heart so you may obey it" (vs. 11, 14 NIV). The traditional proof texts for the sinfulness of babies (Ps. 51:5) fails to take account of the hyperbolic language of biblical poetry. While no text that I am aware of explicitly addresses the issue of the sinfulness or innocence of infants, Deut 1:39 comes closest, "And your little ones . . . Your children who do not know good and evil. . . ." The use of "know," "good," and "evil" has Moses portraying children as having the status of the man and the woman before they ate from the tree of the knowledge of good and evil.

³This view is common in some Jewish interpretations and in Barr's work, *The Garden of Eden and the Hope of Immortality*, who views ch. 3 as narrating the loss of a chance at immortality but as also achieving a form of moral maturity. Brueggemann anticipates Barr's work although he seems to be primarily reacting against the Calvinistic doctrine of original sin.

⁴The NIV's "had planted" in 2:8 is an attempt at forced harmonization. See the commentary below.

⁵The NIV's "had formed" in 2:19 is an attempt at forced harmonization. See the commentary below.

⁶Even if one assumes the existence of J and P, the final author of the

through them us) how to look at the world and their place under the LORD in it. The style is strikingly different from that of chapter 1.[7] The human characters "come alive" in more than one sense! They speak and respond to God and each other for the first time.

1. The Pre-Fall Male (2:4-7)

⁴**This is the account of the heavens and the earth when they were created.**

When the LORD God made the earth and the heavens— ⁵and no shrub of the field had yet appeared on the earth[a] and no plant of the field had yet sprung up, for the LORD God had not sent rain on the earth[a] and there was no man to work the ground, ⁶but streams[b] came up from the earth and watered the whole surface of the ground— ⁷the LORD God formed the man[c] from the dust of the ground and breathed into his nostrils the breath of life, and the man became a living being.

ᵃ5 Or *land*; also in verse 6   ᵇ6 Or *mist*   ᶜ7 The Hebrew for *man (adam)* sounds like and may be related to the Hebrew word for *ground (adamah)*; it is also the name *Adam* (see Gen. 2:20).

In the NIV this passage is one long sentence which describes the circumstances in which the LORD God formed the first man. It begins with the structural formula ("This is the account of") which introduces the next narrative section (see the discussion of Structure in the Introduction to the commentary). Here the formula seems to finish off the previous narrative and introduce the next one. It thus

---

Pentateuch did not see these sources as being in conflict or (s)he would not have juxtaposed them at the beginning of Genesis. A similar point is made by Alter (*Genesis*, p. 7): "Whatever the disparate historical origins of the two accounts, the redaction gives us first a harmonious cosmic overview of creation and then a plunge into the technological nitty-gritty and moral ambiguities of human origins."

⁷Brueggemann (*Genesis*, p. 44): "It will be well to begin with the recognition that this is a shrewdly stated story which moves knowingly through plot development, suspense, and resolution. . . . Whereas 1:1–2:4a permits a summary of its teaching, this narrative resists such summarizing. It prefers to be told according to its own flow and pace. The telling of the story will permit the play of imagination and impression."

serves as a sort of hinge verse concluding one narrative and beginning the next. The story goes back in narrative time before the creation of humanity to describe the exact circumstances of the creation of the first man and the first woman. Certain forms of plant life, at least as they exist later in the fallen world,[8] do not yet exist. Rain as it was later known has not yet come. In this earlier world the LORD God formed the first man.

2:4 This is the account of the heavens and the earth when they were created.

This is the first occurrence of the Hebrew phrase "this is the account of" which gives structure to the Book of Genesis. In every other instance in Genesis the phrase introduces the account which is to follow. This one differs from the other uses of the formula in that an account is given of the "heavens and the earth" while the others give either genealogical material or a narrative about some prominent person. Modern scholarly interpretation has argued that this must be an exception to the rule that this phrase introduces new material. Thus "this is the account of" summarizes and completes the unit which began in 1:1 rather than introducing the account of the garden of Eden. Typically, according to the older consensus, concern with genealogies was a priestly matter, and therefore this formulaic phrase is attributed to the P (Priestly) source, which purportedly is found in 1:1–2:4a.

But this goes against the uniform usage of this phrase in every other instance in Genesis.[9] Skinner argues that the formula is always followed by the genitive of the progenitor, never of the progeny.[10] Thus "the generations of the heavens and the earth" describes not the process by which the heavens and earth are generated, but rather that which is generated by the heavens and the earth. Turner

---

[8]For this possibility see the commentary.

[9]L. Stordalen ("Genesis 2,4: Restudying a *locus classicus*," *ZAW* 104 [1992]: 174) argues that in Genesis 1–11 this formula is "always introducing material which parallels and yet not quite conforms to the preceding text. So this may intelligibly be assumed to be the case also in Gen 2,4." He further argues that the formula has a meaning something like "here is the aftermath of" and tells us that it was Yahweh Elohim who actually did the creating in Genesis 1.

[10]John Skinner, *A Critical and Exegetical Commentary on Genesis*, 2nd ed., ICC (Edinburgh: T & T Clark, 1910), p. 41.

has argued that 2:4a forms an inclusio with 1:1 and functions better as a conclusion than an introduction.

> While *toledot* ('generations') formulas elsewhere in Genesis introduce a section, 2.4a forms a very poor introduction to 2.4bff, which is *not* a description of the creation of the heavens and earth, nor of what heaven and earth generated, but a description of the creation of humans, trees, the garden, land animals and birds. 2.4a functions better as a conclusion, bringing the description of creation week to a natural resting place and forming an inclusion with 1.1:
> 1.1: 'In the beginning God created the heavens and the earth.'
> 2.4a: 'These are the generations of the heavens and the earth when they were created.'

He regards the second half of the verse as the introduction to the following narrative. He notices a chiastic structure between the two halves of the verse.

v. 4a	heavens (šāmayim)	earth (ʼereṣ)	created (bārāʼ)
v. 4b	made (ʻāśāh)	earth (ʼereṣ)	heavens (šāmayim)

He comments:

> The chiasm binds the consecutive episodes together. It provides an invitation to read the two episodes, despite their differences, in an integrated manner, and not simply as two independent units."[11]

While this is a very helpful literary analysis, ultimately I think it is overstated. It is not necessary, in my judgment, to decide between these alternatives. This formula can both finish off the initial section of Genesis and introduce the next and that seems to be the function here.

When the Lord God made the earth and the heavens—
The NIV's adverb "when" is literally "in the day that" and shows that the Hebrew word translated as "day" (יוֹם, *yôm*) does not always

---
[11]Turner, *Genesis,* pp. 25-26.

refer to a 24-hour period of time. This verse has clear echoes of Genesis 1:1 ("In the beginning God created the heavens and the earth."). Here "God" becomes "LORD God"; "created" becomes simply "made"; "the heavens and the earth" becomes "the earth and the heavens"; and the precise "In the beginning" becomes the more generic "when."[12]

The shift in the divine name from God (אֱלֹהִים, 'ĕlōhîm) in 1:1–2:3 to LORD God (יהוה אֱלֹהִים, yhwh 'ĕlōhîm) here is striking and has been the basis of speculation about a shift in sources since the time of Astuc, if not before. The Hebrew word 'ĕlōhîm is the generic term for deity in the Hebrew Bible. In the plural it refers to the gods of other nations, but as a singular to the one God. The short form of 'ĕlōhîm is 'el and this form is found in many of the names in the Bible, i.e., Isra*el*, Ezeki*el*, Dani*el*, Jo*el*, etc. The word translated LORD in the NIV and other modern translations is the four-letter name for Israel's God also known as the "tetragrammaton," i.e., written with four letters. Jewish commentator Plaut explains:

> Adonai (יהוה LORD) is the unique, personal name of God and the name most frequently used in the Bible. The Torah gives the meaning of יהוה in Exod. 3:14, but that explanation is not clear. The original pronunciation was most likely Yahveh, but since Jewish tradition permitted the name to be voiced only by the High Priest, it became customary, after the destruction of the second Temple, to substitute the word Adonai (meaning "my Lord") when reading יהוה. The Masoretes who vocalized the Hebrew text therefore took the vowels from the word Adonai and put them with יהוה to remind the reader not to read Yahveh but Adonai. Hence, all vocalized texts of the Bible now read יהוה with the vowels of Adonai. A Christian writer of the sixteenth century who was unaware of this substitution transcribed יהוה as he saw it, namely, as Jehovah, and this has since entered many Christian Bible translations.[13]

The use of LORD God makes it clear that the LORD of Israel is also the one God of Genesis 1 who created the entire universe. In the text that we have and the one recognized as Scripture by Israel

---

[12]Peter D. Miscall, "Jacques Derrida in the Garden of Eden," *Union Seminary Quarterly Review* 44 (1990): 4.

[13]Plaut, "Genesis," p. 31.

and taken over by the early church there is no conflict between two creation accounts. This second account deals with different issues and has different concerns. The LORD God of Israel is the creator God of the heavens and the earth. The intended audience, Israel on the verge of the promised land, needed to know that the God who brought them out of Egypt is the one and only God who created the heavens and the earth and all that is in them.

2:5 and no shrub of the field had yet appeared on the earth and no plant of the field had yet sprung up, for the Lord God had not sent rain on the earth and there was no man to work the ground,

This verse begins to describe the physical conditions of the earth at the creation of the man and woman. There are two possible ways of taking this verse. Either the verse is describing the incompleteness of creation when the first man was made (the common view), or it refers to the physical creation before it had been affected by the Fall and the subsequent curse on creation (Sailhamer's view).

Futato, who gives the best articulation of the common view, argues that the phrase "shrub of the field" refers exclusively to those plants which only spring up spontaneously after the rain and "plant of the field" refers exclusively to those plants which must be cultivated by humankind.[14] The two-part reason[15] given for this state of affairs (no rain and no man) corresponds to these two types of plants respectively. This noticing of the need for rain to produce the shrubs of the field and then to soften the ground so that human cultivators can help produce the plants of the field, seems to indicate a perspective that only those living in Palestine are able to relate to. The Egyptians and the Mesopotamians relied on river flooding for cultivating and planting and watering crops, not on rain. The word translated "shrub" (שִׂיחַ, *sîyaḥ*) recurs in Genesis 21:15 as a desert shrub under which Ishmael was placed; and twice in Job 30 (vv. 4,7) where desert vegetation or at least wild vegetation is in view. The word translated "plant" (עֵשֶׂב, *'ēśeb*) is used in, e.g., Exodus 9:22,25 of cultivated grains like flax and barley. Perhaps we should translate "wild vegetation" and "cultivated grain." Futato then argues that "streams"

---

[14]Mark D. Futato, "Because It Had Rained: A Study of Gen 2:5-7 with Implications for Gen 2:4-25 and Gen 1:1–2:3," *WTJ* 60 (1998): 1-21.

[15]The Hebrew word is כִּי (*kî*), translated as "for" in the NIV and understood as giving the reason why no shrub or plant had yet arisen.

should be translated "rain cloud" based on Job 36:27 which Dahood translates: "When he draws up drops from the sea, they distill as rain from his rain cloud." While Futato makes a strong case for his understanding of the phrases "shrub of the field" and "plant of the field," his reliance on Dahood's translation is questionable.

Sailhamer, who suggests the Pre-Fall view, argues that the specific types of plants mentioned are referring to the weeds with which the earth is afflicted in the curse of Genesis 3:17; the lack of rain is not the lack of normal rain but the rain of judgment sent in the Flood, and the absence of a man to "work" (literally "serve") the ground is due to the fact that only after the curse is the man to "serve" the ground as a punishment for sin.

> Chapter 2 begins with a description of the condition of the land before the creation of humanity. In this respect it resembles the description of the land in 1:2. The focus of the description is on those parts of the land that were to be directly affected by the Fall (3:8-24). The narrative points to the fact that before the man was created (in 2:7), the effects of the human rebellion and of the Fall had not yet been felt on the land. In the subsequent narratives, each of the parts of the description of the land in verses 4b-6 is specifically identified as a result of the Fall. The "shrub of the field" and "plant of the field" are not a reference to the "vegetation" of chapter 1, but rather anticipate the "thorns and thistles" and "plants of the field" which are to come (in 3:18) as a result of the curse. In the same way, when the narrative says that the Lord God had not yet "caused it to rain upon the land," we can sense the allusion to the Flood narrative at which time the Lord explicitly stated: "I will cause it to rain upon the earth." The reference to "no man to work the ground" (2:4b-5) points us to the time when the man and the woman were to be cast from the garden "to work the ground" (3:23).[16]

Note the following about the Hebrew vocabulary: In 2:5 there is no man to serve (עָבַד, *'ăbōd*) the ground (הָאֲדָמָה, *hā'ădāmāh*). In 3:23 the LORD sent Adam and Eve from the Garden of Eden to serve (*'ăbōd*) the ground (*hā'ădāmāh*). The terminology is strikingly identical. In 2:5 — "every plant (שִׂיחַ, *śîyaḥ*) of the field (הַשָּׂדֶה, *haśśādeh*) was

---

[16]John H. Sailhamer, *Pentateuch as Narrative*, Library of Biblical Interpretation (Grand Rapids: Zondervan, 1992), p. 97.

not yet in the land, and every herb (עֵשֶׂב, 'ēśeb) of the field (haśśādeh) was not yet sprung (יִצְמָח, yiṣmāḥ) up because there was no man to serve the ground." In 3:18 — "thorns (קוֹץ, qôṣ) and thistles (דַּרְדַּר, dardar) it (i.e., the ground) will cause to spring forth (תַּצְמִיחַ, taṣmîaḥ, same verb as in 2:5) to you, and you will eat the herb ('ēśeb) of the field (haśśādeh)." The repetition of the phrase "serve the ground" in 3:23 is a deliberate echo of 2:5. In 3:18 the repetition of the verb "to spring forth" (צמח, ṣmḥ) and the phrase "herb of the field" echoes 2:5 yet again. From this Sailhamer argues that 2:5 is anticipating the conditions of the world after the ground has been cursed and is saying that those conditions had not yet come about.

Sailhamer has not made his case here, in my judgment, although the following considerations support it. Does the rain (הִמְטִיר, himṭîr, Hiphil from מָטַר, māṭar) differ in any way from ordinary rain? I notice the same form of this word is used in Genesis 19:24 where it refers to God *raining* fire and brimstone as judgment on Sodom and Gomorrah. The Hebrew verb *māṭar* is used elsewhere by the narrator of the Pentateuch only in the rain which accompanied the plague of hail. Moses, in Deuteronomy, does, however, use *māṭar* as a sign of God's blessing in the promised land. There are two other roots/words, for rain in Hebrew: יָרָה (yārāh, "to cast or throw"), and גֶּשֶׁם (gešem), a more ordinary word for rain. While *yārāh* would be the more ordinary word for the rain of judgment (pelting down rain), *māṭar* can be used of the rain of judgment. This reading of *māṭar* would obviate the need for positing no rain of any sort prior to the Flood and merely be an affirmation that no rain of judgment had yet occurred. Possibly the Hiphil form (which is usually causative, i.e., "He caused it to rain"), even if the word itself is not exceptional, might hint that while rain may well have fallen by the ordinary processes of nature, God had not yet caused it to rain by special direct intervention as he did at the time of the Flood.

What Sailhamer does not recognize is that the words for thorns and thistles found in the curse on the ground are not found in Genesis 2:5. If they were, it would be difficult to avoid his conclusion. Perhaps the safest reading is to acknowledge the echoes of the post-Fall world without giving up the most natural reading of the text as explained by Futato. The Hebrew Bible does on occasion narrate events in ways that play upon the ambiguity of language. In

149

other words, at times the text deliberately hints of a double meaning.[17] I would suggest that the common view that this text describes the incomplete creation should be sustained while recognizing that the echoes of the Fall narrative suggest the possibility of a double meaning.

for the LORD God had not sent rain on the earth

This is the classic prooftext for the widely held notion that the Bible says there was no rain before the Flood. But this text says no such thing. It merely states that at this preliminary stage of creation the LORD God had not yet sent the rain. Andersen[18] comments on the problematic hermeneutical principle involved here.

> One task of the Reformation and other early modern readers of the Bible was to consider the text in relation to the world. They asked, given that *'ed* means "mist" [which Andersen has just proven wrong] in Genesis 2:6, what do we learn about the history of the weather on this planet? One relevant rule stipulated, "A thing did not happen until the Bible reports it." The other evidence for the weather is abundant. The verse before the one under study, Genesis 2:5 says, "the LORD God had not caused it to rain." And, indeed, rain is first mentioned in Genesis 7:4. The remarks about the "bow" in Genesis 9 were added to the picture, helped out by a late tradition that here the word *qeshet* (קֶשֶׁת) means "rainbow"; this must have been the first rainbow ever, because the Bible had not mentioned any before. We may leave it to the reader to apply this straining logic to the rest of the vocabulary of Scripture.[19]

Once again we should be warned of coming to the biblical text with our own questions in the foreground without the humility to accept that those questions may not be of interest to the text.

and there was no man to work the ground,

The word "work" can as easily be translated "serve." This text is part of the explanation as to why no "plant of the field" had yet

---

[17]See my *Reliable Characters*, ch. 4, for a discussion of the double meaning of the phrase "a double portion of your Spirit" in the Elisha narrative.

[18]Francis I. Andersen, "On Reading Genesis 1–3," in *Backgrounds for the Bible*, ed. by Michael Patrick O'Connor and David Noel Freedman (Winona Lake, IN: Eisenbrauns, 1987), p. 138.

[19]See further the excursus following Genesis 9:17 in the commentary.

sprung up. Such plants required cultivation by human beings, and since none had at this point in the creation process yet arisen, these cultivated plants were not yet present. But this text also echoes the fact that after the Fall the first man was sent from the garden to "serve" the ground. The two types of serving are different. Prior to the Fall the working of the ground was part of humanity's responsibility in creation. After the Fall that "serving" has connotations of subjugation and frustration.

It is commonly assumed that "man" here is the sexually undifferentiated human being (אָדָם, *ādām*, without the definite article 'the') from whom both man (הָאָדָם, *hā'ādām*) and woman (הָאִישׁ, *hā'îš*) will emerge.[20] This has been disputed and may be the result of the desire to read a postmodernist radical egalitarianism into an ancient text.

2:6 but streams came up from the earth and watered the whole surface of the ground—

This text explains the source of moisture prior to the sending of the Flood at this incomplete stage of the creation process. The KJV has "mist" here for the Hebrew word *'ēd* (אֵד) translated as "streams" in the NIV. This has been used to support the "vapor canopy" theory, i.e., that prior to the Flood there was never any rain on the earth and thus no rainbows. Instead a vapor canopy supplied the water, and it incidentally also filtered out the harmful rays of the sun and helps to explain the long lives of the pre-Flood patriarchs. Tsumura,[21] however, has argued effectively that this rare word means "stream" not mist.[22]

---

[20]Phyllis Trible, "Not a Jot, Not a Tittle: Genesis 2–3 after Twenty Years," in *Eve and Adam: Jewish, Christian and Muslim Readings on Genesis and Gender*, ed. by Kristen E. Kvam, Linda S. Shearing, and Valarie H. Ziegler (Bloomington, IN: Indiana University Press, 1995); my copy in *Biblical Studies Alternatively*, ed. by Susanne Scholz (Upper Saddle River, NJ: Prentice Hall, 2003): 101-106. She argues for a nonmale, nongeneric, nonandrogynous meaning for *hā-ādām* prior to the creation of woman. "Instead it signifies a sexually undifferentiated creature: neither male (nor female) nor a combination of the two" (p. 102).

[21]Tsumura, *Earth and Waters*.

[22]Alternatively, Futato ("Because It Had Rained," p. 21) argues for the translation "rain cloud" on the basis of Dahood's translation of Job 36:27. But this verse can be easily translated in other ways. In this context it is hard to imagine what the point would be of saying "the LORD God had not sent rain on

2:7 the LORD God formed the man from the dust of the ground and breathed into his nostrils the breath of life, and the man became a living being.

After the long preparation in verses 4 through 6 the main event finally arrives. Here the creation of the man is given in some detail. Unlike the account in Genesis 1:26-28 the verb is not "create" but "form." The word is used of a potter or woodcarver forming their medium into something.

There is in the Hebrew a wordplay between the word for "the man" (hā'ādām) and the word "the ground" (הָאֲדָמָה, hā'ǎdāmāh). The "earthling" is made from "earth."[23] This is the beginning of a wordplay in the Hebrew text which can only partially be brought over into English. This can be expressed as:

הָאָדָם (hā'ādām, "the man") is to הָאֲדָמָה (hā'ǎdāmāh, "the ground") and אִישׁ ('îš, "man") is to אִשָּׁה, ('iššāh, "woman") as "management" is to "giving life."

The Hebrew hā'ādām ("the man") is taken out of hā'ǎdāmāh ("the ground"), but is to then manage it by tilling it. Every 'îš ("man") after the first one comes from the body of an 'iššāh ("woman").[24] Wolde says this about this set of wordplays:

> In this network the man and the woman, the man and the earth are on the one hand distinct from each other because of their tasks and functions (discontinuity) and on the other hand inseparably tied and committed to each other (continuity). In this network the human is dependent on the earth, for it is his beginning and end and in the time between beginning and end it is his food supply; as a male man he is dependent on the

---

the earth" and then give the reason "but a rain cloud arose from the earth and watered the whole surface of the ground." Alter (*Genesis*, pp. 7-8) suggests, "wetness would well from the earth to water all the surface of the soil."

[23]Alter (*Genesis*, p. 8) translates in order to preserve the wordplay in Hebrew: "then the Lord God fashioned the human, humus from the soil, and blew into his nostrils the breath of life and the human became a living creature."

[24]Notice that both hā'ǎdāmāh and 'iššāh have the appearance of a feminine ending (āh in Hebrew) as though the hā'ǎdāmāh and the 'iššāh were the feminization of the 'ādām and the 'îš. In fact, neither is actually true. The word 'iššāh is not etymologically related to 'îš. While 'ādām is etymologically related to ǎdāmāh, the latter is not the feminization of the former.

woman for she is the one who bears new life. In this network the woman as a human being is dependent on the earth because it is also her beginning and end and food source; as a woman she is dependent on man's management, care and protection. And in this network the earth is dependent on the human being (man and woman) and its tilling of the earth in order to be able to produce vegetation. In this way it becomes clear that the dependence of the woman with respect to the man can therefore not be separated from the man's dependence with respect to the woman, nor can it be separated from the relation of mutual dependence between the human and the earth.[25]

The linking of man and his destiny to the soil through this wordplay[26] has significant implications. While on the one hand man is to serve the ground and owes his existence to it, the ground is dependent on man for cultivation and its destiny is dependent on man managing it in accordance with God's purposes.

After fashioning the man from the ground, the LORD God breathes into his nostrils the breath of life. Man becomes a "living being" once he receives the breath of life. The KJV has "living soul" and many in the history of interpretation thought of the idea of the "immortal soul." But this shows just how much the Greek separation of the physical from the spiritual has affected the reading of the Bible. The Hebrew word translated "soul" (נֶפֶשׁ, *nepheš*) does not refer to the spiritual part of humanity. Animals, in Hebrew vocabulary have a *nepheš*. Since they obviously do not have "immortal souls," another English equivalent must be sought. We speak of animate creatures as opposed to inanimate objects. Perhaps this is a way to express the Hebrew concept.

---

[25]Ellen van Wolde, "A Text-Semantic Study of the Hebrew Bible, Illustrated with Noah and Job," *JBL* 113/1 (1994): 30.

[26]Although fanciful in some ways Jewish interpretation is helpful in bringing this out. According to Rashi (based on Sanhedrin 38a-b) God took dust from the four corners of the earth so that man might be at home everywhere. Plaut comments ("Genesis," p. 32): "According to Islamic legend, the dust was red, white, and black — hence the skin colors of mankind. 'At home' is represented by the possibility of finding a suitable permanent home, i.e., a grave. Every man can rest peacefully anywhere on earth."

2. The Environment of the Pre-Fall Male (2:8-14)

⁸Now the LORD God had planted a garden in the east, in Eden; and there he put the man he had formed. ⁹And the LORD God made all kinds of trees grow out of the ground—trees that were pleasing to the eye and good for food. In the middle of the garden were the tree of life and the tree of the knowledge of good and evil.

¹⁰A river watering the garden flowed from Eden; from there it was separated into four headwaters. ¹¹The name of the first is the Pishon; it winds through the entire land of Havilah, where there is gold. ¹²(The gold of that land is good; aromatic resin[a] and onyx are also there.) ¹³The name of the second river is the Gihon; it winds through the entire land of Cush.[b] ¹⁴The name of the third river is the Tigris; it runs along the east side of Asshur. And the fourth river is the Euphrates.

[a]12 Or *good; pearls*   [b]13 Possibly southeast Mesopotamia

This passage describes the Garden of Eden where the first man was placed after his creation. The description of the Garden finds echoes in the later narrative of the tabernacle. For the imagined audience the tabernacle was a little bit like Eden and provided hope of the restoration of the original relationship between God and humanity in Eden. The Christian reader also sees how the "tabernacling" God of the Old Testament became a man in the Word made flesh (John 1:14)[27] and that the new heavens and new earth of Revelation is a renewed Eden.

The description of Eden here also in various ways anticipates the narrative of the Fall in chapter 3. All of the trees of the garden were pleasing to the eye and good for food. This emphasizes the irony in the woman later focusing only on the prohibited tree of the knowledge of good and evil as though it were the only tree pleasing to the eye and good for food. Both that tree and the tree of life are mentioned, which serve an important role in the later narrative of the Fall in chapter 3. The expulsion of humanity from the direct access to the immediate presence of God which Eden provided is also prepared for in this description.

---

[27]A literalistic translation of the Greek of John 1:14 would be, "And the Word became flesh and made a tabernacle among us. . . ."

EXCURSUS

PARALLELS BETWEEN THE GARDEN OF EDEN AND THE TABERNACLE

The account of the Garden of Eden was written for Israel as they were poised to enter the promised land. As a result the narrative quite naturally is written with the needs, interests, and experiences of Israel in mind. The generation who had recently received the law, including the instructions for the building of the tabernacle and the narrative of its completion, would see what are to us rather subtle parallels between the Garden of Eden narrative and the tabernacle narrative in Exodus 24–40. The most obvious parallel between the Garden of Eden and the tabernacle is the presence of cherubim. These creatures are never described as angels in the Bible despite the popular idea that they are angels. Angels are messengers in the Bible and can be either ordinary humans or spiritual beings who take the form of human beings. In the entire Bible cherubim are only mentioned in relation to the Garden of Eden, the tabernacle, and the temple. In Genesis 3 they guard the entrance to the Tree of Life while in the tabernacle and temple they stand over the ark of the covenant guarding access to the Holy of Holies where the LORD's presence is experienced in its most direct form. Cherubim are also woven into the fabric of the curtains of the tabernacle (Exod 25:1-6).

In both narratives there is access to that direct presence. In Eden the LORD walks about in the windy part of the day to talk with the first human pair directly. In the tabernacle/temple the High Priest, as the representative of the nation, is allowed access to the divine presence on only one day a year, the day of Atonement. Just as the creation account is structured around seven acts, each introduced by the formula, "Then God said" (Gen 1:3,6,9,14,20,24,26; cf. vv. 11,28,29), so the narrative of God's instructions to Moses regarding the tabernacle is structured around seven commands, each introduced by the formula, "And the LORD said" (Exod 25:1; 30:11,17,22, 34; 31:1,12). The descriptions of both the Garden and the tabernacle mention "pure gold."[28] Both are entered from the east. Both have precious jewels. Genesis 2:12b and Exodus 25:7 both refer to onyx

---

[28]Gen 2:12a: *zāhab tôb*; Exod 25:3 just *zāhāb*.

stones, (אֶבֶן שֹׁהַם, *'eben šoham*). The word for "onyx" occurs only in Genesis 2:12; Exodus 25:7; 28:9,13,20; 35:9,27; 39:6,13 (all describing the tabernacle); and elsewhere in the entire Hebrew Bible only in 1 Chronicles 29:2 and Job 28:16. The accounts of the building of the garden and the building of the tabernacle are both followed by "Fall" narratives, mankind into sin and Israel into idol worship. The relatively rare hithpael (reflexive) of the Hebrew verb הָלַךְ (*hālak*) in 3:8, "to walk to and fro," is used to describe the divine presence in Leviticus 26:12; Deuteronomy 23:15; and 2 Samuel 7:6-7.[29] The phrase "to work and take care of" in Genesis 2:15 occurs elsewhere only in Numbers 3:7-8; 8:26; 18:5-6 of the Levites' duties in guarding and serving in the tabernacle. Carol Myers has even suggested that the tabernacle menorah was a stylized tree of life on the basis of archaeology and the description of Exodus 25:31-35.[30] Whether every one of these parallels is completely convincing is beside the point. The total evidence argues strongly for the fact that the original audience would see the connection between the two and realize that in some way the tabernacle is a way for an utterly holy God to maintain in a symbolic way an "Edenic" relationship with humanity.

2:8 Now the LORD God had planted a garden in the east, in Eden;
Interestingly this verse begins with a waw-consecutive form which ordinarily implies narrative sequence. Here the NIV translates it as a past perfect "had planted"[31] in order to imply that the garden had been planted previously. Evidently this avoids the "problem" of chapter 2 seeming to say that the man was created before the plants, contrary to the account in chapter 1. A similar procedure is found in 2:19. In both cases the motivation for a past perfect

---

[29]For this and what follows see Gordon J. Wenham, "Sanctuary Symbolism in the Garden of Eden Story," in *I Studied Inscriptions from Before the Flood. Ancient Near Eastern, Literary, and Linguistic Approaches to Genesis 1–11*, ed. by Richard S. Hess and David Toshio Tsumura (Winona Lake, IN: Eisenbrauns, 1994), pp. 399-404.

[30]For other possible parallels see ibid.

[31]The following also use the pluperfect, i.e., "had planted" or its equivalent: In Latin: the Vulgate and Calvin; in German: Luther, Strack, and Jacob; in French: Calvin, Ostervald, and Crampon.

seems to be a desire to harmonize the account in chapter 2 with the account in chapter 1.[32]

But there are other explanations for this apparent discrepancy that do not require a rare, if not unique, meaning being given for a relatively well-understood Hebrew verb form. Wenham, for example, notes that the establishment of the garden full of plants in chapter 2 more closely parallels the provision of food in 1:29 than the creation of plants in 1:12-13. However we might try to harmonize[33] the two accounts of creation, there is no indication that the author was the least bit concerned about the unevenness which we sometimes sense in the narrative.

The Garden is said to have been planted in the east in Eden. Technically the Garden is in Eden. Eden is not a description of the Garden alone but of the place where the Garden was planted. The meaning of the word "Eden" is somewhat uncertain, although Tsumura[34] and Hess[35] argue convincingly for a meaning which includes the idea of a well-watered place.

---

[32]David E. Timmer points this out in "On Correcting Biblical Errors," *Reformed Journal*, vol. 34, no, 4 (April 1984), pp. 2-3. The NIV began as a project of the Christian Reformed Church and was later expanded to include other evangelicals.

[33]Even if one adopts the traditional source-critical analysis which uses hypothesized sources which purportedly differed in detail from each other, one still needs to explain how the final redactors could juxtapose such divergent sources into a coherent whole.

[34]Tsumura sums up the meaning of Eden (*Earth and Waters*, pp. 136-137): "In the light of the above one might suggest the meaning of *'ēden* as 'a place where there is abundant water-supply' (cf. Gen 13:10); its verbal root **'dn* means primarily 'to make abundant in water-supply,' and secondarily 'to enrich, prosper, make.' The term **'eden* (pl. *'adanim* in Ps 36:9), which means 'pleasure, luxury,' has the same etymology as 'Eden' with this secondary meaning, though MT seems carefully to distinguish *'eden* from **'eden*. This root is also possibly reflected in the personal names, *hmy'dn* and *m'dnh*, which appear on ancient Hebrew seals."

[35]Richard S. Hess, "Eden — A Well-watered Place," *BRev* 7 (1991/6): 28-33, notes that a related Aramaic participle (*m'dn*) occurs in the bilingual inscription from Tell Fakhariyah where context and the Akkadian equivalent means "to make abundant." "This suggests that the word 'Eden' refers to a garden of abundance, that is, a garden that can be described as 'luxuriant and fruitful.'" He notes Tsumura's arguments and Gen 13:10 and extends this to "to make abundant by providing an abundance of water."

The use of "east" to describe the location of the Garden is a hint of the importance of this direction in the ensuing narrative. Adam and Eve were expelled from the Garden to the east. Cain built his city east of Eden. The builders of Babel moved east. This may be yet another narrative anticipation of the trouble that is coming. In these chapters of Genesis when someone moves to the east, trouble usually follows or accompanies the move.

The presence of the ideal place in ancient times is a theme known from the literature of the ancient Near East.[36] While literary dependence is implausible, we do know of a place called the land of Dilmun which has broad parallels to the Garden of Eden narrative. This thematic connection may be another instance of the anti-idolatry polemic that is so prevalent just under the surface of the Genesis text.

2:9 And the LORD God made all kinds of trees grow out of the ground—trees that were pleasing to the eye and good for food. In the middle of the garden were the tree of life and the tree of the knowledge of good and evil.

In the beautiful garden, planted by the LORD God himself, he made all kinds of trees to grow. The use of the word "all" here emphasizes the LORD's generosity. That the LORD himself "made them grow" is another instance of the Bible's portrayal of God as actively involved in and with creation. All of these trees were beautiful and had edible fruit. They provided pleasure and sustenance for humanity. That all the trees of the garden were "pleasing to the eye and good for food" is significant for the story in which part of the motivation for Eve eating of the Tree of the knowledge of good and evil is that it was "good for food and pleasing to the eye" (3:6).

---

[36]From "Enki and Ninhursag":
  The land Dilmun is clean, the land Dilmun is most bright
  In Dilmun the raven utters no cries,
  The ittidu-bird utters not the cry of the ittidu-bird
  The lion kills not,
  The wolf snatches not the lamb,
  Unknown is the kid devouring the wild dog,
  Unknown is the grain-devouring . . .
  The dove droops not the head,
  The sick-eyed says not "I am sick-eyed,"
  The sick-headed says not "I am sick-headed,"
  Its old man says not "I am an old man" (*ANET*, p. 38).

This verse affirms that all of the trees had those characteristics. The only differentiating feature was that it was "desirable for gaining wisdom." God's generosity in providing all kinds of trees, which were beautiful and served as a vital food source, is demonstrated in a remarkably vivid way. It is a failure to trust in that generosity that causes trouble for all Adams and Eves, ancient and modern. How incredibly ironic it is that, when the woman in the temptation scene looks on the prohibited tree, she in part eats of its fruit because it is "pleasing to the eye and good for food." Somehow in that moment the original pair forgot all the other trees that were "pleasing to the eye and good for food."

Two trees in particular are singled out for mention because of the crucial role they will play in the ensuing narrative, the tree of life and the tree of the knowledge of good and evil. The NIV and many other translations are interpretive here. The Hebrew only explicitly says that the tree of life was in the middle of the garden. The tree of the knowledge of good and evil is merely added, and it must be inferred that it also is in the middle of the garden.[37] The tree of life presumably ensured the ongoing life of humanity. By continuing to eat of it, humans would live forever.[38]

The tree of the knowledge of good and evil is the one prohibited tree. What the exact nature of this tree is has been the focus of much speculation. The word "knowledge" derives from the Hebrew root[39] ידע (*yd'*), meaning "to know." It often has connotations of intimate knowledge and is used three times in Genesis 1–11 to refer to sexual relations (Gen 4:1,17,25).

Based partly on this fact and other considerations it is sometimes suggested that the knowledge referred to is sexual knowledge. Milgrom argues that 2 Samuel 19:36 shows that "good and evil" means sex:

---

[37]The potential significance of this seemingly minor detail will be suggested in the commentary on the temptation scene below.

[38]I will argue in the commentary below that it is not a one-time eating of the tree of life that is in view in Gen. 3:22.

[39]While it is typically a questionable exegetical procedure to use the root of a word to determine its meaning, in this case both the noun and verbal form occur in referring to the tree or its effects. Gen 3:22 uses the verbal form to describe the man and the woman after having eaten of the fruit as "knowing good and evil."

Barzillai, David's quartermaster general, says "I am now eighty years old. Can I distinguish between good and evil? Can your servant taste what he eats and drinks? Can I still listen to the singing of men and women?" (2 Samuel 19:36). Of course, Barzillai can "distinguish between good and evil." He has something else in mind. He claims that he can no longer taste food or enjoy music. One need not know Omar Khayyam to realize that the third element after wine and song is — women.[40]

But here Milgrom overstates the case in my judgment. Barzillai may well be saying that his mental faculties are failing and along with that failure the ability to discern good and evil. It is better to regard the knowledge referred to as intimate knowledge or knowledge gained from personal intimate experience rather than focusing on the word's use as a metaphor for sex. I would argue that this chapter is best read in its canonical context where it follows the creation account in chapter 1. There humanity is commanded to be fruitful and multiply. It seems incoherent to read this passage as prohibiting sex when the previous chapter has commended it and given it divine sanction.[41]

Some[42] argue that "good and evil" is a merism for "all things." In 2 Samuel 14:17,20 a woman appeals to David as one like an angel of God, "hearing good and evil," which is in parallel with "all things" in verse 20. If so, the tree promises to enable the person eating its fruit to gain knowledge of all things by disregarding God's will. When the woman is tempted to eat from the tree, she thinks the tree will help her to get wisdom ("a tree to be desired to make one wise"). The Tree of Knowledge of Good and Evil may be referring to that wisdom which is not centered on fear of God and therefore obedience to him. Eating the tree is an attempt to know everything without God. Such an attempt, Genesis tells us, leads to death. Interestingly Proverbs 3:18 speaks of wisdom based on fear of the LORD: "She is a *tree of life* to those who lay hold of her." The tree of life, which was

---

[40]Jacob Milgrom, "Sex and Wisdom: What the Garden of Eden Story Is Saying," *BRev* 10 (1994/6): 21, 51.

[41]If, of course, a goal of interpretation is to set the Bible at odds with itself there is no concern to see the two accounts together as a canonical unity.

[42]E.g., Westermann, *Genesis,* ad loc.

permitted for the original human pair, represents wisdom obtained in obedience to the LORD. Thus two types of wisdom are in view. Wisdom based on the fear of the LORD is a source of life. Wisdom obtained in disobedience to God is the cause of death. Landy notes that the tree of knowledge is the counterpoint to the tree of life and is therefore the tree of death.

The phrase "good and evil" occurs elsewhere in the Pentateuch in Deuteronomy 1:39 where Moses uses it of the innocence of children, who do not "know good and evil." I would argue that the tree prohibits personal, intimate knowledge of evil. Human beings are not created to be God or even gods. God can know everything there is to know about evil and yet not be tempted by it nor tainted by it. Human beings are not so constituted. We have to choose to avoid certain types of knowledge of evil things because we will be tempted by it and then tainted by it. One need only contemplate the trivialized violence in the modern media and the relatively cavalier way in which we participate in state-sanctioned violence to see the connection. Humanity cannot know everything, especially evil, and remain untouched by it. Even comprehensive knowledge of good things can be twisted into pride. Sometimes when we gain knowledge, we are tempted to think that we have no need of God.

2:10 A river watering the garden flowed from Eden; from there it was separated into four headwaters.
2:11 The name of the first is the Pishon; it winds through the entire land of Havilah, where there is gold.
2:12 (The gold of that land is good; aromatic resin and onyx are also there.)
2:13 The name of the second river is the Gihon; it winds through the entire land of Cush.
2:14 The name of the third river is the Tigris; it runs along the east side of Asshur. And the fourth river is the Euphrates.

The garden was watered by a river which flowed out of the land of Eden. The river then broke into "four headwaters," two of which were and are well known, the Tigris and the Euphrates. The other two rivers are unknown. The Tigris and the Euphrates form the borders of what we call "Mesopotamia," i.e., the land between the rivers. The identity of the other two rivers, the Pishon and the Gihon, is unknown. The association of the Gihon with the land of

Cush is perplexing. Usually Cush[43] in the Bible is Ethiopia in northern Africa. A glance at a map makes clear that current topography would not allow a river to be the source for both the Tigris and Euphrates in Mesopotamia and a river in Ethiopia. Further, there is no river currently which feeds both the Tigris and the Euphrates. There is no reason to believe that things were any different in the time of the imagined audience. This could be explained as the result of topographical changes after the Flood. The imagined audience would presumably infer that before the deluge these rivers were somehow connected at their sources. It is equally possible that the imagined audience would regard the description of the location of the garden as unlike the world of their experience. The message would then be, "you cannot go back to the garden of Eden."

The "headwaters" (רָאשִׁים, rā'šîm) of the river in Eden seem to be related to the borders of the Promised land in its ideal form. Genesis 15:18 has God saying to Abram, "To your descendants I will give this land, from the river of Egypt to the great river, the Euphrates." The Euphrates formed the northern border of the idealized promised land. Israel only ever actually had the Euphrates as a border in the time of David and Solomon. The "river of Egypt" could be the Nile or more likely the Wadi el-'Arish.[44] In some sense the promised land is bordered by some of the very same rivers which help to locate the garden of Eden. The implication seems to be that in some vague sense the promised land is to be a little like Eden. The audience would potentially have seen the connection.

The Pishon river is mentioned only here in the OT. Some say the Indus is intended; others the Ganges (Josephus) or one of the rivers of Arabia. Some have suggested that the Pishon is a pun on a verb meaning "to spring up fitfully" and that Gihon is a pun on a verb meaning

---

[43]Speiser (*AB*, p. 72) argues that Cush in Gen 10:8-12 (Nimrod is a "Cushite") is a reference to the Cassites who ruled Babylon in the second millennium. This would make more sense of the mention of Cush here since the Cassites were a Mesopotamian people. But Speiser's interpretation of Cush is questionable and may well cloud the point being made about the location of the garden, i.e., the garden is and is not part of contemporary experience of the world as the imagined audience knew it.

[44]Sarna (*Genesis*, p. 117) notes that the Nile is called *ye'or* in the Bible. The "river of Egypt" marks the boundary between the settled land and the Sinai desert. He suggests that Shihor is the Bible's name for this river.

"to burst forth, bubble."[45] Speiser argues that *soham*-stone (translated "onyx" in NIV) is actually "lapis lazuli" and that the modern Kerkha (in Assyrian Uqnu = blue river) river is the Pishon. In any case the identity of the river is unknown to us and may have been unknown to the original audience. The mention of "good gold" and "onyx" is reminiscent of the description of the tabernacle (see above).

The Gihon is said to wind through the land of Cush. The land of Cush is usually thought to be Ethiopia, and perhaps "the River of Egypt" (Gen 15:18) is meant. Sailhamer argues that, "it can hardly be coincidence that these rivers [Tigris and Euphrates], along with the 'River of Egypt' again play a role in marking boundaries of the land promised to Abraham." Others suggest the Nile. Interestingly, there is a spring in Jerusalem by the name Gihon where Solomon was anointed king (1 Kgs 1:33-45), although the spelling is slightly different (in Gen 2:14 there is a hireq yod, in 1 Kgs 1:33 just a hireq). Perhaps the Gihon is the precursor to the spring in Jerusalem. This would be consistent with the temple/tabernacle imagery within Genesis 1–11. This, of course, would not have been a connection which the imagined audience would have made as the Jebusites controlled Jerusalem until the time of David. The first canonical audience may well, however, have made the connection. Perhaps they would have viewed it as providential that a river[46] which helped to locate the garden would later be the name of the water source for the capital city of the nation.[47]

---

[45]Westermann, *Genesis*, 1:217.

[46]Cf. Ps. 46:5, "There is a river whose streams make glad the city of God," and Ezek 47:1-12 where from the eschatological Jerusalem a great river will flow to sweeten the Dead Sea. The idea of a river flowing out of Jerusalem, when the literal city has no river may well be due to a typological connection seen between Jerusalem and Eden (cf. the next footnote).

[47]A similar sort of thing happens with the location of the near sacrifice of Isaac in Genesis 22. Moriah is the place where Solomon built the temple according to 2 Chronicles 3:1. The imagined audience would not have made the connection, but the canonical audience would have done so.

3. The Pre-Fall Work of Man and the Limitations on his Freedom (2:15-17)

¹⁵**The LORD God took the man and put him in the Garden of Eden to work it and take care of it. ¹⁶And the LORD God commanded the man, "You are free to eat from any tree in the garden; ¹⁷but you must not eat from the tree of the knowledge of good and evil, for when you eat of it you will surely die."**

This section describes the work which the LORD God assigns to the first man. Work in and of itself is thus seen to be something good and part of God's original intention for humanity. The section also describes the boundaries which the LORD God proscribes for the man, both his freedoms and his restrictions. The freedoms are remarkably generous and wide ranging while the single lone restriction is designed to protect humanity from self-destruction.

Brueggemann helpfully notices that these verses explain why humankind is in the garden at all and provide the conditions necessary for plot development. There is a *vocation* in verse 15. The human creature is to care for and tend the garden. There is a *permission* in verse 16. Everything is permitted (cf. 1 Cor 6:12; 10:23). There is a *prohibition* in verse 17. He goes on to comment:

> Nothing is explained. The story has no interest in the character of the tree. What counts is the fact of the prohibition, the authority of the one who speaks and the unqualified expectation of obedience. These three verses together provide a remarkable statement of anthropology. Human beings before God are characterized by *vocation, permission,* and *prohibition.* The primary human task is to find a way to hold the three facets of divine purpose together. Any two of them without the third is surely to pervert life. It is telling and ironic that in the popular understanding of this story, little attention is given the mandate of *vocation* or the gift of *permission.* The divine will for vocation and freedom has been lost. The God of the garden is chiefly remembered as the one who prohibits. But the prohibition only makes sense in terms of the other two.[48]

2:15 The LORD God took the man and put him in the Garden of Eden to work it and take care of it.

---

[48]Brueggemann, *Genesis,* p. 46.

To "work" the garden is literally to "serve" it (עָבַד, *'ābād*). According to Trible it means to "respect, indeed reverence and worship."[49] To "take care" of the garden is literally to "keep" or "protect" it (שָׁמַר, *šāmār*). Notice that in Genesis 3:24 the same word is used of the work of the cherubim in "guarding" the way to the tree of life. We have commented above on the double sense of the first infinitive "to serve" ("work" in NIV). As part of the curse humanity was to "serve" the ground after the expulsion from Eden. This word anticipates the curse on humanity in chapter 3.

But that is not the sense intended here. Trible, who accepts the undifferentiated-man approach, comments helpfully on the implications of the man being given work at creation and prior to the creation of the woman:

> The two infinitives, to till and to keep, connote not plunder and rape but care and attention. They enhance the delight of the garden. By the same token, they give to the earth creature the joy of work. This work changes human life from passivity to participation. Indigenous to creation, work is not a role to be assumed. Moreover, it precedes sexuality to characterize total humanity. Work fulfills both creature and environment, providing dignity and integrity. It testifies to the oneness of humanity and soil at the same time that it establishes the responsibility of the earth creature for the earth. Distinction without opposition, dominion without domination, hierarchy without oppression: to serve and to keep the garden is to live life in harmony and pleasure.[50]

Work is not necessarily something to be dreaded or endured. It has value in and of itself. The fact that humanity is given work to do prior to the debilitating effects of the Fall shows its inherent worth. Pawlikowski, basing his comments on the work of Westermann, highlights the fact that this passage read in light of chapter 1 implies that humanity's created purpose is to both preserve and enhance the creation given to it in grace:

> Contemporary exegetes such as Claus Westermann have emphasized that, in the perspective offered in these passages,

---

[49]Trible, "Not a Jot," p. 85.
[50]Ibid., pp. 85-86.

work in the form of the care and development of inherited creation is viewed as a primal religious duty. Work is integral to the spirituality advocated by the author of this part of Genesis as indeed it is, according to Westermann (*Creation*, Fortress, 1974), to the spirituality of the whole of the Hebrew Scriptures. Contemplation and the striving for personal bliss are never envisioned as the sole reasons for human existence. Rather, the human community has been created by God and through the subsequent covenant with its creator commissioned "to till and keep it." These verbs are to be seen as complementary according to Westermann. "Preservation" and "enhancement" of the creation given humankind as gift by the Creator God are its coequal duties in the eyes of the Genesis author. Neither can be neglected nor can one ever be totally sacrificed to advance the other. Maintaining the proper equilibrium will require great skill and ingenuity on the part of the human family. And it will be an equilibrium in need of periodic readjustment.[51]

Humanity was not designed to live idly in the garden with no task to do. While enjoyment of creation is one of the benefits given to humanity, our responsibility is to take care of the creation as the LORD God's representatives. We live in a distorted and fallen world. We debate the effects of technology on the natural environment. While Genesis gives us no specific guidance on how to solve the problems of pollution in the contemporary world, it does tell God's people that we have a responsibility to creation. While we wait for the redemption of that creation in God's own time, we must live our own lives in anticipation of that redemption and as a sign to the world of what that redemption might look like. When it comes to our relationship with the natural world, God's people should regard the care and development of the creation a "primal religious duty."

2:16 And the LORD God commanded the man, "You are free to eat from any tree in the garden;

The generosity of the LORD God is shown by the abundance of desirable trees in comparison with the single prohibited tree. It is only in light of that generosity that the prohibition of one tree is given.

2:17 but you must not eat from the tree of the knowledge of good and evil, for when you eat of it you will surely die."

---

[51]Pawlikowski, "Participation," pp. 363-369.

Sailhamer notes, "In the remainder of the Pentateuch, the expression *mot tamut* 'you will surely die' means that one has come under the verdict of the death penalty (cf. 20:7; Exod 31:14; Lev 24:16)."[52] The Hebrew construction underlying the NIV's "surely die" (the infinitive absolute followed by the imperfect of the same verb) is used for emphasis. It is important to note that this emphatic expression[53] is omitted in the woman's version of the commandment in Genesis 3. She removes the emphatic character from the commandment and in a sense lessens its impact.

The Hebrew phrase translated as "when" in the NIV literally reads "in the day that." While "when" is a suitable paraphrase for this expression, here it severs this text from its narrative context. The LORD God had warned that the day of death would be the day of the eating of the prohibited tree. The fact that the man and the woman are not immediately struck down after eating of the fruit may well be an indication that God in his grace decided not to carry out the sentence immediately as he had warned. In his grace he allows humanity to live and procreate and only then die.

4. The Completion of the Pre-Fall Male (2:18-25)

¹⁸The LORD God said, "It is not good for the man to be alone. I will make a helper suitable for him."
¹⁹Now the LORD God had formed out of the ground all the beasts of the field and all the birds of the air. He brought them to the man to see what he would name them; and whatever the man called each living creature, that was its name. ²⁰So the man gave names to all the livestock, the birds of the air and all the beasts of the field.

But for Adam[a] no suitable helper was found. ²¹So the LORD God caused the man to fall into a deep sleep; and while he was sleeping, he took one of the man's ribs[b] and closed up the place with flesh. ²²Then the LORD God made a woman from the rib[c] he had taken out of the man, and he brought her to the man.
²³The man said,

---

[52]Sailhamer, *Genesis*, p. 48.
[53]Alter (*Genesis*, p. 8) renders this, "you are doomed to die."

> "This is now bone of my bones
> and flesh of my flesh;
> she shall be called 'woman,'[d]
> for she was taken out of man."

²⁴**For this reason a man will leave his father and mother and be united to his wife, and they will become one flesh.**

²⁵**The man and his wife were both naked, and they felt no shame.**

[a]*20* Or *the man* [b]*21* Or *took part of the man's side* [c]*22* Or *part*
[d]*23* The Hebrew for *woman* sounds like the Hebrew for *man*.

This passage makes it clear that the man was created with the need for partnership with the woman. It describes how the LORD God made this clear to the man and how he met the need by providing the woman for the man. The man's reaction to this gracious gift is recorded. The narrator then, in a sort of "dear reader" comment, explains what the pattern of creation implies about the nature of the relationship between a man and a woman in the experience of the implied audience. The phrase "not good" makes it clear that creation is not finished until the woman has been created. The man is incomplete without her, and the relationship which all later men and women form in marriage must take precedence over all other relationships with other people, including even the man's parents.[54] The creation of the woman thus functions as the high point of chapter 2. She is the capstone of creation.

This text has been the focal point of much heated debate within the Church and within scholarship as to what it might imply about ideal relationships between men and women. Given that it describes creation before it is tainted by the Fall, at least potentially it gives guidance about how male/female or husband/wife relationships are designed to function. From this text scholars have seen both an extraordinary egalitarianism in conflict with the patriarchal societies addressed by the text and an affirmation of the given-ness of some form of subordination. Davidson summarizes the lines of argument from this chapter used to support some type of subordinationism:

---

[54]This is strikingly "countercultural" in a patriarchal society where married men typically lived with their parents after marriage.

The main elements of the narrative which purportedly prove a divinely-ordained hierarchical view of the sexes may be summarized as follows: (a) man is created first and woman last (2:7, 22), and the first is superior and the last is subordinate or inferior; (b) woman is formed for the sake of man — to be his "helpmate" or assistant to cure man's loneliness (vss. 18-20); (c) woman comes out of man (vss. 21-22), which implies a derivative and subordinate position; (d) woman is created from man's rib (vss. 21-22) which indicates her dependence upon him for life; and (e) the man names the woman (vs. 23), which indicates his power and authority over her.[55]

Let us consider these arguments. As to priority in creation [point (a) above] this text ought to be allowed to speak its own message without reading into it what we think the apostle Paul may have been saying in 1 Timothy 2. If being created first in this text automatically implies that "the first is superior and the last is subordinate," how does one explain that the man was created from the ground? If the first is superior, then the ground is superior to man and man is subordinate to the ground. This hardly makes sense of this text in which man is to guard and protect the garden. If we include chapter 1 in our context, humanity is to rule over the creation including the ground. Similarly the fact that the woman comes out of the man does not, in and of itself, imply a subordinate position [Davidson's point (c) above].

The common response to this is to point to what Paul said in 1 Timothy 2:12-14, "I do not permit a woman to teach or to have authority over a man; she must be silent. For Adam was formed first, then Eve. And Adam was not the one deceived; it was the woman who was deceived and became a sinner" (NIV). But Paul does not *explicitly* state that priority in creation is the reason he does not permit a woman to teach or have authority over a man. While it is certainly possible to read the text in that way, there are other ways of reading it.[56] In discussing the issue of head coverings he does point to priority in creation and the fact that the woman was created for the man. But he also says (in 1 Cor 11:11,12): "In the Lord, however,

---

[55]Davidson, "Theology of Sexuality," pp. 13-14.
[56]For further discussion see C. Michael Moss, *1, 2 Timothy and Titus* (Joplin, MO: College Press, 1994), pp. 59-62.

woman is not independent of man, nor is man independent of woman. For as woman came from man, so also man is born of woman." As I understand this, he is saying that, when looked at from a Christian point of view ("in the Lord"), the priority of men in original creation must be seen as complemented by the subordination of men in pro-creation.[57] Just as the first woman was dependent on the first man for her existence, so every subsequent man is dependent on a woman for his existence. The order of creation and procreation prevented there being a conclusive argument in favor of either gender being given an absolutely subordinate position in creation.[58]

Davidson's second point [point (b) above] involves a particular understanding of the word "helpmate" or "assistant." In 2:18 the LORD God decides to make a "helper" suitable for the man. The word translated "helper" (עֵזֶר, *ʿēzer*) does not, in and of itself, imply subordination. Of the nineteen other occurrences of this word in the Hebrew Bible fifteen refer to God as the one who helps. Of the remaining four occurrences: Once David as anointed king is a helper to the nation (Ps 89:19); Daniel 11:34 predicts that the Maccabees will provide "a little help" but not enough to make an ultimate difference; an allied nation is relied upon by an unfaithful Judah for help (Isa 30:5); and the guards of the king of Judah will be unable to help him by protecting him from the Babylonians (Ezek 12:14). Related words are used similarly. In none of these instances is the idea of a "helper" related to subordination. To help someone does not imply being their subordinate.

As to Davidson's point (d) the dependence of the first woman on the first man for life is balanced by the fact that all succeeding men are dependent on the woman for life. As noted above, this is Paul's argument in 1 Corinthians 11:11-12. The naming of the woman by the man [Davidson's point (e) above] may imply subordination in some sense. But what is often not noted is that this naming does not take place until after the Fall (Gen 3:20). As I will argue in the commentary on the woman's curse, in a fallen and distorted world relationships between men and women are distorted along with every

---

[57]For futher discussion see Richard E. Oster, *1 Corinthians* (Joplin, MO: College Press, 1995), pp. 260-262.

[58]That there is a subordinate reality in the fallen world is addressed in the commentary below.

other relationship. This hardly tells us what the ideal relationship should look like.

So far as I can see, nothing in this text, in and of itself, implies subordination. While we live in a fallen world and do not yet experience on a daily basis the ideal relationships of the kingdom, it should be the Christian's goal to live as much as possible in the light of our eternal destiny. Sometimes we are forced to tolerate social institutions and structures which testify to the fallenness of our world.[59] But inasmuch as we are able, we must seek relationships which anticipate the coming kingdom while we pray for its soon arrival. In a world where women are often abused and mistreated, we must also be careful that we do not unwittingly give justification for that abuse by the way we use the Bible.

2:18 The LORD God said, "It is not good for the man to be alone. I will make a helper suitable for him."

The phrase "not good" is striking when one remembers chapter 1. At this preliminary stage of creation something is not good. The man must have a partner and must not be alone. Until that happens creation is not yet complete. It certainly is not worthy of the "very good" of chapter 1 which follows the creation of man and woman and their commissioning.

The Hebrew word translated "the man" (*hā'ādām*) is part of a wordplay with the word for ground in verse 19 (*hā'ădāmāh*) and might be translated "earthling" if it did not carry such fairytale or science fiction connotations. Some have argued that the word does not necessarily at this point in the narrative refer to the male. Mieke Bal says:

> What makes readers assume this creature is male? What, by another equally strange twist, makes them assume that this mistaken priority assumes superiority? Unable to read an unfulfilled character, they supply the lacking features.[60]

Both Trible and Bal think that at this point *hā'ādām* is sexually undifferentiated.[61] But the word is clearly used of the male in Genesis 2:25, only a few verses later.

---

[59]See Ephesians 5:25ff and 1 Pet 3:7.
[60]Mieke Bal, p. 322, quoted in Susan S. Lanser, "(Feminist) Criticism in the Garden: Inferring Genesis 2–3," *Semeia* 44 (1988): 70.
[61]In Lanser, "(Feminist) Criticism," p. 67-84, biblical scholar Trible's and

a helper suitable for him."

A great debate over whether the word "helper" implies subordination has been conducted within recent scholarship (see the comments above). Alter suggests translating this, "a sustainer beside him" and notes that the word elsewhere "connotes active intervention on behalf of someone, especially in military contexts, as often in the Psalms."[62] The word is often used in the Psalms of God's help and cannot therefore imply innate subordination. God is no person's subordinate.

Feminist scholars are divided over whether this text encourages subordination, some (e.g., Exum) arguing that this text is hopelessly patriarchal and others (e.g., Trible) that it is strikingly and counterculturally egalitarian. As I have argued above, I would tentatively suggest that it tends toward being egalitarian, but I do not think that we come to this conclusion by redefining what $hā'ādām$ means. And I recognize that many well-intentioned interpreters who take Scripture just as seriously as I do disagree. I think that in Christ there is no subordination ultimately. We live in a fallen world where we struggle to get relationships to work as God designed them. We should strive to live the "already" of the kingdom while realistically accepting that it is "not yet."

The expression "suitable for him" is difficult to translate. It expresses complementarity, not identity. The woman is the mirror image of the man and because of that is able to genuinely help him.

2:19 Now the LORD God had formed out of the ground all the beasts of the field and all the birds of the air.

Again the NIV translates a waw-consecutive as a past perfect ("had formed") in order to harmonize the order of creation with chapter 1

---

narratologist Mieke Bal's egalitarian readings of Genesis 2–3 are challenged. Both share the following assumptions: man and woman were created not sequentially but simultaneously, from a sexually undifferentiated being; woman is not secondary, dependent, or derivative, but is in fact the "culmination" of creation; the woman is treated less severely than the man for disobeying; and inequality between the woman and the man enters only after 3:16 as a consequence of disobedience, not as a punishment and by no means as a part of the divine plan. Lanser's most telling criticism is her argument that Trible and Bal have a formalist theory of language as opposed to a "speech-act" theory in which context is given more prominence in the determination of the meaning of words.

[62]Alter, *Genesis,* p. 9.

where the animals were created before humankind. GKC does give cases where a waw-consecutive, following and dependent on a preceding perfect, has a pluperfect meaning (Gen 26:18; 28:6ff; 31:19,34; Num 14:36; 1 Sam 28:3; 2 Sam 2:23; Isa 39:1). Only the last of these examples, however, is a waw-consecutive following a perfect which does not already have a pluperfect meaning. The other examples show the waw-consecutive continuing the tense of the preceding perfect. Since those perfects have a pluperfect sense contextually, the waw-consecutive adopts and continues the past perfect sense. But in Isaiah 39:1 we read "Merodach-Baladan sent (simple perfect) scribes with gifts to Hezekiah because he had heard (waw-consecutive) of his illness and recovery." While this demonstrates that a waw-consecutive can have a past-perfect meaning independent of the preceding perfect, it is still not the same construction as we have in 2:19 and 2:8. Here a string of waw-consecutives with simple past tense meaning is suddenly transformed into a pluperfect. Other than a desire for simplistic harmonization I cannot at this point see any reason to translate this as a past perfect. Questions such as the exact order of creation do not seem to be of concern to the author of this narrative.

It is significant that the animals and birds are said to have been formed out of the ground, just as the man was. This would seem to imply a close relationship between them in that they are made of the same substance. The world which the LORD God created did not have the conflict between humanity and animals which is so much a part of human experience east of Eden. While animals and birds are radically different from humans (the LORD God did not breathe into their nostrils the breath of life), they share a common source of origin and so, at least potentially, should live in harmony with the human family. The Bible depicts the eschatological age as one in which this original harmony is restored (e.g., Isa. 11:6-9).

2:20 So the man gave names to all the livestock, the birds of the air and all the beasts of the field. But for Adam no suitable helper was found.

It is interesting that "naming" can be understood as implying the superiority of the "namer." Here Adam "names" the animals, but none of them function as a suitable "helper." When that suitable helper is found, Adam does not "name" her. It is only after the Fall with its distorted relationships between the genders that Adam "names" Eve. It is as though the text were hinting at the notion that in order to find a "helper" one must give up on notions of superiority and look to mutuality.

2:21 So the LORD God caused the man to fall into a deep sleep; and while he was sleeping, he took one of the man's ribs and closed up the place with flesh.

2:22 Then the LORD God made a woman from the rib he had taken out of the man, and he brought her to the man.

Having created a sense of need in the man, the LORD God then makes the woman from the side of the man.[63] This touching passage shows the personal side of creation. It stimulates our curiosity about many things, but unfortunately (or deliberately?) gives few definitive answers. This passage has been the basis for much fanciful (and wonderful) interpretation. Plaut (citing Jacob) suggests that God created woman while Adam slept so as to prevent him from observing the divine power.[64] The deepest mysteries of divine creativity are thus withheld from human gaze. Interpreters have argued over which "rib"[65] the woman was created from, one source asserting, "And from the eighth upper rib of the breast of the right side of Adam was made Eve, so that she should be equal to him."[66] Another medieval source, *Commemoratio Geneseos* asserts:

> Why was the woman formed from a rib? For if she were formed from his foot or hand or some other part she would stand in shame before him. Another interpretation is that it shows the greatest love, for the rib is, after all, closest to the heart, as it is said: the rib is the guardian of the heart.[67]

---

[63]One might ask, Why was the woman made from man and not directly from the ground? Perhaps because otherwise the human race would seem to have two different beginnings, one for males and one for females.

[64]Plaut, "Genesis," 32.

[65]In Christian allegorical interpretation the man and the woman stand for Christ and the church, his bride. The rib signifies the side of Christ from which water and blood flowed, since the Church is the bride of Christ.

[66]Thomas O. Loughlin ["Adam's Rib and the Equality of the Sexes: Some Medieval Exegesis of Gen 2:21-22," *Irish Theological Quarterly* 59 (1993): 44-54] quoting the Prose Version of Saltair na Rann. Targum Jonathan says that woman was created from the 13th rib on the right side.

[67]Ibid., p. 49.

Anderson comments on the long tradition of rabbinical interpretation of this passage. Much of this material has found its way into Christian biblical commentary in one form or another.

> The verse "he built the rib . . . into a woman and led her to him" (Gen 2:22) is understood as a description of the first marriage ceremony. The act of "building" is understood as God's adornment of the bride (*Gen. Rab.* 18:1), and the act of leading is understood as God's acting as Adam's groomsman or sosbin (*Gen. Rab.* 18:3). The precious stones of Eden (Ezek 28:13) are described as the extraordinary huppa under which Adam and Eve were married. There is a definite logical progression implied in these midrashim. In Gen 2:22 God adorns Eve, prepares the huppa and presents the bride to Adam. By the time the snake arrives, just a couple of verses later, Adam and Eve have made love and Adam has gone to sleep (Gen 3:1-2). On the basis of what lies before us, we can see that this union must have occurred before the encounter with the snake and (obviously) after the presentation of Eve to Adam.[68]

Certainly as Christians we gain insight into the nature of our closest relationships from this text. Unscarred by the distorting effects of sin, we see marriage, friendship, and family as God intended it to be.

2:23 The man said, "This is now bone of my bones and flesh of my flesh; she shall be called 'woman,' for she was taken out of man."

When the woman is brought to the now awakened man, he expresses his delight. The phrase translated, "this is now" (זֹאת הַפַּעַם, *zô'th happa'am*) is difficult to translate. It often means "time" or "occasion." We might paraphrase it as, "This is it!" The man's enthusiasm at finally finding a suitable partner for him is hidden in this little phrase.

The closeness of the relationship between man and woman is indicated by the phrase "bone of my bones and flesh of my flesh." In Genesis 29:14 Laban, Jacob's uncle, uses a form of this saying to indicate a familial relationship. She is as close to him as his own bones and flesh. We are not told whether the man knew at this point that she was literally his bones and flesh.

---

[68]Gary Anderson, "Celibacy or Consummation in the Garden? Reflections on Early Jewish Interpretations of the Garden of Eden," *HTR* 82:2 (1989): 124.

In Hebrew and in English there is a wordplay between the words "man" (אִישׁ, *'îš*) and "woman" (אִשָּׁה, *'iššāh*).[69] While the two Hebrew words are unrelated etymologically, they do have a similar sound and the wordplay would have been obvious to the imagined audience. Davidson argues that Adam does not actually name Eve here. The word "woman" is not a name. Adam only names Eve after the Fall in Genesis 3:20. There subordination through naming may be implied.[70]

2:24 For this reason a man will leave his father and mother and be united to his wife, and they will become one flesh.

This verse is a sort of "dear reader" comment in which the author draws a conclusion concerning the implications of her or his narrative for the imagined audience. Its purpose is to assert that the marriage relationship, because it was created at the beginning, must take precedence over every other relationship, even the duty of a son to his parents. Israelite marriage was ordinarily patriarchal and patrilocal, i.e., it was headed by the father of the family and the newly married went to live in the father's household while he was still alive. This text can be read as inferring a matriarchal and/or matrilocal form of marriage.[71] But more likely it is establishing the principle,

---

[69]Samuel Meier ("Linguistic Clues on the Date and Canaanite Origin of Genesis 2:23-24," *CBQ* 53 [1991]: 18-24) notes that the wordplay between "man" (אִישׁ, *'îš*) and "woman" (אִשָּׁה, *'iššāh*) only makes sense in an originally Hebrew story. In Hebrew the original *at* feminine ending has been reduced to a vowel and then lengthened to a qametz he to preserve it. This did not happen in Hebrew until the Iron Age. Further, the wordplay may involve the he-directive signifying motion toward, "woman as the one whom man approaches."

[70]The fact that Adam gives a name to his partner is often taken as some sort of indication of her subservient role. G.W. Ramsey ("Is Name-Giving an Act of Domination in Genesis 2:23 and Elsewhere?" *CBQ* 50 (1988): 24-35) has argued that "taken all together, the evidence indicates that, instead of thinking of name-giving as a *determiner* of an entity's essence, the Hebrews regarded naming as commonly *determined* by circumstances" (p. 34). While I do not find his arguments ultimately convincing, they should give us pause over assuming that the giving of a name necessarily implies that the one receiving the name is in a subordinate position.

[71]Brichto (*Names of God*, p. 79) argues that "a man" in this verse should read, "a person" and that "his" means "his or her." The idea that this is some leftover evidence of an early matriarchal society is based on no solid evidence and on a superficial understanding of Hebrew grammar.

against patriarchal custom, that a marriage comes first, before any other familial relationship. The leaving which is described does not have to be literal in order for the marriage to conform to God's intentions. But the leaving must nevertheless be real. As (post)modern readers we tend to use this as justification for the radical autonomy which our culture propagates in which the extended family has little or no role in our lives after marriage. But this text is responding to an overly coercive patriarchal system in which a man's loyalty to his father often took precedence over his loyalty to his spouse. There is no suggestion here of removing oneself from the extended family in an individualistic search for personal fulfillment. Instead the bond of marriage must supersede every other commitment.

But a married person must not only leave his or her parents but also "be united" to the spouse. The NIV's paraphrase seems a bit weak. The verb (דבק, *dābaq*) means "to stick to" and is used of clinging very closely to another person. Brichto comments on the implications of the narrative: "Every marriage is a union; not a union of two strangers, but rather a reunion, a reconstitution, so to speak, of the primordial unity."[72] Just as sticky things bond to each other, so the partners in marriage are to "cling" to each other.

Notice that the text says, "his wife" in the singular. In a patriarchal society such as Israel's, polygamy was often the accepted right for the male.[73] Here Genesis is saying that marriage as the LORD God designed it was to be monogamous. Whatever it has become through the corrupting effects of sin, it was created as a wonderful relationship between one man and one woman. It may be that this text is an example of the subtle critique of polytheistic society. Kings in the ancient Near East demonstrated their power as rulers by appearing to be so physically virile that they needed numerous wives and concubines who served at their pleasure. Certainly this would have been a temptation for powerful men in Israel from the beginning. In the

---

[72]Ibid., p. 79.

[73]Angelo Tosato, "On Genesis 2:24," *CBQ* 52 (1990): 405, argues that 2:24 is a sort of polemic against the polygamous and divorce-ridden practice of marriage: "It is the very presence of a marriage custom in which the principal actor is the man that justifies a norm (and related etiology) predisposed for the man and not for the woman. In actual fact, Israelite marriage was ad litteram a man "taking a wife"; and it was with the man that in Israel an indiscriminate use of polygamy and divorce usually originated."

postexilic community in Judah when the Pentateuch was canonized the issue of marriage, polygamy, and divorce was a burning one.

The result of leaving one's parents and sticking closely to one's spouse is "becoming one flesh." While certainly sexual expression in marriage is one of the implications of this statement, its primary emphasis is on the unity that the marriage relationship establishes. It is as though the husband and wife shared the same flesh.

2:25 The man and his wife were both naked, and they felt no shame.

The man and his woman were in a state of innocence. They were completely transparent to each other and felt not even a twinge of discomfort at the fact. This verse is anticipating the shame that they feel after sinning against God in Genesis 3. They feel shame and want to hide themselves from God and from each other (Gen 3:7-11). The author wants to make clear that such distorted relationships were not a part of the original creation but are the aftereffects of sin. The Hebrew word for "naked" (עֲרוּמִּים, *'ărûm-mîm*) has a wordplay associated with the Hebrew word "subtle" (עָרוּם, *'ārûm*) describing the serpent in Genesis 3:1 (the very next verse).[74] "Naked" here seems to be the opposite of crafty and means not only physical nakedness but the right sort of naïveté. Adam and Eve are "innocent" in every sense of the word, while the serpent is the opposite of innocent; he is "crafty." Once again this chapter anticipates the narrative of the Fall in the following chapter.

---

[74]The word "naked" is an obvious wordplay on "crafty." But notice the similar word for "naked" in 3:7, *êrumîm*. Sailhamer points to its use in Deut 28:48 where it is used as one of the consequences of exile should the nation rebel against God. The canonical audience, which had experienced the exile, may have been sensitive to this.

GENESIS 3

II. THE RELATIONSHIP BETWEEN GOD AND HUMANITY BROKEN (3:1-24)

A. THE FIRST DISOBEDIENCE (3:1-7)

¹Now the serpent was more crafty than any of the wild animals the LORD God had made. He said to the woman, "Did God really say, 'You must not eat from any tree in the garden'?"
²The woman said to the serpent, "We may eat fruit from the trees in the garden, ³but God did say, 'You must not eat fruit from the tree that is in the middle of the garden, and you must not touch it, or you will die.'"
⁴"You will not surely die," the serpent said to the woman. ⁵"For God knows that when you eat of it your eyes will be opened, and you will be like God, knowing good and evil."
⁶When the woman saw that the fruit of the tree was good for food and pleasing to the eye, and also desirable for gaining wisdom, she took some and ate it. She also gave some to her husband, who was with her, and he ate it. ⁷Then the eyes of both of them were opened, and they realized they were naked; so they sewed fig leaves together and made coverings for themselves.

What chapter 2 anticipates in numerous ways this chapter describes. The created relationship between God and humanity is tragically broken. That brokenness stems from the rebellion of the creature against the Creator. The man and the woman whom the LORD God had fashioned with his own hands reject his simple boundaries. Without realizing it they also reject his freedoms and his protections. They choose to stop trusting in him. That rebellion is elicited by another creature who leads the first human pair to doubt his goodness, generosity, and intentions in placing boundaries around them. The rebellion elicits the LORD God's promised judgment, but also brings forth his grace even in the midst of the judgment.

Among the remarkable aspects of this narrative is the way in which God's commandments are subtly twisted by both the serpent and the woman into a confusing hodgepodge which distorts the nature of reality, the nature of God, and humanity's place within God's creation. The chapter is a sobering reminder of the folly of trying to construct our own lives without regard for God's will and without trusting his wisdom. The original commandment given to the man prior to the creation of the woman is twisted by both the serpent and the woman. The man, who is with the woman during the temptation scene,[1] stands silent and does not speak out. The original recipient of the commandment sees it being disregarded and is mute. In some senses the temptation scene is a meditation on the way in which God's word can be misused and abused with devastating consequences.

In other senses the narrative addresses the issue of human autonomy (lit. "a law to oneself"). Here humanity is faced with the choice of trusting the LORD's goodness and wisdom or trying to construct life on their own. The serpent tells the woman, "You will be like God knowing good and evil." The serpent implies, "God has selfish motives behind his prohibition. He wants deity for himself. You can be just like him." One need not accept Brueggemann's conclusions about date and authorship to appreciate his insights on the ideology of this passage:

> The far agenda (by which is meant the one that is likely intended by the narrator) is how to live with the creation in God's world on God's terms. The narrative appears to be a reflection on what knowledge does to human community. The story is not a counsel to obscurantism, as though knowing nothing is an act of fidelity. But it is an assertion that the recognition and honoring of boundaries leads to well-being. Likely, this narrative

---

[1]Rabbinic and Christian interpretation (including artistic representations) has often assumed that Adam was not present during the temptation, presumably because otherwise he would have stopped it. A typical example is Genesis Rabbah 19:3, "And the woman said unto the serpent . . ." (Gen 3:2). Now where was Adam during this conversation? Abba Halfon b. Qoriah said: "He had engaged in sex and then fell asleep."

reflects the influence of wisdom teachers who are preoccupied with understanding life and probing its mysteries. . . . It may be that this text reflects concern for the Solomonic effort to overcome every mystery and to manufacture knowledge, because knowledge is power. Knowledge leads to freedom to act and the capacity to control. This text may be a reflection on the role of wisdom, perhaps in an aggressive royal context. It probes the question: Are there modes of knowledge that come at too high a cost? (Cf. Prov. 25:2-3). It asks if there are boundaries before which one must bow, even if one could know more. It probes the extent to which one may order one's life autonomously, without reference to any limit or prohibition.[2]

Whether Brueggemann's suggested setting (sometime during or after Solomon's era) is plausible or merely the hangover of the traditional source criticism at the time he wrote, there does seem to be a clear connection with certain themes in what we call wisdom literature. Knowledge or wisdom without the prerequisite fear of the LORD is folly. The LORD God as our creator knows what we are capable of and what we need. He continues:

. . . the God announced in this story is not a petty god who jealously guards holy secrets or who eagerly punishes the disobedient. This story is, rather, the anguished discernment that there is something about life which remains hidden and inscrutable and which will not be trampled upon by human power or knowledge. . . . So what is urged, if not knowledge? Ignorance? No, not ignorance, but trust.[3]

He refers to Paul in 1 Corinthians 1:18-25: "He knew that wisdom taken into human hands may bring death. But the other half of his proclamation is indeed news: the foolish trust of God and the foolish care of neighbor bring life."

The prominence of wisdom themes in this narrative leads Carr to argue that this narrative is actually "polemicizing against the wisdom tradition — more specifically, against the kind of independent human determination of good and evil characteristic of that tradition. For this tradition is characterized by a reasoning based more

---

[2]Brueggemann, *Genesis,* p. 51.
[3]Ibid., p. 52.

on collected human experience than divine fiat."[4] He cites the following evidence:

1. The tree is often used in wisdom literature as an image of wisdom, e.g., Proverbs 3:18;
2. The snake is a frequent symbol of wisdom in the ancient Near East and the word for his "craftiness" only occurs elsewhere in Job and Proverbs;
3. Wisdom terminology abounds in this text — "delight," Proverbs 13:12; "desirable," only elsewhere in Proverbs 21:20 and Psalm 19:11; the infinitive "to become wise" in Proverbs 16:23; 21:11; Psalm 32:8.
4. Carr notes the parallels (and contrasts) with Proverbs 8:

> In this text [Proverbs 8] a female wisdom figure calls for her audience to seek her because of her early role in God's creation. This role in creation then makes it possible for her to grant fame, prosperity, long life, and divine favor to those who seek her. Likewise, in the Garden of Eden story a female figure is prominent in creation and then plays the dominant role in the search for independent, wisdom-like knowledge of good and evil (3:6). But this search is evaluated quite differently in Genesis 2-3 than in Proverbs 8. Here, the eating of the fruit of the tree leads not to fame but to shame (3:7), not to divine favor but to disfavor (3:8-24), not to prosperity but to suffering (3:16-19), and not to long life but to death (3:19).[5]

While Carr's language seems to imply that Genesis 2-3 and Proverbs 8 are at odds with each other, there is no need to posit such conflict. If Genesis is arguing against wisdom, it is the wisdom of the world, not the wisdom that is founded in the fear of the LORD, as in Proverbs. I would argue that Genesis is not specifically targeting the "wisdom school" of Israel (if in fact such a school ever existed), but rather the common human temptation to delude ourselves into thinking that we can reason our way to a life that is healthy and fulfilling without regard to God's wisdom. The imagined audience had recently experienced the cold, hard reality of such a civilization,

---

[4]David M. Carr, "The Politics of Sexual Subversion: A Diachronic Perspective on the Garden of Eden Story," *JBL* 112/4 (1993), 589-590.
[5]Ibid., p. 590.

i.e., Egypt. That life was only built upon the backs of slaves. The Egyptian wisdom tradition failed to address the bare injustice of their social system. The canonical audience would have also experienced the wisdom traditions of great Near Eastern civilizations and also the harsh realities of exile. If this passage in part is critiquing the wisdom tradition, it is the traditions of the polytheistic cultures of Egypt and Babylon, not the wisdom school in Israel.

3:1 Now the serpent was more crafty than any of the wild animals the Lord God had made.

The Hebrew word (עָרוּם, *ārûm* is translated "crafty" (NIV) but is used elsewhere in the Old Testament in a positive sense of wisdom or adroitness. The implication seems to be that the perpetrator of the Fall, the serpent, tempts the original human pair to try to find wisdom without God. The "tree of the knowledge of good and evil" was a temptation because they thought they could become wise through eating of it. Sailhamer takes note of the meaning of the word crafty and notes a further wordplay with the word "curse": "Thus even the serpent is represented as a paragon of wisdom, and archetypal wise man (*'arum*). However, the serpent and his wisdom (*'arum*) lead ultimately to the curse (*'arur*, v. 14)."[6] The wordplay between the word translated "crafty" in this verse and the word "naked" in 2:24 has been noted above. Wenham suggests that it be brought over into English with the words "nude" and "shrewd."[7]

The NIV translation, "more crafty than any of the wild animals the LORD God had made" allows for the possibility that the serpent is not itself one of those animals, but is more crafty than them. The NRSV has, "than any *other* wild animal that the LORD God had made," making it explicit that the serpent was in fact one of those wild animals. The use of the same word is found in the curse on the serpent in Genesis 3:14, and there it seems to imply that the serpent is cursed as one of the animals but his curse is to be more than the other animals receive.

The Hebrew term translated "serpent" (הַנָּחָשׁ, *hannāḥāš*) besides being the generic name for reptile, is also related in its cognate verbal form in the piel to the word for "divination." Perhaps the origi-

---

[6]Sailhamer, *Genesis*, p. 50.
[7]Wenham, *Genesis 1–15*, p. 72.

nal audience would have been reminded of the association between the serpent and Canaanite religion both at a literal level and at an etymological level. The Bible does not answer questions such as "Why a serpent?" "Could animals talk at one time?" etc. But the anti-idolatry polemic which permeates these chapters may give modern readers a hint. In the Semitic world the serpent was not an animal of death. Ellen van Wolde suggests:

> The serpent may, however, be interpreted as a magical animal of life and wisdom, which according to Vriezen, is apparent from texts like 2 Kgs 18:4 and Num 21:9, in which there is mention of a brass serpent in the temple. Because the serpent sheds its skin and renews itself each time, it is an animal of life. Consequently in the Canaanite, Phoenician, Egyptian and Babylonian world the serpent represents fertility, life-giving power or life itself. This general presentation of the serpent as an animal of life and an animal of wisdom has been used by the author of Genesis 2–3. He did so not because he agreed with this presentation but because he wanted to present a polemic contrast and challenge the image.[8]

But this begs many questions. The serpent of Numbers 21:9 is a physical representation of the fiery serpents sent as a judgment for Israel's grumbling against God in the wilderness. The instrument of death and judgment was placed on a pole, evidently to signal the defeat of the instrument of death. In this case, at least, the serpent is an instrument of death, even though looking at its symbolically impaled representation brought healing.

Park has suggested another way to view this text as anti-idolatry polemic. He argues that in Canaanite worship there was a clear association between the fertility goddess Ashtoreth (a consort of Baal), snakes, and women. He concludes:

> Given these associations of snake, woman, and fertility goddess, given the intense competition between the worship of Ashtoreth and Yahweh in ancient Israel, we can see that the story of Eve and the snake, in addition to other readings, is a parody of Canaanite religion. For didactically it says that any

---

[8]Ellen van Wolde, *Words Become Worlds: Semantic Studies of Genesis 1–11*, Biblical Interpretation Series 6 (Leiden: Brill, 1994), pp. 4-5.

religion which claims that through the worship of a lewd goddess and her reptilian attribute we can become as gods is a lie. Wake up Israelites! Here is the woman and the snake, the priestess of fertility in her sacred grove, and what does she lead to? Immortal life? Bliss? Never! Her actions lead to a curse, to expulsion, to suffering, to alienation from God and to death.[9]

Whatever polemic against idolatry this story may suggest to its imagined audience, the irony of this sentence must not be lost. The serpent is a creature which the LORD God had made. A creation of the LORD himself rebels against his created purpose and leads humanity along with him in that rebellion. While the imagined audience would have had only a vague understanding of the doctrine of the devil at best, undoubtedly the original canonical audience would have seen the influence of the devil. Christians reading from the back of the book have no doubt (Rev 12:9; 20:2).

He said to the woman,

As often observed, the serpent approaches the person[10] who had only received the commandment of God at second hand. The command to not eat of the tree was given to the man prior to the creation of the woman. What is often lost on contemporary readers is that the man was there with the woman during the entire conversation and does not utter a word.

"Did God really say, 'You must not eat from any tree in the garden'?"

The serpent poses a question which, if answered affirmatively, would indicate a stinginess and lack of grace on the part of God. The serpent refers to the LORD God merely by the generic word "God," a term which while theologically accurate does not include the connotations of personal commitment and involvement by the LORD God who personally made the man and the woman.[11] The serpent

---

[9]William Park, "Why Eve?" *St. Vladimir's Theological Quarterly* 35 (1991): 130.

[10]It is important to remember that Hebrew (unlike English) distinguishes between the singular and plural in the second person. The serpent uses the plural "you" in addressing the woman throughout this narrative. It is only in verse 6 that we discover what we should have suspected, Adam was there silently watching all the time.

[11]Brueggemann helpfully notes (*Genesis*, p. 48): "God is treated as a third person. God is not a party to the discussion but is the involved object of the

suggests that God may have been so strict as to prohibit the original human pair from eating from any of the many beautiful trees in the garden with their delicious fruit. The questioning of the LORD's graciousness is the first step down the path of rebelling against his will. If the LORD is viewed as a stingy and ungracious person, why should he be obeyed? We may have to tolerate his power but loving trust is out of the question.

EXCURSUS

THE LORD GOD'S WORDS AND THEIR DISTORTION IN THE TEMPTATION SCENE

The LORD God's Words	The Serpent's Words	The Woman's Words
2:16And the LORD God commanded the man, "You are free to eat from any tree in the garden; 17but you must not eat from the tree of the knowledge of good and evil, for when you eat of it you will surely die."	3:1"Did God really say, 'You must not eat from any tree in the garden'?" 3:4"You will not surely die," the serpent said to the woman. 5"For God knows that when you eat of it your eyes will be opened, and you will be like God, knowing good and evil."	3:2The woman said to the serpent, "We may eat fruit from the trees in the garden, 3but God did say, 'You must not eat fruit from the tree that is in the middle of the garden, and you must not touch it, or you will die.'"

Notice the following differences between what the narrator has the LORD God saying and what the serpent and the woman portray him as saying.

---

discussion. This is not speech *to* God or *with* God, but *about* God. God has been objectified. The serpent is the first in the Bible to seem knowing and critical about God and to practice *theology* in the place of *obedience*."

1. Statements which lessen the graciousness of the freedoms which the LORD God granted:
   The serpent suggested that God had prohibited the human pair from eating the fruit of any of the trees of the garden. While the LORD God had said, "You *are free* to eat from any tree in the garden," in the woman's mouth this becomes merely, "We may eat fruit from the trees in the garden." The woman's statement removes the emphasis[12] on the freedom of humanity to enjoy the garden.
2. Statements which directly contradict the LORD's words:
   The serpent asserts "you will not surely die" in direct opposition to the LORD God's original "you will surely die."
3. Statements which add to the LORD's words additional restrictions on humanity:
   As has been often noted, the woman's version of the command adds the restriction "and you must not touch it" to the original prohibition of merely not eating of it.
4. Statements which may indicate confusion about exactly what the LORD God commanded:
   The woman's version reads in part "but God did say, 'You must not eat fruit from the tree that is in the middle of the garden'"; in the LORD God's version in 2:16 the only tree explicitly said to be in the middle of the garden is the tree of life, not the prohibited tree. This may indicate some level of confusion about the precise identity of the prohibited tree. The tree of life was not prohibited, and it was in the middle of the garden.
5. Statements which may lessen the severity of the consequences of disobeying the LORD God's command:
   The woman's version of the threatened punishment is "or you will die" which once again removes the emphatic character of the original prohibition, "you will *surely* die."

3:2 The woman said to the serpent, "We may eat fruit from the trees in the garden,

Once again the woman speaks, and the man remains silent. He has received the commandment directly from the LORD God; she

---

[12]In Hebrew the LORD God's command in 2:17 uses the emphatic construction, infinitive absolute followed by the verb in the same root. This emphatic construction is missing in the woman's version of the command in 3:2.

has not. But when it comes time to explain and defend the gracious character of God, the man remains mute.

The woman responds in a fashion that is technically accurate, but one which loses the generous spirit behind the LORD's original command to Adam. In 2:16 an emphatic Hebrew form is used (infinitive absolute followed by the imperfect of the same verb as in "you shall surely die"). The freedom to eat from any tree is emphasized, and the expectation is there that humankind would avail themselves of that generous freedom. The woman, whom the man has presumably instructed on the divine command, says merely, "we are eating from the trees of the garden." The "may" in NIV is interpretive. In any case the emphatic way that freedom is underscored in the original giving of the command is now lost. So often in communicating God's truth, especially it seems to the "next generation of believers," our passion for the generosity and grace of God, which led us to him to begin with, is lost. What began as "raging holy fire" is now controlled as in a forge where "identikit" Christians are rather boringly mass-produced. The woman, whether through the man's neglect, or her own apathy, has lost a grip on the love and outrageous generosity of a holy God. When the freedom and encouragement to freely eat is minimized to mere permission this may be a subtle indicator that the woman has gone some way toward the attitude toward God which the serpent is encouraging.

3:3 but God did say, 'You must not eat fruit from the tree that is in the middle of the garden, and you must not touch it, or you will die.'"

Just as the serpent referred to the LORD God as merely "God," so the woman here adopts the perspective of the serpent and refers to him as "God." As noted in the excursus, the woman's version of the command differs from the original version given to the man in several ways. She adds a restriction to the commandment of not even touching it. Lapide remarks on Eve's addition to the prohibition:

> The text is silent on the matter, but there are those who believe that the snake demonstrates that she would not die for violating the prohibition by having her touch the fruit. Because nothing happens when she touches the fruit, she supposes she can also eat it with impunity. In this way the snake is able to entice her.[13]

---

[13]Pinchas Lapide, "Touching the Forbidden Fruit," *BRev* 4 (1988): 42-43.

While speculative (and fanciful) it would be consistent with the characterization of the serpent here to attempt subtly to move the woman closer to his perspective before challenging her to directly violate the commandment. In any case the woman has begun to adopt the serpent's perspective. The serpent began the temptation scene by suggesting that God (not the LORD God) was overly restrictive and lacking grace. At one level the woman denies this and corrects the serpent. But at another level her version[14] adds a restriction which the LORD God had not originally given.

The woman's version with its added restriction may have been motivated by a desire to avoid temptation. The Rabbis speak of "placing a fence" around the law; in other words, added restrictions which are not explicitly given in the law may serve a helpful, spiritual purpose. If the abuse of alcohol is a great temptation, it may be wise to construct a rule prohibiting any consumption of alcohol to avoid being tempted to abuse it. The problem with such rules comes when they are confused with the expressed word and will of God and exalted to the place of a badge of spirituality. Others, who do not feel the need to add such a rule, are then judged to be subspiritual, and rather creative exegesis is used to prove that what is in reality legalism is actually scriptural.

The woman's version also softens the emphatic character of the penalty for disobedience. The LORD God's "you will surely die" becomes a more tepid "or you will die." She also may be being portrayed as having a level of confusion about just which tree is prohibited.[15] The tree of life is definitely in the middle of the garden.

---

[14]It is important to note that the woman's version does not necessarily come from her. She could well be repeating with great care and accuracy the version which the man had communicated to her. That the man remains silent and does not correct her version argues in favor of the subtle distortions coming from the man, and not the woman, although the text is silent on the point.

[15]For the woman the tree is in the middle of the garden. But again she is inaccurate. Genesis 2:9 tells us only that the Tree of Life was in the middle of the garden. The location of the tree of knowledge is not specified. Is the woman confused about which tree is prohibited, or only its location? Perhaps the woman did know of the location and it was right beside the Tree of Life. But perhaps the reader is to infer that the woman confused the Tree of Life, which was permitted, with the Tree of Knowledge, which was

The narrator does not explicitly identify the location of the tree of the knowledge of good and evil.[16] The tree of life is not prohibited at this time. While the confusion is minor, there does seem to be a level of confusion about the command. Certainly the woman does not repeat the version given to the man unaltered. The person responsible for the distortion is not explicitly identified. It could be either the man or the woman or both who have changed the expressed will of the LORD God. Regardless the man remains silent and does not intervene to correct the woman.[17]

In some senses this narrative functions as a meditation on how human beings should respond to and apply the word and will of God. When we add to God's word, we ultimately risk being unfaithful to it. Likewise when we convince ourselves that the consequences of rebellion are not as severe as God's word warns, we are prone to disobey his word. When we distrust God's motives and project onto him our own tendencies, we often do so in order to find justification

---

forbidden. Thus in the woman's confused reasoning God deprives her of that which gives Life.

[16]Plaut ("Genesis," pp. 38-40) categorizes the theories about the Tree of Knowledge as:
1) Ethical Interpretation — God provided man with moral discrimination and thereby made him capable of committing sin. Much of Christianity turned this into original sin: "In Adam's Fall We Sinned All"; the Pelagians argued that it was transmitted by bad example. Jewish interpretation does not emphasize the story much and believes humankind is capable of horrendous evil, but also great good.
2) Intellectual Interpretation — "Good and bad" is a merism for "everything." Mankind will attempt to know everything, even things which are harmful for human beings to know; in other words, humanity tries to play God.
3) Sexual Interpretation — The story is of the discovery of sexuality by humankind. Man must now perpetuate himself through procreation, since his disobedience removed the chance for immortality. "As a child he lives in a garden of innocence; when he discovers his sexuality and grows up, he must leave the garden forever.

I would argue that a combination of the "ethical" and the "intellectual" views best fits the narrative.

[17]Lapide ("Touching," p. 43) characterizes Adam's role: "Adam, in fact, reveals himself to be rather reserved, taciturn and, to put it mildly, not terribly energetic. During the entire story he plays a miserable walk-on role, which the Bible refuses to embellish one iota."

for rebellion. When we discuss God's word without talking with him, we often miss the mark and suffer the consequences. When we are confused and unclear about exactly what God's word says, we set ourselves up for failure. When we know God's word and see it being deliberately violated and do not speak up, we also set ourselves up for failure as well as encouraging failure in our faith communities.

3:4 "You will not surely die," the serpent said to the woman.

As is often noted, at one level, the serpent speaks the literal truth. They do not die on the day they eat of it. Their eyes are opened. They have experiential knowledge of both good and evil. But they are not like God. In fact, after eating they are afraid of God. The serpent here directly contradicts the word of the LORD God. While he uses the "you" plural in this text, he only directly speaks to the woman, who has shown real confusion over exactly what the LORD God had said and had already come over to his perspective in some small ways. The serpent does not directly contradict the word of the LORD God until this has happened, and this demonstrates his shrewdness as well as the naïveté of the original human pair.

It is striking that in contradicting the LORD God's warning the serpent quotes him far more exactly than the woman had. The LORD God warned in Genesis 2:16, "You will surely die," using a Hebrew construction indicating emphasis. The serpent uses the exact same emphatic construction in his contradiction of the LORD God's word. The only difference is that the serpent uses the plural form of "you" while the original command is singular since only the man existed at that time. The serpent is better at quoting God's word than the woman is.

3:5 "For God knows that when you eat of it your eyes will be opened, and you will be like God, knowing good and evil."

Once again the LORD God who had given the beautiful garden and its abundance, who is referred to by his covenant name Yahweh, is here called merely the generic "God" by the serpent. The serpent entices the pair to suspect God's motives for placing a prohibition on them. He does not want you to eat because in eating you will be just like him, knowing good and evil in a personal way. The implication is that it is only God's insecurity at creating a rival and his stinginess that led to the command. The man and woman's trust in

God's goodness, despite all the evidence to the contrary all around them in their daily experience, is lost; and when trust in God's goodness and love is lost, sin and its terrible consequences follow as night follows day.

The serpent is once again, in a twisted sort of way, telling the truth. On the day[18] of the eating of the fruit their eyes would be opened. They would "know" good and evil, or at least "evil," in a personal, experiential way. But they would not be like God at all. So often those things which tempt us do so by promising both things they can deliver and things they cannot deliver. During the process of temptation the consequences are often minimized or ignored.

3:6 When the woman saw that the fruit of the tree was good for food and pleasing to the eye, and also desirable for gaining wisdom, she took some and ate it.

It is interesting that the woman sees that the tree was "good for food and pleasing to the eye." That is the same description of the other trees in the garden in Genesis 2. The woman wanted something that she thought she did not already have. But there God had provided it already. This seems to imply that the woman has succumbed to the temptation to doubt God's goodness. She certainly has ignored his generosity.

But the woman is also attracted to the fruit of the tree for another reason. For the woman to "know good and evil" is the same as "gaining wisdom." While she ignores God's generous provision of many trees which are "good for food and pleasing to the eye," this tree also has the potential of giving her wisdom without regard to her relationship with God. The theme verse of the book of Proverbs reads, "The fear of the LORD is the beginning of wisdom." The woman succumbs to the serpent's twisted account and seeks wisdom that is independent of a respectful, reverent, and, yes, fearful awe of the LORD God.

Our modern understanding of this passage has been influenced in a major way by Milton's account and by the artistic depictions of the scene with which we are familiar. For example, readers of the Bible are often surprised to find out that the Bible does not specify

---

[18]The NIV's "when" is literally "on the day that." The serpent once again shows a remarkable ability to exactly quote the LORD God's command and then twist it.

the fruit. Lapide explains where the tradition that the fruit was an apple[19] came from:

> [T]he fruit of the tree in this passage has for almost 2,000 years been painted, sculpted and described as an apple. But the text speaks only of an undefined "fruit." How did we get to the apple, of all things, which was unknown in the Near East until a century ago? In Jerome's fifth-century Latin translation of the Bible, known as the Vulgate, the word for "evil," with which the snake's speech ends (Genesis 3:5), is *malum*. *Malum* can also mean *apple*, and so this false apple was projected back three lines, to end up ultimately in Eve's hands, where it never was in the first place.[20]

She also gave some to her husband, who was with her, and he ate it.
The traditional exegesis of this story wrongly assumes that Adam was not present at the time of the temptation. This verse tells us that he was present, but was strangely silent. Most contemporary interpreters of this narrative have been heavily influenced by this traditional exegesis. Not wanting to blame the man for his complicity in the Fall, there are a series of creative interpretive moves used to vindicate him. The Genesis Rabbah[21] suggests that the man and the woman had engaged in sex and he had fallen asleep. But nothing has influenced us as readers in the west as much as Milton. Milton's powerful description of the sin is found in his Latin Theological Treatise.[22] The sin:

---

[19]"Flora," *ABD*, II:806, notes that the "APRICOT or the quince have been identified as the Heb *tapuah*. . . . It is sometimes associated with the 'apple' tree, but while domesticated apple trees are now found in Israel, wild specimens are not believed to have grown there in biblical times since it is a tree native to the Northern hemisphere. Apricots, however, grow in warmer climes and are native to China: they have long been abundant in Israel and most probably were introduced in biblical times."

[20]Lapide, "Touching," p. 43.

[21]Gen Rabbah 19:3: "And the woman said unto the serpent . . ." (Gen 3:2). Now where was Adam during this conversation? Abba Halfon b. Qoriah said: "He had engaged in sex and then fell asleep."

[22]Quoted in Gordon Campbell, "Milton's Eden," in *A Walk in the Garden: Biblical, Iconographical and Literary Images of Eden*, ed. by Paul Morris and Deborah Sawyer, JSOTSup 136 (1992): 223.

. . . was a most atrocious offence, and . . . broke every part of the law. For what fault is there which man did not commit in commencing this sin? He was to be condemned both for trusting Satan and for not trusting God; he was faithless, ungrateful, disobedient, greedy, uxorious; she, negligent of her husband's welfare; both of them committed theft, robbery with violence, murder against their children (i.e., the whole human race); each was sacrilegious and deceitful, cunningly aspiring to divinity although thoroughly unworthy of it, proud and arrogant.

In Book IX of *Paradise Lost*, however, Milton has a different story. Eve is beguiled by Satan, and Adam chooses to fall *because of his love for Eve*! At the end of the poem we sense the tragic dimensions of which Milton warns. Campbell notes that Milton introduced work, sexual activity, entertaining (of Raphael), and Adam's request for a wife to his account.[23] Interestingly Eve has to convince Adam to work separately, which gives Satan an opportunity.

In this case the traditional picture fails us. It shifts blame totally onto the woman and does not listen to the biblical text. The underlying male chauvinism should embarrass us as Christians. The man was present during the temptation scene. He is addressed along with the woman and shows no hesitation in following her in disobeying the LORD God. His silence during the temptation scene speaks volumes.

3:7 Then the eyes of both of them were opened, and they realized they were naked; so they sewed fig leaves together and made coverings for themselves.

While the complete consequences of the man and woman's sin will be displayed throughout the book of Genesis and the book of world history, the first result is the distorted way in which they begin to look at themselves and each other. Gone is the transparency which knew no shame. The realization that they[24] were naked now

---

[23]Gary A. Anderson (*The Genesis of Perfection* [Louisville, KY: Westminster/John Knox Press, 2001]) shows that Milton is not original in much of this but based his work on the sixth-century A.D. work, "The Lives of Adam and Eve."

[24]According to Jubilees 3 Eve clothed herself with fig leaves before she gave the fruit to Adam, who ate and then made his own garment of fig leaves. But Genesis says that only after both of them ate were their eyes opened.

brought them shame and the desire to hide it. Suddenly the focus of the man and woman is on themselves and not on the task of working and guarding the garden.[25]

The material used to meet that desire, fig leaves, is pitifully inadequate. When we as men and women try to fix our problems by ourselves which our sins against God have brought upon us, our remedies are just as pitiful. Fig leaves will serve as clothing no better than our own self-help strategies. It is possible that for the imagined audience fig trees had sexually suggestive connotations and that they might see a critique against the fertility cults of Canaan.[26]

---

[25]Brueggemann, referring to his previous exposition of chapter 2, says (*Genesis,* p. 48): "The couple stands exposed beyond the safe parameters of vocation/permission/prohibition, now having taken life into their own hands. The prohibition of 2:17 is violated. The permission of verse 16 is perverted. The vocation of verse 15 is neglected. There is no more mention of tending and feeding. They have no energy for that. Their interest has focused completely on self, on their new freedom and the terror that comes with it."

[26]Stephen N. Lambden ("From Fig Leaves to Fingernails: Some Notes on the Garments of Adam and Eve in the Hebrew Bible and Select Early Postbiblical Jewish Writings," in *A Walk in the Garden,* p. 76): "It is important for the understanding of Genesis 2-3 to note that the very first act of the first couple after eating of the fruit of the forbidden tree was the making of fig-leaf 'aprons.' Modern commentators are generally disappointing in explaining the significance of this act — if indeed, it is commented on at all. The view that the first couple made specifically fig-leaf 'aprons' because of the leaves of the fig tree, being the largest on any Palestinian tree, were most suitable for sewing together and making 'aprons,' is not very convincing. Also inadequate is the view that the first couple made fig-leaf 'aprons' because the forbidden tree itself, allegedly being a fig tree, provided them with the necessary material. Rather, it seems to me, the first couple's act of making fig-leaf 'aprons' is an indication of the fact that, despite their becoming sophisticated or wise as a result of eating of the fruit of the forbidden tree, they were still so foolish as to imagine that they could adequately cover their 'nakedness.' Gen 3.7b points to the folly of the first couple and also, perhaps, in terms of the sexually suggestive associations of the fig tree, to the dangers of participation in fertility cults and rites." I find Wright's [David P. Wright, "Holiness, Sex and Death in the Garden of Eden," *Biblica* 77 (1996): 305-329] suggestion of parallels with Gilgamesh and its equation of sexuality and acquisition of knowledge far-fetched.

B. THE DISCOVERY AND PUNISHMENT OF THE DISOBEDIENCE (3:8-19)

⁸Then the man and his wife heard the sound of the LORD God as he was walking in the garden in the cool of the day, and they hid from the LORD God among the trees of the garden. ⁹But the LORD God called to the man, "Where are you?"

¹⁰He answered, "I heard you in the garden, and I was afraid because I was naked; so I hid."

¹¹And he said, "Who told you that you were naked? Have you eaten from the tree that I commanded you not to eat from?"

¹²The man said, "The woman you put here with me—she gave me some fruit from the tree, and I ate it."

¹³Then the LORD God said to the woman, "What is this you have done?"

The woman said, "The serpent deceived me, and I ate."

¹⁴So the LORD God said to the serpent, "Because you have done this,

"Cursed are you above all the livestock
    and all the wild animals!
You will crawl on your belly
    and you will eat dust
    all the days of your life.
¹⁵And I will put enmity
    between you and the woman,
    and between your offspringᵃ and hers;
he will crushᵇ your head,
    and you will strike his heel."

¹⁶To the woman he said,

"I will greatly increase your pains in childbearing;
    with pain you will give birth to children.
Your desire will be for your husband,
    and he will rule over you."

¹⁷To Adam he said, "Because you listened to your wife and ate from the tree about which I commanded you, 'You must not eat of it,'

"Cursed is the ground because of you;
    through painful toil you will eat of it
    all the days of your life.

> ¹⁸It will produce thorns and thistles for you,
>   and you will eat the plants of the field.
> ¹⁹By the sweat of your brow
>   you will eat your food
> until you return to the ground,
>   since from it you were taken;
> for dust you are
>   and to dust you will return."

ᵃ*15 Or seed*   ᵇ*15 Or strike*

In this section the man and woman's sin is discovered and punished. We discover that one of the effects of the Fall is the tendency to be so ashamed of our behavior that we seek to shift responsibility for it to others. This refusal to accept the consequences only further exacerbates the broken relationship with the LORD which underlies the rest of the Bible's story. The punishment is announced in the opposite order in which the sin is discovered. The net result of the sin and its punishment is the distortion of every relationship between the LORD God and his creation. Some of these distortions happen spontaneously with the act of disobedience. Humanity's relationship with the LORD is damaged as they hide from him and the man blames the LORD for giving the woman to him. The relationships between men and women are scarred as the man passes off blame to the woman and they must cover themselves from seeing each other's nakedness. The man and the woman have distorted views of themselves as they are suddenly ashamed of their nakedness. The relationship with the animal kingdom is marred as the woman in part blames the deception of the serpent for her own decisions.

Other distortions come as the result of the LORD's announced punishment. The physical creation is under his curse as is the animal kingdom, the serpent in particular. Humanity's relationship with the animal kingdom is also distorted by the predicted enmity of the descendants of the woman and the serpent. Humanity's relationship with the physical creation is dramatically changed. The fulfilling vocation of caring for creation will now be a frustrating process of fighting thorns and thistles in order to live. The relationship of the man and the woman is also spoiled. The process of procreation will become incredibly painful for the woman, and there will be a struggle for power between the genders with the stronger winning. And of course the man and the woman will be estranged from the LORD God as they struggle to reestablish and sustain a relationship with him.

1. The Discovery of the Disobedience (3:8-13)

3:8 Then the man and his wife heard the sound of the LORD God as he was walking in the garden in the cool of the day, and they hid from the LORD God among the trees of the garden.

The next manifestation of the fallen condition of the man and the woman is when they are confronted with the possibility of direct interaction with the LORD God. They hear him walking in the garden. Instead of being drawn into fellowship with him, they hide themselves. The trees of the garden were created by the LORD to provide food for humanity. They are now turned into the means of trying to hide from the LORD! How often God's good gifts are twisted into something for which they were never designed.

The verb translated "was walking" is in a relatively rare verb stem, the hithpael, usually the intensive reflexive. The hithpael of *hālāk* may point forward to Deuteronomy 23:15 "For Yahweh your God walks about [Hithpael participle of *hālāk*] in the midst of your camp" and Leviticus 26:12 where an obedient future Israel is promised, "I will walk [Hithpael of *hālāk*] among you and be your God and you will be my people."

Niehaus has argued that by using another homonymous Hebrew root for the Hebrew word translated "day" (יוֹם, *yōm*) this word should be translated as "storm." He also suggests using rarer, although well-attested meanings, for the Hebrew words translated "cool of" and "voice" as "wind" and "thunder." This verse should then be translated, "Then the man and his wife heard the *thunder* of Yahweh God as he was going back and forth in the garden in the *wind* of the *storm*, and they hid from Yahweh." What is being described according to Neihaus is a theophany. The fear recalls the reaction of Israel at Sinai (Exod 20:18) and the accounts of theophanies in Ezekiel 1:13 and Psalm 77:17-19.[27] I am also reminded of the voice of the

---

[27]Jeffrey Niehaus, "In the Wind of the Storm: Another Look at Genesis III 8," *VT* XLIV (1994): 263-267.

"shriveled whisper" in 1 Kings 19:10-13.[28] While this is possible, it seems more likely to me that the fearsomeness of a theophany is a result of the Fall and its punishment. At this point the LORD is still seeking the intimate fellowship with the man and the woman that he has always enjoyed.

3:9 But the LORD God called to the man, "Where are you?"

The LORD God seeks out humankind in the garden, and he has been seeking ever since. Even when we would prefer to hide from God, he seeks us. He does not merely speak to the man, but he "calls" to him because man is not where he should be. Presumably the LORD does not ask "Where are you?" because he needs information; he wants the human pair to realize where they really are. His question is addressed to the man in particular since he bears primary responsibility for obedience to the commandment since he, and not the woman, was given it directly.

3:10 He answered, "I heard you in the garden, and I was afraid because I was naked; so I hid."

The man answers the LORD God's call. But his answer is strikingly self-focused. Instead of the free and unfettered access which they had enjoyed together, the man is now afraid of the LORD, ashamed of himself, and embarrassed to be in the LORD's presence. Brueggemann helpfully teases out the selfish preoccupation of the man:

> The speech of the indicted couple is revealing, for it is all "I." Therein lies the primal offense: " I heard . . . I was afraid . . . I was naked; I hid . . . I ate . . . I ate" (3:10-13). Their own speech indicts them. It makes clear that their preoccupation with the Gardener, with his vocation, his permission, his prohibition, has been given up. Now the preoccupation is "I."[29]

What Brueggemann fails to notice is that it is only the man, and not the woman also, who demonstrates this self-focus. Interestingly the man was not afraid of the LORD God's warnings prior to the eating of the fruit. Now he is afraid of the LORD's very presence.

3:11 And he said, "Who told you that you were naked? Have you eaten from the tree that I commanded you not to eat from?"

---

[28]See Kissling, *Reliable Characters*, ch. 3.
[29]Brueggemann, *Genesis*, p. 49.

The LORD God asks not for information, but for explanation. The LORD God addresses Adam here in the singular. The command was given to him alone. He knew better and is thus the first to face the questioning and the last to receive his punishment. The man only knew of his nakedness because he was suddenly ashamed of it. That shame could only come from the distorting effects of sin. The LORD gives the man the opportunity to confess his sin and face the consequences of it.

3:12 The man said, "The woman you put here with me—she gave me some fruit from the tree, and I ate it."

Instead of acknowledging his sin the man shifts the blame to the woman and to the LORD who had given him the woman. His response to the LORD's gift of the woman here is very different from his initial response. The man refuses to accept his own responsibility.

If the woman was confused about the specifics of God's command, it was the man's responsibility to clarify since only he was the original recipient of the command. Either the man distorted the message, communicated it poorly, or failed to correct the woman in her misunderstandings. For the man to stand silently by while the serpent and the woman distort the commandment of the LORD is inexcusable. The man in part blames the LORD for even allowing the possibility of his own fall by giving him the woman to begin with. She is no longer "bone of my bone and flesh of my flesh." Now she is the problem.

3:13 Then the LORD God said to the woman, "What is this you have done?" The woman said, "The serpent deceived me, and I ate."

Having been informed that the woman gave the man the fruit, the LORD addresses the woman. The woman in part blames the serpent. The serpent had deceived her. But she also, in contrast to the man, quickly takes personal responsibility.[30] The woman is correct in her evaluation. She was deceived. She does not blame the man or the LORD.

---

[30]Park, "Why Eve?" p. 127-135: "That she listens to the serpent and Adam to her implies a hierarchy: God, Adam, Eve, the serpent (and animal kingdom). She is closer to nature; Adam to God. God's actions seem to affirm this hierarchy when he discovers the crime, for he first asks Adam why he ate the fruit, and Adam blames Eve. He then asks Eve why she ate, and one would expect her to blame the serpent. But no, the Bible disrupts the structure it is creating by having Eve blame herself. 'The serpent tricked me, and

2. The Punishment of the Disobedience (3:14-19)

The Punishment of the Serpent (3:14-15)

3:14 So the LORD God said to the serpent, "Because you have done this, "Cursed are you above all the livestock and all the wild animals! You will crawl on your belly and you will eat dust all the days of your life.

The serpent, who was in part blamed by the woman for her disobedience, has his punishment announced first. He is specifically said to be cursed. His curse is to be above that of all the livestock and wild animals. This seems to imply that all animals also receive a curse but that the serpent's curse is more severe than that of the other animals. This is not an invitation to speculation as to whether snakes originally walked upright. Just as the eating of the dust is not literal, so the crawling on the belly as a new physical phenomena is not likely to be literal. Instead the LORD God announces that the serpent will have a subordinate position in creation. He will not hold his head up but will crawl on his belly. His perpetual food will be dust not in some literal sense but as a sign of his low status.

3:15 And I will put enmity between you and the woman, and between your offspring and hers; he will crush your head, and you will strike his heel."

The LORD God announces to the serpent that there will be intense conflict between the progeny of the serpent and the progeny of the woman. While a distorted relationship between the animal kingdom and the human family is already implied in verse 14, this verse focuses in on the conflict of the serpent's descendants and the woman's descendants. The conflict will harm both sides, but the serpent's offspring will get the worst of it. While a strike on the heel is painful, a strike to the head is lethal.[31]

This is one of only two places in the Hebrew bible where the word "seed" or "offspring" refers to the progeny of a woman (cf.

I ate.' In other words, she has more dignity than Adam, for she takes the responsibility upon herself, something he was too weak or cowardly to do."

[31]The words "crush" and "strike" in the NIV are actually the same Hebrew verb (שׁוּף, *šûph*). The blow to the head is the same as the blow to the heel. The difference is in the result because of the relative vulnerability of the heel and head to a lethal injury.

Gen 16:10, Hagar). Usually it is a man's seed that is mentioned. Some see in the singulars ("he" and "your") a hint that a single descendant of the woman is meant. This seems unlikely for a number of reasons. Consistency would seem to require that the serpent also have a single "seed" which would be in conflict with the woman's seed. It is not obvious who this singular descendant would be. Further the word for "offspring" or "seed" is usually a collective noun which is singular in form but plural in meaning. The word translated "he" is better translated "it" or more likely "they."

This text is traditionally known as the *proto-evangelium* or first prediction of the gospel and its savior Jesus Christ. It seems unlikely that the original audience would have understood it that way. More likely they would have thought of conflict between the animal kingdom and the human descendants of the woman. It is worthy of note that the only two allusions (it is never quoted) in the New Testament to this passage interpret it collectively. Luke 10:19 has Jesus telling the 70 after they had returned from their "mini-Great Commission" that he had given them "authority to tread on serpents and scorpions and over all of the power of the enemy." In Romans 16:19 Paul assures the Roman Christians that "the God of peace will soon crush Satan under your feet." It is never used of Jesus personally crushing Satan's head.

But as Christians we might well ask, "Doesn't the broader message of the Bible lead us quite naturally to see at least a hint of the LORD's ultimate plan through Christ? Does not the fuller sense of Scripture, the so-called *sensus plenior* guide us?" Certainly Christ, as *the* seed of Abraham and the new Adam, fulfills in himself God's ultimate purpose for creation. While the original audience would probably not have seen the prophecy of an individual messiah in this passage, it seems quite appropriate for Christians who have read the back of the book to see the anticipation if not the specific prediction of the work of Christ in defeating the devil.

The Punishment of the Woman (3:16)

3:16 To the woman he said, "I will greatly increase your pains in childbearing; with pain you will give birth to children. Your desire will be for your husband, and he will rule over you."

The woman here receives her punishment.[32] The woman's pun-

---

[32]While it is true that the specific word "curse" does not occur in the pun-

ishment relates to her ability to bear children.³³ The process will be distorted into one that is extremely painful. It is not as though there was to be no pain associated with birth prior to the Fall; instead that pain will be greatly increased. The process designed by the creator to bring forth new life will also serve as a stark reminder of the consequences of attempting to live life on one's own terms and not on God's.³⁴

The second part of the punishment has been discussed and debated for centuries. The first debated issue is the nature of the woman's desire. In the history of interpretation this has often been interpreted as meaning sexual desire. The point would then be that women would sexually desire their husbands, but ironically be dominated (ruled over) by their husbands. The Hebrew word translated "desire" occurs only two other times in the Hebrew Bible, in Genesis 4:7 and Song of Songs 7:10. The latter text, "I am my beloved's and his desire is for me," obviously has sexual connotations in its context. But a safer guide to the connotation of a general word such as "desire"³⁵ is the same author's use of it. In Genesis 4:7 the LORD says

---

ishment of the woman, I fail to see the cogency of the fine distinction between punishment and curse that some scholars have attempted to make, e.g., John J. Schmitt. "Like Eve, Like Adam: *mšl* in Gen 3,16." *Biblica* 72 (1991): 1-22. See also Adrien Janis Bledstein. "Was Eve Cursed?" *BRev* 9 (1993/1): 42-45.

³³Julie Galambush ("'ADAM FROM 'ADAMA, 'SSA FROM 'IS: Derivation and Subordination in Genesis 2.4b–3.24," in *History and Interpretation: Essays in Honour of John H. Hayes,* ed. by M. Patrick Graham, William P. Brown, and Jeffrey K. Kuan, JSOTSup 173 [Sheffield: Sheffield Academic Press, 1993]) has argued that the different type of suffering that each is assigned here derives from the differences in the substances from which the first couple was formed; Adam from the soil and Eve from Adam.

³⁴Bledstein, "Was Eve Cursed?" p. 44, argues that there may be another instance of anti-idolatry polemic here. She notes, "Goddesses, however, unlike women bear children easily — after nine days of pregnancy in a Sumerian paradise myth, according to Sumerologist Samuel Noah Kramer. To an ancient audience, well aware that goddesses give birth painlessly, increased pain in childbirth would seem an especially appropriate punishment for this woman who aspired to be a goddess. The author is cleverly satirizing the human tendency to play god."

³⁵Bledstein argues that the word translated "desire" could mean "desirable" arguing that 4:7 means that sin is "desirable to you." But this makes little sense in 4:7. Why would the LORD say to Cain, "sin is desirable to you but you must master it"? Doesn't this in effect mean that you can either submit to sin (which will rule over you if you let it) or you can master it?

to Cain, "If you do what is right, will you not be accepted? But if you do not do what is right, sin is crouching at your door; it *desires* to have you, but you must *master* it." Here sin is portrayed as a crouching animal ready to pounce on the unsuspecting victim. Sin's desire is to dominate and destroy Cain. Cain, however, has the ability to rule[36] over sin and not be ruled by it. It seems much more sensible exegetically to me to gain insight on the meaning of a rare word from a similar text by the same narrator than to find its connotation from Song of Songs, a text widely separated in time, genre, and style from Genesis. In fact Genesis 3:16 and 4:7 are remarkably similar to one another with the latter text deliberately echoing the former[37] as Vogels shows:

3:16b — אֶל־אִישֵׁךְ תְּשׁוּקָתֵךְ וְהוּא יִמְשָׁל־בָּךְ
4:7b — וְאֵלֶיךָ תְּשׁוּקָתוֹ וְאַתָּה תִּמְשָׁל־בּוֹ

The woman will desire to dominate in the relationship and will frustratingly lose the battle for control to which history amply testifies.

Some[38] have argued that in the wider context women do not act out the predicted subservient role. Both Eve and Sarah name their sons. But that is only an argument for the fact that the curse is not mechanical in its outworking and that the effects of the curse can be mitigated at various times and in various ways. This text is not telling us what should be, but what is. The subjugation of the woman is a sad effect of the Fall. Wenham helpfully traces how the distorted relationship between men and women plays itself out in the rest of Genesis:

---

[36]Schmitt has argued that *mašal*, usually translated "rule," is only one of three verbal roots for the Hebrew letters משל: I. "to represent, be like"; II. "to use a proverb, speak in parables"; III. "to rule, have dominion over." He thinks that this verse is saying that the woman will have sexual desire for the man and the man will be like her in having that desire. I find his reasoning unconvincing, not least because the earliest translation, the LXX understands it to mean "rule," cf. *kyrieusei*, i.e., "He will lord it over" you.

[37]Walter Vogels, "The Power Struggle between Man and Woman," *Biblica* 77 (1996): 197-209.

[38]Schmitt, "Like Eve," pp. 1-22. He asserts: "This study proposes that the idea of male domination is not really present in the text of Gen 3,16. Regardless of how some readers of the Bible interpret other texts, this verse does not support the idea of a husband's controlling power over his wife. This study argues that the original idea in Gen 3,16 is the male's 'similarity to' the woman rather than his 'domination over' her" (p. 1).

But more than short-term disharmony blights male-female relationships, for 3:16 spells out long-term problems for women, such as pain in pregnancy and childbirth, and ongoing conflict with men. "Your desire shall be for your husband" is obscure. It may be suggesting that women will go to unreasonable lengths to please their man, or that they will seek a degree of independence. Both situations are described in the patriarchal stories (e.g., chs 30, 16), but the latter meaning fits better in 4:7, the only other mention of "desire" in Genesis. "He shall rule over you" may suggest a harsh use of male authority as opposed to the more benign patriarchy envisaged in chapter 2.

Reading further in Genesis, the harsh realism of chapter 3 seems more in evidence than the ideals of chapter 2. Lamech, the first bigamist, is a vicious thug, boasting that he will take seventy-sevenfold vengeance on those who attack him (4:23-24). Sarah's resort to surrogate motherhood, though a well-known practice in the ancient Near East, is described in terms that echo Genesis 3 and causes great tension between Sarah, Hagar and Abraham. Jacob's involuntary bigamy leads to a most unhappy marriage for all concerned. As Leah and Rachel name their sons, they pour out their feelings of rejection on the one hand and their desire for more children on the other (29:32–30:24).

But polygamy is not the only problem between the sexes. Husbands too frequently seem to put their own interests before their wife's: twice Sarah lands up in a foreign harem because of Abraham's lack of candour about their marriage (12:10-20; 20) and Rebekah nearly suffers the same way (26:6-11). For her part it is Sarah who persuades Abraham to go in for surrogacy and it is Rebekah who persuades Jacob to deceive his father Isaac (27:5-17) — hardly the action of a loyal wife. Most of the patriarchs' wives have difficulty in becoming pregnant, and when they succeed they suffer as 3:16 predicts. Rebekah experiences the pain of pregnancy as Esau and Jacob smash into each other inside her womb, while Rachel dies in childbirth (25:22; 35:16-19). Thus the gloomy picture of married life in Genesis 3 is illustrated in the following narratives.[39]

---

[39]Gordon Wenham, *Torah as Story: Reading the Old Testament Narrative Ethically* (London, T & T Clark, 2000), pp. 32-33.

But there is an up side. While relationships between men and women are distorted by the Fall, there are still signs of hope. Positive relationships between the genders are possible even in the fallen world east of Eden.[40]

This text should not be used as justification for the subjugation of women. If men try to subjugate women, they only act as people under the curse. In Christ we are a new creation, and we anticipate the new heavens and the new earth where every evidence of the curse will be removed. In light of that destiny we seek, so far as it is possible in this fallen world, to live our lives in light of the kingdom which is already here but not yet completely instituted.

The Punishment of the Man (3:17-19)

3:17 To Adam he said, "Because you listened to your wife and ate from the tree about which I commanded you, 'You must not eat of it,' "Cursed is the ground because of you; through painful toil you will eat of it all the days of your life.

Unlike the woman, Adam receives a punishment that is actually called a curse. That curse relates to his originally created function. As guardian of Eden, the material creation was intended to be a source of food and enjoyment for him. With the ground being cursed the fruit of the ground would become difficult to obtain. Obtaining food would now only happen through painful toil. The life which God gave to Adam and intended to be unending would have an end. Adam and his descendants will face famine, even in the promised land which near the Jordan was "well-watered like the Garden of Eden" (Gen 13:11). At other times the ground will not be productive.

All of this will happen because Adam obeyed (lit. Hebrew, NIV has "listened to") his wife's voice rather than the LORD God's com-

---

[40]Wenham, ibid., p. 33: "However there are glimpses of joy, showing that the idealism of Genesis 2 is not completely overshadowed. Eve ascribes the birth of both Cain and Seth to God's help. The birth of children to the patriarchs is not merely the fulfillment of God's promises but an answer to their prayers (15:2; 25:21; 30:22,24). Birth is an occasion for joy as the names given to children at birth show (21:6; 29:32,35; 41:51,52). And as for happiness between partners, we are told that Jacob's seven years of engagement to Rachel 'seemed to him but a few days because of the love he had for her' (29:20)."

mandment. The LORD had commanded the man individually.[41] The woman had not directly received the commandment. Adam is held accountable for having personally received the commandment and deliberately rejecting it. Adam listened to his wife silently and obeyed in a sheepish fashion. He uttered no protest and did nothing to even attempt to stop his wife. He is therefore held accountable, and because of his inaction and sheepish following of the woman into sin the entire ground is under the LORD's curse.

It is significant that neither the man nor the woman die immediately as had been warned. It is an act of grace on the part of the LORD not to carry out the sentence with strict exactitude. But death is coming nevertheless. Adam's life will involve painful toil until the very end. There will be an end to his life. The painful toil is not an eternal sentence. But death is coming as the LORD had warned in Genesis 2:16.

3:18 It will produce thorns and thistles for you, and you will eat the plants of the field.

The ground from which the man was formed will now produce useless plants. The thorns and thistles will spontaneously sprout up[42] but will yield nothing edible for humanity. No longer will the fruit of the trees of the garden feed him and his woman. He will now have to depend on the "plants of the field" which he must search for and gather or else carefully cultivate. In either case it seems clear that this will be done outside of the garden.

3:19 By the sweat of your brow you will eat your food until you return to the ground, since from it you were taken; for dust you are and to dust you will return."

In order to obtain this food the man and his descendants will have to work in a difficult and frustrating way ("by the sweat of your brow"). Man's service of the ground will no longer be enjoyable and easily productive work. It will now be a battle with creation for survival. That battle will ultimately be won by the creation, for humanity will eventually turn into dust once again. The irony of the punishment must not be lost. The man was created from the earth but to work and preserve it. He is thus created in an exalted position

---

[41]The "you" in 2:16 is singular in Hebrew.

[42]The Hebrew verb צָמַח (ṣāmaḥ) means "to sprout up spontaneously."

over the very stuff of which he was created. But in this curse humanity will again become subordinate to the ground. He will die, his body will rot, and it will turn into dust. Because he has chosen to reject the good life which the good LORD had provided and make his own way in the world, he will end up as dust, the very thing which the LORD used to make him!

It is a commonplace in Christian theology to argue that humanity inherits the sins of Adam. This is supposedly justified by a specific reading of certain statements of Paul (Rom 5:12ff.; 1 Cor 15:21ff., 45ff.). But Paul never explicitly says that Adam passed on a sinful nature to future generations. In Romans 5:12 (NASB) he says, "Therefore, just as through one man sin entered the world and death through sin, and so death spread to all men because all sinned."[43] While Adam is responsible for sin and death entering the world, it spreads to "all men" because all of them sin, not because they were predestined to do so. Physical death is a consequence of the Fall, but spiritual death is based on the choice of human beings to sin. In 1 Corinthians 15:21,22 (NASB) Paul says, "For since by a man came death, by a man also came the resurrection of the dead. For as in Adam all die, so also in Christ all will be made alive." For this text to be saying that all who are born of Adam spiritually die because they inherit sin from him. it must also be affirming universalism. If "all" sin in Adam and sin is universal, then by Paul's logic "all" are made alive in Christ, i.e., "all" will be saved. Since this clearly contradicts the rest of Scripture which does not teach universal salvation, Paul must be saying something else. In the context he is talking about the physical death of the body and the physical resurrection of it, not spiritual death and spiritual resurrection. Paul could be saying something like, "those who follow Adam in sinning receive Adam's penalty, death, while those who follow Christ receive Christ's reward for faithfulness, resurrection." Barr comments on this:

> . . . when we go back to the Old Testament, we find two similarly significant facts. Firstly, after the story of Adam and Eve is first narrated in Genesis, nowhere in the books of the Hebrew canon does anyone go back to that incident in order to use it as an explanation for the origin of sin, evil, and death.

---

[43]Paul here never completes the sentence grammatically as is common in his epistles.

It just does not happen. . . . The Hebrew Bible is certainly deeply conscious of the actuality and pervasiveness of sin and evil. But nowhere in all the books of the Hebrew canon is the existence or profundity of evil accounted for on the grounds that Adam's disobedience originated it or made it inevitable. It is not surprising, therefore, that Judaism, as we know it, has no doctrine corresponding to the Christian traditions of "original sin," no idea that sin and evil exist as a heritage passed on from the first human beings.[44]

Certainly the world after the Fall is distorted and damaged by human sin and the LORD's judgment on it. But evil is not so pervasive that human beings have no choice but to sin, and there certainly is no suggestion in Genesis that children inherit a sin nature. The LORD expects Cain to be able to fight off the sin that desires to control him.

C. GRACE IN THE MIDST OF JUDGMENT (3:20-24)

[20]Adam[a] named his wife Eve,[b] because she would become the mother of all the living.
[21]The LORD God made garments of skin for Adam and his wife and clothed them. [22]And the LORD God said, "The man has now become like one of us, knowing good and evil. He must not be allowed to reach out his hand and take also from the tree of life and eat, and live forever." [23]So the LORD God banished him from the Garden of Eden to work the ground from which he had been taken. [24]After he drove the man out, he placed on the east side[c] of the Garden of Eden cherubim and a flaming sword flashing back and forth to guard the way to the tree of life.

[a]*20 Or The man*   [b]*20 Eve probably means living.*   [c]*24 Or placed in front*

This section narrates events after the announcing of judgment by the LORD. The effects of the Fall continue to be felt as Adam regards his woman as a subordinate by naming her. But the LORD's forgiveness and grace are also evident. He personally clothes them

---

[44]James Barr, *Biblical Faith and Natural Theology* (Oxford: Clarendon, 1993), p. x. Similar thoughts occur in Barr, *Garden of Eden*, p. 6.

with garments of skin which will do a much better job of covering them than the fig leaves. He also banishes them from the garden. This at first seems like another judgment, and in some senses it is. But in reality this, too, is an act of grace. Not wanting humanity to be forever stuck in never-ending alienation with him, with each other, and with creation, the expulsion from the garden and the denial of access to eternal life prevents humanity being trapped. With free access to the direct presence of the LORD God but without a relationship that would desire access, eternal life would be a never-ending series of experiences of fearing the LORD without ever enjoying his presence. Death, though undesirable from one point of view, at least ends the alienation and frustration of a cursed creation and a cursed humanity.

3:20 Adam named his wife Eve, because she would become the mother of all the living.

The fact that Adam gives a name to his partner is often taken as some sort of indication of her subservient role. If this is so,[45] then the fact that Adam only names Eve after the Fall is highly significant. As I have argued above, a form of subordination is one of the consequences of the Fall. This subordination is not what the LORD intended in creation but is a tragic consequence of a broken world in which the strong dominate the weak.

But while the act of naming may carry connotations of subjugation, the name that Adam chooses seems to be an affirmation of faith. Humanity was commanded in chapter 1 to be fruitful and multiply. In naming the woman "Eve" (which means something like "life"[46]) Adam expresses faith that at least part of the creation commission will be realized. She will be bringing forth life.

---

[45]In fact G.W. Ramsey ["Is Name-Giving an Act of Domination in Genesis 2:23 and Elsewhere?" *CBQ* 50 (1988): 34] has argued that "taken all together, the evidence indicates that, instead of thinking of name-giving as a *determiner* of an entity's essence, the Hebrews regarded naming as commonly *determined* by circumstances." While I am not necessarily persuaded by Ramsey's arguments, his work does give one pause about a false sense of certainty about exegetical conclusions that are inferences.

[46]See the careful discussion of Richard S. Hess, *Studies in the Personal Names of Genesis 1–11,* AOAT (Neukirchen-Vluyn: Neukirchen Verlag, 1993), pp. 19-24.

3:21 The LORD God made garments of skin for Adam and his wife and clothed them.

Since von Rad this has been viewed as an amelioration of divine punishment with divine grace. The garments cover the nakedness of Adam and his wife because they are now ashamed of it. The garments of skin (lit., "tunics") are far superior and longer lasting than the fig-leaf apron invented by the man and the woman. This text has led to much speculation. Spina wonders,

> One recalls that the human couple clothed themselves with the products of vegetation — fig leaves — after their disobedience (Gen 3,7), while God subsequently clothed them with skins, i.e. animal products (3,21). Was the deity thereby demonstrating that animals were available to human beings in ways they had not previously considered?[47]

Speculation abounds as to what sort of skin the garments were made from. Targum Pseudo-Jonathan to Genesis 3:21 has it that the garments of glory were made from the "skin cast off by the serpent."[48] Ginzberg refers to an unknown Midrash which argued that the skin was from Leviathan.[49] Lambden discusses speculation that the original "clothing" of Adam was a transparent coat of fingernails and that our fingernails are the only remnants of the original glorious "clothing."[50] Wolde notes the similarity between the Hebrew word for "animal skins" (עוֹר, 'ôr) and the two words in obvious wordplay, "naked" (עֲרוּמִּים, 'ărûmîm) and "crafty" (עָרוּם, 'ārûm). She, rather fancifully suggests:

> While the serpent helped the human being to become aware of his nakedness, the other animals helped him to cover that nakedness. As the serpent does not possess a furry skin, it is

---

[47]F.A. Spina, "The 'Ground' for Cain's Rejection (Gen 4): 'adamah in the Context of Gen 1–11," *ZAW* 104 (1992): 319-332.

[48]Lambden, "From Fig Leaves," p. 86.

[49]Quoted in Lambden.

[50]Exodus 20:26 commands priests to be clothed when offering sacrifices at the altar. Intertestamental and early Christian era literature refer, based on a literalistic reading of Ezek 28:11-15, to the priestly garments of Adam. Adam was evidently believed to be clothed with jewels. The LXX at Ezek 28:13 lists twelve jewels, the number set on the high priest's breastplate instead of the nine precious jewels of MT.

not suited for clothing the human being. But because of the frequent shedding of its skin, the serpent is suited for the function of intermediary of the knowledge of ever-renewing life.[51]

Clearly the Bible is far less interested in such questions than we are.

3:22 And the LORD God said, "The man has now become like one of us, knowing good and evil. He must not be allowed to reach out his hand and take also from the tree of life and eat, and live forever."

Now that the man and the woman have intimate knowledge of good and evil, and in that respect they are like divine beings, the LORD realizes the difficulty they are in. If they were to live forever in such a state without any hope of it ending, that would be tragic. The knowledge they have received through disobedience to the LORD has damaged them. They are ashamed of themselves, afraid of the LORD, and embarrassed to be in each other's presence. In what seems at first sight as a protective statement[52] designed to keep humanity from the divine status which the LORD has, there is actually grace. There must be an end to the brokenness. It must not go on forever.

3:23 So the LORD God banished him from the Garden of Eden to work the ground from which he had been taken.

Because[53] the LORD God did not want to leave humanity eternally in their broken state, he sends[54] them from the garden to "work the ground." The Hebrew text of this phrase reads literally, "to serve the ground." Adam, who was created from the ground, had acted in

---

[51]Wolde, *Words Become Worlds*, p. 12.

[52]This passage has parallels to Gen 11:6 "Look, they are one people, and they have all one language; and this is only the beginning of what they will do; nothing that they propose to do will now be impossible for them." Both of these passages can be taken out of the wider biblical context and interpreted in such a way as to portray the LORD as an insecure deity trying to protect his turf. But that can only be done at the expense of the wider biblical portrait of God as all-powerful and all-knowing and having no insecurities. That the text could be read in this way, and is sometimes so read in deconstructive readings, should serve as a warning to keep the larger biblical context in view when interpreting a specific passage. That principle is especially important here.

[53]The waw-consecutive here can be read as either a logical or temporal result.

[54]The Hebrew uses a piel (intensive) of the common verb שָׁלַח (šālaḥ).

such a way that the ground was cursed. That cursed ground would now be Adam's master. He would "serve"[55] it. While the man was to "serve" the ground before the Fall, he must now do so in its cursed state, and that will prove to be frustrating and difficult.

It is to be noticed that the text only mentions the man being sent out, although clearly the wider context indicates that both the man and the woman were banished. It may be that the Hebrew is using the word הָאָדָם (hā'ādām) in a double sense. The man stands for humanity as a whole even though he is spoken of as though singular.

3:24 After he drove the man out, he placed on the east side of the Garden of Eden cherubim and a flaming sword flashing back and forth to guard the way to the tree of life.

Since the original humans were driven out of Eden to the east, it is on the east that the entrance to the garden is guarded by the cherubim. Cherubim (the singular is cherub) are winged creatures who live in the direct presence of God. While traditional interpretation assumes that they are angels, this is nowhere stated in Scripture. The tradition that angels have wings, despite every description of an actual angel in the Bible looking like a man and not having wings, comes from assuming that cherubim and the similar seraphim of Isaiah 6 are angels. The cherubim serve as a warning and as an impediment to sinful human beings presuming that it is permissible for them to walk into the unmediated presence of the LORD.

The tabernacle/temple imagery of both creation accounts is perhaps most obvious here. The tabernacle was entered from the east, and cherubim "guarded" the way to the direct presence of God.[56]

---

[55]Heb. עבד ('bd).
[56]See the excursus on the Garden of Eden and tabernacle imagery in chapter 2.

GENESIS 4

III. HUMAN SOCIETY WITHOUT THE DIVINE-HUMAN RELATIONSHIP (4:1-26)

¹Adam[a] lay with his wife Eve, and she became pregnant and gave birth to Cain.[b] She said, "With the help of the LORD I have brought forth[c] a man." ²Later she gave birth to his brother Abel.

Now Abel kept flocks, and Cain worked the soil. ³In the course of time Cain brought some of the fruits of the soil as an offering to the LORD. ⁴But Abel brought fat portions from some of the firstborn of his flock. The LORD looked with favor on Abel and his offering, ⁵but on Cain and his offering he did not look with favor. So Cain was very angry, and his face was downcast.

⁶Then the LORD said to Cain, "Why are you angry? Why is your face downcast? ⁷If you do what is right, will you not be accepted? But if you do not do what is right, sin is crouching at your door; it desires to have you, but you must master it."

⁸Now Cain said to his brother Abel, "Let's go out to the field."[d] And while they were in the field, Cain attacked his brother Abel and killed him.

⁹Then the LORD said to Cain, "Where is your brother Abel?"

"I don't know," he replied. "Am I my brother's keeper?"

¹⁰The LORD said, "What have you done? Listen! Your brother's blood cries out to me from the ground. ¹¹Now you are under a curse and driven from the ground, which opened its mouth to receive your brother's blood from your hand. ¹²When you work the ground, it will no longer yield its crops for you. You will be a restless wanderer on the earth."

¹³Cain said to the LORD, "My punishment is more than I can bear. ¹⁴Today you are driving me from the land, and I will be hidden from your presence; I will be a restless wanderer on the earth, and whoever finds me will kill me."

¹⁵But the LORD said to him, "Not soᵉ; if anyone kills Cain, he will suffer vengeance seven times over." Then the LORD put a mark on Cain so that no one who found him would kill him. ¹⁶So Cain went out from the Lord's presence and lived in the land of Nod,ᶠ east of Eden.

ᵃ*1* Or *The man*   ᵇ*1 Cain* sounds like the Hebrew for *brought forth* or *acquired.*   ᶜ*1* Or *have acquired*   ᵈ*8* Samaritan Pentateuch, Septuagint, Vulgate and Syriac; Masoretic Text does not have *"Let's go out to the field."*   ᵉ*15* Septuagint, Vulgate and Syriac; Hebrew *Very well*   ᶠ*16 Nod* means *wandering* (see verses 12 and 14).

This text describes human life outside of the Garden, east of Eden.¹ The curse which the LORD has announced on humanity, both male and female, as well as the animal kingdom and the creation in chapter 3 begins to play itself out. In childbirth Eve experiences for the first time the distorting effects of the Fall. Adam and Eve and their children have to struggle with the cursed ground to eke out a living. The first child mentioned from the union of Adam and Eve kills the second child. Wenham helpfully summarizes the ideology of this chapter:

> However the immediate sequel to the Garden of Eden story is gloomy. The Cain and Abel story contains many echoes of Genesis 2 and 3, all to the detriment of Cain. His offence is not only more serious than his father's, but he is the more brazen and impenitent sinner. But if he was bad, Lamech several generations later was much worse still, bragging to his two wives 'If Cain is avenged sevenfold, truly Lamech seventy-sevenfold' (4:24).²

Cain and his descendants have a checkered history. On the one hand they are given credit for some of the fundamental tools of civilization. Cain is the first person mentioned to live in a city. His descendants are portrayed as pioneers in music, metallurgy, and nomadic shepherding. But from his line there also flows the first recorded case of polygamy. It ends with Lamech who would dare to presume upon God's grace to Cain in order to escape culpability for

---

¹John Steinbeck's *East of Eden* is a sort of meditation on this passage, especially ch. 24 and the end where it is explicit.
²Wenham, *Genesis 1–15*, p. 33.

his own violence. The contemporary reader must be careful not to import into this text her or his own assumptions about progress and modernity. We live in an era in which technology and urbanization permeate our lives and can scarcely imagine it being any other way. But urban centers in the ancient world were centers of imperial power and the violence which undergirded them, whether it be economic, military, or sexual in nature. The same steel can be turned into a surgeon's scalpel or a gun, and this text reflects the ambiguity of technology and progress.

A. THE SACRIFICES OF CAIN AND ABEL (4:1-7)

1. The Birth of Cain and Abel (4:1-2a)

4:1 Adam lay with his wife Eve, and she became pregnant and gave birth to Cain. She said, "With the help of the LORD I have brought forth a man."

The Hebrew reads literally, "Adam *knew* his wife and she became pregnant." The Hebrew word "know" (יָדַע, *yādāʻ*) often connotes personal or even intimate knowledge as here. The curse on woman in Genesis 3:16 begins to play itself out as she experiences extraordinary pain in childbirth. Her statement which the NIV renders as "with the help of the LORD I have brought forth a man" is difficult. In Hebrew it contains a wordplay between the verb translated "I have brought forth" (in Hebrew קָנִיתִי, *qnyty*) and the proper name, Cain (in Hebrew קַיִן, *qyn*). Wenham (*ad loc.*) suggests "Cain, with the help of the LORD I have gained" as a way of bringing the wordplay over to English. Cain's name may mean "smith" and may allude forward to his descendants who were the first to perfect metallurgy. This is, however, uncertain and based on parallels in Arabic from a different time period.[3]

The use of the Hebrew word אֵת (*'eth*, NIV "with the help of") is perplexing. Usually this word is used as a sign that the next word is the beginning of the direct object of the sentence and is therefore left untranslated. Occasionally the word is a preposition meaning "with." If we assume that the word is the sign of the direct object, we

---
[3]Hess, *Studies*, pp. 24-25.

would translate, "I have gained a man, the LORD." Cain is thus viewed by Eve as the LORD himself. But this requires an unusual construal of the Hebrew, and it seems more likely that the word *'eth* is the preposition "with." The meaning would then be, "I have gotten a man with (the help of) the LORD." This could then be construed as an act of praise for the LORD's help through the difficult and painful process of childbirth.

But these words could also be understood in a way which is less complimentary to Eve. Cassuto, among others, argues for the translation, "I have created a man equally with the Lord,"[4] which implies arrogance on Eve's part. Sailhamer contrasts Eve's words here with her words in 4:25.[5] Here she takes credit for the birth of the child; in 4:25 she speaks of what God has done for her. From this Sailhamer infers an attitude change on the part of Eve. She comes to accept God's gift gratefully and gives up on the attempt to accomplish God's work for him. This text would then be the first of many texts in Genesis in which the folly of humankind trying to do what only God can do is highlighted. The creature resisting the Creator is a common theme in Genesis.

The text is ambiguous at this point and Eve's words could be construed as either a statement of grateful praise or as a somewhat presumptuous and arrogant statement in which Eve does not acknowledge the Creator's primacy.

4:2a Later she gave birth to his brother Abel.

The Hebrew word transliterated as the name Abel, probably means something ephemeral like "breath" or "vapor." Perhaps this is a hint to the reader that his life will not last long. It is the word translated "vanity" in Ecclesiastes' famous discourse on the seeming meaninglessness of life.

2. The First Offerings to the Lord (4:2b-4a)

4:2b Now Abel kept flocks, and Cain worked the soil.

The occupations of the brothers are given to prepare the reader

---

[4]Umberto Cassuto, *A Commentary on the Book of Genesis. Part One: From Adam to Noah* (Jerusalem: Magnes Press, 1961), pp. 198-199.
[5]Sailhamer, *Genesis*, pp. 60-61.

for the story to come. Cain's occupation is literally "servant of the ground." While this phrase can mean simply "farmer," it is possible that it echoes the curse on the ground because of Adam's sin (3:17). Cain serves the cursed ground as a consequence of his father's disobedience. Abel's occupation may also hint that we are being introduced to the distorted life outside of the garden, east of Eden. At creation humanity is given plants for food (Gen 1:29; 2:9). Here animals have become a food source. While domesticating sheep and breeding them for food is not the same thing as a deep-seated conflict between humanity and the animal kingdom, it is possible that it is to be viewed as a step along the road to that conflict. That conflict was anticipated in the curse on the serpent. Animals are explicitly given as a food source to humanity only after the Flood in Genesis 9:3.

But perhaps the entire discussion of vegetarianism as an either/or issue is too simplistic. In the ancient world most people were vegetarians most of the time out of necessity. But there were exceptional times such as at feasts when meat was eaten. Perhaps the intended audience would read this narrative in that way. Sacrifices were exceptions to a typically vegetarian existence which would have been the experience of the intended audience.

4:3 In the course of time Cain brought some of the fruits of the soil as an offering to the LORD.

The estrangement in the relationship between God and humankind implied in chapter 3 is escalating. Instead of intimate conversations and immediate access, humankind east of Eden must now come to the LORD with or through an offering. Interestingly the text does not inform us as to how Cain and Abel knew that offerings were expected. The imagined audience, Israel about to enter the promised land, would undoubtedly see something significant here. The sacrifices that they were commanded to perform in the Laws revealed at Sinai were not new inventions imposed by an arbitrary God who suddenly had a whim. Instead the particular sacrifices they were commanded to bring were specific embodiments of the principles of how a sinful and fallen humanity relates to a holy God east of Eden. They are based upon principles from the earliest days of humanity's relationship with God in a fallen world.

The phrase translated "in the course of time" is literally, "And it was from the end of days." Why? What does this mean? Is this related to eschatology in some fashion? The phrase can, however, refer to a specific time such as a year.⁶ After the year of planting the harvesting of the grains would supply Cain with something to bring.

The word "some" seems innocuous enough, until the reader compares it with the description of Abel's offering. When read in light of the entire Pentateuch, the implication seems clear that Cain did not obey the most basic principle of sacrifice, give the first and the best. Cain did not give the firstfruits, but only "some" of the fruits. Behind Cain's actions lies an attitude which is problematic.

Commentators have speculated for centuries on the problem with Cain's offering. Among the more well known views are: 1) God prefers shepherds to gardeners (Gunkel); 2) animal offerings are more acceptable than vegetable; 3) the mystery of divine election — pattern of choice of younger over older; 4) Hebrews 11:4 — "by faith" the attitude of Cain was wrong; 5) Cain's offering came from the cursed ground and therefore is to be viewed as something not acceptable as a sacrifice to a holy God; 6) Abel offered the firstlings while Cain just offered some, not necessarily the firstfruits. Gunkel's view has few supporters today. The law allows for vegetable sacrifices as well as animal sacrifices so it seems unlikely that the imagined audience would think of this view. The mystery of divine election reading is weakened by the fact that God only starts the process of election in the time of Abram. This view seems to read the later development of election as a divine strategy into a text which depicts circumstances where divine election is not yet operating. Certainly Cain's attitude is wrong (view 4) and the outworking of the cursing of the ground⁷ is a motif in this passage (view 5). But view 6 seems to make the most sense for an imagined audience that has recently received the law at Sinai. The principle of giving God the first and best is based on the notion that ultimately as Creator he already owns it all and is deserving of our very best when we acknowledge his ownership.

---

⁶Westermann, *Genesis*, p. 294.

⁷Spina, "The 'Ground,'" pp. 319-332, argues that God rejects Cain's offering for no discernible reason, but it is Cain's reaction to that rejection which is the issue. He then moves on to argue that it is the fact that Cain's offering is from the ground cursed by Yahweh in chapter 3 that results in the rejection. He then notes how often the Hebrew word *'adamah* occurs in this text (4:3,10,11,12).

4:4a But Abel brought fat portions from some of the firstborn of his flock.

Abel's offering was from the firstlings [pl] and from the fat of them [pl]. The plurals may imply an abundant offering as opposed to a minimal one. In Israel the fat portions were regarded as the best portions and were specifically reserved for the LORD. The contrast between Abel's offering (fat portions of the firstborn) and Cain's (some of the fruits) would have been especially obvious to the ancient audience. Abel gave the first and the best while Cain just gave some.

3. The LORD's Evaluation of the Offerings (4:4b-5a)

4:4b The LORD looked with favor on Abel and his offering,

The terminology "fat portions from some of the firstborn of his flock" is reminiscent of the law and is likely another evidence of the anticipation of the law in Genesis. Other examples include Noah's knowledge of clean and unclean animals, Abraham's and Jacob's tithing, and the parallels between the tabernacle and the garden of Eden. The point of these anticipations of the law seems to be that the law given to Israel after they come out of Egypt is not to be regarded as something that is given out of the blue, but is based on the most ancient principles of humankind's relationship to the LORD.

4:5a but on Cain and his offering he did not look with favor.

In 2 Samuel 24:24 David is quoted as saying, "I will not offer burnt offerings to the Lord . . . that cost me nothing." Since this is the first reference to offerings in the Bible, it is not surprising that this fundamental principle is highlighted. Cain did not give the first and best as Abel did.

4. Cain's Reaction to the Rejection of His Offering (4:5b)

4:5b So Cain was very angry, and his face was downcast.

Cain's reaction shows a wrong attitude toward God. It is the creator's prerogative to decide what is acceptable in sacrifice and what is not acceptable. For Cain to be angry and to express that anger in violence shows a completely distorted view of a human being's relationship with God. Human beings are not in competition with each other for a relationship with God. God's love for one does not diminish his love for someone else. Our only competition should be with the person we used to be.

5. The LORD Warns Cain about His Reaction (4:6-7)

4:6 Then the LORD said to Cain, "Why are you angry? Why is your face downcast?

The LORD confronts Cain with his attitude. Cain expects God to accept his gift whatever it might be. When he does not, Cain's anger and downcast face show his wrong attitude toward God. How often, when confronted with our own sin, our tendency is to react with defensive anger and bitterness toward others and God. The Lord addresses the manifestations of the attitude, anger and a downcast face, through a series of questions. What right does Cain have to be angry? None. Why should his face be downcast? Cain brought God's rejection of his sacrifice upon himself.

4:7 If you do what is right, will you not be accepted? But if you do not do what is right, sin is crouching at your door; it desires to have you, but you must master it."

While the NIV's "right" gets at the sense of God's question, literally the Hebrew reads "good." Whatever we conclude was wrong with Cain's offering, he did not do something good in offering it.[8] The LORD assumes that even in a fallen world east of Eden Cain is able, and therefore accountable, to do good.[9] Sin is here spoken of as though it was a crouching animal ready to pounce upon Cain unexpectedly. If Cain does what is good, sin will have no power over

---

[8]Whatever was wrong with Cain's offering, this verse makes it clear that his actions were not good. The popular idea that there was nothing wrong just because it is challenging to discover cannot be sustained.

[9]Brueggemann (*Genesis*, p. 56) helpfully comments: "The first alternative, 'to do well,' is instructive. It suggests that a post-Genesis 3 man can do well (cf. Amos 5:15). He is not "fallen." He is not victim of any original sin. He can choose and act for the good. Such an affirmation by the narrator suggests that chapter 3 must not be permitted to control chapter 4. Cain in this story is free and capable of faithful living."

him. If, however, he does not, sin will pounce on him and consume him. Sin "desires" to control Cain just as the woman[10] would desire to control her husband (Gen 3:16). Cain is able and is expected to master the sin which desires to control him.

B. THE ONSET AND PUNISHMENT OF VIOLENCE (4:8-12)

1. Cain Becomes the First Murderer (4:8)

4:8 Now Cain said to his brother Abel, "Let's go out to the field." And while they were in the field, Cain attacked his brother Abel and killed him.

By describing the location of the murder of Abel as "in the field" the narrator may be suggesting that Cain's offense was punishable by death. Crimes committed in the field away from the help of others are regarded in the law as indicative of premeditation (Deut 22:23-27). The narrator carefully describes Abel twice as "his brother" in order to show the special heinousness of the crime.

2. The LORD Confronts Cain for His Violence (4:9)

4:9 Then the LORD said to Cain, "Where is your brother Abel?" "I don't know," he replied. "Am I my brother's keeper?"

As in chapter 3, when God is confronting sin he already knows about, he begins by asking questions. As in verse 8 twice Abel is referred to as "brother." The word "keeper" means "guardian" (participle of שׁמר, *šmr*). Cain claims that he has no responsibility to protect and guard his brother, all the while hiding the fact that not only has he not protected him but has brutally murdered him. The "Fall" of Adam and Eve does not remove the freedom of humanity, but the effects of the distorted and fallen world begin to make themselves known. Just as Adam and Eve deflected responsibility for their sin, so also does Cain. But Cain goes further. He, unlike Adam and Eve,

---

[10]The Hebrew word for desire (תְּשׁוּקָה, *t°šûqāh*) is a rare one and occurs only in these two texts (Gen. 3:16; 4:7) in the Pentateuch and only once elsewhere.

refuses to acknowledge the sin when confronted with it. The portrayal of the escalation of evil "east of Eden" has begun. The violence which escalates until it is temporarily wiped out in the Flood begins here. It is ironic that the first baby born of the human process of birth kills the second one and is banished. The effects of sin are also shown in that Cain refuses to accept the fact that we as human beings are created to protect and guard each other.

3. The LORD's Punishment of Cain for His Violence (4:10-12)

4:10 The LORD said, "What have you done? Listen! Your brother's blood cries out to me from the ground.

The LORD does not ask the question, "What have you done?" because he needed information. It appears to mean something like, "Do you understand the magnitude of your actions? Do you know what you have set in motion by your petty jealousy and senseless violence?" Once again Abel is referred to as Cain's "brother." The blood which Cain shed was that of someone with the closest of relationships to him. The audience, who had recently received the law, would understand the metaphor of blood crying out to the LORD from the ground. Wenham helpfully explains:

> Compressed into [these words] is a whole theology whose principles inform much of the criminal and cultic law of Israel. Life is in the blood (Lev. 17:11), so shed blood is the most polluting of all substances. Consequently, un-atoned-for murders pollute the holy land, making it unfit for the divine presence. To prevent such a catastrophe, the cities of refuge were established (Num 35:9-34; Deut 19:1-13). In cases where the murderer could not be traced, the rite prescribed in Deut 21:1-9 had to be carried out. Because man is made in God's image, homicide must be avenged (Gen 9:5). Here Abel's blood is pictured "crying" to God for vengeance. [The Hebrew word] צעק "cry" is the desperate cry of men without food (Gen 41:55), expecting to die (Exod 14:10), or oppressed by their enemies (Judg 4:3). It is the scream for help of a woman being raped (Deut 22:24,27). It is the plea to God of the victims of injustice (Exod 22:22 [23],26,27). The law, the prophets (Isa 19:20; cf. 5:7), and the Psalms (34:18[17]; 106:28) unite with narratives

like this (cf. 2 Sam 23; 1 Kgs 21) to assert that God does hear his people's desperate cries for help.[11]

Abel's life turns out to be just a vapor because of Cain's cynical violence. If his sacrifice is not acceptable to the LORD, no one's sacrifice will be! Such violence stains the promised land. The inhabitants of Canaan perpetuate such violence, and Israel must take great care that she not continue the pattern. Just as Cain is to be banished from the land for such violence, so also the Canaanites are to be banished. Israel, however, is not exempt. Should they perpetuate such violence, they too will be vomited out, just like the Canaanites (Lev 18:25-28). The canonical audience, who has experienced this firsthand in the exile, knows the truth of this. Chosen people or not, a society which lives by violence will be ground into the dust of history.

4:11 Now you are under a curse and driven from the ground, which opened its mouth to receive your brother's blood from your hand.

The punishment fits the crime. Cain's offering was from the ground. That offering was not acceptable, and in anger and jealousy he lashed out at his brother and put his blood in that same ground. Cain's curse is therefore a curse on the ground. But it is an intensification of the original curse on the ground. For Cain, it is not only that making a living from the ground would be difficult (as it was to be for Adam); now it would be impossible. Cain is under a further curse and driven from the ground from which he had obtained his livelihood. That ground was designed to receive the seeds of plants which would produce food. Cain used it to hide his own violence. The gift of God, though cursed in chapter 3, is still a gift. Cain turns it into a means of hiding his own sin much as Adam and Eve hid their own nakedness with fig leaves. Yet again Abel is referred to as Cain's brother to reinforce the seriousness of his sin.

4:12 When you work the ground, it will no longer yield its crops for you. You will be a restless wanderer on the earth."

God's curse is an intensifying of the original curse on the ground. In Eden Adam could freely eat of the fruit of the trees of the garden without the slow and toilsome labor necessary to grow

---

[11]Wenham, *Genesis 1-15*, p. 107.

one's own food. East of Eden the ground is cursed, and only by hard labor will it yield enough to live on. But Cain will not even be able to work hard to live. Instead he is sentenced to restless wandering on the earth.[12]

C. THE MITIGATION OF THE PUNISHMENT (4:13-16)

1. Cain's Plea to the LORD (4:13-14)

4:13 Cain said to the LORD, "My punishment is more than I can bear.

This text is usually read as though Cain, who has just murdered his own brother, is trying to evade the consequences of his callous actions. He wants to avoid such strict punishment. The word translated "punishment" (עֲוֹנִי, *'ăwōnî*) could be translated as "sin." If translated as "sin" here, it would imply an expression of regret and a plea for mercy on Cain's part. This would make God's merciful response seem less mysterious. It is impossible to be certain, but it is intriguing to ponder the notion that even Cain may have regrets for his sinful actions. The word, however, usually refers to the consequences of sin whether that be guilt or punishment rather than the sin by itself. I would favor the NIV's rendering here, "punishment" which would imply that Cain wants to minimize the consequences of his own actions.

4:14 Today you are driving me from the land, and I will be hidden from your presence; I will be a restless wanderer on the earth, and whoever finds me will kill me."

A literalistic translation might read, "Here, you drive me away today from the *face* of the soil, and from your *face* must I conceal myself." Notice the play on the word "face." Exactly who the people are whom Cain fears will kill him has been the source of much inventive exegesis. The text as we have it shows no interest in the question. It merely presumes that other people are present without

---

[12]Everett Fox (*The Five Books of Moses*, Schocken Bible, vol. 1 [New York: Schocken Books, 1995], p. 27) has "wavering and wandering must you be on the earth" as an attempt to bring over the assonance of the Hebrew נָע וָנָד (*nā' wānād*).

explaining how that came about. Part of the responsibility of reading the Scriptures faithfully is to recognize what Scripture regards as important and to focus on those questions and not our idle curiosities. The early chapters of Genesis are not an attempt to answer every curious question which might arise but to focus on the meaning and theology of the pre-Abrahamic world for Israel newly in the promised land.

Whether Cain is repentant or regretful of the consequences of his actions, he does say that lack of access to God's presence is an intolerable thing. The canonical audience would relate to being driven from the land and being hidden from God's presence. They had experienced those things in exile. Even the imagined audience would relate to their time in Egypt as a sort of exile away from the land promised to their forefathers. While in exile or in Egypt they did not have free access to worship the LORD.

Part of Cain's argument against his sentence is that it will result in further acts of violence when he is found out and killed, presumably in revenge for the murder of Abel. Violence usually begets more violence. If violence stains the land with blood, the revenge of that violence will stain it even further.

2. The Protective Sign for Cain (4:15)

4:15 But the LORD said to him, "Not so; if anyone kills Cain, he will suffer vengeance seven times over." Then the LORD put a mark on Cain so that no one who found him would kill him.

The final argument of Cain is accepted by the LORD. In order to contain the outbreak of violence the LORD warns of severe, sevenfold repercussions.

The mark of Cain may not be anything on his person. The Hebrew word for 'mark' is often to be translated as 'sign.' If understood in this way, we should perhaps translate, "The LORD made a sign for Cain." Sailhamer suggests that the sign is the city which Cain builds. He suggests that the audience would understand this as a sort of "prototype" of the later cities of refuge (Numbers 35).[13] The cities of refuge were places where someone who had killed someone

---

[13]Sailhamer, *Genesis*, p. 67.

might flee to avoid immediate revenge killings. Those who killed someone accidentally were allowed to take up residence there while those eventually found guilty of murder through the legal system would receive punishment. This interpretation is suggestive and would make this narrative especially relevant to the imagined audience, but it is impossible to be certain about it.

In the history of interpretation the mark of Cain has sometimes been assumed to be black skin. Since black-skinned people were enslaved in large numbers, it was assumed that they must be under God's judgment. This perplexing misreading warns us of the potential for the Bible to be abused to support whatever oppressive social practice we are guilty of. This reading makes no sense of the narrative. There is no reason to believe that the mark of Cain was some genetic change which affected future generations even if we assume it was a physical mark and not a sign. Even if it was some genetic change, it was presumably wiped out in the Flood.

3. Cain Settles East of Eden (4:16)

4:16 So Cain went out from the LORD's presence and lived in the land of Nod, east of Eden.

The Hebrew for Nod is from the same root as "wandering" in verse 12. A preferable way to translate this verse may be, "So Cain went out from the LORD's presence and lived in the land of wandering, east of Eden." When human beings move to the east in these chapters, it not only signifies geography but is a sign of their moving further and further away from God.

D. THE FAMILY HISTORY FROM CAIN TO LAMECH (4:17-24)

17Cain lay with his wife, and she became pregnant and gave birth to Enoch. Cain was then building a city, and he named it after his son Enoch. 18To Enoch was born Irad, and Irad was the father of Mehujael, and Mehujael was the father of Methushael, and Methushael was the father of Lamech.

19Lamech married two women, one named Adah and the other Zillah. 20Adah gave birth to Jabal; he was the father of those who

live in tents and raise livestock. ²¹His brother's name was Jubal; he was the father of all who play the harp and flute. ²²Zillah also had a son, Tubal-Cain, who forged all kinds of tools out of ᵃ bronze and iron. Tubal-Cain's sister was Naamah.

²³Lamech said to his wives,

"Adah and Zillah, listen to me;
wives of Lamech, hear my words.
I have killed ᵇ a man for wounding me,
a young man for injuring me.
²⁴If Cain is avenged seven times,
then Lamech seventy-seven times."

ᵃ22 Or *who instructed all who work in*   ᵇ23 Or *I will kill*

This passage is the first of the Bible's famous genealogies. While I have discussed the nature of biblical genealogies in more detail in chapter 10, here a few brief remarks will hopefully help to orient the reader. Robert Wilson discusses the Genealogy of the Hammurapi Dynasty and the Assyrian King List along with research from "contemporary primitive" genealogies for insight into the forms and functions of ancient genealogies.[14] Anthropologists say that oral genealogies have two forms: segmented (several lines are traced simultaneously for breadth) and linear (a single line is traced for depth). Segmented ones have at least two generations but such depth is not the chief characteristic as in linear genealogies. Both types of genealogies are fluid and change with circumstances and needs. Genealogies function in the domestic sphere where kinship terminology can represent biological ties or status or economic or geographical relationships. Such genealogies are segmented. They also function in the politico-juridical sphere where monarchical forms of government are legitimated by linear genealogies or in nonmonarchical governments by segmented ones. They also function in the religious sphere. He comments:

> In any given society, genealogies may function in more than one of the three spheres mentioned above. Therefore, it would

---

[14]Robert R. Wilson, "The Old Testament Genealogies in Recent Research," in *I Studied Inscriptions from before the Flood: Ancient Near Eastern, Literary, and Linguistic Approaches to Genesis 1–11*, ed. by Richard S. Hess and David Tsumura (Winona Lake, IN: Eisenbrauns, 1994), pp. 200-223.

be possible for a society to have a number of apparently conflicting genealogies, each of which could be considered accurate in terms of its function. The structure of the society for political purposes may well be different from the structure of the society for domestic or religious purposes, and for this reason genealogies functioning politically may be different from genealogies functioning in other spheres. It would be a mistake to ask which of the conflicting genealogies is historically accurate. All of them are accurate when their differing functions are taken into consideration.[15]

It may well be that some or all of these characteristics are true of biblical genealogies. For example genealogical fluidity may help explain the striking similarities between this genealogy in chapter 4 of Cain's line and the genealogy of Seth's line in chapter 5.[16] However, the similarities could as easily be explained as a way of making the comparison and contrast between the lines of Cain and Seth all that much more apparent. The two lines share much in common, but they are very different. The two names which appear in both genealogies, Enoch and Lamech, are given additional commentary so as to avoid confusion between them.

This passage may also have a polemical intent. Mesopotamian tradition tells of seven *apkallus*, sages, who lived before the Flood and taught humanity the arts of civilization. The parallels between Genesis 4:17-26 and such extrabiblical traditions are too distant to suggest direct borrowing. It is possible, though, that the author knew something of these ideas and wanted to critique them. For the author technology was a human achievement, not something given to humanity by one of the gods. It therefore carries with it all the

---

[15]Ibid., pp. 214-215.

[16]On the similarities between this genealogy and the one in chapter 5, David T. Bryant, "A Reevaluation of Gen 4 and 5 in Light of Recent Studies in Genealogical Fluidity," *ZAW* 99 (1987): 180-188, argues that the similarities are more easily explained by two originally separate genealogies which have conflated toward each other over time. This is because of the numerous differences between the two genealogies as well as similarities; the notion of a Flood hero in Seth's line, the inclusion of a final segmented generation with a female element in Cain's line, the Cainite contribution to culture, the exaggerated life spans in chapter 5, and ancient comments about individuals in each genealogy. See further the discussion on chapters 5 and 10.

ambiguities of other human creations. As Wenham suggests, "By linking urbanization and nomadism, music and metalworking to the genealogy of Cain, [the author] seems to be suggesting that all aspects of human culture are in some way tainted by Cain's sin."[17]

1. The Line from Cain to Lamech (4:17-18)

4:17 Cain lay with his wife, and she became pregnant and gave birth to Enoch. Cain was then building a city, and he named it after his son Enoch.

Cain, like his father Adam, "knew" (NIV "lay with") his wife and she gave birth to Enoch. The name probably means "founder"[18] Cain's building of a city may be read as a necessity given that he is under a curse in terms of agricultural pursuits, his previous livelihood. The city may also function for the imagined audience as an early prototype of the cities of refuge (Deut 19:11). If so, this would be yet another example of the anticipation of the law in Genesis.

4:18 To Enoch was born Irad, and Irad was the father of Mehujael, and Mehujael was the father of Methushael, and Methushael was the father of Lamech.

Irad's[19] name is of uncertain meaning although it may plausibly be related to the early city Eridu.[20] Mehujael's name probably means something like "God enlivens" or "enlivened by God." This may indicate an expression of thanks at the birth. Even in the line of Cain there was still faith during this period. Nothing is known about Irad or Mehujael. Often in ancient genealogies the most important names are at the beginning and end and at crucial turning points. Methushael may mean "man of God," but could as easily mean "man of Sheol" or "man of asking [in prayer]" or "man of desire." Lamech's

---

[17]Wenham, *Genesis 1–15*, p. 111.
[18]Hess, *Studies*, p. 39.
[19]On the etymology of these names see ibid., pp. 40-46.
[20]The oldest city in the Mesopotamian tradition is Eridu. Some suggest emending the text to read, "he was building a city, and he called the name of the city after his son's name." In context Enoch, not Cain would be the builder; Enoch's son Irad (עִירָד, *'irād*) has the city (עִיר, *'îr*) named after him. This would preserve a Hebrew wordplay, a common feature of these narratives.

name is also of uncertain meaning, although Hess mentions the discovery of tribal names in Oman which may give evidence of an as of yet unattested Semitic root. Lamech is the seventh from Adam and thus is given more "press" in this genealogy as is the seventh from Adam in chapter 5, Enoch.

2. The Polygamous Family Line of Lamech (4:19)

4:19 Lamech married two women, one named Adah and the other Zillah.

This is the first recorded case of polygamy in the Bible, although it is difficult to know whether the author subtly critiques polygamy by pointing out the unsavory character of the first polygamist. Certainly the narrator's comment to the reader in Genesis 2:24 ("A man shall leave his father and mother and cleave to his *wife*") seems to indicate that God's creation intention for marriage was monogamy. While polygamy was not rare in the ancient Near East and among prominent biblical characters (e.g., Abraham, Jacob), it is striking that it is never given approval by the Bible. It is in the line of Cain that polygamy first arises. "Adah" is also the name of one of Esau's wives (Gen 36:2) and probably means "pretty" or "ornament." Zillah may mean "shadow" referring to the relief of the shade in an arid, and often hot, climate. Westermann and Cassuto suggest deriving the name from "to tinkle" referring to the beauty of the feminine voice (S of S 2:14, "a sweet voice and a pretty face").[21] Perhaps the author is hinting at the fact that Lamech succumbed to sensuality by being unable to resist the pretty Adah or the lovely-voiced Zillah.

3. Civilization Begins (4:20-22)

4:20 Adah gave birth to Jabal; he was the father of those who live in tents and raise livestock.

The two wives bring forth three sons in total, each of them with names derived from the same Hebrew word, *yebul*, meaning "produce." This perhaps refers to their being inventors or producers of

---

[21]Westermann, *Genesis 1–11*, p. 331; Cassuto, *Genesis: Part One*, p. 234.

various skills. Jabal not only replaced Abel's shepherding, but "advanced" things by raising livestock which could be sold for transportation, etc. But like all human "advancement" it is tinged with human imperfection.

4:21 His brother's name was Jubal; he was the father of all who play the harp and flute.

Giving two siblings similarly sounding names is common in the OT, e.g., Medan/Midian (Gen 25:2); Ephah/Epher (25:4); Ishavah/Ishvi (46:17); Oholah/Oholibah (Ezek 23:4). Jubal is credited with the invention of musical instruments both wind and stringed. The gift of music has the inherent ambiguities of all things created by sinful human beings. With the same lips we praise God and curse our brothers in Christ. With the same music we praise God and manipulate emotions for undesirable ends.

4:22 Zillah also had a son, Tubal-Cain, who forged all kinds of tools out of bronze and iron. Tubal-Cain's sister was Naamah.

The word "Cain" in Tubal-Cain probably means "smith." The Cain element of the name is missing in the Septuagint which leads some scholars to regard it as an explanatory gloss. Tubal could be a geographic name. It appears in Ezekiel 27:13 with Javan and Meshech in relation to the trading of slaves and metal goods with the king of Tyre. Alternatively Tubal could be read as related to Jabal and Jubal with the meaning "producer of." If so the complete name would indicate a close relationship to work with metals.[22] Wenham thinks that the word translated "forged" should be translated "sharpened." Copper (NIV "bronze") was the first metal to be worked, from the fourth millennium B.C. Since iron working did not develop until the second millennium, it is sometimes suggested that the cold forging of meteoric iron (which is an ancient technology) is meant. But perhaps this is expecting too much specificity. Once again the ambiguity of human creations is being hinted at. In Cain's line, the descendants of the first murderer, the forging of metal arises. Whether that will result in plowshares and pruning hooks which alleviate human toil or sword and spears which perpetuate human violence remains to be determined.

Naamah is one of the few women to be named in this section of Genesis. Her name could mean either "to comfort" or "to sing."

---

[22]See the thorough discussion in Hess, *Studies*.

Given the fact that her half-brother Jubal was ancestor of instrumental musicians, the latter seems plausible. The mention of her name then serves the function of noting that the founder of vocal music was half-sister to the founder of instrumental music.[23]

4. Lamech's Cynical Boast (4:23-24)

4:23 Lamech said to his wives, "Adah and Zillah, listen to me; wives of Lamech, hear my words. I have killed a man for wounding me, a young man for injuring me.
4:24 If Cain is avenged seven times, then Lamech seventy-seven times."

Lamech's words are often understood as arrogant boasting. The mercy which the LORD extends to Cain is presumed upon by Lamech as a sort of entitlement. Sailhamer suggests that Lamech appeals to *lex talionis*, i.e., if Cain, who killed his brother with malice of forethought, was not to be the object of revenge, Lamech could surely be avenged for killing a man in self-defense. While this is possible, it seems unlikely given that this chapter seems to consistently point to ambiguity if not outright moral decline in the descendants of Cain who live east of Eden.

Lamech's words are in a form of Hebrew poetry usually termed "synonymous parallelism" in which the repetition with variation of lines is used to emphasize the point. The text can be laid out in the following way:

A	Ada and Zillah,	hear my voice
A'	Wives of Lamech	give ear to my speech
B	A man I have killed	for my wound
B'	a boy (ellipsis)	for my bruising
C	If sevenfold avenged	is Cain
C'	Lamech then (ellipsis)	seventy-seven[24]

---

[23]Carol Meyers, "Naamah 1," *Women in Scripture,* ed. by Carol Meyers. Grand Rapids: Eerdmans, 2000, p. 129, comments: "The intimate connection between women and song, going back to the maternal tuneful, rhythmic soothing of infants and found widely across cultures, would support the idea that Naamah is the archetypal founder of vocal music."

[24]See Robert Alter's discussion of this passage in *The Art of Biblical Poetry* (New York: Harper Collins, 1985), pp. 5ff.

Notice the precise parallelism between lines A, B, and C and respectively A', B', and C'. But lines C and C' show inverted word order (chiastic structure) in order to underscore the contrast between Lamech and Cain. The stress patterns in the Hebrew are 4/4, 3/2, and 3/3 for each of the three sets of lines. The irregularity in the stress patterns in the B/B' lines focuses attention there. Lamech seems to try to minimize his crime. At first it is a man whom Lamech has killed and that in revenge for a wound. It is only in the second line that we realize it is not a mature adult but a boy, and Lamech has only suffered a bruise. Cain murdered Abel even though Abel had not harmed him. Lamech reasons that, if Cain is protected from revenge for a premeditated murder, how much more should he be absolved for protecting himself and retaliating. But Lamech oversells the case. It was only a boy and only a wound. Interestingly he addresses his wives and not the LORD nor the people around him. The LORD could potentially grant Lamech immunity or grace if he would appeal to him as he had when Cain appealed to him. The people around could potentially stop the spread of violence. But Lamech addresses neither the LORD nor the people, but his wives. Did Lamech kill someone close to his wives, perhaps a child? We can only speculate. In any case it seems a rather poor attempt to prevent revenge. If it is boasting to his wives, as Wenham suggests, Lamech shows that the end of the line of Cain has made no real progress.

E. PARTIAL REHABILITATION OF DIVINE-HUMAN RELATIONSHIPS (4:25-26)

²⁵Adam lay with his wife again, and she gave birth to a son and named him Seth,ª saying, "God has granted me another child in place of Abel, since Cain killed him." ²⁶Seth also had a son, and he named him Enosh.
At that time men began to call onᵇ the name of the LORD.

ª*25 Seth* probably means *granted*. ᵇ*26* Or *to proclaim*

The scene shifts from the line of Cain to the line of Seth. Instead of murder, polygamy, and presuming on the LORD's mercy, these descendants of Adam and Eve begin to call on the name of the LORD in worship. This is a partial rehabilitation of the divine-human relationship which was broken in Eden. This rapprochement with the LORD is in stark contrast to the narrative of Cain and his descendants, especially Lamech.

1. The Birth of Seth to Replace Abel (4:25)

4:25 Adam lay with his wife again, and she gave birth to a son and named him Seth, saying, "God has granted me another child in place of Abel, since Cain killed him."

Adam and Eve (here termed "his wife") had another child. Once again, she names him. In the ancient world this was unusual, although by no means unknown. Here she does not speak of what she has done in bringing forth a son but of what God has given to her. Sailhamer construes this as indicating a change of attitude on her part. In any case she recognizes in the very act of naming Seth that life, and especially the lives of children, are gifts from God. There is a wordplay in the Hebrew between the Seth (שֵׁת, šēth) and the verb "granted" (שָׁת, šāth), only the vowel being different.

The form of the Hebrew verb "lay" (lit. "knew")[25] is difficult here. Ordinarily it would imply the next thing after the previous account, in this case the previous instance of Adam having intimate relations with Eve. If the birth of Seth is the next son[26] born, and is a sort of replacement for the murdered Abel, the population which Cain fears and the origins of his wife are perplexing. This may indicate that Seth was not at all the third son, but merely the next son after the death of Abel, and once again the Bible is silent on something we are quite curious about. Certainly the text shows no interest in satisfying our curiosity about such questions.

2. Humanity Begins to Call on the Name of the LORD (4:26)

4:26 Seth also had a son, and he named him Enosh. At that time men began to call on the name of the LORD.

---

[25]Waw-consecutive with imperfect.

[26]Luther notes that neither Cain nor Abel are called 'son.' He suggests that this is because of what happens to each of them — Abel perishes physically and leaves no descendants while Cain perishes spiritually and his descendants remain under God's judgment. It is only with Seth that a male child is given the description, 'son.'

For the first time the father names the child. The name Enosh means "mortal" according to Fox. It is the less common word for "human" and is often viewed as emphasizing the weakness of humanity (e.g., Ps 8:5). If so, the point would seem to be that after the tragedy of Cain and Abel the confidence of humans in humanity has taken a blow. They are mere mortals. But here it may (also) be a sign of the start of a new humanity and therefore something more hopeful. Enosh is a sort of "new Adam." Perhaps the ambiguity is the point. Humanity is made up of mortals, but their continued existence means that there is still hope, despite the violence in the early years east of Eden.

That hope is given an added boost by the fact that in the time of the mere mortal Enosh people began to call on the name of the LORD. This seems to signify a desire and an attempt by humanity to reestablish a relationship with the LORD that had been lost in the Fall and the early period after the expulsion from Eden. This stands in stark contrast with the line of Cain. Since the line of Seth and Enosh is given in genealogical form in chapter 5, it seems likely that the two lines are being distinguished. Cain's line is ambiguous at best while Seth's line leads to the godly Enoch and the blameless Noah.

One perplexing aspect of this statement is the affirmation that in the earliest days of humanity people called on the name of the LORD in prayer and worship. This has often been taken to mean that this was the first time men began to address God in prayer with the special name Yahweh or LORD. Whereas the purported source documents E (Exod. 3:14-15) and P (Exod 6:3) date the first use of the LORD as the name of the one God to the time of Moses, this passage supposedly from J (for "Jahwist" or "Yahwist") asserts that the LORD's name was known from the earliest of times. But this reading assumes a lot and seems bent on finding a way to read the text in conflict with itself. More likely this passage is asserting either that the LORD's name was known from the earliest times and then largely forgotten or that the focus of this text is not upon the exact name used in worship at all but rather the fact of worship.[27] This text perhaps helps to explain the presence of Melchizedek and Abimelech, who worship

---

[27]Wenham (*Genesis 1-15*, p. 116) comments: "These stories are concerned with universal human institutions and experiences, not with a particular event in the history of Israel. It makes better sense to take this remark as a

and are faithful even though they have not experienced the revelation which was given to Abraham and his descendants. In any case, far too much has been made of this passage in source-critical analysis.

---

comment on the fact that all nations worship, not as a comment on the name under which they worship God."

GENESIS 5

IV. THE DESTRUCTION AND RESTORATION OF CREATION (5:1–9:17)

A. THE FAMILY LINE FROM SETH TO NOAH (5:1-32)

¹This is the written account of Adam's line.

When God created man, he made him in the likeness of God. ²He created them male and female and blessed them. And when they were created, he called them "man.ᵃ"

³When Adam had lived 130 years, he had a son in his own likeness, in his own image; and he named him Seth. ⁴After Seth was born, Adam lived 800 years and had other sons and daughters. ⁵Altogether, Adam lived 930 years, and then he died.

⁶When Seth had lived 105 years, he became the fatherᵇ of Enosh. ⁷And after he became the father of Enosh, Seth lived 807 years and had other sons and daughters. ⁸Altogether, Seth lived 912 years, and then he died.

⁹When Enosh had lived 90 years, he became the father of Kenan. ¹⁰And after he became the father of Kenan, Enosh lived 815 years and had other sons and daughters. ¹¹Altogether, Enosh lived 905 years, and then he died.

¹²When Kenan had lived 70 years, he became the father of Mahalalel. ¹³And after he became the father of Mahalalel, Kenan lived 840 years and had other sons and daughters. ¹⁴Altogether, Kenan lived 910 years, and then he died.

¹⁵When Mahalalel had lived 65 years, he became the father of Jared. ¹⁶And after he became the father of Jared, Mahalalel lived 830 years and had other sons and daughters. ¹⁷Altogether, Mahalalel lived 895 years, and then he died.

¹⁸When Jared had lived 162 years, he became the father of

Enoch. ¹⁹And after he became the father of Enoch, Jared lived 800 years and had other sons and daughters. ²⁰Altogether, Jared lived 962 years, and then he died.

²¹When Enoch had lived 65 years, he became the father of Methuselah. ²²And after he became the father of Methuselah, Enoch walked with God 300 years and had other sons and daughters. ²³Altogether, Enoch lived 365 years. ²⁴Enoch walked with God; then he was no more, because God took him away.

²⁵When Methuselah had lived 187 years, he became the father of Lamech. ²⁶And after he became the father of Lamech, Methuselah lived 782 years and had other sons and daughters. ²⁷Altogether, Methuselah lived 969 years, and then he died.

²⁸When Lamech had lived 182 years, he had a son. ²⁹He named him Noahᶜ and said, "He will comfort us in the labor and painful toil of our hands caused by the ground the LORD has cursed." ³⁰After Noah was born, Lamech lived 595 years and had other sons and daughters. ³¹Altogether, Lamech lived 777 years, and then he died.

³²After Noah was 500 years old, he became the father of Shem, Ham and Japheth.

ᵃ*2* Hebrew *adam*   ᵇ*6 Father* may mean *ancestor*; also in verses 7-26.
ᶜ*29 Noah* sounds like the Hebrew for *comfort*.

This passage follows on from 4:25-26 with the line of Seth. The initial contrast between the line of Cain and the line of Seth is already established in 4:25-26. The genealogy here traces the line all the way from Seth to Noah and his sons. The passage functions in several ways. God's curse on humanity for sin is shown to work itself out in history as the repetitive phrase "and he died" hammers home the point with each repetition. Death was the penalty for rebellion against God's one simple command in Eden. Here that penalty is shown to be operative.

This passage functions also to show that, even in the midst of the free choices of humankind to resist God's will, history inexorably progresses in the direction which God intends. This genealogy goes somewhere. Like its counterpart in Genesis 11:10-26 it leads somewhere. God's ultimate purposes will not be frustrated even by the sin and rebellion of humanity.[1]

---

[1]Robert B. Robinson, "Literary Functions of the Genealogies of Genesis," *CBQ* 48 (1986): 608, relates the function of combining narrative and geneal-

But this passage also functions to remind its readers of God's grace. The penalty is not immediately operative, as many of the descendants of Seth live nearly 1,000 years. And then there is the case of Enoch, seventh in the list, whose shorter life span resulted from his relationship with God. By his grace Enoch is allowed to forgo physical death. The naming of Noah expresses the hope that humanity will receive comfort from the manual labor and painful toil involved in making a living from the cursed ground. His name expresses hope that the LORD will ease the burden.

This text is not a genealogy in the modern sense.[2] It is neither comprehensive in its coverage nor is it designed to be used to reconstruct prediluvian history. Like other biblical genealogies it operates with ancient conventions which are very different from our conventions about genealogical material. While a more thorough discussion of biblical genealogical material may be found in the introduction to chapter 10, a few remarks here will help orient the reader.[3] The recitation of a person's ancestors in what today we would view as primitive societies was designed to help an individual identify her or his proper place in society. Modern genealogies are mainly used as a source of past history; ancient genealogies such as are found in the Bible point to the present roles and status of people within their societies. Modern genealogies cannot change. They can be correct-

---

ogy in Genesis: "The delicate interplay between the narratives and the non-narrative genealogies places Genesis at a fluctuating, never specifiable point between the complete predestination of events embodied in the strict prophecy-fulfillment structure of the Odyssey and the nearly complete autonomy of successive events familiar from modern plots. That point is not meant to be fixed. Events retain their full contingency, characters the moral control of their wills; yet somehow God is in charge, and creation follows the will of its creator. The interplay of story and genealogy, narrative and non-narrative, is a literary strategy which, in a sense, defies the restrictions and reductions of the neat logical oppositions of free will versus determinism or contingency versus foreordination which, perforce, we use in our analysis. Logic cannot affirm both sides of these oppositions without contradiction. But the literary structure of Genesis has found a way to maintain both sides and thus to give expression to a deeper reality."

[2]For the evidence that biblical genealogies do not operate by modern conventions see the special study below.

[3]For what follows see the helpful article by Lawrence Boadt, "Chronicles and Genealogies," *TBT* 26 (1988): 203-208.

ed with new information, but by their very nature they do not change; ancient genealogies are changeable. A person can have more than one "true" genealogy. They are not designed to be a scientifically accurate listing of all of one's biological ancestors in their proper historical order. In ancient genealogies many generations are often skipped[4] and the important names are usually the first and last in the list; others are only of significance if they appear at a crucial turning point in the history of the people or are somehow famous for an accomplishment or their character. Anthropologists distinguish between *linear* genealogies which have depth and trace a single line and *segmented* genealogies which have breadth and do not focus on the single line. Boadt comments on the different functions of these two types of genealogies:

> In judging the value and importance of any ancient genealogy we must ask the *function* it plays in its *setting*. In general, a *segmented* genealogy traces the relationships of one group to another or of one class of persons to another. A *linear* genealogy, on the other hand, often establishes a claim to power or authority [italics mine].[5]

Genesis 5 is a linear genealogy. As such it establishes the godly line which leads from Seth through Enoch to Noah.

The similarities between the genealogies in Genesis 4 and 5 are remarkable. Enoch and Lamech appear in both. The seventh name in each (Enoch and Lamech) is given special prominence. The similarities (cf. the chart below) might be explained as an example of genealogical fluidity or the reflection of ancient intermarrying followed by periods of social separation between the two lines. It could also be that the names are common enough that they refer to different individuals. The last view tends to be the modern assumption, but it is just that, an assumption, and is based upon the shaky premise that ancient conventions were very similar to modern conventions regarding genealogies.

---

[4]Boadt refers to the great Assyrian king Esarhaddon (680–669 B.C.) who listed his ancestors on an inscription in which he jumped from his father and grandfather back sixty-two generations to the third name, a remote king from whom he traces the beginning of his dynasty.

[5]Ibid., p. 207.

Gen 5 Sethites	Gen 4 Cainites
1. 1 Adam	1. 1 Adam
2. 6 Seth	
3. 9 Enosh	
4. 12 Qenan	2. 17 Cain
5. 15 Mahalalel	3. 17 Enoch
6. 18 Yared	4. 18 Irad
7. 21 Enoch	5. 18 Mehuya'el
8. 25 Methuselah	6. 18 Methusha'el
9. 28 Lamech	7. 18 Lamech
10. 32 Noah	8. 20 Yabal, Yubal, Tubal-Cain

The text of Genesis 5 is difficult to establish in as much as the three earliest sources (the Massoretic Hebrew (M); the Greek Septuagint (G); the Samaritan Pentateuch (S) differ in significant ways in supplying the numbers. Hendel has done an exhaustive study of the text. The chart below gives the information and his proposed original text ("Archetype").

The Chronology of Gen 5:3-32: Major Versions and Archetype

Name	Age at:	Massoretic	Samaritan	Greek	# Archetype
Adam	b	130	130	230	130
	r	800	800	700	800
	t	930	930	930	930
	A.M.	(1–930)	(1–930)	(1–930)	(1–930)
Seth	b	105	105	205	105
	r	807	807	707	807
	t	912	912	912	912
	A.M.	(130–1042)	(130–1042)	(230–1042)	(130–1042)
Enosh	b	90	90	190	90
	r	815	815	715	815
	t	905	905	905	905
	A.M.	(235–1140)	(235–1140)	(435–1140)	(235–1140)
Kenan	b	70	70	170	70
	r	840	840	740	840
	t	910	910	910	910
	A.M.	(325–1235)	(325–1235)	(625–1535)	(325–1235)
Mehalalel	b	65	65	165	65
	r	830	830	730	830
	t	895	895	895	895
	A.M.	(395–1290)	(395–1290)	(795–1690)	(395–1290)

Name	Age at:	Massoretic	Samaritan	Greek	# Archetype
*Jared	b	162	62	162	62
	r	800	785	800	*900
	t	962	847	962	962
	A.M.	(460–1422)	(460–1307)	(960–1922)	(460–1422)
Enoch	b	65	65	65	65
	r	300	300	300	300
	t	365	365	365	365
	A.M.	(622–987)	(522–887)	(1122–1487)	(522–987)
Methuselah	b	187	67	167	67
	r	782	653	802	902
	t	969	720	969	969
	A.M.	(687–1656)	(587–1307)	(1287–2256*)	(587–1556)
Lamech	b	182	53	188	*88
	r	595	600	565	*665
	t	777	653	753	753
	A.M.	(874–1651)	(654–1307)	(1454–2207)	(654–1407)
Flood	A.M.	(1656)	(1307)	(2242)	(1342)

b = age at begetting   r = remainder   t = total life span   A.M. = year after creation
(anno mundi)
= Hendel   * = note especially
Assumes no partial year issues and a complete genealogy.

Explanation of the Proposed Archetype

In light of the probability that G is a systematic revision Hendel posits that with the exceptions of Jared, Methuselah, and Lamech, the archetypal numbers can be ascertained in the following way:

b = M, S, or G − 100[6]
r = M, S, or G + 100[7]
t = M, S, or G[8]

---

[6]That is, the original age of begetting the next generation is preserved in either the Hebrew or Samaritan Pentateuch. The Septuagint's number must be reduced by 100.

[7]That is, the original years lived after begetting the next generation is preserved in either the Hebrew or Samaritan Pentateuch. The Septuagint's number must be increased by 100.

[8]That is, the total life span can be found in any of the three early sources.

Hendel's Discussion of the Exceptions

Jared

Jared's t is 962 in M and G but 847 in S. Since agreement between M and G preserves the archetype elsewhere, S is suspect of revision due to some theological or other motivation. Since S has the year of the Flood at 1307 and 847 ensures that Jared dies during the year of the Flood, this seems to be the most likely explanation.

Jared's b is 162 in M and G but 62 in S. Since elsewhere S = G − 100, one looks for the motivation of M in increasing Jared's age at begetting. In M the extra 100 years delays the onset of the Flood so that Jared dies before the Flood.

Methuselah

Methusaleh's t is 969 in G and M but 720 in S. S is therefore suspect, and since it places Methuselah's death in the year of the Flood in S, the rationale for revision seems clear.

Methuselah's b is 187 in M but 67 in S and 167 in G. Since G consistently adds 100 to the archetype, S gives the original of 67. M is suspect since by adding 120 years to the archetype the Flood is delayed so that Methuselah dies the year of the Flood.

Interestingly, G has Methuselah surviving the Flood by 14 years!

Lamech

The situation with Lamech is more complicated. Lamech's t is 777 in M, 653 in S, and 753 in G. Since S has Lamech die in the year of the Flood, it is probably a revision. M has 777 which seems, according to Hendel, to be influenced by the Cainite Lamech who called for 77-fold vengeance (4:24). The issue is whether M has an intentional revision here or accidental assimilation. In any case M seems secondary. This leaves G, but the 653 in S gives one pause.

Lamech's b is difficult to discern since M's 182, S's 53, and G's 188 show no discernible pattern. Klein argues that G − 100 equals the archetypal b, i.e., 188 − 100 = 88.[9] But how does one explain M? M originally added 100 years and then a scribal error in which the 82 from Methuselah's r is accidentally transferred to Lamech (see 5:26, Methuselah two and eighty years; 5:28 Lamech, two and eighty

---

[9]R.W. Klein, "Archaic Chronologies and the Textual History of the Old Testament," *HTR* 67 (1974): 255-263.

years). But why would M add 100 years to the archetype? S's reading is explained by a similar scribal reminiscence (5:28 in S, Lamech three and fifty years; 5:31 G, Lamech three and fifty years). This is mere speculation.

Hendel's Summary

> Aside from the residue of uncertainty in the numbers for Lamech, the archetypal numbers for the chronology of Genesis 5 are easily ascertainable by this analysis, predicated on the desire of ancient scribes to have the antediluvian ancestors of Noah die at or before the year of the flood. In proto-G, the solution adopted was to revise upward by 100 years each year of begetting, thereby delaying by 900 years (100×9) the date of the onset of the flood. In proto-M and proto-S, the textual revisions were confined to the ages of the three problematic patriarchs, Jared, Methuselah, and Lamech. Proto-M revised upward the year of begetting for each of the three, and proto-S revised downward the year of death for each of the three. By these three different strategies of revision, the problem was solved, with the notorious exception of Methuselah in G.[10]

Evaluation of Hendel's Work

Hendel fails to remark upon the assumptions which led to these revisions. The archetype (i.e., original text) is assumed to be a complete chronology and the basis for calculating the date of the creation of the world. In fact, the archetype is either naive in the extreme and doesn't do math well, or never intended the list of ten generations to be taken as the basis for a chronology and a complete genealogy. Certainly by the time of the translation of the Hebrew into Greek there was an interest in such questions. But the genealogy in the Septuagint (G), if taken in the way that Hendel assumes it was taken has Methuselah surviving the Flood! This should warn us about Hendel's assumptions, not about the reliability of the G text. Further, this approach does not do justice to ancient Near Eastern genealogies. The Bible shows no interest in adding up the numbers or calculating the date of creation. Hendel does establish that the Hebrew

---

[10]Ronald S. Hendel, *The Text of Genesis 1–11* (New York: Oxford University Press, 1998), pp. 68-69.

text MT cannot be taken as the archetype in some simplistic sense. His suggestions for the most likely original text have merit. But we must be cautious about the assumptions which undergird his work.

SPECIAL STUDY

CONCRETE EVIDENCE THAT BIBLICAL GENEALOGIES ARE NOT MODERN

I. The Birth Order of Noah's Sons

Genesis 5:32 lists the sons of Noah in the order Shem, Ham, and Japheth. But the following evidence makes clear that this is not their order of birth. Rather it speaks of their future significance in the narrative and to the imagined audience.

1. Gen 7:6: Noah was six hundred years old when the floodwaters came on the earth.
2. Gen 9:24: When Noah awoke from his wine and found out what his *youngest* son [Ham] had done to him,
3. Gen 10:21: Sons were born to Shem, he was the father of all the sons of Eber, the brother of Japheth, the oldest.
4. Gen 11:10,11: This is the account of Shem. Two years after the Flood, when Shem was 100 years old, he became the father of Arphaxad.

From this it seems obvious that the birth order was Japheth, Shem, and Ham, not Shem, Ham, and Japheth. We only inaccurately assume that the sons are listed in their birth order because we come to the text with modern assumptions about how names should be listed.

II. The Birth Order of Terah's Sons

Gen 11:26 — After Terah had lived 70 years he became the father of Abram, Nahor, and Haran.
Gen 11:32 — Terah lived 205 years, and he died in Charan. 12:2 Then the LORD said to Abram, "Leave your country, your people and your father's household and go to the land I will show you.

Gen 12:4 — So Abram left, as the LORD had told him, and Lot went with him. Abram was 75 years old when he set out from Charan.

If 11:26 is in birth order, we have a contradiction here. But the waw-consecutive in 11:31 hints that Haran was significantly older than Abram and Nahor, and 11:26 does not give their birth order, but second oldest first, youngest second, and oldest third as in 5:32.

III. Matthew's and Luke's genealogies compared with OT

Matthew	Old Testament	Luke
1. Abraham	1. Abraham	1. Abraham
2. Isaac	2. Isaac	2. Isaac
3. Jacob	3. Jacob	3. Jacob
4. Judah	4. Judah	4. Judah
5. Perez	5. Perez	5. Perez
6. Hezron	6. Hezron	6. Hezron
7. Ram	7. Ram	7. Ram
8. Amminadab	8. Amminadab	8. Amminadab
9. Nashon	9. Nashon	9. Nashon
10. Salmon	10. Salmon	10. Salmon
11. Boaz	11. Boaz	11. Boaz
12. Obed	12. Obed	12. Obed
13. Jesse	13. Jesse	13. Jesse
14. David	14. David	14. David
15. Solomon	15. Solomon	15. Nathan*
16. Rehoboam	16. Rehoboam	16. Mattatha
17. Abijah	17. Abijah	17. Menna
18. Asa	18. Asa	18. Melea
19. Jehoshaphat	19. Jehoshaphat	19. Eliakim
20. Jehoram	20. Jehoram	20. Jonam
	21. Ahaziah	21. Joseph
	22. Joash	22. Judah
	23. Amaziah	23. Simeon
21. Uzziah	24. Uzziah	24. Levi
22. Jotham	25. Jotham	25. Matthat
23. Ahaz	26. Ahaz	26. Jorim
24. Hezekiah	27. Hezekiah	27. Eliezer
25. Manasseh	28. Manasseh	28. Joshua
26. Amon	29. Amon	29. Er
27. Josiah	30. Josiah	30. Elmadam
28. Jeconiah	31. Jehoahaz	
29. Jeconiah	32. Jehoiakim	31. Cosam

30. Shealtiel	33. Jehoiachin (Jeconiah)	32. Addi
31. Zerubbabel	34. Zedekiah	33. Melchi
32. Abiud		34. Neri
33. Eliakim		35. Shealtiel
34. Azor		36. Zerubbabel
35. Zadok		37. Rhesa
36. Akim		38. Joanan
37. Eliud		39. Joda
38. Eleazar		40. Josech
39. Mattan		41. Semein
40. Jacob		42. Mattathias
41. Joseph		43. Joseph
42. Jesus		44. Maath
		45. Naggai
		46. Hesli
		47. Nahum
		48. Amos
		49. Mattathias
		50. Joseph
		51. Jannai
		52. Melchi
		53. Levi
		54. Matthat
		55. Heli
		56. Joseph, father of Jesus

Notice that Matthew only gets three sets of 14 generations by repeating one name (Jeconiah), by skipping several of the royal line of David (Ahaziah, Joash, Amaziah) and by apparently skipping a large number of generations in the intertestamental period (notice the many extra generations which Luke has during this time period). Matthew obviously is not attempting to give a comprehensive genealogy in the modern sense.

Conclusion

Even without other parallel evidence from the ancient Near East and the genealogies of modern primitives it is clear that the Bible's genealogies: 1) are not comprehensive, 2) do not follow modern conventions of order, 3) are sometimes based upon numerical patterns, 4) often skip generations, and 5) are more concerned with establishing the present legitimacy of a person than with comprehensive descriptions of biological descent.

1. Resumptive Repetition of Creation (5:1-2)

5:1a This is the written account of Adam's line.

Here the wordplay on the Hebrew word *'ādām* recurs, which can refer to the person Adam or simply be a common Hebrew noun for humankind. The NIV in this verse first renders it "Adam" (1a) and then "man." (1b). The Hebrew phrase rendered, "This is the written account of" is a formula which Genesis consistently uses to introduce the next segment of the narrative (see Introduction under "Structure of Genesis").

5:1b When God created man, he made him in the likeness of God. 5:2 He created them male and female and blessed them. And when they were created, he called them "man."

The author obviously repeats with slight variations the account in chapter 1 here. Notice the repetition of the words and/or phrases: "created," "likeness of God," "male and female," "blessed," and "called." Why retell the information in these verses in this way? Perhaps because, as Sailhamer[11] suggests, God is being portrayed as being like a father. He made a son in his own likeness. He named him and blessed them, just as the patriarchs are portrayed as doing.

2. Ten "Generations" from Adam to Noah (5:3-31)

5:3 When Adam had lived 130 years, he had a son in his own likeness, in his own image; and he named him Seth.

Notice the echo of the creation account in Genesis 1:26-28. That passage has the words "likeness" and "image" in reverse order. This may indicate the difference between the action of God in creation and the action of mankind in procreation. While humanity's procreation has similarities to God's creation it is not the same as God's creation.

The length of time which Adam lived before giving birth to Seth could be an indication of how removed the lives of prediluvian people were from the experience of Israel. It could also be an indication that many other children were born prior to the birth of Seth. Another possibility is that the reader is to infer that the extraordi-

---

[11]Sailhamer, *Genesis*, p. 70.

nary life spans prior to and just after the Flood resulted in the entire life span being elongated from childhood to maturation to death.

The name "Seth" is derived from the common West Semitic root "to place, set." It is common in West Semitic languages for the root to have a divine name appended to it to form a name meaning, "God places." It may be that the original audience would have understood that the one who does the "placing" is God. God set a person in place to begin again after the murder of Abel and the banishment of Cain.

5:4 After Seth was born, Adam lived 800 years and had other sons and daughters.

The phrase, "sons and daughters" shows the blessings of procreation and reminds the reader of God's original commission to humanity, "be fruitful and multiply." It also makes clear that we are not being given a comprehensive account of all humanity, but are focused on a single line of descendants, as we are told nothing about the other sons and daughters other than their existence.

5:5 Altogether, Adam lived 930 years, and then he died.

The phrase "and then he died" (in Hebrew a single word) is a solemn chorus in this chapter which shows the working out in history of God's curse in chapter 3. With each repetition the point is hammered home about the consequences of sin. The death spoken of here is what we would call physical death, not spiritual death. This rather obvious fact is often lost when reading Paul's comments and applications of these chapters in Romans 5. That Adam lived as long as 930 years before the sentence of the garden is carried out is a manifestation of God's grace in the midst of his judgment. The return to such long life is a part of the picture of the eschatological age (Isa 65:20).[12] Whether that age be viewed as the millennium or as a picture of the eternal state must be decided on other grounds.

5:6 When Seth had lived 105 years, he became the father of Enosh.

Enosh (אֱנוֹשׁ, *'ĕnôš*) means "human" in Hebrew and is a synonym of the word *'ādām*, translated as the proper name Adam, or as a

---

[12]Kenneth A. Matthews comments (*Genesis 1–11:26*, New American Commentary [Nashville: Broadman & Holman, 1996], p. 310): "strikingly, apart from the patriarchs of Genesis, in the Old Testament only Job (140), Moses (120), Joshua (110), and Jehoiada (130) lived longer than a century of years."

common word for a human being. It often occurs in poetic texts where parallelism demands a synonym for, *'ādām*, "human." Since this word never occurs again as a proper name in Hebrew or in any other West Semitic language, it seems likely that it has a literary function here. Seth, after the disaster of Cain and Abel, begins a new line of humanity. Enosh is a sort of second Adam. The name Enosh derives from a verb meaning "to be weak, feeble, ill." At times it does seem to be used in contexts which suggest the frailty of humankind. This does not necessarily mean that every time the word is used it does so.[13] The question is, however, whether this text is such an instance. There is no way to be certain, but given the context of the working out of the curse through the generations descended from Adam in chapters 4 and 5, it is reasonable to suggest that the original audience would see significance in the fact that the "new Adam" is named Enosh ("Frail one"). Seth's descendants provide the start of a new humanity, but that humanity is also frail and weak.

5:7 And after he became the father of Enosh, Seth lived 807 years and had other sons and daughters.

Once again the blessing of procreation is emphasized with the statement, Seth "had other sons and daughters." At the same time this reminds the reader that only a partial and selective story of humankind is being given. The blessing of procreation is emphasized perhaps to echo the original commission to humanity in Genesis 1:26-28.

5:8 Altogether, Seth lived 912 years, and then he died.

The phrase, "and he died" occurs with haunting regularity in this chapter and serves to remind the reader of one of the consequences of Adam and Eve's original transgression. While the LORD had graciously delayed the execution date of Adam and Eve, they and all their descendants, died. That it takes 912 years for the sentence to be carried out is yet another demonstration of God's remarkable grace.

5:9 When Enosh had lived 90 years, he became the father of Kenan.

Kenan's name has the same three consonants as Cain's. In fact, Kenan has a nun ending (a second n) added to the name Cain as is

---

[13]NIDOTTE 1:454.

common in West Semitic names.[14] This could be the result of genealogical fluidity or merely the coincidence of two people bearing the same name.

5:10 And after he became the father of Kenan, Enosh lived 815 years and had other sons and daughters.

The blessings of procreation are mentioned yet again. While the consequences of sin — death — are reiterated time and again, so are the blessings of procreation. Since we are given no other information about the other sons and daughters the selectivity of the account is emphasized yet again.

5:11 Altogether, Enosh lived 905 years, and then he died.

While Enosh is a sort of "new Adam" (his name meaning "humankind") he too receives the consequences of the curse — physical death. That Enosh lasts 905 years is pure grace from a patient and just God.

5:12 When Kenan had lived 70 years, he became the father of Mahalalel.

Mahalalel seems to be derived from the verb הלל (*hll*), "to praise" (cf. our word "hallelujah") and the common Semitic word for God, אל (*'el*). The מ (*m*) may indicate an original participle yielding "one who praises God" or "praising God" or even "praise of God." The verb *hālāl* is relatively rare in West Semitic names, the few examples other than the Bible coming from the late third and early second millennia B.C. Perhaps the name hints at the more spiritual nature of the line of Seth compared to the line of Cain. The name also occurs in Nehemiah 11:4.

5:13 And after he became the father of Mahalalel, Kenan lived 840 years and had other sons and daughters.

The death of Kenan is offset by his own prolific fruitfulness (for 840 years!) as the dual themes of grace and judgment play themselves out in the narrative.

5:14 Altogether, Kenan lived 910 years, and then he died.

Kenan's death reminds the readers yet again of the consequences of sin. His long life is, by contrast, a reminder of God's grace. The repeated death knell of this chapter intensifies with every repetition of the phrase, "and he died."

---

[14]Hess, *Studies,* p. 68.

5:15 When Mahalalel had lived 65 years, he became the father of Jared.

According to Hess,[15] Jared comes from a root meaning "to descend" and may refer to a deity "descending" to give help in time of need. The age at the birth of the first recorded child (65 years) is gradually decreasing.

5:16 And after he became the father of Jared, Mahalalel lived 830 years and had other sons and daughters.

The blessings of procreation (other sons and daughters) and a long life span are emphasized once again. We are given no other information about the other sons and daughters.

5:17 Altogether, Mahalalel lived 895 years, and then he died.

The repetition of the haunting toll "and he died" reminds the readers of God's curse and yet Mahalalel's long life shows God's grace in not immediately carrying out his judgment.

5:18 When Jared had lived 162 years, he became the father of Enoch.

Enoch is the seventh in the list of ten generations. He contrasts with the Cainite Lamech who is also seventh in the genealogy traced through Cain in chapter 4. The name Enoch may be derived from a West Semitic root $ḥnk$ meaning "to introduce, initiate"[16] It is not clear what if any symbolic significance the name may have in this context.

5:19 And after he became the father of Enoch, Jared lived 800 years and had other sons and daughters.

The blessing of fertility (other sons and daughters) and a limited life span (a result of the curse) are here, as elsewhere, juxtaposed. As sin and its consequences work themselves out in the experience of humanity the subtle indications of the spread of God's grace are also there. Since we are given no other information about the other sons and daughters, the selectivity of the account is highlighted.

5:20 Altogether, Jared lived 962 years, and then he died.

The bell toll of death and the long life of Jared pull the reader in opposite (complimentary, but paradoxical?) directions. God's just sentence is reiterated yet again as is his grace of a long and fruitful life.

---

[15]Ibid., pp. 69-70.
[16]Hess, *ABD*, II:508.

5:21 When Enoch had lived 65 years, he became the father of Methuselah.

The one person who does not die and escapes the death sentence of the curse is the father of the one with the longest recorded life. Enoch gives birth to the one who comes closest to beating death. Hess argues that Methuselah comes from two elements: *mt* = "man, husband" and *slh*.[17] The latter may be a divine name, or a divine epithet of some sort.

5:22 And after he became the father of Methuselah, Enoch walked with God 300 years and had other sons and daughters.

Notice that the Enoch passage does not begin "Altogether Enoch lived" but "and Enoch walked with God" to contrast his life with those who preceded and followed him. The verb "walked with" is the hithpael of *halak*, which is used of God walking in the Garden in 3:8. By thus echoing the experience of Eden, Enoch's relationship with God is compared to that of Adam and Eve prior to the Fall. That Enoch, who walked with God, had other sons and daughters perhaps hints at the fulfillment of God's intended purpose for humanity. They were created to rule over the earth as God's representative. In order to do this in such a large world they must be fruitful and multiply. That Enoch did this while walking with God brings together the two creation accounts. He lived an "Edenlike" existence (Genesis 2) while fulfilling the creation mandate (Genesis 1). We are given no other information about the other sons and daughters.

5:23 Altogether, Enoch lived 365 years.

Scholars often remark on the fact that Enoch's years of life correspond to the days of a solar year and infer from this that some symbolical significance is to be found here. One wonders whether the original audience would have been as conscious as we are of the number of days in a year given the competing lunar and solar calendars of the ancient world. What is striking in this account is the lack of the refrain, "and he died."

5:24 Enoch walked with God; then he was no more, because God took him away.

Why did the author add "and he died" after each of the other characters in this genealogy, when the length of his life implies this?

---

[17]Hess, *Studies*, p. 43.

Perhaps this was to contrast and highlight Enoch who did not die although his life ended.[18] Because Enoch's fellowship with God was Edenlike, he is given the unique privilege of forgoing death. He is "translated" into the invisible realm of God long before "natural death" would have taken him. This passage is allusive and elliptical. It does not even begin to answer the many questions which we quite naturally have as readers. Later on in the history of interpretation several long works were written under the name of Enoch and much speculation about such questions is given. These speculative pseudepigraphical works were known among Jewish people in the time of the New Testament and one of them is even quoted in the book of Jude. But Genesis is very guarded.

5:25 When Methuselah had lived 187 years, he became the father of Lamech.

Lamech's name has no known meaning, although there is an Arabic root meaning "strong man" which may be related.[19] This Lamech contrasts sharply with the Lamech in chapter 4. This Lamech sires Noah, whom he hopes will bring relief from the curse. The Cainite Lamech shows the continuing effect of the curse.

5:26 And after he became the father of Lamech, Methuselah lived 782 years and had other sons and daughters.

Since we are given no other information about the other sons and daughters, the selectivity of the account is emphasized yet again as well as the blessing of fertility.

5:27 Altogether, Methuselah lived 969 years, and then he died.

While Methuselah has the longest recorded life span, he too succumbs ultimately to the curse and dies. Even under God's grace the longest cursed human being is slightly under a day in God's reckoning. If the genealogy is read as complete and exhaustive, Methuselah dies the same year as the Flood.

5:28 When Lamech had lived 182 years, he had a son.
5:29 He named him Noah and said, "He will comfort us in the labor

---

[18]Timothy J. Cole, "Enoch, a Man Who Walked with God," *BibSac* 148 (1991): 289: "In a plot where a funeral bell continually tolls out its mournful drone there is a disjunctive ray of hope, another example of the spread-of-sin, spread-of- grace theme."

[19]Hess, *ABD*, IV:136.

and painful toil of our hands caused by the ground the LORD has cursed."

Spina says, "The Cainite Lamech increases human violence and sin; the Sethite Lamech promises that his issue will reduce one of the terrible effects of sin."[20] Noah is the first person born after the death of Adam, if the genealogy is read consecutively. Sarna has suggested that "until you return to the earth" in 3:19 applies to Adam as an individual. Noah's vineyard is then taken as a sign of the alleviating of the curse on the ground because it produces something not essential, but pleasurable. But while this is interesting, it fails to recognize the selective nature of ancient genealogies. Lamech's prophecy (hope?) turns out not to be true in any ordinary sense. In Noah's time the greatest manifestation of the curse on the ground unfolds (the Flood). While Noah and his family survive the Flood and receive God's promise to never again destroy the entire cosmos in that fashion, it is not obvious that Noah comforted humankind in the labor and painful toil of working the cursed ground.

5:30 After Noah was born, Lamech lived 595 years and had other sons and daughters.

That Lamech has other sons and daughters and lived a long life is yet another recurrence of the dual theme of judgment and grace. There is, however, a decreasing of the life span. Also as we come near to the end of the "genealogy," literal descent from father to son is given without the gaps of the middle portion of the genealogy. The sons and daughters of Lamech are the sisters and brothers of Noah who do not survive the Flood. We are given no other information about the other sons and daughters.

5:31 Altogether, Lamech lived 777 years, and then he died.

Jacob sees significance in the number patterns; Cain is avenged 7-fold; the Cainite Lamech is avenged 77-fold, and the Sethite Lamech lives 777 years![21] While it is difficult to know the exact significance of this pattern, it is striking and leads the reader to compare and contrast Cain and the two Lamechs.

---

[20]Spina, "The 'Ground,'" pp. 328-329.
[21]B. Jacob, *Das Erste Buch der Tora* (New York: KTAV, 1974 rep.; 1934), pp. 156-157.

3. The Sons of Noah (5:32)

5:32 After Noah was 500 years old, he became the father of Shem, Ham and Japheth.

Unless we assume that the three boys were triplets, only one of the sons was born when Noah was 500 years old. Ham is later mentioned as the youngest son, and therefore they are not given in the order of their birth. Shem is said to be 100 years old two years after the Flood (Gen 11:10). Since Noah was 600 years old when the Flood came (i.e. 500 + 100; Gen 7:6) Shem must have been born two years or so after his older brother Japheth. Also not included is the statement that Noah "had other sons and daughters." Is this because there were none or because they were not relevant to the story line? The sons of Terah are similarly listed out of birth order as Abram, Nahor, and Haran in Genesis 11:27. Certainly by limiting the account to the three sons the theme of the new humanity through Noah after the Flood is highlighted.

GENESIS 6

B. THE TWO LINES INTERMARRY (6:1-4)

¹When men began to increase in number on the earth and daughters were born to them, ²the sons of God saw that the daughters of men were beautiful, and they married any of them they chose. ³Then the LORD said, "My Spirit will not contend with[a] man forever, for he is mortal[b]; his days will be a hundred and twenty years."

⁴The Nephilim were on the earth in those days—and also afterward—when the sons of God went to the daughters of men and had children by them. They were the heroes of old, men of renown.

[a]*3 Or My spirit will not remain in*   [b]*3 Or corrupt*

This controversial passage reads most naturally as the introduction to the Flood narrative, giving an explanation for the flood in terms of the pervasive evil in humanity that arises. As such it serves as a critique of the polytheistic myths about the flood with which the audience was familiar. In those myths morally trivial reasons are given which depict the gods as rather less mature than the men and women they supposedly have created. For example, in one widespread story the flood comes because the population explosion of humanity has resulted in such noise that the gods cannot sleep.[1] By contrast Genesis asserts that it is human corruption, particularly as it relates to violence (including sexual violence), which saturates the creation and brings God's reluctant judgment.

But several other matters in the interpretation of this passage are fraught with difficulty and uncertainty. The identity of the sons of God and the daughters of men is a matter of great controversy, and there is no way to be certain about the matter. Hamilton comments helpfully:

---

[1]*COS*, I:451.

Enter the problematic sons of God. Who are they? From whence do they come? They appear without fanfare or explanation. The narrator's assumption is that they are readily identifiable by his audience. But if his audience knew their identity, it has been lost to subsequent readers.[2]

Without being able to identify the sons of God and daughters of men, the sin and its relation to God's decision to destroy the world is also less than clear. The Nephilim mentioned in verse 4 have been the basis of much fanciful speculation. The text does not explicitly say that the Nephilim are the result of the union of the sons of God and the daughters of men, although many interpreters have assumed this. The point of the comment about man's days being 120 years is also capable of at least two interpretations, neither of which is certain. With this much uncertainty both about the purpose of this passage and of several key details within it we would do well to hold our opinions with an extra measure of humility and to take care not to base other exegetical conclusions on one of the possible interpretations of it.

In this commentary I will attempt to represent the opinions fairly and to give my own opinions tentatively. If I have anything to add to the thorough discussions already in print, it would be to keep the anti-idolatry polemic underlying these chapters in clear view. I also have chosen for reasons discussed in the Introduction to read over the shoulder of the original canonical reader. That reader is a committed monotheist. I therefore regard any view which swims against the flow of an anti-idolatry polemical reading of this passage as unlikely. Those who regarded the Torah as Scripture for God's people in the postexilic period were committed monotheists and would have rejected out of hand a text which seemed to affirm polytheism in any way. While this consideration does not solve the dilemmas of this passage it does rule out certain theories about the potential meaning of the sons of God.

---

[2]Hamilton, *Genesis 1–17,* p. 262.

1. The Sons of God and the Daughters of Men (6:1-2)

6:1 When men began to increase in number on the earth and daughters were born to them,
This verse provides the background situation in which the sons of God "took women to themselves"[3] (verse 2). With the increased population and the birth of numerous daughters who grew into women there were more women available than previously.

6:2 the sons of God saw that the daughters of men were beautiful, and they married any of them they chose.
The identity of "the sons of God" in this passage is fraught with uncertainty. Essentially there are three views. First, the oldest theory is that the "sons of God" are divine beings of some sort, either angels or lesser gods.[4] The lesser god subtheory is based on the fact that in the oldest sources in parallel cultures with which we are familiar the phrase "sons of God" refers to subordinate deities.[5] The problem with this theory is that, while it is certainly possible that it

---

[3]The NIV translates the Hebrew (וַיִּקְחוּ לָהֶם נָשִׁים, *wayyiqḥû lāhem nāšîm*) "they married them." While this is a common idiom for marriage, it literally reads, "and they took women to themselves" and can be used of forcible abduction or even rape (e.g. Gen 20:2,3; 34:2; 2 Sam 11:4). The NIV here limits the ambiguity by giving a less literal rendering.

[4]Ronald S. Hendel, "Of Demigods and the Deluge: Toward an Interpretation of Genesis 6:1-4," *JBL* 106/1 (1987): 23, represents this view well: "Gen 6:1-4 presents a mixing of categories — of gods and mortals — and the procreation of a hybrid category of demigods which it is in the nature of the myth to suppress. Mary Douglas has pointed out the preoccupation of ancient Israelite thought with the suppression of anomaly in dietary laws and in the laws of kinship. These 'purity laws' as she calls them, serve to keep "distinct the categories of creation." The same tendency is at work in Gen 6:1-4. The sexual mingling of the sons of God and the daughters of men creates an imbalance and a confusion in the cosmic order. The birth of the demigods threatens the fabric of the cosmos. The natural response in myth, as exemplified by the Babylonian flood tradition and the Greek Trojan War tradition, is to suppress the imbalance by destroying the cause of the imbalance. In the *Atrahasis* myth, humanity is destroyed so that its noise might be eliminated; in the Trojan War tradition, humanity is to be destroyed so that the demigods might be eliminated."

[5]See Christopher A. Rollston, "The Rise of Monotheism in Ancient Israel: Biblical and Epigraphic Evidence," *SCJ* 6.1 (2003): 102-104.

would be read that way in the early period when polytheism was so popular in Israel, it seems unlikely that when the book of Genesis was accepted along with the rest of the Torah as Scripture for Israel in the postexilic period that a text which was believed to affirm the existence of lesser deities would be accepted as divine, authoritative revelation for Israel.

The view that the sons of God are angels, however, is a plausible view for the original canonical audience. The earliest translation from the Hebrew, the Septuagint, reads *angeloi tou theou*, i.e., "angels of God." The main evidence is from other usages of the phrase in the OT for angels, both in prose (Job 1:6; 2:1) and poetry (Job 38:7; Ps 29:1; 82:6; 89:7 [Eng; 6]; and possibly Dan 3:25). Another strength of this view is that several early sources apparently read it this way including Enoch and many readings of Jude 6 and 2 Peter 2:4. The main argument against it is the NT teaching that angels *do not* marry (Matt 22:29-30; Mark 12:24-25; Luke 20:34-36). But these texts do not say angels *cannot* marry, but *do not* marry. Another problem is that if angels are culpable, why does God not punish them, instead of humankind? But the context shows clear human responsibility on other counts which do explain God's decision to send the flood adequately.

While this view is certainly plausible and it is hard to argue against the Septuagint and several early sources including perhaps two New Testament books, I do not personally find it persuasive. It is far from certain that Jude and 2 Peter affirm the angel interpretation of this passage. The fact that the speculative and fanciful Enoch literature affirms this view is not a strong argument in its favor. In my judgment it also adds a mythological tone to a decidedly antimythological text. However, I am aware that, as a person raised in a cultural environment which exalts science and is suspicious of the miraculous, I may find difficulties with the angel interpretation of this text because I have unconsciously swallowed the modern suspicion of the miraculous to a degree.[6] Certainly this view cannot be ruled out.

---

[6]Wenham, who supports the angel marriage view says (*Genesis 1–15*, p. 140), "If the modern reader finds this story incredible, that reflects a materialism that tends to doubt the existence of spirits good or ill. But those who believe that the creator could unite himself to human nature in the Virgin's womb will not find this story intrinsically beyond belief."

The second view regards the sons of God as dynastic rulers ("kings") who use their power in, and display their virility by, creating harems. In the Ugaritic Keret Epic, King Keret is called a "*bn il*" = "son of El." The word "elohim" is sometimes used of human figures (Exod 21:6; 22:7,8,27), and a son of David is implicitly referred to as (a) son of God (2 Sam 7:14; 1 Chr 17:13). The advantages to this view are: it removes what seems to us as a mythological element from the Bible, it makes sense of the context as the introduction to the Flood, and it continues the two-lines approach from earlier chapters. The chief weakness is that kings as a group are never called "sons of God" in the Hebrew Bible. Another potential problem is that this interpretation requires that the Hebrew phrase, "they took women/wives to themselves" be understood as forcible abduction and not marriage as it typically means.

The third view interprets the Sethites as the "godly" line while "the daughters of men" are the "ungodly" Cainites. The strength of this view is that it carries forward the contrast (implied by narrative juxtaposition) between the line of Cain in Genesis 4:1-24 and the line of Seth, whose line attempts to reestablish a relationship with the LORD in worship (Gen. 4:26), and whose line includes the godly Enoch who walked with God and was able to forgo physical death (Gen 5:21-24), as well as the blameless Noah (Gen 6:8-9). The fact that the chosen nation Israel is called God's son (Exod 4:22; Deut 4:11) is a possible argument in favor of the view, although the entire nation is a single "son" of God whereas here the group of individually faithful men are termed "sons" of God. It has for a long period of time been the most popular Christian interpretation. The fact that Paul refers to Christians as "sons of God" has little relevance here. But there are problems with this view. This interpretation forces upon the Hebrew word *'ādām* a different meaning in verse 1 ('humankind') from the meaning in verse 2 ('Cainite'). Also the phrase "son(s) of God" never elsewhere refers to Sethites or the "godly" line of mankind. The biggest weakness is that the view is based on supposition without much evidence.

I would tentatively suggest that, while any of these three views is possible, a combination of the second and the third views has many attractions. Chapters 4 and 5 do contrast the descendants of Cain and Seth. The fact that godly leaders from the line of Seth take (by force?) whomever they choose without regard for their own commitment to the Lord leads to a situation where (sexual) violence fills the earth. When those who lead (the word "king" may be somewhat anachronistic) depart from their godly traditions and use their power to take any woman they deem to be "good," the result is a sort of moral dissolution of the world. Israel faced the temptations of intermarrying with those who did not recognize the LORD in the land of Canaan. They are warned in the strongest of terms to avoid assimilating to the polytheistic practices of both the Egypt they have left and the Canaan they are entering (Lev 18:3). Intermarriage, whether arranged or not, is not an option because of the danger which such marriages presented for Israel (Deut 7:3-4: "for they will turn your sons away from following me to serve other gods . . ."). Postexilic Israel faced the very same issue (Ezra 9:14). This passage may be read as a warning to Israel. When those who are committed to God take partners who are not committed to a covenantal relationship with God, the danger is for those who are committed to God to be drawn away from faithfulness to him and not vice versa. The fact that kings as a group are not called "sons of God" and the fact that the godly individual is not termed "a son of God" elsewhere in the Hebrew Bible is perhaps not ultimately all that significant. It is of interest that both the church and the synagogue ultimately favored either the royal or godly line interpretation. This was in part motivated by the specious nature of the speculation that arose from the angel marriage view.[7]

Whoever the sons of God are, they "saw" that the daughters of men were "good." The NIV paraphrases this word as "beautiful." But this translation, while accurate, loses the connection between this passage and the preceding chapters. To begin with it is the Creator God in Genesis 1 who "sees" that something is "good." It may be that a subtle hint is being given that the sons of God are taking over the creator's prerogative by defining what is good. But there may also be an echo of Genesis 3:6 where during the temptation scene the woman *saw* that the fruit of the tree of the knowledge of good and evil was *good* and *took* it.[8] These intertextual echoes, so common in Genesis, inform the reader that this is a "Fall" narrative.

---

[7]P.S. Alexander, "The Targumim and Early Exegesis of 'Sons of God' in Gen 6," *JJS* 23 (1972): 60-71, argues this for the adopting of the royal interpretation in the Aramaic paraphrases of the Hebrew Bible, the Targumim.

[8]Wenham, *Genesis 1–15,* p. 141.

The fact that the "sons of God" took women for themselves as "they chose" may hint at the fact that these unions were not legitimate. There is no mention of their parents arranging marriages as would have been typical in Israel. They chose whomever they wanted and regarded to be good without regard to what God and parents regarded as good. The fact that they "took" them may indicate that the taking was by force, as noted above.[9] In this reading the sons of God are thus guilty of misusing their power for sexual advantage and of forging relationships with those who do not share their godly heritage, which leads them away from God.

2. The Decision to Reduce the Life Span of Humanity (6:3)

6:3 Then the LORD said, "My Spirit will not contend with man forever, for he is mortal; his days will be a hundred and twenty years."

This verse is fraught with translational difficulties. The word translated "contend" (יָדוֹן, *yādôn*) is a *hapax legomenon* that has been variously understood. The Septuagint and Vulgate suggest "remain" (followed by NRSV) while NASB in agreement with the NIV's "contend" suggests "strive."[10] The word translated "mortal" is more literally

---

[9]The *BBC* (p. 36): "The practice of marrying 'any of them they chose' has been interpreted by some to be a reference to polygamy. While it is not to be doubted that polygamy was practiced, it is difficult to imagine why that would be worthy of note, since polygamy was an acceptable practice even in Israel in Old Testament times. It is more likely that this is a reference to the 'right of the first night,' cited as one of the oppressive practices of kings in the *Gilgamesh Epic. The king could exercise his right, as representative of the gods, to spend the wedding night with any woman who was being given in marriage. This presumably was construed as a *fertility rite. If this is the practice referred to here, it would offer an explanation of the nature of the offense." While this is a possibility, I think it is safer to leave the exact nature of the taking undetermined although rape, abductions for harems, or even the right of first night are possibilities.

[10]Hendel ("Of Demigods," p. 15) argues that "contend" should be understood as a stative qal imperfect from the geminate root דנן (*dnn*) = "to be strong." He notes that it is twice attested in Ugaritic and the place name Dannah in Josh 15:49 near Debir in the relatively unpopulated hill country of Judea, is probably an Israelite settlement with a Hebrew name meaning "stronghold" or "fortress" from this same geminate verbal stem. To say "My

"flesh" in contrast to Spirit. The word translated "for" (בְּשַׁגַּם, *bᵊšaggam*) in NIV is found only here in the entire OT.[11] It seems to be composed of three elements בְּ = "in," שׁ = a shortened form of *ăsher* = "which," and גַּם = "also." All three of the most popular standard translations (NIV, NRSV, NASB) give "for" or "because" for this word.[12]

After the sons of God event is recorded, the LORD comes to a conclusion about humanity. Depending on the translation of the word *yādôn* ("contend" or "remain") the LORD announces either that an unending fight will not work or that his Spirit will not remain forever in human flesh. The first alternative is adopted by the NIV. The fact that humanity is flesh (NIV "mortal") is a sign of weakness both morally and physically. The LORD decides to stop fighting with a resistant humanity and end it. This translation tends to favor the view that the hundred and twenty years refers to the time leading up to the Flood. This reading would tend to favor the view that the initial divine decision was to wipe out humanity in its entirety until Noah found favor in the eyes of the LORD (Gen 6:8).

Alternatively, if we translate, "My Spirit will not remain in humanity forever" the sense seems to be that he will remove his Spirit and consequently humanity's flesh will die. The reference to a hundred and twenty years would then most naturally refer to the successive shortening of the expected life span from slightly less than 1,000 years to a mere 120. Both of these readings are plausible. I would tentatively favor the second since the last recorded death in the Pentateuch, Moses', occurs at 120 years (Deut 34:7), and the imagined audience,

---

Spirit will not remain strong in humanity" is similar in thought to "remain" in humankind.

[11]Roy A. Rosenberg ("*Besaggam* and *Shiloh*," ZAW 105 [1993]: 258-261) thinks that this was a neologism created because its value in gemmatria is 345 (b = 2; sh = 300; g = 3; and m = 40), the value of Moses's name in Hebrew. Thereby the 'initiated' meaning would be: "My spirit will not remain strong in the man forever; Moses is flesh and his days will be 120 years." This does coincide with Sailhamer's contention that the death of Moses is in view in this passage, since in the Pentateuch we see the decline of ages (not without exceptions) until the last person who dies is Moses at 120 years. I am not certain I buy into this, but it is interesting. Both of these correspondences were noticed by the Rabbis (Pirque de Rabbi Eliezer, ch. 32; Zohar 1.25b).

[12]The NASB footnote suggests "in his going astray" as an alternative.

Israel on the verge of the promised land, might naturally connect the two. This reading can also be plausibly understood as a critique of polytheistic accounts of the search for immortality.[13]

3. The Nephilim (6:4a)

6:4a The Nephilim were on the earth in those days—and also afterward—

This text has been the supposed basis for much unhelpful speculation in popular circles. This text does not say that the Nephilim are the children of the union of the sons of God and the daughters of men. The meaning of the phrase "and also afterward" and the punctuation of this verse is key to understanding it. The NIV punctuation seems to be suggesting, "The Nephilim were on the earth in those days when the sons of God went to the daughters of men and had children by them." Even this punctuation, however, comes short of saying that the children of the union are the Nephilim. If one assumes that the Nephilim are the children the phrase "and also afterward" seems to suggest that after the Flood there was another union(s) of the sons of God and daughters of men which resulted in more Nephilim being born. And if it happened then, why not now? Perhaps angels are still on the hunt for human women! The speciousness of such interpretations should warn us about the dangers of using the Bible speculatively.

4. The Warrior Children Born from the Illicit Unions (6:4b)

6:4b when the sons of God went to the daughters of men and had children by them. They were the heroes of old, men of renown.

---

[13]*BBC*, p. 36 "The limitation of 120 years most likely refers to a reduction of the life span of humans, since it is in the context of a statement about mortality. While the verse **is** notoriously difficult to translate, modern consensus is moving toward translating it "My spirit will not remain in man forever," thus affirming mortality. Just as the offense can be understood in light of information from the Gilgamesh Epic, so this statement may refer to the never ending quest for immortality; a quest such as is at the core of the Gilgamesh Epic. Though Gilgamesh lived after the flood, these elements of the narrative resonate with universal human experience."

I would suggest the following punctuation, "The Nephilim were on the earth in those days and also afterwards. When the sons of God went to the daughters of men and had children by them, they were the heroes of old, men of renown." In this reading *Nephilim* is not an ethnic designation but a description of a particular type of individual. In Numbers 13:33, the only other time they appear in the Pentateuch,[14] they are identified along with the descendants of Anak as some of the inhabitants of the land of Canaan. The latter are described as giants, but there is no necessary reason to consider the Nephilim to be giants. Instead the imagined audience would understand that the great warrior figures that they were about to face in the land of Canaan were also present prior to the Flood. Their violent natures were part of the reason for the sending of the Flood. Just as the LORD destroyed the Nephilim in the Flood, so the Nephilim which Israel will face will likewise receive his judgment. Israel's fear of the spies' description of the Nephilim and the sons of Anak resulted in an entire generation perishing in the wilderness. Here the Torah is telling its imagined audience that there is no reason to fear the inhabitants of the land as the Exodus generation had done. The LORD, long ago, demonstrated his ability to defeat any sort of violent warrior who works against his purposes.

It seems possible that even the word Nephilim itself is an ironic description. It means "fallen ones" in Hebrew. Perhaps this is the Torah's way of anticipating their defeat at the LORD's hand!

The children of the union of the sons of God and the daughters of men are described as "heroes of old, men of renown." The Nephilim are violent warrior figures that arise throughout history. They are paired with the violent children of the illicit union of the sons of God and the daughters of men to reinforce the theme of human violence as one of the principal reasons for the Flood. The phrase, "men of renown" is literally in Hebrew "men of the name" (אַנְשֵׁי הַשֵּׁם, *'anšê hašēm*). This is the beginning of a repeated wordplay in the Hebrew text which becomes a theme linking the generation which perished in the Flood to the generation of Babel ("Let us

---

[14]According to Zimmerli (*Ezekiel 2*, Hermeneia [Philadelphia: Fortress Press, 1983], pp. 168, 175) Ezek 32:27 refers to the Nephilim. NRSV has "fallen warriors of long ago," treating the word as an adjective rather than a noun.

make a name for ourselves," Gen 11:4). They are deliberately contrasted with those who receive a name through God's promise ("I will make your name great" Gen 12:2). Those who achieve a name by their own efforts perish, while those who trust in God's promise receive a great and lasting name through God's grace.

C. THE DECISION TO SEND THE FLOOD (6:5-13)

⁵The LORD saw how great man's wickedness on the earth had become, and that every inclination of the thoughts of his heart was only evil all the time. ⁶The LORD was grieved that he had made man on the earth, and his heart was filled with pain. ⁷So the LORD said, "I will wipe mankind, whom I have created, from the face of the earth—men and animals, and creatures that move along the ground, and birds of the air—for I am grieved that I have made them." ⁸But Noah found favor in the eyes of the LORD.

1. The LORD Recognizes the Extent of the Evil (6:5)

6:5 The LORD saw how great man's wickedness on the earth had become, and that every inclination of the thoughts of his heart was only evil all the time.
This text expresses in a powerful way just how pervasive and damaging human sinfulness can become. Humanity's wickedness had become great and humanity's inmost thoughts were continually thoughts of evil. This must be paired with 8:21 which is worded in a remarkably similar way but evaluates humanity after the cleansing through Noah's election. There God concludes that man's nature will not change. Even the Flood will not drive evil from the heart of mankind. His strategy must change. The Flood, then, starts the game over, with a realistic understanding of just how difficult it will be for the Lord to see humankind fulfill his purposes without his intervention. Christians know that ultimately the intervention required was incarnation of the Divine Son. This text is the beginning of the Bible's explanation of why such drastic action was required.

2. The LORD's Regret at Having Made Humankind (6:6)

6:6 The LORD was grieved that he had made man on the earth, and his heart was filled with pain.

Often this statement is viewed as anthropomorphism, i.e., speaking of God as though he were a human person in order for us to understand him better. The argument is that the creator God of the universe does not experience emotions since emotions flow from our limited and flawed human perspectives. But if it is anthropomorphism, then it is necessary anthropomorphism. God does not have the power to prevent humanity from making bad choices without turning us into puppets. He does, however, as the Creator have the power to start over with his creation.

3. Decision to Destroy Creation (6:7)

6:7 So the LORD said, "I will wipe mankind, whom I have created, from the face of the earth—men and animals, and creatures that move along the ground, and birds of the air—for I am grieved that I have made them."

The initial decision is to destroy humankind *en toto* and the rest of the animate creation along with it. This suggests that in some fashion the destinies of humanity and creation are indissolubly linked as in the account of the curses in chapter 3. God's grief at having made humanity stems from having provided everything for the good of humanity only to see them reject his good gifts and drift further and further away from his purposes for them. The divine pain at the sight of such grievous rebellion by the creatures he made is an important biblical theme which leads ultimately to the cross.

4. The Exception of Noah (6:8)

6:8 But Noah found favor in the eyes of the LORD.

When it seems hopeless, seemingly out of nowhere Noah is said to find favor in the eyes of the LORD. Creation will not be totally erased. The LORD will begin again with a chosen person, a sort of "new Adam." In Hebrew the name Noah (נֹחַ, *nōaḥ*) and the verb found favor (חֵן, *ḥēn*) is a reversal of letters and may be a wordplay. It is also possible that there is a further echo of the verb "he grieved" in verse 6 (וַיִּנָּחֶם, *wayyinnāḥem*) which has a root beginning with the same two Hebrew letters as Noah's name (נֹחַ). The LORD's grief (נחם, *nḥm*) at the (sexually) violent human world is contrasted with his grace (חֵן, *ḥn*) to a faithful man (נֹחַ, *nḥ*). The first-time reader breathes a sigh of relief. The LORD has not given up. We know from the rest of Scripture (a second-time reading) that he will never give up!

Rolf Rendtorff has helpfully observed a parallel between the structure of the Primeval History in Genesis 1–11 and the Sinai story in Exodus 19–34. He argues that they show a parallel structure. In both cases the first gift of God (creation/covenant) is endangered by human sin and threatened to be destroyed by God's wrath. In both cases God changes his mind because of (the intervention of) one man (Noah/Moses). In both cases God promises not to bring destruction again (on humanity/on Israel), and in order to confirm that he (re)establishes his covenant (*berith*).[15] This reading would be especially apropos to the imagined audience, Israel on the verge of entering the promised land. That generation had experienced the near miss at Sinai when the LORD was seemingly on the verge of wiping out Israel and starting over with Moses (Exod 32:9,10). They begin to see (and the rest of Scripture reassures us) that even the defection of God's own people will not defeat God's gracious purposes.

INTRODUCTION TO THE FLOOD NARRATIVE

In order to understand the Flood narrative on its own terms (post)modern readers must learn to put their contemporary questions about the Flood on the margins. The Flood narrative is carefully crafted to emphasize the key point that, after the appalling corruption which humanity had fallen into, the LORD decides to begin anew with a new creation. The garden of Eden had not worked as a strategy for sustaining the type of relationship which the LORD desires with the people he has created. Life east of Eden fared even

---

[15]Robert Rendtorff, "'Covenant' as a Structuring Concept in Genesis and Exodus," *JBL* 108/3 (1989): 385-393.

worse. The escalating moral corruption and violence to which humanity degenerated brought the painful decision to begin anew. The Flood narrative's structure and theology make this clear.

THE STRUCTURE OF THE FLOOD NARRATIVE

The Flood narrative has a chiastic or inverted structure such that the events which unfold and the statements made in the first half of the narrative are repeated in reverse order in the second half. The Flood narrative has 7 stages or episodes:
1) 6:11,12: Divine speech — the decision to send the flood and rescue Noah;
2) 6:13-22: the command to build the ark;
3) 7:1-5: the command to enter the ark
4) 7:6-24: the flood comes;
5) 8:1-14: the flood abates;
6) 8:15-19: the command to exit the ark
7) 8:20–9:17: the building of the altar and the covenant

Notice that elements 4 and 5, and 3 and 6 obviously mirror each other. What is perhaps less obvious is that elements 2 and 7 both have something built (an ark and an altar). Elements 1 and 7 are speeches by God regarding his relationship with humanity. Another way of showing the inverted structure of the Flood narrative is provided in the chart below.

The Flood Narrative as a Palistrophe[16]

```
1] 6:1-12                                          1˥ 9:1-17
   2] 6:13-22                                   2˥ 8:20-22
      3] 7:1-10                              3˥ 8:15-19
         4] 7:11-16                    4˥ 8:6-14
            5] 7:17-24          5˥ 8:1-5
               6] 8:1
```

---

[16]For a similar analysis see Wenham, *Genesis 1–15,* pp. 156-158.

Analysis

1 and 1'] resolve to destroy order and resolve to preserve order
2 and 2'] divine speeches to Noah
3 and 3'] entering the ark and leaving the ark
4 and 4'] flooding of the earth and drying of the earth
5 and 5'] rising of the flood and receding of the flood
    6   ] God remembers and the process is reversed

Wenham has noted the palistrophic structure of the waiting periods during the flood.[17]

Waiting Periods in the Flood Narrative

7:4	7 DAYS		
7:10	7		
7:17		40	
7:24			150 WATER PREVAILING
8:3			150 DECLINING OF WATER
8:6		40	
8:1	7		
8:12	7		

In addition if one imagines the narrative playing itself out pictorially, there is a striking parallelism between the second half of the narrative and the creation account in Genesis 1 beginning with verse 2. The earth is covered with water, and as yet there is no expanse or firmament which creates the space where we breathe and birds fly. The expanse is then created which separates the water in the clouds above the expanse from the waters which now cover the earth. Then the waters are gathered into seas and lakes and rivers and the dry ground appears. Plants grow on that dry ground. Birds then fill the air. Finally animals and then humans fill the dry ground.

The last half of the Flood narrative is strikingly parallel. The rain stops and the expanse is reestablished. Birds are sent out from the ark to fly in that air space. Eventually a dove returns with an olive leaf in its beak demonstrating that the dry land has appeared and plants have begun to grow on it once again. When the ark is opened, the animals depart followed by Noah and his family. The point being

---

[17]Ibid., p. 157.

made by this description is that a new creation has begun. There is a new physical creation and there is a new humanity. The commission given to Noah and his family after the Flood is deliberately reminiscent of the commission given to humanity at creation. They are to be fruitful and multiply and fill the earth just as humankind, both male and female, are commanded in Genesis 1:26-28.

THE THEOLOGY OF THE FLOOD NARRATIVE

The structure of the Flood narrative as discussed above portrays the Flood as de-creation followed by re-creation. But the re-creation world, while similar in many ways to the world prior to its de-creation, is also different. The postdiluvian world is the last universalistic divine strategy. God related to humanity as a whole in the Garden and in the world east of Eden. But in both cases the relationship became estranged by human rebellion. The Flood functions theologically or ideologically as the last attempt by the LORD to relate to humanity as a whole, on a universal basis. The fact that this third universal strategy also fails leads to the introduction of election, the divine choosing of specific persons as the primary channel of the outworking of his purposes. The persistent echoing of words, phrases, ideas, and persons from the creation account is too prevalent to be fortuitous. The narrator's deliberate strategy is to compare and contrast the first creation with the "second creation" in the time of Noah. Bergant has even argued that the Flood and creation stories are variants of the same story.

> Scholars currently agree that the narrative of the flood and the eventual recession of the waters is a second creation story, coming from the same theological tradition and highlighting much of the same theology as found in Genesis 1. In fact, in the traditions of many early civilizations, the flood narrative was identical with the creation narrative. The destructive flood was really the primeval flood, and the individual saved was the first created human being. This suggests that both creation and flood were viewed as primeval happenings, not as historical events. Israel's flood account contains some of the very vocabulary found in the creation report. The abyss (*tehom*) was in place before God separated the waters (Gen 1:2). This same

abyss burst open, causing the flood (Gen 7:11), and was closed when God decreed its end (8:2). Both narratives mention a wind (*ruah*) that swept over the cosmic abyss (1:2; 8:1). It was God's intent that the animals "be fertile and multiply" (1:22; 8:17). The same blessing with the commission to rule over the animals is given to humankind in both passages (1:28; 9:1-2).[18]

But Bergant confuses the re-creation of the post-Flood era with the original creation, which in the Bible is not a flood narrative, unlike other ancient Near Eastern stories.[19] Instead the point must be understood in its narrative context as a third strategy for accomplishing God's purposes in creation. God is portrayed as having a purpose in creation which is temporarily frustrated by the appalling rebellion of humanity against him. The Flood narrative demonstrates that God is not a God who will give up on his purposes. There is and will always be a Noah who finds grace in God's eyes. He is also a God who will not tolerate a world of violence and corruption.

Humankind is portrayed as prone to rebellion. Even the Flood will not remove the tendency toward evil in the human heart as a comparison of Genesis 6:5 and 8:21 makes clear, as does the story of the fall of Noah and his son Ham in Genesis 9:18-27. But even though the evil in the human heart has not been driven out by the Flood, humanity is still the focus of God's creative purposes. They are still the image of God and still have the responsibility to be fruitful and multiply and fill the earth in order to rule over it.

The fact that the Flood does not change human nature is striking. When God promises, in spite of this fact, never again to curse the ground on account of humanity (Gen 8:21), there has obviously been a shift in the divine strategy. The destiny of the physical creation is no longer tied so directly to the destiny of humanity as it was previously.[20] If future generations of humanity return to the violence and corruption which brought on divine judgment through a flood, there will be no flood! Instead God will deal with the outbreak of

---

[18]Dianne Bergant, "Is the Biblical Worldview Anthropocentric?" *New Theology Review* 4 (1991): 11.

[19]This may well be another point of polemic against the polytheistic myths of creation and flood.

[20]I am not implying that there is a complete severing of the relationship, cf. Romans 8:22.

human evil in other ways. The Flood then functions as a sort of warning of the potential severity of God's judgment (see Gen 9:11).[21]

The relationship of humanity to the rest of creation is also changed in other ways after the Flood. The diet of humanity had been limited (with possible exceptions for sacrifices and feasts) to a vegetarian one. After the Flood God allows humanity to eat animal flesh as food also. He protects the animal kingdom from being hunted into extinction by making them innately afraid of humans. He also limits human consumption of animals to those which are dead. They cannot be eaten with their life's blood still in them (Gen 9:1-5).

THE BIBLICAL FLOOD STORY AND THE FLOOD STORIES OF THE ANCIENT NEAR EAST

No biblical narrative in Genesis has more striking parallels in ancient Near Eastern Culture than the Flood narrative. The Mesopotamian stories in particular make it obvious that Genesis is telling the same story but from its own monotheistic point of view. The following parallels argue strongly for some connection between the narratives.

1. The Atrahasis epic and the Gilgamesh epic depict the chief god Enlil as angry at humanity while Genesis depicts the one God as angry.
2. Enlil decides to destroy humanity with a flood just as God does in Genesis.
3. In both accounts the hero of the flood is warned of its coming.
4. The hero is commanded to build an ark which is sealed with bitumen, has decks, and is covered.
5. The hero obeys and saves his family, animals, and necessary supplies for them to eat.
6. The ark is boarded and closed up.
7. The flood and the destruction of humanity is described.
8. The rain ends and the ark settles on a specific mountain.
9. The hero opens the window and sends out birds to determine

---

[21]See my unpublished paper, "Touching Evil: Yahweh's Changing Strategies," delivered at the Stone-Campbell Journal Conference, Cincinnati, Ohio, March 27, 2004, available from the author.

whether the flood waters have abated enough to make it safe to depart.
10. After exiting the ark, the hero offers a sacrifice which God/the gods smell as a sweet savor.
11. The hero receives a divine blessing.

These common elements make a strong case for Genesis telling the same story,[22] but in a way that fits the needs of its audience and the worldview of the author. It is particularly in the differences between the monotheistic biblical account and the polytheistic flood stories of Israel's context that this is most apparent.

THE FLOOD AS ANTI-IDOLATRY POLEMIC

Genesis' Flood story is a counterstory. Israel was familiar with the polytheistic stories of the flood. Those stories were closely related to the creation myths, since creation was viewed as a sort of battle with the primordial Chaos in the sea. Just as the creation account serves as an argument (a polemic) against polytheistic views, the same is true of the Flood narrative. The ancient world had a memory of a flood of universal proportions from which only a small remnant of humanity emerged. Genesis is subtly (and sometimes not so subtly) undermining the polytheistic form of the story. The following selection of differences with the ancient Near Eastern flood stories should make this come into clearer focus.

1. In the biblical account there is only one God, not a pantheon of gods in conflict.
2. The God of the Bible is not frightened by the flood as the gods of the flood stories are.[23] He alone is God, and he alone sends the flood. In the myths the high god Enlil sends the flood, and the other gods are afraid of it.
3. The God of the Bible reluctantly and with a heavy heart sends

---

[22]I am not claiming that the author of Genesis had actually read the flood stories which have been excavated.

[23]Tablet 11, line 113 of the Gilgamesh Epic reads, "The gods were frightened by the deluge. And, shrinking back, they ascended to the heaven of Anu. The gods cowered like dogs crouched against the outer wall" (*ANET*, p. 94).

the flood in order to eliminate the outbreak of human sin, violence, and corruption. In the myths Enlil sends the flood because of the noise of humanity caused by its overpopulation.

4. God finds Noah blameless and commands him to build an ark to preserve humanity and the animal kingdom. In other words the same God who is responsible for sending the flood is also responsible for preserving the remnant. In the myths the god Ea, against the wishes and without the knowledge of the chief god Enlil and the pantheon which accepted his decision, secretly preserves the remnant of humanity. Noah does not survive because of divine favoritism but because of God's grace.

5. In the myths the hero, Atrahasis, is a king while Noah is an ordinary but godly person.

6. In the myths after the flood the hero is elevated to divine status, and his name is changed to Utnapishtim. In the Bible Noah remains a human being and even lives to show his imperfections.

7. In the myths the ark has no connection to reality. It is shaped as a cube and takes only seven days to build. In the Bible the ark has dimensions that reminds one of a boat which could float and does not suggest an unimaginably short time for its building.

8. In the Bible God shuts the ark in order to show that he is in control. In the myths the hero shuts the ark.

9. In the myths the gods are "'crowding like flies around the sacrifice,' greedily jostling for places at the open-air barbecue."[24] Humanity had been created to provide the gods with food through sacrifices. The flood had stopped their food supply and they were hungry. In Genesis God smells the sweet savor of a sacrifice performed in humble gratitude to him. He is not hungry, and sacrifices do not feed him.

10. God is the hero of the biblical flood story. He is in control. Noah obeys God but does not speak a single word during the entire narrative. By contrast the hero of the myths is valorized. His achievements are emphasized. He ultimately is divinized.

While this is not intended to be an exhaustive listing of the differences between the flood stories of the ancient world and Genesis, the above should make clear that Genesis is telling a counterstory.

---

[24]Wenham, *Genesis 1–15*, p. 165.

Its imagined audience was familiar with the myths of creation and flood in the polytheistic cultures in which they lived and by which they were surrounded. Those stories portray the gods as competitive, political, greedy, ignorant, unreasonable, unreliable, fearful, petty, insecure, and unjust. They are no more moral, and sometimes less so, than the human beings they had created. Genesis portrays God as moral, just, righteous, holy, gracious, secure, fearless, all-knowing, and all-powerful. Israel, as they were about to enter the promised land, needed to know that God could be relied upon and that God would not tolerate a plague of human evil.

THE FLOOD LOCAL OR UNIVERSAL?

One of the questions that modern readers of the Flood narrative often have is how the biblical account interfaces with contemporary geology. We ask such questions as, "Is the Flood responsible for the fossils which have been discovered?" "Is there physical evidence from around the world of a flood of physically universal proportions?" And "Was the physical environment of the world so different prior to the Flood that it is impossible to project currently operating physical processes into the distant past?" Certainly the ideology of the Flood narrative is that it is universal. The pounding repetition of the words "all" and "every" in the narrative[25] make it clear that just as the moral corruption of humankind (the cause of the Flood) is universal, so also the judgment for that corruption is universal. But does this necessarily translate into a physically universal flood?

One concern with this understandable assumption is that the Hebrew word for "earth" can also, and is often to be, translated "land." We do not have that ambiguity of meaning in English. Secondly there is no reason to believe that the writers or audience of the Bible were aware of the extent of the physical earth. They were not asking questions about the fossil record, the geological evidence of a physically universal flood, or any number of other modern questions. Sometimes the word "all" is used in the Bible in a less strictly universal sense than might be supposed. For example the

---

[25]A grammcord search reveals 63 uses of the Hebrew word for "all" or "every" in the Flood narrative.

apostle Paul writing in the early 60s A.D. says of the gospel message that it had already come to the Colossians just as it had come to "all the world" (Col 1:6). Surely the gospel had not yet gone to all the world in some literalistic sense by the sixth decade of the Christian era! The point the book of Genesis is making is a theological one. Universal corruption brings universal condemnation from a holy and righteous God. Third, the physical evidence that we currently have is, according to some scholars, inconclusive when it comes to a universal flood. Jack P. Lewis, who taught for 35 years at Harding University, summarizes the evidence in light of popular-level assertions regarding evidence for the Flood:

> Scholars are agreed that archaeological evidence for a universal flood in the historical past is wanting. The silt layers noticed at Ur and Kish by Wooley and Langdon (and similar silting at Nineveh, Shuruppak, Uruk, and Lagash) are of differing dates, and lack convincing connection with the biblical narrative. Extremely old sites in Palestine, such as Jericho, have revealed no flood deposits. (Aquatic fossils found at mountainous elevations were once seized upon as evidence of a universal flood, but they may be more reasonably explained as resulting from geologic upheavals than as evidence of a cataclysmic flood.) Claims that remains of the biblical ark have been found on the 17,000 foot Agri Dagh peak northwest of Lake Van in Turkey (traditional Mt. Ararat) are unconvincing; such claims ignore the text of the Bible, which does not mention a specific mountain but mountains (pl.), and are misguided in their certainty that Agri Dagh is the correct location. Carbon 14 dating of the wood allegedly found there dates the samples tested no earlier than A.D. 450, about the time Christian tradition began to center on this mountain. Claims formerly made of living persons who had seen remains of the ark, when examined, prove themselves incredible.[26]

While attempts to refute the fossil evidence and current geological theories are undoubtedly well intentioned, they may also result in focusing interpretation on questions that the text was not trying to answer (and thus distracting attention from the lessons of the narrative). In addition such attempts may in the long run bring

---

[26]Jack P. Lewis, "Flood," *ABD* 2:798-803.

discredit on the Bible. The Bible is, in my judgment, concerned with other matters.

⁹**This is the account of Noah.**

Noah was a righteous man, blameless among the people of his time, and he walked with God. ¹⁰Noah had three sons: Shem, Ham and Japheth.

¹¹Now the earth was corrupt in God's sight and was full of violence. ¹²God saw how corrupt the earth had become, for all the people on earth had corrupted their ways. ¹³So God said to Noah, "I am going to put an end to all people, for the earth is filled with violence because of them. I am surely going to destroy both them and the earth.

5. Noah Introduced (6:9-10)

6:9 This is the account of Noah. Noah was a righteous man, blameless among the people of his time, and he walked with God. The account of Noah begins with the standard marker of structure in the book of Genesis. He had been introduced in the previous section and in the genealogy of chapter 5. Here he is given a moral and spiritual evaluation by the author. Noah was a man of righteousness in contrast to the corrupt and violent society in which he lived. Compared to them he was blameless. "Noah is the only person in Genesis described as blameless or perfect. Abraham is told to be perfect and walk before [God] (17:1) but he is never said to have achieved it."[27] Noah is not only described by the narrator as a "righteous" man; God himself describes him so in 7:1. The word often describes the innocent in contrast to the guilty, who are described as "wicked." Abraham is concerned about the "righteous" of Sodom receiving judgment along with the "wicked" or "guilty." The word "blameless" is often used in sacrificial contexts of the "perfect" animal. "He walked with God" recalls the statement about Enoch in 5:23. The verb "walked" is in the hithpael (reflexive "he walked himself") form and reminds the reader of the Garden scene in 3:8 where the same verb form occurs of the LORD's walking in the garden in

---

[27]Wenham, *Torah as Story*, p. 35.

the cool part of the day. To walk with God is to enjoy the same sort of direct and easy access to the LORD's presence as Adam and Eve had in the garden.

Noah functions in this story as a sort of Adam *redivivus*. Forrest comments, "Compared with the first Adam (humanity), Noah's potential to vindicate the divine confidence in humanity seems assured." He also notes some contrast with the characterization of Utnapishtim, the hero of the Gilgamesh Epic:

> Unlike Noah, Utnapishtim has a steersman, Puzur-Amurri, but Noah's ark is implicitly directed by God himself. In the construction of the craft, Noah is merely the instrument of the divine will, whereas in the Gilgamesh account Utnapishtim shows considerable initiative of his own. It is only when the flood waters have subsided and Noah is returned to earth that Noah shows some initiative in planting a vineyard. Until that point he is the epitome of acquiescence and obedience.[28]

6:10 Noah had three sons: Shem, Ham and Japheth.

The sons of Noah are not listed in order of birth, but in order of significance in the story. Shem, the second born, is chosen by God. Ham, the youngest plays a key role in 9:18-29. Japheth, apparently the oldest, is listed last. Their names are listed here according to their importance in the ensuing narrative.

6. Reiteration of the Corruption and God's Recognition of It (6:11-12)

6:11 Now the earth was corrupt in God's sight and was full of violence.

The abrupt shift of tone in this verse seems to be deliberate. Even though Noah was a righteous man, the earth was still corrupt in God's sight and full of violence. The verse begins with a waw-consecutive, implying a sort of sequence. Noah was a righteous man, then he had three sons; then the earth became corrupt and full of violence. The outbreak of violence is one of the primary signs of the

---

[28]Robert W.E. Forrest, "Paradise Lost Again: Violence and Obedience in the Flood Narrative," *JSOT* 62 (1994): 10.

distortion of the world because of sin. The violence has escalated to such an extent that it requires divine intervention. Humanity had been commissioned to be fruitful and multiply and *fill* the earth. Instead they *filled* the earth with violence.

6:12 God saw how corrupt the earth had become, for all the people on earth had corrupted their ways.

Notice the parallel between this verse and God's evaluation of his completed creation in 1:31: "and God saw everything that he had made, and behold, it was very good." Here he saw how corrupt the earth had become. This verse refers to God *seeing* his creation, and the Hebrew word "behold" also occurs as in 1:31. But God's response in chapter 6 is the direct opposite of 1:31. There it was "very good." Here it was "corrupt." That corruption comes from the decisions of human beings who "corrupted their ways." And this was not the pattern of a few; "all" people on earth had corrupted their ways.

7. Announcement to Noah of Decision to Judge Humanity (6:13)

6:13 So God said to Noah, "I am going to put an end to all people, for the earth is filled with violence because of them. I am surely going to destroy both them and the earth.[29]

Because the corruption has spread to *all* people, God tells Noah that he is going to put an end to *all* people. God confirms to Noah what the narrator had just told his readers, the earth is full of violence. In this way the narrator makes clear that the narrator shares God's perspective. God announces that both the people who have filled the earth with violence and the earth that has been so filled will be destroyed. Just as in the garden of Eden the physical creation was cursed along with humanity, so here the creation receives God's judgment along with the people who caused God's judgment to come. The destiny of the creation itself is tied up with the destiny of

---

[29]P.J. Harland ("Vertical or Horizontal: The Sin of Babel," *VT* XLVIII/4 (1998): 515-533) argues that the last sentence should read "and behold! I will destroy them with the earth," interpreting the direct object marker as the preposition "with" in a similar way that Eve's statement in 4:1 is understood.

humanity. This should lead us to appreciate the significant place we have been given in God's purpose and the responsibility we have toward the rest of creation to live in conformity with God's will. If the creation's destiny is tied up with the destiny of humanity, we are responsible for what we do in and with creation.

In the Atrahasis Epic's account of the flood the reason that the gods decide to send the flood is the "noise" of mankind. This is not necessarily different from the biblical reason in that "noise" can be the result of violence. Abel's blood cries out from the ground (4:10), and the outcry against Sodom and Gomorrah is great (Gen 18:20). The noise could be generated either by the number of petitions being made to the gods to respond to the violence and bloodshed or by the victims who cry out in their distress. But given the overall portrayal of the gods in the ancient flood stories as rather less mature and rather more self-focused than many humans, it seems more likely that all sorts of human noise interrupts the sleep of the gods. If so, Genesis is critiquing the flood stories' rationale for the flood. It is not something trivial like the noise of humanity but something deadly serious, the violence and moral corruption of humankind.

D. THE DIRECTIVE TO BUILD THE ARK (6:14-22)

[14] So make yourself an ark of cypress[a] wood; make rooms in it and coat it with pitch inside and out. [15] This is how you are to build it: The ark is to be 450 feet long, 75 feet wide and 45 feet high.[b] [16] Make a roof for it and finish[c] the ark to within 18 inches[d] of the top. Put a door in the side of the ark and make lower, middle and upper decks. [17] I am going to bring floodwaters on the earth to destroy all life under the heavens, every creature that has the breath of life in it. Everything on earth will perish. [18] But I will establish my covenant with you, and you will enter the ark—you and your sons and your wife and your sons' wives with you. [19] You are to bring into the ark two of all living creatures, male and female, to keep them alive with you. [20] Two of every kind of bird, of every kind of animal and of every kind of creature that moves along the ground will come to you to be kept alive. [21] You are to take every kind of food that is to be eaten and store it away as food for you and for them."

²²Noah did everything just as God commanded him.

ᵃ*14 The meaning of the Hebrew for this word is uncertain.*
ᵇ*15 Hebrew 300 cubits long, 50 cubits wide and 30 cubits high* (about 140 meters long, 23 meters wide and 13. 5 meters high)   ᶜ*16 Or Make an opening for light by finishing*   ᵈ*16 Hebrew a cubit*

This section corresponds in the chiastic or palistrophic structure of the Flood narrative to the narrative after the Flood when Noah builds an altar. He builds the ark because God has decided to start over with a new humanity while destroying the old humanity and the old creation. Noah builds the altar in response the LORD promises to never repeat the Flood and to preserve the created order with its seasons (Gen 8:20-22). The ark preserves life through the Flood while the altar leads to the LORD's promise that he will preserve the created order so that life can continue.

Since this passage is a part of the Flood narrative with its metatheme of de-creation followed by re-creation, it has many echoes with the original creation narrative. For example, we read of male and female, kinds, creatures which move along the ground, and the provision of food for the creatures.

1. Command to Build the Ark with Detailed Instructions (6:14-16)

6:14 So make yourself an ark of cypress wood; make rooms in it and coat it with pitch inside and out.

The use of the word "ark" for Noah's boat may point forward for English readers to the ark of the covenant in the tabernacle. But actually the word used, (תֵּבָה, *tēbath*) is not the word used for the ark of the tabernacle, (הָאָרֹן, *hā'ārōn*). Its only other occurrence outside of the Flood narrative is in the story of Moses' birth where it refers to the papyrus vessel used to float the infant Moses down the Nile. Just as Moses was preserved in dangerous circumstances and was saved out of the Nile, so Noah was preserved from a larger body of water and brought safely out by God. The original readers, Israel on the edge of entering the promised land, would undoubtedly make this connection.

Despite this, Blenkinsopp has argued that (in the purported source P) the construction of the ark parallels that of the tabernacle:[30]

---

[30]Blenkinsopp, *Prophecy and Canon*. His chapter on the Priestly work notes

Construction of the Ark	Construction of the sanctuary
Noah did according to all that God had commanded him; thus did he (Gen 6:22).	According to all that the LORD had commanded Moses, thus did the Israelites all the work (Ex 39:42).

Blenkinsopp also says:

> If, as suggested earlier, the P-edited story of the great deluge functions as a parable of Israel's inundation by the *goyim*, the history of spiritual decline which led up to it (with the emphasis in P on violence) corresponds with the history of Israel's failure under the monarchy. The message is then one of hope, for judgment is seen to lie in the past and, in a sense, the end of the world has already taken place.[31]

This is going way beyond what can legitimately be inferred from the narrative. But the parallel between the construction of the ark and the construction of the tabernacle may be something the imagined audience would have noticed. Both are built at God's direction and require the careful and total obedience of human beings. Both the ark and the tabernacle are means of saving those people who have a relationship with God. Other parallels between the Flood narrative and the events surrounding the Exodus are discussed in the body of the commentary.

We do not know what wood is referred to in this passage. "Cypress wood" is only a guess by the NIV translators (cf. the KJV's "gopher wood"). Undoubtedly it refers to some tree which could be effectively waterproofed and which possesses great strength and durability. Cypress was often used in shipbuilding in the ancient Near East, but cedars of Lebanon were also prized by the Egyptians in barge construction.[32]

The NIV's "rooms" translates a Hebrew word which in the singular means "nest." The plural seems to be used here as something like "compartments" for the animals and human occupants.[33]

---

the conclusion formula which occurs only at certain key points in the narrative: creation of the world (Gen 2:1,2), construction of the tabernacle (Exod 39:32; 40:33), and distribution of the land (Josh 19:51).

[31]Ibid., p. 75.
[32]*BBC*, p. 36.
[33]Sarna, *Genesis*, p. 52.

Wenham suggests (following Jacob) that the word be re-pointed to mean "reeds." If so it would be another building material.

6:15 This is how you are to build it: The ark is to be 450 feet long, 75 feet wide and 45 feet high.

The majority opinion of scholars is that a cubit equals approximately 18 inches or 45 centimeters. From this estimate the NIV gives the dimensions in feet. The ark constructed by Utnapishtim in the Gilgamesh Epic was a cube of 120 cubits or 180 feet. This would produce an extraordinarily unstable boat. It may be that Genesis is critiquing this part of the myth by providing measurements which would make a more realistic boat. But we should not overstate the case. The ark has no rudder or sail that is mentioned. If Noah's family is to survive the Flood it can only be by the miraculous hand of God. Utnapishtim's boat had a navigator. Its shape was evidently magical[34] since there was no all-powerful God protecting and preserving it.

6:16 Make a roof for it and finish the ark to within 18 inches of the top. Put a door in the side of the ark and make lower, middle and upper decks.

The word translated "roof" (צֹהַר, ṣōhar) could also be translated as "opening for daylight."[35] It is not clear what "finish the ark to within 18 inches of the top" means. It could mean that there was to be 18 inches from the top of the opening to the roof or that the opening was to be 18 inches or that the (slanting) roof extended 18 inches beyond the side of the ark as a sort of overhang.

The Gilgamesh Epic ark has seven decks while the Atrahasis version of the story may imply that there are only two decks. I cannot see how the three decks of the Bible would be a critique of these stories at this point. If the word translated "roof" is read as "opening" it would make sense of the ensuing narrative. The door was to be on the side of the ark and thus it could not be opened until the flood waters were gone. The opening provides a way to view the outside world without opening the door. But in Genesis 8:6 the word used for "window" is different from this word. But the word for "covering," i.e., a roof in

---

[34]It is sometimes suggested that only the base of Utnapishtim's boat was 120 cubits and that actually it was shaped like a ziggurat, a tiered temple with seven ascending levels, each one smaller than its base level. This shape may have been believed to have innately magical properties as would a cube.

[35]Sarna, *Genesis*, p. 52.

Genesis 8:13 is also a different word. The fact that there is much uncertainty about exactly what the ark looked like and how it was constructed should warn us of asking the wrong questions of this text.

2. Warning of the Flood (6:17)

6:17 I am going to bring floodwaters on the earth to destroy all life under the heavens, every creature that has the breath of life in it. Everything on earth will perish.

Here God announces to Noah why he needs to build an ark. Three times the word "all" or "every" is used in this verse. This emphasizes to Noah the comprehensiveness of the judgment that is coming. "All life under the heavens" will be destroyed. This is further specified by noting that "every creature which has the breath of life in it" will be destroyed. The point is further emphasized by stating that "everything on earth will perish."

The word translated "floodwaters" here (הַמַּבּוּל, *hammabbûl*) is found only in this narrative and in Psalm 29:10. It seems to refer to the first phase of the Flood with its rising destructive waters and not to the Flood as a whole.

3. God's Promise of a Covenant with Noah and Family (6:18)

6:18 But I will establish my covenant with you, and you will enter the ark—you and your sons and your wife and your sons' wives with you.

This is the first time the word "covenant" occurs in the Bible. The word can mean something like "pact" or "contract" when it is bilateral; or it can mean something more like "commitment" or "pledge" or even "promise" when it is more unilateral, i.e., something which God commits himself to do. Here it seems to be bilateral, in that Noah has to trust and obey by building and then entering the ark.

4. Command to Preserve Animals (6:19-20)

6:19 You are to bring into the ark two of all living creatures, male and female, to keep them alive with you.

6:20 Two of every kind of bird, of every kind of animal and of every kind of creature that moves along the ground will come to you to be kept alive.

Here the motivation for the pairs of various types of animals is the re-creation of life after the de-creation of the Flood ("to keep them alive with you"). The terminology here is reminiscent of the creation account in chapter 1. We have here "male and female," "kinds," "birds," etc. The motivation is the preservation of life which can be fruitful and multiply and fill the re-created earth after the Flood. It is significant that the terminology goes back to the universal creation story in chapter 1, rather than the more particular creation story in chapter 2. The LORD's control over the situation is alluded to when Noah is commanded to bring the animals into the ark, but the LORD promises that he will not have to collect them; they will come to Noah of their own accord.

5. Food for Noah's Family and the Animals (6:21)

6:21 You are to take every kind of food that is to be eaten and store it away as food for you and for them."

Every sort of edible food was stored away for the year-long ordeal Noah, his family, and the animals were about to endure. This is reminiscent of the first chapter where in 1:29 God granted every sort of vegetation as food. We are not told how Noah knew of the correct quantity of food. Was he somehow informed that the Flood would take a year? We are not told.

6. Noah's Obedience (6:22)

6:22 Noah did everything just as God commanded him.

Literally this reads, "Then Noah did according to all that God commanded him. Thus he did." This is a sort of Janus parallelism (the same thought repeated in reverse order):

Noah did according to all that God commanded him.
According to all that God commanded him, thus he did.

289

In any case, Noah conforms his actions perfectly to the commandments of God. He does not speak a word; he simply obeys. We are given no information as to how Noah felt about the commandment or whether he had questions of God. That is not the point being made in the narrative. The focus is on God and God alone.

GENESIS 7

E. THE COMMAND TO ENTER THE ARK (7:1-10)

¹The LORD then said to Noah, "Go into the ark, you and your whole family, because I have found you righteous in this generation. ²Take with you seven[a] of every kind of clean animal, a male and its mate, and two of every kind of unclean animal, a male and its mate, ³and also seven of every kind of bird, male and female, to keep their various kinds alive throughout the earth. ⁴Seven days from now I will send rain on the earth for forty days and forty nights, and I will wipe from the face of the earth every living creature I have made."

⁵And Noah did all that the LORD commanded him.

⁶Noah was six hundred years old when the floodwaters came on the earth. ⁷And Noah and his sons and his wife and his sons' wives entered the ark to escape the waters of the flood. ⁸Pairs of clean and unclean animals, of birds and of all creatures that move along the ground, ⁹male and female, came to Noah and entered the ark, as God had commanded Noah. ¹⁰And after the seven days the floodwaters came on the earth.

[a]2 Or *seven pairs*; also in verse 3

This passage records the command to load the ark which has just been built, with the animals and people who will start over in the new creation promised after the Flood, and the actual fulfillment of the command. In the structure of the Flood narrative it corresponds with Genesis 8:15-19 where the command to depart from the ark and its fulfillment is narrated.

1. The Command to Enter (7:1)

7:1 The LORD then said to Noah, "Go into the ark, you and your whole family, because I have found you righteous in this generation.

After the completion of the ark in obedience to the LORD's command, Noah and his family are directed to enter the ark. The reason the LORD[1] gives Noah that he and his family were chosen to be preserved through the Flood is that the LORD sees[2] Noah as righteous in his generation. Notice that it is only Noah who is seen to be righteous.[3] Here the LORD confirms what the narrator has already informed us about. Noah was a righteous man, and because of that righteousness he is chosen to be the new Adam for the new humanity that will emerge after the Flood. His family is not mentioned as being particularly righteous, but they are spared with Noah so that he can restart humanity after the Flood.

2. Provision for Clean and Unclean Animals (7:2-3)

7:2 Take with you seven of every kind of clean animal, a male and its mate, and two of every kind of unclean animal, a male and its mate,

In Genesis 6:19-20 Noah had been commanded to bring a pair of every animal into the ark. Here an additional command is given. He is also to bring seven pairs of all clean animals. The NIV text[4] can be confusing here. The Hebrew literally reads, "From every clean beast you will take for yourself seven, seven — a male and its mate." The repetition makes it clear that there are to be seven males and seven females of each clean animal.

This verse has been used as a classic proof text for the docu-

---

[1]The Samaritan Pentateuch reads "God" instead of "LORD." The LXX has "LORD God." While the presence of the divine name Yahweh ("LORD") here is taken as a sign that this section must be J, the repetition of the words "righteous" and "generation" from 6:9 (supposedly P) shows the problems with the traditional source analysis.

[2]"I found you righteous" in NIV is interpretive. Literally it reads, "I have seen/saw you righteous before me in this generation."

[3]The Hebrew "you" is singular here.

[4]Cf. The NIV footnote correctly translates "seven pairs."

mentary hypothesis. According to the theory the J source knows of seven pairs of clean animals while the P source knows of only a single pair. The additional clean animals make sacrifice immediately after the Flood possible since only animals regarded as clean would be sacrificed. Without this provision either sacrifice would soon end for lack of suitable animals or it would have to be delayed until breeding had taken place.

The concept of clean animals would have been very familiar to the imagined audience of Genesis, Israel on the verge of entering the promised land. They had received the laws which defined clean and unclean animals. For them this text would seem to imply that the distinction was not an arbitrary innovation first introduced at Sinai. The laws given to Israel were particular instances based upon long-standing principles. For Noah and his family, who are not given permission to eat animals until after the Flood, the category of "clean" must have meant something like "acceptable to sacrifice." But the categories clean and unclean come from the earliest times of God's relationship with humanity. Later laws which were specific to Israel as they lived in covenant with God in Canaan used the concepts of clean and unclean, even though the particular regulations were appropriate for their circumstances and not the time of Noah.

7:3 and also seven of every kind of bird, male and female, to keep their various kinds alive throughout the earth.

In addition to the sacrificial animals, extra birds are included both for sacrificial purposes and to reconnoiter the earth after the Flood (8:7-12). Without extra pairs of these animals, sacrifice would have caused the extinction of the clean animals and birds and would very soon bring sacrifice to an end.

3. God's Pronouncement of Imminent Destruction (7:4)

7:4 Seven days from now I will send rain on the earth for forty days and forty nights, and I will wipe from the face of the earth every living creature I have made."

In 6:17 Noah had been warned about the impending flood and instructed to build the ark. Here, with the command to enter, more specific timing about the onset of the flood and its duration are given. The Gilgamesh Epic seems to imply that only seven days were needed to build the ship and the storm lasted only seven days. "Forty days and nights" is a conventional expression for "a long time" and seems more suited to a flood of universal proportions.

4. Noah's Obedience (7:5)

7:5 And Noah did all that the LORD commanded him.

This seems to be an exact repetition of 6:22, except for the name of the deity used (Yahweh instead of Elohim) and the lack of the Janus parallelism there. Noah obeys the LORD's commandments. The Gilgamesh Epic goes into elaborate detail about the heroic achievement of building the ark. Here the emphasis is on obedience to God, not Noah's architectural achievement.

5. Noah's Family and the Animals Actually Enter the Ark (7:6-9)

7:6 Noah was six hundred years old when the floodwaters came on the earth.

The age of Noah is apparently the basis for the chronology of the Flood. This demonstrates the narrator's respect for Noah by dividing time in terms of the chronology of his life.

7:7 And Noah and his sons and his wife and his sons' wives entered the ark to escape the waters of the flood.

This verse begins with a waw-consecutive, usually to be translated as "then," not "and." The command in 7:1 is fulfilled, although the terminology is closer to the prediction of that entrance in 6:18. This verse along with 7:1 forms a sort of inclusio around its pericope. He is commanded to enter the ark, and without speaking a word he obeys. This is another instance of Noah's portrayal as the quietly obedient and trustful one. There is no hint of any hesitation or questioning of God. He and his family obey.

7:8 Pairs of clean and unclean animals, of birds and of all creatures that move along the ground,
7:9 male and female, came to Noah and entered the ark, as God had commanded Noah.

"Came" here should better be translated "had come," a perfectly possible reading of a simple perfect in Hebrew. Here "pairs" apparently included the single pair for the preservation of each species and the seven additional pairs for the purposes of sacrifice and reconnaisance. God had commanded that Noah take these animals with him and had further promised that Noah would not have to go out and gather up the animals. As God had promised in 6:20 the animals to be preserved came to Noah. God had commanded Noah to take them, and he never asks us to do that which we are incapable of doing without his help.

6. Seven Day Waiting Period for the Flood (7:10)

7:10 And after the seven days the floodwaters came on the earth.

As predicted in 7:4 the flood came within seven days. God is true to his word. The ability of God to control the precise timing of the processes of nature would have been remarkable to the original readers. Our own scientific age tends to use the explanatory power of the "laws of nature" to remove the element of mystery and wonder from nature. Our own experiences of "aberrations"[5] in nature (hurricanes, for example) remind us, however, of the unimaginable power of nature. For Christians, the normal processes of nature should be a cause of wonder and praise to God, just as the more unusual processes should be a cause of reverent fear of him.

F. THE FLOODWATERS RISE (7:11-24)

[11]In the six hundredth year of Noah's life, on the seventeenth day of the second month—on that day all the springs of the great deep burst forth, and the floodgates of the heavens were opened. [12]And rain fell on the earth forty days and forty nights.

---

[5]Miracles are sometimes defined as the violation of natural law. But for a Christian this is a problematic view. It implies a sort of deistic God who creates natural laws and allows them to run their course only to break the very laws he has created. A more biblical way to define a miracle would seem to be an unusual work of God. God is always at work in processes of nature. He does not create laws of nature and then break them.

¹³On that very day Noah and his sons, Shem, Ham and Japheth, together with his wife and the wives of his three sons, entered the ark. ¹⁴They had with them every wild animal according to its kind, all livestock according to their kinds, every creature that moves along the ground according to its kind and every bird according to its kind, everything with wings. ¹⁵Pairs of all creatures that have the breath of life in them came to Noah and entered the ark. ¹⁶The animals going in were male and female of every living thing, as God had commanded Noah. Then the LORD shut him in.

¹⁷For forty days the flood kept coming on the earth, and as the waters increased they lifted the ark high above the earth. ¹⁸The waters rose and increased greatly on the earth, and the ark floated on the surface of the water. ¹⁹They rose greatly on the earth, and all the high mountains under the entire heavens were covered. ²⁰The waters rose and covered the mountains to a depth of more than twenty feet.[a,b] ²¹Every living thing that moved on the earth perished—birds, livestock, wild animals, all the creatures that swarm over the earth, and all mankind. ²²Everything on dry land that had the breath of life in its nostrils died. ²³Every living thing on the face of the earth was wiped out; men and animals and the creatures that move along the ground and the birds of the air were wiped from the earth. Only Noah was left, and those with him in the ark. ²⁴The waters flooded the earth for a hundred and fifty days.

[a]*20* Hebrew *15 cubits* (about 6.9 meters)   [b]*20* Or *rose more than twenty feet, and the mountains were covered*

This passage corresponds in the structure of the Flood narrative with Genesis 8:6-14, where the floodwaters abate. Here the Flood is described as a sort of reversal of creation. The expanse (KJV "firmament") is taken away. The breathing space inhabited by animals was created on day one of creation. It was created to separate the waters above and below it from each other. Here the expanse is taken away so that the breathing space is filled with water and the water covers the ground. The destructive effects of the Flood as a de-creation are graphically portrayed.

1. The Underground and Aboveground Waters Begin (7:11-12)

7:11 In the six hundredth year of Noah's life, on the seventeenth

day of the second month—on that day all the springs of the great deep burst forth, and the floodgates of the heavens were opened.

Noah's age is used as the basis for the chronology of the Flood. The fullness and precision of the dates in the Flood narrative are remarkable, rivaled only by Ezekiel's dating of his prophecies in the entire Old Testament.[6] Other than to emphasize the factuality of the events described, it is difficult to understand why these details have been given.

The first and last dates in the Flood narrative (7:11; 8:14) yield one year and eleven days. Since a solar year (365 days) and a lunar year (354) differ by eleven days it has sometimes been suggested that the author of Genesis was using a lunar calendar to describe a flood of exactly one solar year. But what exactly the point would be of using a lunar calendar to describe a flood of exactly one solar year is less than clear. Cassuto suggested that the narrative has omitted to state explicitly that it took forty days to build the ark.[7] If Noah started on "January" 1 of his year 600, then spent 40 days in building the ark and seven waiting (7:10), we arrive at "February" 17 of that same year 600, the exact date of the start of the Flood. But even if we accept this inference, it is less than clear what the point would be.

Wenham has suggested that the exact dates of the Flood may serve to suggest that the LORD and Noah were observant of the Sabbath in their work in regard to the Flood. He suggests the following schema[8]:

Dates of the Flood:

1)	Announcement of the Flood	7:4	10.2.600	Sunday
2)	Flood begins	7:11	17.2.600	Sunday
3)	Flood lasts 40 days and ends	7:12	27.3.600	Friday
4)	Waters triumph and abate for 150 days (The 40 days are included in the 150)	8:4	17.7.600	Friday
5)	Mountaintops appear	8:5	1.10.600	Wednesday
6)	Raven sent out (after 40 days)	8:6	10.11.600	Sunday
7)	Dove's second flight	8:10	24.11.600	Sunday
8)	Dove's third flight	8:12	1.12.600	Sunday ➤

---

[6]Wenham, *Genesis 1–15*, p. 179.

[7]Umberto Cassuto, *A Commentary on the Book of Genesis. Part Two: From Noah to Abraham* (Jerusalem: Magnes Press, 1964), p. 71.

[8]Wenham, *Genesis 1–15*, p. 180.

9) Waters dry up	8:13	1.1.601	Wednesday
10) Noah leaves ark	8:14	27.2.601	Wednesday

But this is far from conclusive. For one thing he must assume that the LORD begins his work on a Sunday. But it may be that the imagined audience, Israel about to enter the promised land, would make the same assumption since for them the Sabbath was a living reality. Certainty is impossible at this remove. It is perhaps safest to leave the question of the exact purpose of the dating unanswered.[9]

Waters from under the earth, which had been confined to their appropriate spot at creation, are now unleashed with their terrible destructive force. The opening of the "floodgates of heaven" describes in popular language[10] the removal of the expanse so that the water held in the clouds is emptied upon the earth. The combination of these two sources of water, subterranean and torrential rain from the clouds, creates a frightening picture of the flood. The verbal echoes between this account and the creation account in Genesis 1 emphasize yet again the "de-creation" motif in this narrative. The springs come from the "great deep," which echoes the "deep" in Genesis 1:2.

7:12 And rain fell on the earth forty days and forty nights.

As promised the length of actual, continual rainfall was 40 days and nights. For people familiar with the early and latter rain cycle, as was Israel, this shows the tremendous power of God over his creation. Baal, the god of thunder and rain, could only be cajoled into sporadically giving it as the Elijah narrative makes clear. Here the rain comes as a judgment on human evil. There is no difficulty for God to produce it. He only regrets that he has to do so.

The Hebrew word for rain used here (גֶּשֶׁם, *gašem*) is "used of the heavy winter rain."[11] Unlike the more common מָטָר (*matar*), this

---

[9]Another suggestion by A. Jaubert (*La Date de la Cene* [Paris: Gabalde, 1957], p. 33, cited in Wenham, *Genesis 1–15*, p. 180) is that Genesis adopts the same 364-day calendar as found in the book of Jubilees. This calendar would result in significant events always falling on the same day of the week. This requires that one assume, among other things, that the 364-day calendar was known to the author of Genesis.

[10]This is not scientific language but reflects the perspective of the observer, much as we would speak of the sun "setting."

[11]Skinner, *Genesis*, p. 154.

word signifies abnormal rainfall. While Israel lived in a dry climate where rain was precious, here it is the rain of judgment which falls. The number 40 often has symbolic significance in the Bible and can mean merely a long time. Israel spent 40 years in the wilderness as a judgment for their lack of faith and would perhaps attach symbolic significance to the 40 days and nights of judgment.

2. Noah's Family and Creatures Safe in the Ark (7:13-16)

7:13 On that very day Noah and his sons, Shem, Ham and Japheth, together with his wife and the wives of his three sons, entered the ark.

"On that very day" (lit., "bone of that day") is an unusual expression used to stress that an occasion was particularly noteworthy. The phrase is used of the Exodus, of the Day of Atonement, regarding the celebration of the firstfruits of Canaan and at the death of Moses. The entering of the ark signals the salvation of humanity from total destruction. Interestingly Noah's sons are named here, unlike earlier in the narrative (cf. 7:6). This could be an indication of the event's importance (although why are the women never named?) or in preparation for the significant role his sons will play in the narrative after the Flood.

7:14 They had with them every wild animal according to its kind, all livestock according to their kinds, every creature that moves along the ground according to its kind and every bird according to its kind, everything with wings.

The full roll call of the animals echoes chapter 1 and is part of the narrative strategy of showing the universality of the de-creation, just as chapter 1 dealt with the universal creation. The repetition of the vocabulary from chapter 1 makes this connection clear ("according to its kind," "every creature that moves along the ground," etc.).

7:15 Pairs of all creatures that have the breath of life in them came to Noah and entered the ark.

Here the creation account in 2:7 is echoed although a different word for breath is used here. The breath of life is literally "spirit of life" here. Again the fact that God brought the animals to Noah and even apparently had them enter the ark shows God's control of the situation and of his creation. This could in part be explained by the fact that the conflict between the animal and human kingdoms announced in 9:2 has not yet been realized. But clearly they come to Noah and enter the ark at the behest of the LORD.

7:16 The animals going in were male and female of every living thing, as God had commanded Noah. Then the LORD shut him in.

The animals who entered the ark were the ones God had commanded Noah to keep safe in the ark. Noah's obedience to the LORD's command is noted yet again although here that obedience comes from trusting God to bring the animals to Noah as he had promised. Gilgamesh mentions that Utnapishtim closed the door himself. By attributing this action to the LORD Genesis is reminding the reader that Noah was saved by divine grace, not heroic human efforts.

3. The Rising of the Floodwaters to Their Peak (7:17-24)

7:17 For forty days the flood kept coming on the earth, and as the waters increased they lifted the ark high above the earth.

"Increased" is literally "multiplied," a somber "anti-echo" of the injunction at the creation to "be fruitful and multiply." The continual rising of the flood lifts the ark high above the land. The ark serves its purpose. No matter how severe the floodwaters became, it protected its passengers, both animal and human.

7:18 The waters rose and increased greatly on the earth, and the ark floated on the surface of the water.

The word translated "increased" is a military word for succeeding in battle (Exod 17:11) often translated "prevailed." At this stage the waters are winning the battle with creation. This verse is largely repetitive of the previous and is reminiscent of the phenomenon of parallelism in Hebrew poetry. This does not mean, however, that the account is not intended to be a narrative description of actual events.

7:19 They rose greatly on the earth, and all the high mountains under the entire heavens were covered.

Even the "high" mountains were covered. This shows just how devastating the Flood was. Contemporary readers should remember that the Hebrew word for "mountain" often refers to nothing more than "hills" in our terms. The point is that the Flood was to bring universal judgment on humanity because of the universal evil to which humanity had degenerated.

7:20 The waters rose and covered the mountains to a depth of more than twenty feet.

The NIV's "more than twenty feet" is literally "fifteen cubits." If the standard measure of the cubit is used this would be twenty-two and one half feet. Apparently the story assumes that the ark's draft was half (15 cubits) its height of thirty cubits or 45 feet and thus could not scrape bottom when even the mountains were covered in fifteen cubits of water.

7:21 Every living thing that moved on the earth perished—birds, livestock, wild animals, all the creatures that swarm over the earth, and all mankind.

The order of creation is used to describe the deaths in the Flood, thus mankind is mentioned last. The detailed listing of the victims leads the reader to ponder the consequences of rebellion against God. Again the words "all" and "every" occur to emphasize the totality of the destruction.

7:22 Everything on dry land that had the breath of life in its nostrils died.

The words "breath" and "nostrils" echo 2:7, and are similar to 6:17 and 7:5. The LORD who gave the breath of life now takes it. Again the totality of the destruction is indicated by the word "everything."

7:23 Every living thing on the face of the earth was wiped out; men and animals and the creatures that move along the ground and the birds of the air were wiped from the earth. Only Noah was left, and those with him in the ark.

Life did not merely die, it was "wiped out." The totality of the judgment is indicated yet again by the word "every." The exception is Noah. A wordplay between the verb "wiped out" (*mḥh*) and the name of Noah (*nḥ*) subtly shows the contrast. He and his family are "left" (שָׁאַר, *šā'ar*), a verb used in passages that refer to the remnant of Israel. Noah and family are the righteous remnant, spared from the judgment, who give hope for the re-creation of humanity. In the midst of the horrific and terrifying universal judgment there is one man and his family who are spared.

7:24 The waters flooded the earth for a hundred and fifty days.

In order for the Flood chronology to make sense, the 150 days must cover the five months from the coming of the Flood on "February" 17 (7:11) to the grounding of the ark on "July" 17 (8:4). Evidently the 40 days of rain were followed by 110 days of the triumph of the waters. Once again Genesis leaves details such as this like loose threads. Unfortunately some interpreters have been tempted to pull on those threads and cause a coherent narrative to unravel into pieces before their eyes. In order for a narrative to be understood it needs to be read sympathetically. Unfortunately the traditional source analysis of Genesis discourages such readings.

GENESIS 8

G. THE TURNING POINT OF THE FLOOD: GOD REMEMBERS NOAH (8:1a)

This section narrates the reversal in the Flood narrative. The floodwaters had reached their highest point in the previous section. Here God remembers Noah so that he stops the waters and causes them to begin decreasing.

H. THE FLOODWATERS ABATE (8:1b-14)

The reversal of the flood begins with a "wind" or the Spirit followed by the reestablishment of the expanse by closing the subterranean water springs and stopping the rain. The water then recedes until the dry land begins to emerge as the ark hits bottom. The mountaintops reemerge as the water continues to abate. Finally Noah discovers that the land is dry once again so that it is safe to leave the ark. This passage parallels the rising of the floodwaters narrated in the previous section.

But perhaps more significantly it parallels the creation account in Genesis 1. The drying of the earth from the floodwaters mirrors the creation account from Genesis 1:2-30. The emergence of the earth from the floodwaters is strikingly similar to its first emergence from the watery mass which was without form or void. When the rains stop the cycle of light and darkness, day and night is resumed. Light can now be seen once again. Day one and the fourth day of creation are reenacted. Also the expanse is (re)established. This separates the water covering the earth from the water in the clouds and provides a space where birds and eventually animals and people can breathe and live. The second day of creation is reenacted. As the water recedes the ark settles on one of the mountains of Ararat. Thus the dry land appears. When the dove returns with an olive leaf in its beak, it is clear that plants are growing on that dry land. The plants will provide food for the animals and humanity when they emerge on the earth. The third day of creation is reenacted. When Noah sends the birds from the ark, the expanse is populated once again.[1] The fifth day of creation is reenacted. Finally the animals and humans leave the ark to take up residence on the newly dry land. The sixth day of creation is reenacted. Theologically this emergence is a new creation with a new Adam and a new creation mandate to be fruitful and multiply and fill the earth.

¹But God remembered Noah and all the wild animals and the livestock that were with him in the ark, and he sent a wind over the earth, and the waters receded. ²Now the springs of the deep and the floodgates of the heavens had been closed, and the rain had stopped falling from the sky. ³The water receded steadily from the earth. At the end of the hundred and fifty days the water had gone down, ⁴and on the seventeenth day of the seventh month the ark came to rest on the mountains of Ararat. ⁵The waters continued to recede until the tenth month, and on the first day of the tenth month the tops of the mountains became visible.

⁶After forty days Noah opened the window he had made in the ark ⁷and sent out a raven, and it kept flying back and forth until the water had dried up from the earth. ⁸Then he sent out a dove to see if the water had receded from the surface of the ground. ⁹But the dove could find no place to set its feet because there was water over all the surface of the earth; so it returned to Noah in the ark. He reached out his hand and took the dove and brought it back to himself in the ark. ¹⁰He waited seven more days and again sent out the dove from the ark. ¹¹When the dove returned to him in the evening, there in its beak was a freshly plucked olive leaf! Then Noah knew that the water had receded from the earth. ¹²He waited seven more days and sent the dove out again, but this time it did not return to him.

¹³By the first day of the first month of Noah's six hundred and

---

[1]Presumably the water creatures would have survived the flood and therefore have no need for re-creation.

first year, the water had dried up from the earth. Noah then removed the covering from the ark and saw that the surface of the ground was dry. ¹⁴By the twenty-seventh day of the second month the earth was completely dry.

1. The Rain Stops and the Flood Begins to Abate (8:1b-3)

8:1 But God remembered Noah and all the wild animals and the livestock that were with him in the ark, and he sent a wind over the earth, and the waters receded.

The hinge point in the narrative is the record of God remembering Noah. The Bible does not mean that due to some mental dysfunction God had forgotten Noah during the flood. Here memory is not just a mental event that happens to the mind. Instead it is a deliberate decision by God to act for the sake of Noah and the remnant of the new creation hidden in the ark. The watery unformed and unfilled mass now has to be formed and filled again. As in Genesis 1:2 where the Spirit (or wind) was God's agent in the original creation, so here a wind (or Spirit?) is God's agent in the re-creation.

It is interesting that God is said to have remembered Noah and the animals, but not Noah's family. One wonders whether there is a subtle hint of the problems that he will have with his family after the Flood (cf. the discussion of Gen 9:18-27).

The NIV chooses to translate the Hebrew word רוּחַ (*rûaḥ*) as "wind" here. But if "Spirit" is an appropriate translation in Genesis 1:2 (the Hebrew word can mean either), I cannot see why it should be changed here when we recognize the deliberate allusions this passage makes to the original creation account. Just as in the original creation account God does his work through his Spirit, so also in the re-creation account. Just as God empowered Oholiab and Bezalel to build the tabernacle with his Spirit, here he does the work of creation with his Spirit.

8:2 Now the springs of the deep and the floodgates of the heavens had been closed, and the rain had stopped falling from the sky.

The closing of the springs and floodgates and the stopping of the rain is the reversal of 7:11 and 12 respectively. The two sources of water which fueled the flood are now cut off. The sea is contained² and the rainwaters have been stopped. There is no longer enough water to keep the flood at its heights. With the closing of the floodgates the expanse is reestablished and presumably the light of the sun is once again visible. The reappearance of the light echoes day one of creation when God said, "Let there be light." Creation is beginning again. The stopping of the rain reestablishes the expanse which was created on the second day of creation. Once again water is confined to the liquid form covering the land and rainwater in the clouds. The continual raining had effectively removed the expanse from the creation. With the cessation of the rain the expanse which separates the liquid water from the water in rain clouds once again

---

²The danger that the original readers would have undoubtedly felt about the abyss is illustrated from (admittedly much later) Rabbinic sources. Steven W. Holloway ("What Ship Goes There: The Flood Narratives in the Gilgamesh Epic and Genesis Considered in Light of Ancient Near Eastern Temple Ideology," *ZAW* 103 [1991]: 328-355) notes that according to 1 Kgs 8:2,65 Solomon's Temple was dedicated at Succoth, the fall festival where the Songs of Ascents were read to ensure the fall of rain. He quotes a Jewish legend:

Rabbi Johanan said . . . When David dug the Pits [that is, the perpendicular shafts reaching down under the Temple to the Deep], the Deep arose and threatened to submerge the world. "Is there anyone" inquired David, "who knows whether it is permitted to inscribe the [Ineffable] Name upon a sherd, and cast it into the Deep that its waves should subside?" There was none who answered a word. Said David, "Whoever knows the answer and does not speak, may he be suffocated! Whereupon Ahitophel . . . said to him, "It is permitted." [David] thereupon inscribed the [Ineffable] Name upon a sherd, cast it into the Deep and it subsided sixteen thousand cubits. When he saw that it had subsided to such a great extent, he said, "The nearer it is to the [surface of the] earth, the better the earth can be kept watered," and he uttered the fifteen Songs of Ascents and the Deep re-ascended fifteen thousand cubits and remained one thousand cubits [below the surface].

The legend is explicitly related to the creation of the world in this version:

When God created heaven and earth, he also created the stone over the Deep, and engraved on it the Ineffable Name consisting of forty-two letters, and fixed the stone over the Deep in order to keep down its water. . . . But when the generation of the deluge sinned, he removed the stone and immediately all the sources of the great Deep sprang up. And when David dug the shafts, the stone rolled aside and the waters came out and filled the whole world. . . . David took the stone and threw it back on the Deep whereupon the waters returned.

appears. There is now once again the cycle of light and darkness and air available to breathe. The preparation for the inhabiting of the earth by animals and humanity has begun.

2. The Floodwaters Dry Up and the Dry Land Reappears (8:4-14)

8:3 The water receded steadily from the earth. At the end of the hundred and fifty days the water had gone down,
8:4 and on the seventeenth day of the seventh month the ark came to rest on the mountains of Ararat.

This passage describes the receding of the water so that the dry ground once again appears. The third day of creation is reoccurring before the reader's eyes. We only discover later, when the dove returns with an olive leaf in its beak, that as the ground dries, it generates the plants which will be necessary for food for the animals and humans who come out of the ark.

Exactly the same description (NIV, "The water receded steadily from the earth") is given of the Red Sea returning to its normal state in Exodus 14:26,28 and of the Jordan returning after being parted in Joshua 4:18. The imagined audience may have noticed the connection. In some sense the re-creation is an act of salvation, of redemptive history, as well as being a repetition of the creation. Or perhaps the parting of the Red Sea and the Jordan have such momentous significance in the working out of God's purpose that they are described in terms of creation. These events of salvation history are just as momentous as the first acts of creation! It may be that our way of categorizing things as either acts of creation or acts of salvation history (but not both) is flawed. For the imagined audience these may not have been such distinct categories as they are for us. Given the near worship of science and technology in the modern world, we tend to separate sharply between acts of creation which we associate with the so-called laws of nature and miraculous interventions which we tend to regard as violations of the laws of nature.

The hundred and fifty days (five months of 30 days) is the period of time in which the waters decreased. At the end of this period the waters had receded. This corresponds symmetrically with the hundred and fifty days during which the waters increased (Gen 7:24).

The use of the word "rest" to describe the ark settling on one of the mountains of Ararat is unusual. The word (וַתָּנַח, *wattanaḥ*) may be a rhyming allusion to Noah's name (נֹחַ, *nōaḥ*) as in 5:29. Noah's father in naming him had hoped that he would bring rest from the toilsome labor with the cursed ground. Instead Noah is protected by God as the ark comes to rest on one of the mountains of Ararat after the Flood. There may be the suggestion of irony here.

It has commonly been assumed that the Bible identifies a specific mountain for the resting place of the ark. In fact Ararat is a region (known as Urartu in Assyrian inscriptions) in eastern Turkey near Lake Van. There is a range of mountains there, but the Bible does not specify a single mountain but only the region where the mountain was located. Attempts to identify a specific mountain are therefore dubious as are the reported sightings of the ark. In the Gilgamesh epic a specific mountain, Mount Nisir[3] in modern Kurdistan is mentioned. Our curiosity about the exact location of the ark often leads us to read into Scripture things that are not there and are of no apparent interest to the author.

8:5 The waters continued to recede until the tenth month, and on the first day of the tenth month the tops of the mountains became visible.

This verse corresponds to 7:19-20 where the hills are covered. Here they become visible again as the floodwaters recede. With the reappearance of the mountaintops the dry ground has begun to reappear. The third day of creation is beginning to be reenacted before the reader's eyes. In the ancient world the power of the sea was so fearsome that the Sea was often divinized into a god with a prickly personality which needed to be either massaged or controlled. Here there is no battle with the waters. They recede quite naturally after the rain has stopped sufficiently long to allow the waters to return to their normal levels.

8:6 After forty days Noah opened the window he had made in the ark 8:7 and sent out a raven, and it kept flying back and forth until the water had dried up from the earth.

Hamilton remarks: "The forty days can refer only to the period of time that Noah waited from the time the peaks of the mountain

---

[3]Foster reads this as Nimush (*COS* 1.132, p. 460).

became visible (8:5) until he sent out the birds. Perhaps Noah thought that such a period would give even more time for more of the submerged earth to reappear."[4] Usually this verse is cited as part of J's chronology which is supposedly in conflict with P's chronology. But in the text that we have it makes perfect sense. Further it corresponds with the forty-day period in Genesis 7:17 of the floodwaters rising and floating the ark (see Introduction to the Flood Narrative above). There is a striking resemblance between this text and the Gilgamesh Epic in terms of the sending of the birds from the ark.

> When the seventh day arrived,
> I released a dove to go free,
> The dove went and returned,
> No landing place came to view, it turned back.
> I released a swallow to go free,
> The swallow went and returned,
> No landing place came to view, it turned back.
> I sent a raven to go free,
> The raven went forth, saw the ebbing of the waters,
> It ate, circled, left droppings, did not turn back.
> I released (all) to the four cardinal points.[5]

It seems likely that the biblical narrative is telling the same story but with a completely different set of concerns. Birds were used for navigation purposes at sea in the ancient world. Ravens apparently would choose the most direct line of flight to land, and this would provide navigational guidance for seamen who could not see land.[6] But here the ark has landed and no navigation was needed.

8:8 Then he sent out a dove to see if the water had receded from the surface of the ground.
8:9 But the dove could find no place to set its feet because there was water over all the surface of the earth; so it returned to Noah

---

[4]Hamilton, *Genesis 1–17*, p. 303.
[5]Foster, *COS* 1.132, p. 460.
[6]*BBC, ad loc*: "Unlike pigeons or doves, which will return after being released, a raven's use to seamen is based on its line of flight. By noting the direction it chooses, a sailor may determine where land is located. The most sensible strategy is to release a raven first and then use other birds to determine the depth of the water and the likelihood of a place to land. A raven by habit, lives on carrion and would therefore have sufficient food available."

in the ark. He reached out his hand and took the dove and brought it back to himself in the ark.

The dove was a clean animal used in sacrifices (Lev 1:14; 12:6).[7] Doves would return if they found no dry land, and that seems to be Noah's purpose here. They have limited flight capabilities and so would naturally return if there was no landing place nearby.

8:10 He waited seven more days and again sent out the dove from the ark.
8:11 When the dove returned to him in the evening, there in its beak was a freshly plucked olive leaf! Then Noah knew that the water had receded from the earth.

The number seven occurs once again in this narrative. The seven days mentioned here is probably the amount of time it would take for an olive tree to leaf out after being under water. In the chronological structure of the Flood narrative it corresponds with the seven-day period in Genesis 7:10 where the sending of the Flood comes seven days after the announcement in verse 4. The leaf shows Noah that the water had receded significantly from the earth. The return of the dove indicates, however, that more time is still needed before it is safe to depart from the ark.

8:12 He waited seven more days and sent the dove out again, but this time it did not return to him.

The assumption is that the dove has now found acceptable habitation and the time for leaving the ark was nearing. Yet again seven days occur. This period corresponds with the seven day period in Genesis 7:4 announcing the onset of the Flood.

8:13 By the first day of the first month of Noah's six hundred and first year, the water had dried up from the earth. Noah then removed the covering from the ark and saw that the surface of the ground was dry.

On Noah's "birthday" he was given the joy of seeing the restored cosmos. Once again, however, Noah's emotions are not described. In the Hebrew Bible, the sanctuary in the wilderness was dedicated on the same day that the floodwaters receded from the

---

[7]Hosea 7:11; 11:11 uses the dove as a symbol for Israel. The original canonical audience may have made a connection between this text and Israel's exile and salvation from exile.

land of the new world — the first day of the first month of the second year after the great event — the Exodus or the beginning of the Flood. This shows a parallel between the Flood and the crossing of the Red Sea which the audience would have undoubtedly recognized. The word used for the covering of the ark is also used of the skins used to cover the tabernacle. The Exodus, so fresh in the minds of the imagined audience, is yet again echoed in the last half of the Flood narrative.

With the earth now dry Noah removed the covering of the ark. The reader is then drawn into Noah's experience. Literally the Hebrew reads, "Then Noah saw and behold! The surface of the ground was laid waste." The NIV among other translations opts for translating the Hebrew verb חָרַב (ḥārāb) "was dry." But often this word speaks of devastation and ruin[8] (sometimes as here following a cataclysmic event). It seems more likely that the author is playing on the double meaning of this verb. The earth is dry, but it is also devastated by the Flood.

8:14 By the twenty-seventh day of the second month the earth was completely dry.

According to the Hebrew text the Flood lasted one year and ten[9] days. While the earth was dry on the first day of the first month, it had not yet returned to be in the state that it was on the third day of creation. It took another 56 days to complete the drying out process.[10]

---

[8]*HALOT*, p. 349.

[9]Or eleven if we follow Cassuto (*Genesis: Part One*, pp. 113-114) in counting both the first and the last day. For those familiar with a lunar calendar this would be exactly one solar year which is eleven days longer than a lunar year. Cassuto argues that the LXX (of Egyptian provenance) used the solar calendar and therefore wrote 27 instead of 17 in Gen 7:11 and 8:4 making it last exactly one solar year. But we do not know whether the imagined audience would have known of both the lunar and solar calendars as this view presupposes. Hendel, "4Q252 and the Flood Chronology of Genesis 7–8: A Text Critical Solution," *Dead Sea Discoveries* 2 (1995): 72-79, argues that the odd one-year and ten-day duration of the Flood in MT of 8:14 comes from MT's misreading an original "ten" as "tens" = "twenty" and then adding "day" yielding "twenty days." Again he assumes a flood of exactly one year was original.

[10]The sequence of חָרַב (ḥārāb) "was dry" followed by יָבֵשׁ (yābāš) is also found in a parallel usage Isa 19:5 and Job 14:11.

I. EXITING THE ARK (8:15-19)

¹⁵Then God said to Noah, ¹⁶"Come out of the ark, you and your wife and your sons and their wives. ¹⁷Bring out every kind of living creature that is with you—the birds, the animals, and all the creatures that move along the ground—so they can multiply on the earth and be fruitful and increase in number upon it."

¹⁸So Noah came out, together with his sons and his wife and his sons' wives. ¹⁹All the animals and all the creatures that move along the ground and all the birds—everything that moves on the earth—came out of the ark, one kind after another.

This section corresponds with Genesis 7:1-10 where Noah is commanded to enter the ark and does so. Even though Noah has used the birds to determine when it is safe to leave the ark, when the time comes, he waits for God's command. Noah's obedience does not mean that it is mindless. His research by means of sending out the raven and doves prepares him for God's command. The people exit first, followed by the animals which are given their new commission. Once again this section echoes the creation account: the animals are told to be fruitful and multiply; kinds of animals are carefully distinguished; the same terminology is used to describe the animals — e.g., "all the creatures than move along the ground"; etc.

1. The Command to Exit the Ark (8:15-17)

8:15 Then God said to Noah,
8:16 "Come out of the ark, you and your wife and your sons and their wives.

Here the NIV correctly translates the waw-consecutive with "then." God's first concern is with people, so their departure from the ark is mentioned first. The animals must wait for verse 17. Mention is specifically made of Noah's wife, his sons, and his daughters-in-law since they will be responsible to repopulate the earth. Both the males and females have been preserved through the Flood and both are necessary for the human family to continue.

8:17 Bring out every kind of living creature that is with you—the birds, the animals, and all the creatures that move along the

ground—so they can multiply on the earth and be fruitful and increase in number upon it."

The commands originally given at creation just to the fish and the birds (1:20,22) are now extended to all the land animals, perhaps a hint that the re-creation is something new.[11] "Every kind of living creature" may be something more specific than the NIV's translation sounds. Wenham translates "wild animals." These animals quite understandably head the list, since being cooped up in the ark for over a year would have been difficult for them. The use of three words to describe the procreative activity of the animals makes it emphatic. This may be due to the special circumstances immediately following the flood. If they were not extremely prolific, they would be in severe danger of extinction.

2. The Exiting of the Ark (8:18-19)

8:18 So Noah came out, together with his sons and his wife and his sons' wives.

Once again, Noah is obedient to God's command. He waits for God's directions before doing anything. His sons, his wife and his daughters-in-law also show the same obedience. Whether this stems from Noah's influence or their own commitment to God or both is impossible to determine. The order of their mention as they depart together is slightly different from the order in which God mentioned them (cf. v. 16). This may be a merely stylistic variation with no real significance to be attached to it. The new humanity enters the chastened world once again. There is the opportunity to start over, having learned the hard lessons of the consequences of building a life without obedience and faithfulness to God. Once again the Bible shows no concern for the emotional impact of the event. They obeyed and in that obedience are given the opportunity to start again with God and the entire creation before them.

---

[11]I am reminded of Paul's comment in 1 Corinthians 11:11: "However, in the Lord, neither is woman independent of man nor man independent of woman." Somehow the new creation is the same, and yet different from the original creation.

8:19 All the animals and all the creatures that move along the ground and all the birds—everything that moves on the earth—came out of the ark, one kind after another.

Noah has been commanded to bring out the animals, and he does so. The "wild animals" head the list as in verse 17. Apparently they filed out in pairs, one kind after another. Their filing out is like a re-creation of the sixth day of Genesis 1.

J. YAHWEH'S GRACIOUS RESPONSE TO NOAH'S ALTAR (8:20-22)

[20]Then Noah built an altar to the LORD and, taking some of all the clean animals and clean birds, he sacrificed burnt offerings on it. [21]The LORD smelled the pleasing aroma and said in his heart: "Never again will I curse the ground because of man, even though[a] every inclination of his heart is evil from childhood. And never again will I destroy all living creatures, as I have done.

[22]"As long as the earth endures,
  seedtime and harvest,
  cold and heat,
  summer and winter,
  day and night
  will never cease."

[a]*21 Or* man, for

This paragraph corresponds to the section where Noah is commanded to build the ark prior to the Flood. There God commands Noah, and Noah silently and completely obeys. Here Noah initiates things. He decides to build an altar and sacrifice burnt offerings to the LORD on it. Noah uses the right sort of sacrificial animals (clean ones), and he offers them in their totality to the LORD. Burnt offerings were completely burned up on the altar. The audience would see the significance of Noah's actions. Before there is a law of sacrifice given, Noah obeys the principles of sacrifice. He gives the holy God only what is clean, and he gives it in its totality. Nothing is left over for him or his family to enjoy. It is a burnt offering. God's response to this faithful obedience is striking. It is a pleasing aroma because it is offered in faithful and grateful acknowledgment of the

LORD. The LORD determines that, even though the nature of humanity has not changed (cf. Gen 6:5), he will never again judge the entire creation because of human sin. As long as the present creation remains, the cycles of nature will continue. There must be a different strategy for dealing with the sin of humanity. This is in direct contradiction to the flood stories of the ancient world. In Genesis God's actions contrast with the mythological cycle of capricious gods sending unpredictable catastrophes upon humanity. The LORD faces the inescapable fact of human sin and yet still, in his grace, provides another way for atonement of sins.

1. The Altar and Sacrifice of Noah (8:20)

8:20 Then Noah built an altar to the LORD and, taking some of all the clean animals and clean birds, he sacrificed burnt offerings on it.

Noah takes the initiative here and builds an altar to the LORD. In the early period described here this may have been no more than a rock shelf or a pile of stones. The seven pairs of clean animals and birds which Noah had taken with him on the ark now serve their sacrificial purpose. He does not use all of them, only "some" since they will need to breed and multiply even more quickly than other animals if they are to serve sacrificial purposes. Noah offers "burnt offerings" in which the entire animal was given completely over to God. This was symbolized by the burning up of the whole animal. None was to be shared with the offerer or priests as in many other sacrifices.

Noah here functions as a priest in offering a sacrifice. This was not unusual in the early period in the Bible before the establishment of the priesthood at Sinai. The father or patriarch of the family served as the priest. It may be, however, that Genesis is critiquing the notion of the royal figure being preserved during the flood as in the Gilgamesh epic. In Genesis Noah is a commoner, not a king, and acts more like a priestly mediator than a powerful ruler.[12]

---

[12]Notice however, that James R. Davila ("The Flood Hero as King and Priest," *JNES* 54 [1995]: 199-214) has argued that the *original* Mesopotamian flood story did not have a royal hero, but a priestly one.

2. Yahweh's Response (8:21-22)

8:21 The LORD smelled the pleasing aroma and said in his heart: "Never again will I curse the ground because of man, even though every inclination of his heart is evil from childhood. And never again will I destroy all living creatures, as I have done.

In the Gilgamesh epic Utnapishtim also made an altar and provided sacrifices. The gods smell the pleasing aroma ("sweet savor") as in Genesis. But the similarity ends there. In Gilgamesh the gods, having been deprived of sacrifices during the flood, crowd around the offering like flies:

> I set up an offering stand on the top of the mountain,
> Seven and seven cult vessels I set out,
> I heaped reeds, cedar, and myrtle in their bowls,
> The gods smelled the savor,
> The gods smelled the sweet savor,
> The gods crowded around the sacrificer like flies.[13]

Humanity was created in order to relieve the gods of the drudgery of having to provide their own food.[14] Sacrifices were viewed as food for the gods. Genesis implicitly critiques such notions. God did not create humanity to meet his own needs. He does not need food nor sacrifices. His reaction to the faithful obedience of Noah is the declaration of a determination never again to destroy all of creation because of the sinfulness of humanity. The link is severed. The offering is not a sin offering nor specifically a thank offering. In contrast:

> [T]he sacrifice offered after the flood in the *Gilgamesh Epic and in the earlier *Sumerian version of the flood story feature libations and grain offerings as well as meat sacrifices in order to provide a feast for the gods. The general purpose for sacrifice in the ancient world was to appease the anger of the gods by gifts of food and drink, and that is probably the intention of the flood hero in the Mesopotamian accounts.[15]

---

[13]*COS* 1.132, p. 460.
[14]Atra-hasis, ibid., p. 450-451.
[15]*BBC, ad loc.*

The LORD does not say that he is removing the curse from the ground but that he would never again curse it with a flood. The ground is still under the curse of Genesis 3. This decision has not removed the original curse. The LORD only promises to use something other than a de-creating flood to deal with humanity's tendency to sin. That tendency has not been completely removed by the Flood. The re-creation after the Flood does not mean a return to Eden, although it keeps the eventual possibility alive. That possibility is assured in the book of Revelation's depiction of the new heavens and new earth in "Edenic" terms.

In 8:21b essentially the same thing is being said as in 6:5; every human thought from its inception tends toward evil (cf. the chart below). Wenham notices: "But it is put more gently the second time to explain God's mercy towards human sin, whereas on the first occasion it was explaining his determination to destroy mankind."[16] Humanity has not been fundamentally changed by the Flood as the story of Noah's fall makes clear. In 6:5 even the thoughts of humanity's hearts were evil whereas in 8:21b it is only his heart. In 6:5 the thoughts of the human heart were *only* evil; in 8:21b they are simply evil. In 6:5 humanity's evil was "all the time" whereas in 8:21b it is only "from his youth."[17]

6:5	8:21b
The LORD saw how great man's wickedness on the earth had become, and that every inclination of the thoughts of his heart was only evil all the time.	". . . even though every inclination of his heart is evil from his youth."

That God will never again curse the ground because of humankind implies a separation between the destinies of humankind and nature. Earth (*hā'ădāmāh*) could be cursed because of Adam's sin because they were of the same substance. Noah is distinct from the

---

[16]Wenham, *Torah as Story*, p. 35.

[17]The NIV translates "from his childhood." But the Hebrew word usually refers to a young man old enough to make moral decisions. It refers to Ishmael when he is banished after the birth of Isaac (older than 13), Joseph at 17 and at 30, the young soldiers of Abraham (Gen. 14:24), etc.

earth, and so his actions and those of his progeny will not inevitably cause the earth's destruction.

8:22 "As long as the earth endures, seedtime and harvest, cold and heat, summer and winter, day and night will never cease."

The LORD promises that he will never again curse the ground through sending a flood as he has done. By promising that the seasonal agricultural cycle will never again be interrupted, he clearly is referring to the disruption of that cycle which the Flood caused. This text functions as a sort of mitigation of the curse on the ground. Davies comments:

> But it is not simply a matter of undoing what has been done. The problem of the curse is resolved, but the curse itself is not revoked. What occurs is a *volte face* in which the original, negative curse is "resolved" by a positive "counter-curse" — effectively a blessing; the blessing of the seasonal cycle. . . . The divine statement presupposes that the effects of the original curse will continue; but they will be offset by divine help in promoting agriculture through regular ordering of the seasons.[18]

This is perhaps overstating the matter but Davies' insight remains. There is no longer any danger of a disruption of seasonal cycle with this promise. The cursed earth can at least be relied upon to bring the seasonal changes which make it possible to grow crops.

Davies[19] notices the following chiastic-like structure in the broader narrative:

A	2.5	Man as a "servant"' of the ground (cf. 3.23)
B	3.17	Curse on the ground "because of man"
C	4.4	Rejection of human offering
C'	8.20	Acceptance of human offering
B'	8.21	Curse on the ground "because of man"' not to recur
A'	9.20	Noah a "man" of the ground

---

[18]Philip R. Davies, "Sons of Cain," in *A Word in Season: Essays in Honor of William McKane*, ed. by James D. Martin and Philip R. Davies, JSOTSup 42 (Sheffield: JSOT Press, 1986), p. 37. Davies in an endnote sees a parallel to the book of Esther where the irrevocable law of the Medes and Persians is counteracted by a decree arming the Jews and allowing them to defend themselves.

[19]I have modified his wording slightly.

He sees in this structure a subtle clue that there may be development in the relationship between God and man. At the end of the narrative Noah is not a "servant" of the ground as man was cursed to be in 3:23, but merely "a man" of the ground and this seems like progress. One problem with his analysis is that it seems to imply a sort of arbitrariness on the part of God. But Cain's offering was not rejected for arbitrary reasons (see commentary above) nor presumably was Noah's accepted for arbitrary reasons. Noah was a blameless man in his generation and walked with God in a way reminiscent of the Garden of Eden. His silent obedience and reverent sacrifice gives the reader hope for the future of humanity in its relationship with God.

I think it is preferable to realize that, while the Flood in part cleanses humanity of sin, there is a bigger purpose for it in the working out of God's relationship with humanity. The Flood is a warning to future generations of the seriousness of the consequences of attempting to construct a life without God. Such a life will invariably bring an "eat, drink, and be merry for tomorrow we die" attitude to the strong, and inevitably the weak are trampled under their feet. This is an offense to God's holy nature and will inevitably bring the sternest form of judgment. Since God's holy nature does not change and since he has committed himself to never again include all creation in his judgment, those who would construct such a life should take warning. He will no longer tolerate evil getting out of hand. He will intervene before such evil has produced its offspring. The Sodom and Gomorrah narrative with its persistent echoing of the Flood narrative makes it clear what God's new strategy would be. Judgment will be more confined and will not encompass the cosmos, but it will also be swifter and no less severe for the perpetrators.

Why then, did God tolerate it prior to the Flood? The Bible does not answer such questions directly. But in this narrative God is portrayed as being in a reciprocal relationship with humankind. The Flood seems to serve as a sort of demonstration of what happens when humanity attempts to live life without God at the center. It also is a part of the narrative in which humanity is given the freedom to interface in a variety of ways until it is finally determined that only a relationship which God initiates and preserves in his grace will work.[20]

---

[20]See further Paul J. Kissling, *A Sketch of Old Testament Theology*.

GENESIS 9

K. THE PRESERVATION OF NOAH'S LINE (9:1-7)

¹Then God blessed Noah and his sons, saying to them, "Be fruitful and increase in number and fill the earth. ²The fear and dread of you will fall upon all the beasts of the earth and all the birds of the air, upon every creature that moves along the ground, and upon all the fish of the sea; they are given into your hands. ³Everything that lives and moves will be food for you. Just as I gave you the green plants, I now give you everything.

⁴"But you must not eat meat that has its lifeblood still in it. ⁵And for your lifeblood I will surely demand an accounting. I will demand an accounting from every animal. And from each man, too, I will demand an accounting for the life of his fellow man.

⁶"Whoever sheds the blood of man,
    by man shall his blood be shed;
for in the image of God
    has God made man.

⁷As for you, be fruitful and increase in number; multiply on the earth and increase upon it."

This section and the following one record a speech from God to Noah after the Flood. Within the structure of the Flood narrative it corresponds to the divine speech in 6:9-22 prior to the Flood. Although the creation narrative is echoed in various ways throughout the Flood narrative, this section has perhaps the most overt echoes. Humanity has a new Adam named Noah. With his sons Noah is recommissioned to be fruitful and multiply and fill the earth. This is referred to as a "blessing" as it was in chapter 1. Food is designated for the new humanity just as it was for the original humanity. The image of God is mentioned again as the rationale for the prohibition of murder just as it was in Genesis 1:26-28. The passage has a sort of chiastic structure in which the first verse is repeated in the last.

1. The Recommissioning of Humanity (9:1)

9:1 Then God blessed Noah and his sons, saying to them, "Be fruitful and increase in number and fill the earth.

God's blessing on the new humanity repeats almost verbatim his blessing on the old (1:28).

1:28a	9:1-7
28 God blessed them and said to them, "Be fruitful and increase in number; fill the earth and subdue it."	v. 1 Then God blessed Noah and his sons, saying to them, "Be fruitful and increase in number and fill the earth."

This is the third time God has blessed humankind (1:28; 5:2) and the third time humankind has been told to be "fruitful and multiply" (1:28; 8:17). The fulfillment of that command happens in a new way in chapter 10 with its record of how the descendants of Noah spread throughout the world after the Flood. In the modern world with its concerns about overpopulation it is very difficult for us to appreciate fully the blessing of fertility. But the Bible clearly and consistently portrays procreation and the fertility needed for it to happen as the gift of God. It is interesting that there is no repetition of the command to "subdue" the earth to Noah. This may be because humanity's subduing of the earth prior to the Flood was a cause for concern. It is also possible that the new relationship with the animals, i.e., as a possible food source, could easily be abused if subduing the earth was done in a sinful way without regard to God's will.

2. The Conditions under Which Animals May Now Be Eaten (9:2-5a)

9:2 The fear and dread of you will fall upon all the beasts of the earth and all the birds of the air, upon every creature that moves

along the ground, and upon all the fish of the sea; they are given into your hands.
9:3 Everything that lives and moves will be food for you. Just as I gave you the green plants, I now give you everything.

In the process of filling the earth the descendants of Noah will undoubtedly interact with the animals and other creatures which have survived the flood. Before God announces that now humanity's diet will be expanded to include meat and fish, he informs Noah and his family that they will no longer be easy to catch. Instead they will run in fear from humanity. Given that the animals at least are in a very vulnerable state (actually on the edge of extinction) at this time, this shows God's concern for the continued existence of the animals he had created. The fear and dread which animals will now experience when they meet humans is God's protection of them which prevents their being hunted into extinction too easily.

While the fear which animals will have for humanity is a protection, it is also an indication that the harmony in which God created the world is gone. The curse on the serpent is in a sense here extended to all of the animal world. There is a new sense of estrangement between the human family and the animal family. Isaiah 11:6-9 refers to a time when this estranged relationship between humankind and the animal kingdom will be healed. Leviticus 26:6 within the context of an Edenic description of the promised land (26:3-13) has God promising to "rid evil beasts from the land." In other words one of the reflex reactions in animals to fear of humankind is aggressive violence. While in many senses the post-Flood era is a sort of new creation this trajectory must not be overemphasized. The new creation after the Flood sees an intensifying of some of the disharmony introduced by the Fall.

But why did God make this choice? One possibility is that the emergency circumstances after the Flood required it. It would take time for the earth to fructify itself again after it was so disrupted by the deluge. The granting of permission to eat animals could be out of necessity given the state of the earth after the Flood. Steinmetz suggests another possible narrative rationale for this development:

> Noah has taken responsibility for animal life, and so he and his family enjoy new rights over the animal kingdom; but gone is

the relative harmony between human being and animal suggested in the first two chapters of Genesis.¹

This suggests that the granting of humanity the right to eat animals is a sort of reward for Noah working to preserve them through the flood. But we must be cautious here. The Cain and Abel narrative seems to suggest that it was perfectly acceptable to raise flocks prior to the Flood. A total vegetarian existence prior to the Flood therefore seems unlikely. It also seems implausible to suggest that humanity is portrayed as suddenly eating a diet as rich in meat and fish as contemporary diets. Whatever reason we choose to infer for the giving of this new freedom in the ideology of Genesis, it is a sign of further brokenness of God's originally created harmony.

Even though meat and fish are now granted as food sources, there are restrictions. Everything that lives and moves is to be a potential food source. This would seem to restrict the eating of animals that have died of "natural causes." Further restrictions are found in verse 4 below.

9:4 "But you must not eat meat that has its lifeblood still in it. 9:5a And for your lifeblood I will surely demand an accounting.

The meat of animals and fish is a potential food source only if it does not have its lifeblood still in it. Some read this as prohibiting the eating of animals while they are still alive and their blood is coursing through their veins.² Others³ suggest that it really would prohibit such things as blood sausage. Blood must be drained and not eaten. Certainly life is in the blood according to biblical law (Deut 12:23). It might be natural to assume that the imagined audience would read this text in that way. If so, this would be yet another example of the laws which Israel received at Sinai being based

---

¹Devora Steinmetz, "Vineyard, Farm, and Garden: The Drunkenness of Noah in the Context of Primeval History," *JBL* 113/2 (1994): 196.

²Wenham, *Genesis 1–15*, p. 193.

³*BBC*, p. 39: "The prohibition does not require that no blood at all be consumed, but only that the blood must be drained. The draining of the blood before eating the meat was a way of returning the life force of the animal to the God who gave it life. This offers recognition that they have taken the life with permission and are partaking of God's bounty as his guests. Its function is not unlike that of the blessing said before a meal in modern practice. No comparable prohibition is known in the ancient world."

upon universal principles which come from the earliest days of God's relationship with the world. In the end it is difficult to know for certain which of these views to adopt. Certainly the text calls upon its readers to exercise the utmost respect for life, even animal and fish life which is given as food to feed us.[4]

3. Prohibition of Killing Other Humans (9:5b-6)

9:5b I will demand an accounting from every animal. And from each man, too, I will demand an accounting for the life of his fellow man.

In this text God makes it very clear that life is valuable, even sacred. Any life that is taken violently and without respect for the life that God has given demands an accounting. Violent animals will be held accountable as well as violent people. God himself values life and will therefore personally hold accountable any animal or human who takes life in a foolish way.

9:6 "Whoever sheds the blood of man, by man shall his blood be shed; for in the image of God has God made man.

In order to limit human-on-human violence God authorizes other humans to take vengeance. Certainly the imagined audience was familiar with the death penalty which was prescribed in the law revealed at Sinai. The rationale for such vengeance is the created nature and divinely given purpose of humanity. They are the image of God and authorized by him to rule over creation on his behalf. The violence which brought on the Flood must be stopped before it fills the earth. Since God has promised never again to use a universal flood to wipe out human violence, that violence must be stopped in its tracks. It will not be allowed to spread. It is interesting that God does not explicitly command the death penalty here. It is impossible to know whether he is making a prediction or a recommendation.

Certainly Christians struggle with the notion of personally taking revenge in light of Jesus' clear teaching about forgiving even our enemies. While this passage might suggest that as a means of limit-

---

[4]It is interesting that at the so-called Jerusalem Council in Acts 15 one of the practices which James advocates that Gentile believers must abstain from is the eating of blood.

ing violence the death penalty is permissible, it is very different from advocating it for Christians or giving support for it today in contemporary secular nations.

4. Reminder of the Recommissioning (9:7)

9:7 As for you, be fruitful and increase in number; multiply on the earth and increase upon it."

This verse forms an inclusio with 9:1 and a reminder of its importance, especially in light of the fact that there are so few people left with which to populate the world. While the conditions of the new creation are both different from and similar to the first creation, in one respect they are identical. Humanity is responsible to multiply through procreation and fill the earth. Only in doing so will they be able to effectively rule over creation as they have been commissioned. Humanity is God's image, his representative in the world. To be that effectively required that the new humanity procreate.

L. THE COVENANT AND ITS SIGN (9:8-17)

Covenants in the ancient world were solemn agreements between two parties. They were typically formalized in some ritualized way and often included a sign which reminded both parties and others of their obligations to the other party. Having reestablished humanity's creational purpose in verses 1-7, here God formally establishes the new covenant and announces the sign of that covenant, the bow in the clouds.

⁸Then God said to Noah and to his sons with him: ⁹"I now establish my covenant with you and with your descendants after you ¹⁰and with every living creature that was with you—the birds, the livestock and all the wild animals, all those that came out of the ark with you—every living creature on earth. ¹¹I establish my covenant with you: Never again will all life be cut off by the waters of a flood; never again will there be a flood to destroy the earth."

¹²And God said, "This is the sign of the covenant I am making between me and you and every living creature with you, a covenant

for all generations to come: ¹³I have set my rainbow in the clouds, and it will be the sign of the covenant between me and the earth. ¹⁴Whenever I bring clouds over the earth and the rainbow appears in the clouds, ¹⁵I will remember my covenant between me and you and all living creatures of every kind. Never again will the waters become a flood to destroy all life. ¹⁶Whenever the rainbow appears in the clouds, I will see it and remember the everlasting covenant between God and all living creatures of every kind on the earth."

¹⁷So God said to Noah, "This is the sign of the covenant I have established between me and all life on the earth."

1. The Covenant with the New Creation (9:8-11)

9:8 Then God said to Noah and to his sons with him:
The waw-consecutive (cf. "then" in NIV) is logical here perhaps as well as temporal. After the responsibility is given to humankind in the restored creation and on that basis, God speaks to Noah and family about the establishment of a covenant. The fact that his sons are addressed along with Noah probably implies that the covenant is understood to continue beyond the time of Noah.

9:9 "I now establish my covenant with you and with your descendants after you
9:10 and with every living creature that was with you—the birds, the livestock and all the wild animals, all those that came out of the ark with you—every living creature on earth.
In Genesis 6:18 God promised to establish a covenant with Noah sometime in the future which would enable Noah to remain alive and repopulate the earth. Now that promise reaches its formal fulfillment. Because the destiny of humankind and the destiny of creation are intertwined, the covenant (commitment) that God grants (gives) is made not only with humankind, but with that part of the animate creation that was saved on the ark as well. Sea creatures, unaffected by the flood, are not included in the covenant. The fact that it is with Noah's descendants as well as Noah himself indicates that this is a lasting (eternal?) covenant.

A covenant is a solemn, formal agreement between two parties. Most covenants are bilateral and have responsibilities and rights for both parties. In this case the parties are God on the one hand and Noah, his descendants, and the animals protected on the ark on the other. In this covenant the responsibilities of Noah and the animals have already been fulfilled. Noah did build the ark as he was instructed, and he did preserve the animals alive. In this covenant God makes promises without laying any further responsibilities on Noah or the rest of creation. God takes on the obligations of the covenant himself. There is no response required of Noah, his family, or the animals. In this sense it is a unilateral covenant which God bestows in his grace. This covenant differs, however, from the covenants with Abra(ha)m and Israel in that this is a covenant with all humanity and not with an elect line.

9:11 I establish my covenant with you: Never again will all life be cut off by the waters of a flood; never again will there be a flood to destroy the earth."

In saying, "I establish my covenant with you," God makes a "performative utterance," i.e., a statement which merely by its being spoken actually does something. A common example would be the words "I do" spoken at a wedding ceremony by the bride or groom. Since God is God, for him to say "I establish my covenant with you" is to do it. God commits himself to never again using the universal de-creation of a flood to deal with the wickedness of humankind. The Flood thus becomes an object lesson for future generations, and a warning that God will act in the future before the evil of humankind escalates to such de-creating proportions. The many echoes between the Flood narrative and the creation account emphasize this point. The "you" is plural in Hebrew and makes clear that this is not just a covenant with Noah as an individual but with the new humanity of which Noah is the head.

The parallelistic repetition which God uses in this covenant promise shows its solemnity. Modern western readers often find this repetition tiresome, but it is the Bible's way of clarifying and emphasizing an important point:

| Never again | will all life be cut off | by the waters of a flood; |
| Never again | will there be a flood | to destroy the earth." |

2. The Sign of the Covenant: The Bow (9:12-17)

**9:12 And God said, "This is the sign of the covenant I am making between me and you and every living creature with you, a covenant for all generations to come:
9:13 I have set my rainbow in the clouds, and it will be the sign of the covenant between me and the earth.**

This passage has been examined in detail in the excursus below. The "bow in the cloud" (not the "rainbow in the clouds" in the NIV) may be what we call a rainbow, or it may refer to God hanging up his bow signifying that the war with creation is over, or it may signify the shape of the expanse which has been reestablished to keep the floodwaters at bay. I have suggested in the following excursus that there may be deliberate ambiguity between these three readings, a sort of *triple entendre*.

As I have tentatively argued in the excursus, the Hebrew seems to imply that the rainbow had previously been given and was only now designated as the sign of the covenant God makes with creation. There is no reason to believe the popular idea that there was no rain prior to the Flood and consequently no rainbows.

The covenant which God makes here is for all generations. As long as the present creation exists, there will never be a disruption of the seasonal cycle as occurred in the Flood. Further revelation informs us that the next cataclysmic judgment will be the final one, and it will come through fire. The new heavens and new earth that emerge from that cataclysmic event will remain forever and will never be spoiled by sin (2 Pet 3:8-13).

**9:14 Whenever I bring clouds over the earth and the rainbow appears in the clouds,
9:15 I will remember my covenant between me and you and all living creatures of every kind. Never again will the waters become a flood to destroy all life.**

Notice how close God is to the processes of what we call nature. He brings clouds over the earth. He is not the distant creator who runs the universe by default on natural law and only rarely "breaks" his own laws in what we call miracles. He is the creator and the sustainer of the universe.

Just as the Flood narrative "hinges" or "pivots" on 8:1 ("Then

329

God remembered Noah"), so here God promises to remember the commitment he has made at the key moment. Clouds with rain threaten the destruction of the creation, but at the very moment when the threatening clouds appear, it is then that God promises to remember his covenant. That covenant is not only with humanity but with "all living creatures of every kind." Creation itself will no longer bear the brunt of human iniquity.

9:16 Whenever the rainbow appears in the clouds, I will see it and remember the everlasting covenant between God and all living creatures of every kind on the earth."

Here the covenant is called "everlasting" (עוֹלָם, 'ôlām). The word does not necessarily mean absolutely eternal in some mathematical sense. It means at least "for a long time" or "into the distant future." But the rest of the Bible makes it clear that this is a covenant that God will never go back on.

The universal nature of this solemn promise is indicated by the double use of the word "all" or "every" (in Hebrew כֹּל, kōl). All living creatures of all kinds receive this promise. God will remember every time the bow appears in the clouds.

9:17 So God said to Noah, "This is the sign of the covenant I have established between me and all life on the earth."

God tells Noah a second time for emphasis to summarize and conclude the passage, and to underscore the importance of the covenant. The covenant is not just with humanity who tends to break and undermine God's covenants. The covenant is with all life on earth, human or animal. Since the covenant is thus universal, so also the sign of the covenant is similarly universal.

EXCURSUS

THE BOW IN GENESIS 9:12-17[5]

INTRODUCTION

If the current fashion of being attracted to holistic methodologies has furthered the scholarly investigation of Hebrew Narrative at all, it certainly has taught us to read more carefully and grant to the narrators a greater degree of subtlety than previously thought plausible. Often much that is below the surface is merely hinted at on the surface; sometimes in the most delicate of ways. *Double entendres* (or at least scholarly suggestions of them) abound. The אֶרֶץ (*'ereṣ*) of Genesis one, is it the earth or is it the promised land, or is it in some sense both?[6] The "double portion" which Elisha desires of Elijah's spirit, is it the extra share that the firstborn receives according to Deuteronomy 21:17 or is it "literally" double the amount which Elijah possesses, or is it both?[7] Is the garden of Eden merely the actual garden where Adam and Eve resided, or is it also a presage of the Promised Land, or perhaps, *vice versa*?[8] A *desideratum* would be a cataloguing of such suggestions.

Here I would like to investigate the possibility of a *triple entendre*. In Genesis 9:12-17 we read:

> 12) Then God said, "This (is) a sign of the covenant which I am giving (part. of נָתַן) between me and between you all and between every animate living being which is with you all for countless (עוֹלָם) generations. 13) My bow I have given in the cloud. And it will be for a sign of the covenant between me and between the earth. 14) And it will be when I bring the cloud

---

[5]This is a slightly edited version of an article originally delivered at the Fellowship of Professors Meeting at St. Louis Christian College and later published in *Stone-Campbell Journal* 4 (2001): 249-261. Used by permission.

[6]Cf. Sailhamer, *Genesis,* p. 19, "In translating the Hebrew word הָאָרֶץ 'earth' in 1:1 and 1:2, the EVs have blurred the connection of these early verses of Genesis to the central theme of the "land," (*'ereṣ*) in the Pentateuch."

[7]Cf. Kissling, *Reliable Characters*, pp. 161-199.

[8]E.g., the "ideal" borders of the promised land in Gen 15:18 bear a striking resemblance to the borders of Eden in Gen 2:10-14.

upon the earth and the bow will be seen in the cloud 15) then (lit. 'and') I will remember my covenant which (is) between me and between you all and between every animate living being of (lit. 'in') all flesh; and there will never again be the waters of a flood to spoil (piel) all flesh. 16) And the bow will be in the cloud and I will see it to remember the enduring (עוֹלָם) covenant between God and between every animate being of (lit. 'in') all flesh which (is) upon the earth. 17) Then God said unto Noah, "this is a sign, which I have raised up (hiph.), of the covenant between me and between all flesh which (is) upon the earth.[9]

Traditionally the bow referred in this passage is assumed to be what we call a "rainbow." Just as the rainbow appears after the rain, so it is argued, the rainbow here is a reminder that God has promised to never again spoil all flesh with the waters of the flood. A second view, popular at least since the time of Wellhausen, notes that the word translated "bow" (קֶשֶׁת, *qešeth*) is almost invariably[10] used in reference to the weapon used to propel arrows. What exactly this sort of bow might mean in this context is debated. I would like to suggest a third possibility and suggest that any of the three views are plausible and investigate the possibility that an "intentional" triple entendre might be in view.

I. THE BOW AS THE RAINBOW

If interpretation were evaluated by means democratic, this view would win hands down. The rainbow after the rain is such a memorable and seemingly almost universal human experience that interpreters throughout the ages have been drawn to it.

There has been discussion among those who subscribe to this view about whether the text is claiming that this was the first occurrence of a rainbow, Luther followed by some proponents of "creation science" claiming yes, Calvin no. The Hebrew verbs may be of some help. In verse 12 a participial form of נָתַן (*nāthān*), נֹתֵן (*nōthēn*), occurs. God says, "I am giving a sign." In verse 13, however, we have

---

[9] My literalistic translation.
[10] The only seeming exception is Ezek 1:28.

the same verb, *nāthān*, but as a perfect, "I have given (placed) my bow." While I would not place too much weight on this given the quicksand which tense and aspect in Classical Hebrew have become for contemporary scholars, I would argue that the giving of the rainbow in all probability is to be understood as preceding the giving of the sign. The rainbow has already been given by God, presumably in creation, but its significance as a sign is something new.[11]

Even without the argument from the Hebrew, however, the view that the rainbow was created *de novo* after the Flood seems to be based on arguments from silence and the rather absurd, albeit unconscious, hermeneutical principle that things should not be assumed to be in existence in creation until they are explicitly mentioned for the first time in the Bible. Related to the creation-science interpretation of this text is the interpretation of the word אֵד (*'d*, "mist" in KJV) in Genesis 2:6 and the statement in Genesis 2:5 that, "the LORD God had not caused it to rain." Francis Andersen remarks helpfully on the problem:

> One task of the Reformation and other early modern readers of the Bible was to consider the text in relation to the world. They asked, given that *'ed* means "mist" [which Andersen has just argued against rather conclusively] in Genesis 2:6, what do we learn about the history of the weather on this planet? One relevant rule stipulated, "A thing did not happen until the Bible reports it." The other evidence for the weather is abundant. The verse before the one under study, Genesis 2:5 says, "the LORD God had not caused it to rain." And, indeed, rain is first mentioned in Genesis 7:4. The remarks about the "bow" in Genesis 9 were added to the picture, helped out by a late tradition that here the word *qešeth* (קשת) means "rainbow"; this must have been the first rainbow ever, because the Bible had not mentioned any before. We may leave it to the reader to apply this straining logic to the rest of the vocabulary of

---

[11]*BBC*, p. 30, "The designation of the rainbow as a sign of the covenant does not suggest that it was the first rainbow ever seen. The function of a sign is connected to the significance attached to it. In like manner, circumcision is designated as a sign of the covenant with Abraham, yet that was an ancient practice, not new with Abraham and his family. In the *Gilgamesh Epic the goddess *Ishtar identified the lapis lazuli . . . of her necklace as the basis of an oath by which she would never forget the days of the flood."

Scripture. One scholar of our own time, C.T. Schwarze, notes that "sunlight is not mentioned in the Bible until Genesis 15:12" and therefore constructs a vast shell of ice around the earth to explain, not only the lack of sunlight, but also the absence of rain before Noah's flood, and incidentally, ice ages, coal deposits, the continent of Atlantis, etc. Between the supposed "mist" of chapter 2 and the supposed "rainbow" of chapter 9, the meteorological history of this planet from Creation to Flood was worked out in early modern times; this history was believed to be "the teaching of the word of God." The inerrancy of the Bible was thus identified with materials in two academic subjects — the Hebrew dictionary (*'ed* means "mist") and the history of rainfall (no rain before the Flood); both subjects are distinct from the biblical text.[12]

While I do not question the sincerity of those who hold such views (I once held them), and am myself no proponent of mindless genetic happenstance as an explanation for the origins of the universe,[13] such views seem implausible at best.

But whether the bow in 9:12-17 is to be understood as a rainbow is another matter. Besides a long and venerable history, this view has the following considerations in its favor. First the use of the Hebrew phrase בֶּעָנָן (*be'ānān*, "in the cloud[s]") with *qešeth* ("bow") both here and in Ezekiel 1:28 argues for a special "metaphorical" use of *qešeth* ("bow") here meaning something like, "the bow-shaped object seen in the clouds." The fact that *'ānān* is clearly a collective noun in Hebrew[14] is a further argument. While *'ānān* usually refers to "the cloud," which is a moving or at least moveable theophany of God's presence in the wilderness, and its tabernacle and later the temple, there is ample attestation of its use in the singular of the physical phenomenon we call clouds.

There is also the general context of the passage. The flood has ended, and the "re-creation" mandates are given to Noah and family

---

[12] Andersen, "On Reading Genesis 1–3," p. 138

[13] Cf. William S. Dembski, ed., *Mere Creation* (Downers Grove, IL: InterVarsity, 1998).

[14] The only occurrence of the Hebrew plural is in Jer 4:13. While some of these are disputable, the plural "clouds" seems to be an appropriate translation for the singular in Job 7:9; 26:8,9; 37:11,15; 38:9; Ps 97:2; Ezek 30:3; 32:7; 34:12; 38:9,16; Hos 6:4; 13:3; Joel 2:2; Nahum 1:3; Zeph 1:15.

(9:1-6). Since (notice the כִּי, *kî*) the Flood has done little to change the fundamental nature of humankind (8:21 with 6:5), Yahweh makes a unilateral commitment to himself to never again curse the ground nor destroy every living creature because of humankind's propensity to evil (8:21). He must turn to another stratagem or face an endless cycle of de-creation followed by re-creation followed by de-creation. The designation of a sign of that unilateral commitment (בְּרִית, *bᵊrîth*) naturally follows from the fact that Yahweh has already made the commitment in 8:21.[15] That the sign should be a rainbow is appropriate in that a rainbow follows and signals the end of the rain. Since the bow is a sign for God (9:15,16), and not directly for humankind, the exact sequence of the rainbow following the rain is not necessarily relevant. God has already given the bow in creation (9:13). When he brings clouds upon the earth, he will "see" the bow and remember his commitment. It is not necessary for the clouds first to dump the rain and cause a flood for him to see it and remember his commitment to never use a flood again.

Further, Ezekiel 1:28, the only other place to qualify *qešeth* with the phrase *beʿānān* seems at first sight to be referring to a rainbow since it is further qualified by the phrase בְּיוֹם הַגֶּשֶׁם (*bᵊyôm hagešem*) "on the day of rain."

While these arguments do carry considerable weight, there are other considerations which give the interpreter pause. To begin with, of the 74 verses in which the word *qešeth* appears, it always refers to the weapon, except possibly here, the text at issue, and in Ezekiel 1:28. The latter passage may well be based on this one.[16] Further, while I would not want to press this very far, the Hebrew word for cloud, *ʿānān*, is articular in 9:12-17.[17] In the Pentateuch this phrase, *the* cloud, uniformly refers to the theophanic cloud which signaled God's presence and was the signal for the camp of Israelites to move on. While occasionally the word *ʿānān*, "cloud" is anarthrous when referring to this cloud,[18] the articular form always refers to this

---

[15]Gen 8:21 is usually viewed as J. While 9:12-17 is P, this does not materially affect my point. P or the redactor(s) which followed placed the commitment in 8:21 prior to the sign of the covenant in 9:12-17.

[16]That is, canonically speaking where the Pentateuch is first.

[17]The seeming exception is 9:14a, *bᵊʿanᵊnî ʿānān*, but it is clear from the final word of v. 14, *beʿānān*, that *the* cloud is referred to here.

[18]By my count 8 out of 43 cases, most of which are parts of phrases such

theophanic cloud. The point is that, given that Genesis 9:12-17 is found within the canonical context of the Pentateuch, it seems plausible that the reader is being reminded of the theophanic presence of God with his people Israel in the desert. This would be consistent with what I take to be one of the dominant themes of Genesis. The institutions, laws, and revelations given to Israel from the Exodus on are anticipated in the book of Genesis in the most remarkable of ways. So Noah obeys clean and unclean food laws before they are given; Abraham and Jacob tithe; the Sabbath is anticipated in creation, etc.[19] While the suggestion of the theophanic cloud does not rule out the "rainbow" interpretation, it does, I would argue, suggest a deeper and more "theological" meaning.

There are other difficulties with the "rainbow" interpretation. One is that ordinarily rainbows follow the rain and are a sign of its abatement. If a literal rainbow is in view, one could argue that the sign would not help God remember until, oops, he had already sent another flood. As Brichto remarks, "the rainbow would function as a signal to lock the barn door after the horse has left!"[20] Further, rainbows are usually seen against the background of a clear blue sky, not in the clouds.[21] Further still, the sign of the bow is a sign for God. He is the one who will see it.

Now, none of these difficulties so far as I am able to judge matters, *exclude* the "rainbow" interpretation. But they are significant enough to make one wonder whether the text is being more subtle than it at first seems. The strongest argument in favor of the "rainbow" view is the parallel text, Ezekiel 1:28. But if that text is some-

---

as "pillar of cloud" or "cloud of Yahweh" (Exod 13:21; 14:24; 40:38; Num 10:34; 12:5; 14:14; Deut 4:11; 31:15).

[19]See my unpublished paper on natural law in Gen 9:1-6 delivered at the Midwest Regional SBL meeting at Wheaton College in 1996.

[20]Brichto, *The Names of God*, p. 157.

[21]Note, however, F. Delitzsch's comment (*A New Commentary on Genesis*, trans. by S. Taylor [Edinburgh: T & T Clark, 1888], 1:289-290): "The label of the rainbow is sufficiently legible. Shining upon a dark ground . . . it represents the victory of the light of love over the fiery darkness of wrath. Originating from the effect of the sun upon a dark cloud, it typifies the willingness of the heavenly to penetrate the earthly. Stretched between heaven and earth, it is a bond of peace between both, and, spanning the horizon, it points to the all-embracing universality of the Divine mercy."

how reflecting this one, the matter is not so simple. And Ezekiel 1:28 is, after all, found in a remarkably symbolic description of a theophany. My point is that choosing between these alternatives in a yes/no fashion may be a rather naïve way of reading this subtle text.

II. THE BOW AS A WEAPON OF WAR

While apparently there was rabbinic discussion of this very point,[22] among modern interpreters, so far as I am aware, Wellhausen was the first to suggest that the bow was God's discarded weapon. For him, of course, this was the remnant of a flood story in which a great battle with the watery forces of chaos resulted in a narrow escape for the forces of order. But the idea that the battle is over and therefore the bow, the battle weapon, is no longer needed, is a plausible meaning. We to this day speak of "burying the hatchet,"[23] and the giving of the bow as a sign could well be the Hebrew equivalent.

Gunkel among others notices that Enuma Elish apparently speaks of Marduk's bow being hung among the stars after his defeat of Tiamat and her allies. After the construction of the temple of Marduk in Babylon the myth records a banquet hosted by Marduk. The gods drink and celebrate and then take their seats. The gods Enlil and then Anu speak:

> Enlil lifted up the bow [Marduk's] weapon and laid it before them.
> The gods, his fathers, also beheld the net which he had made.
> When they saw how skillfully the bow had been constructed
> His fathers praised the work which he had done.
> Anu lifted up the bow and spoke in the assembly of the gods
> He kissed the bow saying, "This is my daughter!"

---

[22]Matthews, *Genesis 1–11:26*, p. 411, note 144. Laurence A. Turner, "The Rainbow as the Sign of the Covenant in Genesis IX 11-13," *VT* 43/1 (1993): 119-124, refers to Ramban's Commentary on the Torah: *Genesis* (New York, 1971), pp. 136-137, who notes that several Rabbis viewed the bow as shooting arrows upwards, away from the earth and therefore as a sign of peace.

[23]Brichto, *Names of God*, p. 158.

He named the names of the bow as follows:
Longwood is first, the second is Achiever;
Its third name is ***Bow-star***
In the heavens I have made it shine.[24]

Interestingly, the bow, according to Enuma Elish VI:125 was actually a "rain-flood" or "flood-storm."[25] The arrows are apparently bolts of lightning.

Mendenhall discusses the textual and visual evidence for a winged solar disk. In one such instance the disk is surrounded by heavy rain clouds and the god Assur, depicted as riding on the disk, is holding a *drawn bow* aimed at his enemies.[26] A slightly earlier broken obelisk depicts the disk with the cloud and two hands extending from it, one in a gesture of blessing and the other holding an upright, but *undrawn bow*.[27] An even more interesting and relevant piece from the reign of Assur-nasir-pal II shows the triumphant entry of the king after a victory, undrawn bow in hand. Above him is the winged disk representing the king's "divine air power." The figure in the disk, the god Assur, a mirror image of the king, is holding an undrawn bow, but it is oriented *horizontally* like a rainbow. Mendenhall argues that the Flood narrative is consciously reflecting on such traditions by sub/in-verting them. In the ancient Near Eastern theology the king is the god of the state incarnate. But in Genesis 9 the imagery is used differently and as a deliberate counterpoint to that theology:

> The undrawn bow of the Assyrian triumph becomes a symbol, then, not of the all-powerful king's glorious victory which enhances the well-being (i.e., the "peace") of all his subjects, but

---

[24]My paraphrase based on Alexander Heidel, *The Babylonian Genesis* (Chicago: The University of Chicago Press, 1942), pp. 49-50; and Speiser's translation in *ANET*, p. 69. That "the fixing of the stations" refers to placing a god as a star or series of stars in the heavens is clear from *Enuma Elish* V.1-10 and VI.78-79.

[25]Ibid.

[26]George E. Mendenhall, *The Tenth Generation* (Baltimore: John Hopkins University Press, 1973), pp. 44-45.

[27]K. Jaritz, "The Problem of the 'Broken Obelisk,'" *JSS* 4 (1959): 204 ff., cited in Mendenhall, *Tenth Generation*, p. 44.

of the determination that never again can the evil and chaos of mankind provoke God into returning the world to chaos (i.e., the Flood) as a just punishment. The undrawn bow is the "sign" of the unilateral covenant by which God binds Himself to guarantee the security even of His enemies from the violence of such overwhelming power that it reduces to insignificance the petty triumphs and proud gloating of man. . . .[28]

There is also ample evidence within the Hebrew Bible itself of Yahweh being depicted as a warrior who wins battles of cosmic proportions with the bow.[29] Habakkuk 3:9 depicts Yahweh coming to save his people in terms of a cosmic battle won with his bow. A bow with arrows is a symbol of his judgment in Psalm 7:13 (v. 12 in Eng.), and Lamentations 2:4 while in Lamentations 3:12 the bow symbolizes the difficulties which prophets experience in being faithful to their callings.[30]

The chief strength of the weapon view is the Hebrew usage of *qešeth*. While this passage and the related Ezekiel 1:28 might be exceptions, the semantic range for this word seems quite limited. In addition, the use of literal bows and arrows as metaphors for divine action within the realm of what we call nature is well attested in the Hebrew Bible.[31]

Some versions of this view, however, fail at one crucial point. The sustained anti-idolatry polemic, so manifestly a major concern of this section of the Pentateuch,[32] fits poorly with approaches which imply that the remnants of that very same idolatry still show up in Genesis. One cannot coherently argue that Genesis critiques ancient Near Eastern idolatrous notions and myths in the most exclusive terms and then argue that it leaves traces of the very myths it is critiquing, unless one lives in a sort of Derridaian multiverse. Either these texts are monotheistic or they are not. The alternative, partially monotheistic, sounds like being a little less than completely pregnant. That the community which canonized these texts[33] read

---

[28]Mendenhall, *Tenth Generation*, pp. 47-48.
[29]See Heidel's discussion, *Babylonian Genesis*, pp. 82-140.
[30]God's arrows are referred to in Num 24:8; Deut 32:23,42; 2 Sam 22:15 = Ps 18:15; Hab 3:11; Zech 9:14; Ps 38:2; 64:8; 144:6; and Job 6:4.
[31]2 Sam 22:15 = Ps 18:15; Hab 3:11; Ps 144:6.
[32]See Matthews, Wenham, and Hamilton.
[33]I am, of course, revealing my own bias with these comments.

them as monotheistic in an exclusive sense seems beyond reasonable doubt. That the putative sources behind the Pentateuch, P, D, and any redactors, granting for the moment their existence, were exclusivists seems highly likely also. Read as Scripture for the church the case is even stronger.[34] To claim that the bow is the remnant of an earlier account of some primordial battle with the forces of chaos stretches credulity. Even Sarna's comment gives me pause:

> This weapon is frequently featured in ancient Near Eastern mythology. In the Mesopotamian creation epic Enuma Elish (6.82-90), Marduk suspended in the sky and set as a constellation the victorious bow with which he had defeated Tiamat. In Babylonian astronomy, a group of stars in the shape of a bow was mythologically identified with the accouterments of the war goddess. In the Ugaritic myth dealing with the relationship of Aqhat and the bellicose goddess Anath, a bow plays a prominent role. In the Bible itself, numerous poetic texts figuratively refer to God's bow and arrows and are probably echoes of some now lost ancient Hebrew epic. Against this background, the rainbow in our narrative takes on added significance as a departure from Near Eastern notions. The symbol of divine bellicosity and hostility has been transformed into a token of reconciliation between God and man.[35]

While there is for Sarna "a departure from Near Eastern notions," it is only a partial one. For him, Genesis borrows the mythological detail, but transforms it into something more biblical. But this seems not to have been the case with the sun, moon, and stars, the רָקִיעַ (raqia'), the primordial ocean (תְּהוֹם, t°hôm), etc. where virtually every vestige of polytheistic cosmology has been deliberately excised. Why should this be any different with the bow? The narratives of Genesis 1–11, unlike some poetic texts, seem to be uniformly anti-idolatry.

A further problem with this view is that the bow as a weapon only corresponds in shape to the bow in the clouds when it is strung. Mendenhall's distinction between drawn and undrawn bows in

---

[34]One is reminded of Gerhard Hasel's suggestion (*Old Testament Theology: Basic Issues in the Current Debate,* 4th ed. [Grand Rapids: Eerdmans, 1991], pp. 162-171) of God as the center for Old Testament Theology and House's recent attempt to write an Old Testament Theology on that basis (Paul House, *Old Testament Theology* [Downers Grove, IL: InterVarsity, 1998]).

[35]Sarna, *Genesis,* p. 63.

ancient Near Eastern iconography is helpful so far as it goes, but even an undrawn bow is still a usable weapon and at a moment's notice can be converted into such a weapon. The peace which the undrawn bow symbolizes is peace at the end of a sword. This is indicative of the fundamental dualism in polytheism. A god who has put down his bow can quite quickly and quite capriciously take it up again. The defeat of the primordial waters in ancient Near East flood traditions is always and only a temporary or uncertain defeat. Guards keep the half of Tiamat's body that forms the sky and contains life-threatening waters at bay (*Enuma Elish*, IV.139-140), but what if the guards are bribed or alienated by the great Marduk? Are the two hands reaching out from the clouds in the Assyrian relief (*Bible Background Commentary*) offering blessing and peace, or the choice of blessing or war? Or is it, blessing and peace at the tip of the arrow of the still strung bow? The weapon view falters if it is too closely linked to ancient Near Eastern iconographic or textual evidence from cultures with worldviews in diametric opposition to that of the narrator of Genesis.

When, however, the anti-idolatry polemic of this text is taken into account, the view that the bow be seen as a weapon does have merit.

III. THE BOW AS A SIGN OF THE REESTABLISHMENT OF THE *RAQÎA'*

In a short note in *Vetus Testamentum*[36] and in his *Readings Commentary on Genesis* my friend Laurence Turner has suggested another possibility.

> The rainbow does not signify God's war bow set to one side (a notion for which there is no contextual support nor any strong ancient near eastern parallels), but rather it provides a pictorial representation of the firmament. As the domed firmament restrains the *mabbul*, so the arched rainbow stands as a guarantee of the permanence of the cosmological structure.

Turner points to Ezekiel 1:22-28 where the invisible, but dome-shaped *raqîa'* ("firmament" or "dome" or "vault") no longer sepa-

---

[36]Turner, "Rainbow," p. 123.

rates the waters as in Genesis 1:6-8, but separates the creatures below from God's throne above. When this suggestion is combined with the fact that "the cloud" is used of the theophany of God's presence throughout the Pentateuch, a plausible case for a new reading emerges. The bow in the cloud is a sign that God is present in the cloud, and will in the future keep the bow-shaped *raqîaʻ* intact. While it cannot be proven that the *raqîaʻ* was conceived as being dome-shaped, this does seem likely.[37] Job 22:14 has Eliphaz, after reminding Job of God's transcendent glory (22:12), mock what he supposes Job's position to be. To Eliphaz Job seems to regard that very transcendence as remoteness. God is so distant from us that he does not see. He walks on the circle of the heavens, not here on earth. God is thus pictured, as in Ezekiel 1:28, as above the firmament which is viewed, at least poetically as circular or dome shaped. Isaiah 40:22 similarly has God sitting upon the half circle of the earth and there stretches out the heavens as a tent to live in. Proverbs 8:27 has personified Wisdom claiming to be there with God "when he drew a circle on the face of the deep" (תְהוֹם, *tehōm*). It is hard to imagine that a complete circle is in view here. Rather a half circle seems to be implied. Since this is a poetic description of the creation of the *raqîaʻ*, at least in this poetic text the idea is expressed that the shape of the firmament is like a half circle. Job 26:10 uses the verbal form of הוג (*hwg*) to describe the inscribing of a half circle upon the waters at the boundary of light and darkness, evidently the horizon. The verbal root for the expanse is רקע (*rqʻ*) which in the piel refers to the beating out of thin sheets of metal as in gold leaf.[38] The beauty of the bow may in fact signal the theophanic splendor as well as the splendor of the *raqîaʻ* (Dan 12:3!). Its shape, however, serves as a reminder to God, to whom the shape is visible,[39] to never again allow it to be breached by a flood.

---

[37]*HALOT*, 3:1292, gives "bow" as a meaning. Wenham, *Genesis 1–15*, p. 20, noting that Ezek 1:22 and Dan 12:3 describe it as shiny, remarks, "Such comments may suggest that the firmament was viewed as a glass dome over the earth, but since the most vivid descriptions occur in poetic texts, the language may be figurative."

[38]*HALOT*, 3:1292.

[39]Presumably it is not visible to humankind. Ezek 1:22 describes its appearance as like "the splendor of ice."

CONCLUSION

Are these three views mutually exclusive? I can see no convincing reason why they should be. None of them is without its strengths and weaknesses. The Hebrew word *qešeth* almost always refers to the weapon, but the qualification *be'ānān* ("in the cloud(s)") here and in Ezekiel 1:28 makes an equally strong linguistic argument. The timing of the rainbow and the shape of a strung bow create difficulties, although not insurmountable ones. The cloud as the theophany of God's presence supports the dome view, but is consistent with the other views. It cannot be proven that the Hebrews conceived of the *raqîaʿ* as in the shape of the bow, although this seems likely. While certitude is unavailable, perhaps we have here an example of a triple entendre. Our need to find one and only one meaning may get in the way of reading these subtle narratives as they were intended. Perhaps what we lack is the necessary imagination to read texts in their sometimes intentional ambiguity.

V. THE FALL OF THE POST-FLOOD GENERATIONS (9:18–11:32)

A. THE FALL OF NOAH (9:18-29)

¹⁸The sons of Noah who came out of the ark were Shem, Ham and Japheth. (Ham was the father of Canaan.) ¹⁹These were the three sons of Noah, and from them came the people who were scattered over the earth.

²⁰Noah, a man of the soil, proceeded^a to plant a vineyard. ²¹When he drank some of its wine, he became drunk and lay uncovered inside his tent. ²²Ham, the father of Canaan, saw his father's nakedness and told his two brothers outside. ²³But Shem and Japheth took a garment and laid it across their shoulders; then they walked in backward and covered their father's nakedness. Their faces were turned the other way so that they would not see their father's nakedness.

²⁴When Noah awoke from his wine and found out what his youngest son had done to him, ²⁵he said,

"Cursed be Canaan!
The lowest of slaves
will he be to his brothers."

²⁶He also said,

"Blessed be the LORD, the God of Shem!
May Canaan be the slave of Shem.ᵇ
²⁷May God extend the territory of Japhethᶜ;
may Japheth live in the tents of Shem,
and may Canaan be hisᵈ slave."

²⁸After the flood Noah lived 350 years. ²⁹Altogether, Noah lived 950 years, and then he died.

ᵃ*20 Or soil, was the first*   ᵇ*26 Or be his slave*   ᶜ*27 Japheth* sounds like the Hebrew word for *extend.*   ᵈ*27 Or their*

This text describes the "fall" of Noah and his descendants through his son Ham after the Flood and, as such, parallels the "falls" of Adam and Eve, and Cain respectively. Coupled with the Babel episode this narrative explains why it was necessary for God to move on to a new strategy in Genesis 12 from attempting to work through all of humankind to choosing a single faithful individual and working primarily through him and his descendants. In a sort of "three strikes and yer out" humanity proves that another way must be found that is far less dependent upon the obedient and faithful response of the human race to God.

In each of the three "fall" texts something planted is significant to the narrative (the tree of knowledge; the crops of Cain; the vineyard of Noah), a key character is described as a man or servant of the ground (Gen 2:5,15; 4:2; 9:20), and in each case the use of the Hebrew verb *yādāʻ* = "to know (often with connotations of intimate knowledge)" plays a key role in the story (Gen 3:7; 4:1,9; 9:24). A curse follows each of the falls (Gen 3:14-19; 4:11,12; 9:24,25). Davies notices the following chiastic structure when the story of the fall of Adam and Eve, the fall of Cain, and the fall of Noah are read intertextually:[40]

---

[40]Davies, "Sons of Cain," p. 36.

A	2.5	Man (*'ādām*) as a "servant of the ground" (*la'ăbōd 'eth hā'ădāmāh*; cf. 3.23)
B	3.17	Curse (*'rr*) on the ground "because of" (*ba'ăbûr*) man
C	4.4	Rejection of human offering
C'	8.20	Acceptance of human offering
B'	8.21	Curse (*qll*) on the ground "because of" (*ba'ăbûr*) man not to recur
A'	9.20	Noah "a man of the ground" (*'îš hā'ădāmāh*)

He notes that Noah is not a "servant" of the ground but merely "a man" of the ground and this seems like progress. He concludes:

> In the new order of things inaugurated by the countering of the divine curse, we see mankind left to its own devices. It is not created to work in God's garden; its fruit is not provided for it; but neither is any forbidden, nor is it subject to a curse. Rather, it now finds its own way, doing its own planting, eating its own fruit, doing its own cursing. Its fate, in other words, is now in its own hands, more or less.[41]

While God has, as Davies notes, changed strategies in relation to humanity as a whole, he has not given up on his ultimate purpose of blessing the entire creation with humanity at its head. This passage explains the switch in strategy and with the Babel narrative provides a narrative-based explanation for the calling of Abram.

This passage has a long history of being used to justify racial superiority and the enslavement of Africans in the seventeenth through nineteenth centuries. By a strange twist of logic the curse on Canaan (Ham's son) is transferred back to Ham's other descendants who inhabit what we call Africa today.[42] Some have even suggested that the curse on Canaan was to have black skin and therefore those with darker skin today are assumed to be under God's curse. Frei Betto[43] personally interviewed Fidel Castro about religion and dis-

---

[41] Ibid., p. 39.

[42] Thomas Virgil Peterson, *Ham and Japheth: The Mythic World of Whites in the Antebellum South*, ATLA Monograph Series 12 (Metuchen, NJ: Scarecrow Press, 1978).

[43] Frei Betto, *Fidel and Religion* (Sydney: Pathfinder, 1986), p. 108: "*Castro*: There's something I've never forgotten about biblical history, though. I'm

covered that Castro had been taught as a child that in the curse on Noah's son's descendants they were condemned to be black skinned. But in this narrative it is some of the other descendants of Ham (e.g., Cush, Put) who are "black" skinned, not the Canaanites.

1. Introduction (9:18-19)

9:18 The sons of Noah who came out of the ark were Shem, Ham and Japheth. (Ham was the father of Canaan.)
This introductory statement prepares the reader for what is to follow. The sons of Noah are not listed in the order of their birth. **Ham** is the youngest (9:24) and **Japheth** is the oldest (10:21). But **Shem** is put in first place because from him Abraham arose, the father of the nation of Israel. He, as the second son, is chosen over the first son to be the primary recipient of God's promise. Ham is listed next as the ensuing story focuses on him. The parenthetical remark, "Ham was the father of Canaan," prepares the reader for the surprising fact that even though Ham sins, it is his descendant Canaan who receives the consequences.

9:19 These were the three sons of Noah, and from them came the people who were scattered over the earth.

---

not sure if it's actually mentioned in the Bible or not, but if it is, I think it will require some analysis. It's this: after the flood one of Noah's sons — was it one of Noah's sons? — mocked his father. Noah made wine from grapes and drank so much that he became drunk. One of his sons made fun of him, and as a result his descendants were condemned to be black. I can't recall if the son mentioned in biblical history was Canaan. Who were Noah's sons?

Betto: Shem, Ham, and Japheth. In the Bible in Genesis, Canaan appears as the son of Ham — and therefore as one of Noah's offspring. Noah cursed Canaan and condemned him to be the last of the slaves. Since the slaves in Latin America were blacks, some old translations use the term black as a synonym for slave. Moreover, Canaan's descendants became the peoples of Egypt, Ethiopia, and Arabia, who are dark skinned. But in the Bible his descendants weren't included in the curse, unless you make a slanted interpretation in order to seek religious justification for apartheid.

Castro: Well, I was taught that one of Noah's sons was punished by having black descendants. Somebody should check to see if this is being taught today and if it's really proper for religion to teach that being black is a punishment of God."

This verse anticipates the Babel episode in which the scattering actually takes place. A first-time reading yields the impression that God's command in 9:2,7 is being obeyed. It is only after the Babel episode that the reader realizes that the command's fulfillment requires God's judgment on humankind's attempt at a false unity.

2. The Sin of Ham (9:20-22)

9:20 Noah, a man of the soil, proceeded to plant a vineyard.

Cain was also a man of the soil (*'ădāmāh*, 4:2), but here at least some of the effects of the curse on the ground have been partially mitigated. Noah is the first tiller of the soil under the new circumstances. The harvest is so abundant that there is enough extra to make Noah drunk. Cain's cursed crops are now "uncursed" (8:21). Noah had provided relief as his father Lamech had anticipated (5:29).

9:21 and lay uncovered inside his tent.

The Hebrew text reads אהלה (*'hlh*) which at first sight seems to mean "her tent." Wenham argues that this text has an archaic third masculine singular pronominal suffix. The Samaritan Pentateuch and the Masoretic marginal note (the Qere) suggest that the text be read אהלו (*'hlw*) "his tent." But what if this was originally a standard third feminine singular pronominal suffix (i.e., "her tent")? F.W. Bassett suggests that Noah's intoxication had aroused his sexual desire and thus he is in his wife's tent, but fell asleep.[44] Kikawada and Quinn suggest that "her tent" be retained and argue that Ham is, through euphemism, being depicted as having illicit sexual relations with Noah's wife, a union which produced their child Canaan. Canaan is cursed as the product of that illicit union. They argue that Noah has no more children after the three sons because he is no longer potent. Another possibility would be that after the illicit union Noah breaks off further sexual relations with his wife. The biggest strength in their argument is based upon the palistrophic structure of the Flood narrative:

---

[44]F.W. Bassett, "Noah's Nakedness and the Curse of Canaan: A Case of Incest?" *VT* 21 (1971): 232-237.

The parallel episode with the sons of God may be of some help here. In this episode there was illicit sexual activity, activity which violated the natural order. The flood was God's curse on the issue from this union, the mighty and renowned men of old. In contrast with the curse, God blessed his good "son" Noah, much as Noah himself would bless his good sons. If these parallels are correct (and the general chiastic structure of the Flood story leads us to think that they probably are), then Canaan would be cursed as the product of illicit sexual intercourse by Ham. Certainly the line of Ham produced men of renown — among them Nimrod, "the first on earth to be a mighty man," whose kingdom is associated with "Babel" and "Accad." If Canaan is the product of illicit intercourse by Ham, when and with whom did it occur? One answer suggests itself. Ham commits incest with his mother after his father is rendered incapacitated by drink (and after Noah arouses the mother but proves incapable of satisfying her). Ham supplants his father, much as the sons of God before supplanted other potential human fathers.[45]

While speculative, this does draw the parallel with the Sodom and Gomorrah incident more closely, and it does make sense of why Canaan is cursed even though it is his parent who committed the incest. This is strikingly parallel to the cases of Moab and Ammon who are the children of the drunken Lot and his daughters after the destruction of Sodom and Gomorrah.

9:22 Ham, the father of Canaan, saw his father's nakedness and told his two brothers outside.

In Leviticus 20:17 "seeing" nakedness and "uncovering" nakedness are apparently identical.[46] "Uncovering" is euphemistic for sexual intercourse in Leviticus 18 and 20. Whatever it is precisely that Ham did (וַיַּרְא אֵת עֶרְוַת, *wayyar' 'ēth 'erwath*), it was probably sexual in nature. It could be that Ham homosexually raped his father or that he had intercourse with his father's wife while Noah was inebriated. Ham is here identified once again as the father of Canaan

---

[45]Kikawada and Quinn, *Before Abraham Was*, pp. 102-103.

[46]The NIV confuses this by translating the Hebrew "he sees her nakedness and she sees his nakedness" by "they have sexual relations." The NIV's "dishonored his sister" is literally "uncovered his sister's nakedness."

to prepare the reader for the curse on Ham's sin being given to one of his descendants, Canaan.

3. The Contrasting Respectfulness of Shem and Japheth (9:23)

9:23 But Shem and Japheth took a garment and laid it across their shoulders; then they walked in backward and covered their father's nakedness. Their faces were turned the other way so that they would not see their father's nakedness.

Steinmetz argues that the "almost redundant specificity" of the narrative of Shem's and Japheth's actions indicate that they deal with two issues, not one. They cover Noah's nakedness, and they do not look upon his nakedness. Just as "seeing" one's father's nakedness is probably euphemistic for some sexually immoral act, the refusal to see his nakedness is more than literally not seeing it.[47] Their discretion is in marked contrast to Ham, and their actions paint the heinousness of Ham's crime more clearly.

4. The Curse of Ham's Son Canaan (9:24-25)

9:24 When Noah awoke from his wine and found out what his youngest son had done to him,

Notice that Ham is here identified as the youngest son even though he is listed second in verse 18. That something other than just

---

[47]Steinmetz, "Vineyard," p. xx, says, "Who then violates and who is violated? Noah is violated, but I suggest that it is not just by Ham that he is violated. The narrative implies that Noah takes part in his own humiliation, that he, in effect, sets the stage for the son's violation of his father. Not only does Noah make himself drunk; he becomes 'uncovered within his tent' (9:21). Just as 'seeing' nakedness is more than seeing, 'uncovering' is more than uncovering. To 'uncover' nakedness is the other term which the Bible uses to describe sexual immorality. [E.g., throughout Leviticus 18 and 20; in 20:17 the terms 'to see' and 'to uncover' nakedness are both used to describe the same act] That there are two parts to Noah's humiliation is supported by the verse which describes the actions of Shem and Japheth: 'Shem and Japheth took the garment, and they put it on the shoulder of both of them, and they walked backwards, and they covered their father's nakedness; and their faces were backwards, and they did not see their father's nakedness' (9:23)."

literal seeing is involved is hinted at by the fact that Noah knew (NIV here translates "found out" for Hebrew *yd'* meaning "to know") what his youngest son had done (*'śh*) to him. If it was merely looking, how did Noah know? The verb "he knew" is used of intimate knowledge and sometimes is euphemistic for sexual activity as in Genesis 4:1. While it is not so used here, the association of the word with intimate sexual knowledge may have hinted in yet another way at the sexual nature of Ham's offense for the imagined audience.

9:25 he said, "Cursed be Canaan! The lowest of slaves will he be to his brothers."

Notice that according to Noah's curse Canaan will be slave to both Shem and Japheth, not just Shem. Usually this verse is read as though it said, "to his brother Shem." The pronouncements of patriarchs in Genesis, without explicit divine warrant, are complicated as to their resolution in the book of Genesis. They are not, therefore, to be taken as absolute prophecies. An example is Joseph's dreams; another is Jacob's "blessing" of his twelve sons and how those blessings work themselves out in the nation's canonical history.[48] Since God does not direct Noah to utter these words, the reader must be careful not to assume more than is warranted by such pronouncements. Why Canaan is cursed, rather than Ham the offender, is difficult to determine. It could be that the curse was on all of the sons of Ham and only Canaan's is mentioned as being the most directly relevant to the audience about to enter Canaan. Alternatively, this may be an instance of the sins of the fathers being visited upon the sons to the third and fourth generation. But then why is only Canaan singled out? Perhaps because only the destiny of Canaan's descendants is in the immediate foreground in the Pentateuch. Israel is on the verge of entering Canaan at the end of the Pentateuch. One could also argue that the other descendants of Ham, Cush (Ethiopia), Egypt, and Put (Libya), received judgment in the plagues on Egypt.

Exactly how Canaan can be described as the lowest of slaves to the descendants of both Shem and Japheth is perplexing. This may be yet another example of seemingly prophetic pronouncements which are only partially fulfilled. The partial fulfillment could be due to their conditional nature as seems to be the case with Jacob's curse of Levi in Genesis 49:5-7, or to the fact that they are somehow a mixture of human words and God's intentions as seems to be the case with Joseph's second dream. In any case, the use of this text to justify the enslavement of Africans by Europeans is an egregious example of how easily we fall into using the Bible to justify ourselves and our own sinful structures.[49]

5. The Blessing of Shem and Japheth (9:26-27)

**9:26 He also said, "Blessed be the LORD, the God of Shem! May Canaan be the slave of Shem.
9:27 May God extend the territory of Japheth; may Japheth live in the tents of Shem, and may Canaan be his slave."**

These verses expand upon verse 25. Each of the brothers of Ham are to be given an exalted position over one of Ham's descendants. They are associated with blessing, while Canaan is associated with curse and servitude. Interestingly just as Canaan, not Ham, receives the curse, it is the LORD, not Shem who is to receive the blessing in verse 26. The imagined audience would read this as hope for their future life in the promised land. As descendants of Shem both their Hamite oppressors in Egypt and the Hamite occupants of the promised land would be defeated by them. They had already seen the defeat of the Egyptians in their own experience and looked forward to God's judgment on the descendants of Canaan.

The second clause of verse 27 reads literally "may he live in the tents of Shem." Kaiser, rather unconvincingly, argues that the "he"

---

[48]See Laurence Turner, *Announcements of Plot in Genesis,* JSOTSup 96 (Sheffield: Sheffield Academic Press, 1990).

[49]Peterson (*Ham and Japheth*) has analyzed how this story was used in the pre-Civil War south to justify the practice of slavery. Interestingly, Shem was viewed as the red or brown race including American Indians, persons of Oriental descent, and Jews; Ham as the black race, and Japheth as the spiritual or white race. Philip Schaff, famous historian, believed in this myth and that one day blacks would take Christianity back to Africa and thus fulfill Ps 68:31: "Envoys will come from Egypt; Cush will submit herself to God." Only the Jews of the descendants of Shem performed their spiritual function. However, the Jews rejected their Messiah and thus became subordinate to Japheth, the white race. Jews were regarded as coming from the same racial group as Orientals.

is not Japheth, but God.⁵⁰ The Japhethites were generally settled in areas distant to the experience of Israel. The blessing of Noah seems to indicate that the descendants of Japheth will live peacefully with the descendants of Shem. The descendants of Ham, the Canaanites, in particular will become subordinate to Japheth.

6. The Remainder of Noah's Life and His Death (9:28-29)

9:28 After the flood Noah lived 350 years.
9:29 Altogether, Noah lived 950 years, and then he died.

This passage completes the genealogical information from 5:32 and 7:6. We are not told how long after the flood the incident with Ham occurred. Certainly there was time for Canaan to be born. Shem's son Arphaxad was born only two years after the flood (Genesis 11:10), and one might presume that Ham began his family at about the same time. If it was soon after the flood, the family lived with the estranged relationship between Noah and Ham for most of the 350 remaining years of Noah's life. Noah is the last of the line of Adam whose life span came close to a millennium. But eventually he also dies. The judgment of death which all of the descendants of Adam, save Enoch, experienced also comes to the new Adam, Noah. His story ends like those of all his predecessors, with death. Even though he walked with God as did Enoch, Noah was, unlike Enoch, unable to bypass death. As the new Adam he also "fell" and received the same sentence as his predecessor.

---

⁵⁰Walter C. Kaiser, *Toward an Old Testament Theology* (Grand Rapids: Zondervan, 1978), p. 82.

GENESIS 10

B. THE FAMILIES OF THE SONS OF NOAH (10:1-32)

¹This is the account of Shem, Ham and Japheth, Noah's sons, who themselves had sons after the flood.

²The sons[a] of Japheth:
Gomer, Magog, Madai, Javan, Tubal, Meshech and Tiras.
³The sons of Gomer:
Ashkenaz, Riphath and Togarmah.
⁴The sons of Javan:
Elishah, Tarshish, the Kittim and the Rodanim.[b] ⁵(From these the maritime peoples spread out into their territories by their clans within their nations, each with its own language.)
⁶The sons of Ham:
Cush, Mizraim,[c] Put and Canaan.
⁷The sons of Cush:
Seba, Havilah, Sabtah, Raamah and Sabteca.
The sons of Raamah:
Sheba and Dedan.
⁸Cush was the father[d] of Nimrod, who grew to be a mighty warrior on the earth. ⁹He was a mighty hunter before the LORD; that is why it is said, "Like Nimrod, a mighty hunter before the LORD." ¹⁰The first centers of his kingdom were Babylon, Erech, Akkad and Calneh, in[e] Shinar.[f] ¹¹From that land he went to Assyria, where he built Nineveh, Rehoboth Ir,[g] Calah ¹²and Resen, which is between Nineveh and Calah; that is the great city.

¹³Mizraim was the father of
the Ludites, Anamites, Lehabites, Naphtuhites, ¹⁴Pathrusites, Casluhites (from whom the Philistines came) and Caphtorites.

¹⁵Canaan was the father of
>   Sidon his firstborn,ʰ and of the Hittites, ¹⁶Jebusites, Amorites, Girgashites, ¹⁷Hivites, Arkites, Sinites, ¹⁸Arvadites, Zemarites and Hamathites.

Later the Canaanite clans scattered ¹⁹and the borders of Canaan reached from Sidon toward Gerar as far as Gaza, and then toward Sodom, Gomorrah, Admah and Zeboiim, as far as Lasha.

²⁰These are the sons of Ham by their clans and languages, in their territories and nations.

²¹Sons were also born to Shem, whose older brother wasⁱ Japheth; Shem was the ancestor of all the sons of Eber.

²²The sons of Shem:
>   Elam, Asshur, Arphaxad, Lud and Aram.

²³The sons of Aram:
>   Uz, Hul, Gether and Meshech.ʲ

²⁴Arphaxad was the father ofᵏ Shelah,
>   and Shelah the father of Eber.

²⁵Two sons were born to Eber:
>   One was named Peleg,ˡ because in his time the earth was divided; his brother was named Joktan.

²⁶Joktan was the father of Almodad,
>   Sheleph, Hazarmaveth, Jerah, ²⁷Hadoram, Uzal, Diklah, ²⁸Obal, Abimael, Sheba, ²⁹Ophir, Havilah and Jobab. All these were sons of Joktan.

³⁰The region where they lived stretched from Mesha toward Sephar, in the eastern hill country.

³¹These are the sons of Shem by their clans and languages, in their territories and nations.

³²These are the clans of Noah's sons, according to their lines of descent, within their nations. From these the nations spread out over the earth after the flood.

ᵃ*2 Sons* may mean *descendants* or *successors* or *nations*; also in verses 3, 4, 6, 7, 20-23, 29 and 31.   ᵇ*4* Some manuscripts of the Masoretic Text and Samaritan Pentateuch (see also Septuagint and 1 Chron. 1:7); most manuscripts of the Masoretic Text *Dodanim*   ᶜ*6* That is, Egypt; also in verse 13   ᵈ*8 Father* may mean *ancestor* or *predecessor* or *founder*; also in verses 13, 15, 24 and 26.   ᵉ*10* Or *Erech and Akkad—all of them in*   ᶠ*10* That is, Babylonia   ᵍ*11* Or *Nineveh with its city squares*   ʰ*15* Or *of the Sidonians, the foremost*   ⁱ*21* Or *Shem, the older brother of*   ʲ*23* See Septuagint

and 1 Chron. 1:17; Hebrew *Mash* *k24 Hebrew; Septuagint father of Cainan, and Cainan was the father of* *l25 Peleg means division.*

The list of descendants of Noah's sons in this chapter anticipates the aftermath of the Babel episode. It is only because of God's judgment at Babel that humanity does spread out and fill the earth, speaking a multitude of diverse languages. Chapter 10 is thus out of narrative sequence. Its placement here accomplishes at least two purposes. First, God's command to Noah in 9:1 is to be fruitful and multiply and thus fill the earth. This narrative highlights the fact that this command is in fact fulfilled. Second, by placing the Babel episode after this chapter the theme of "name" in the Babel episode ("Let us make a name for ourselves"), in the genealogy of Shem ("Name"), and in the promise to Abram ("I will make your name great") is given greater emphasis.

Many of the difficulties which texts like Genesis 10 create for the contemporary interpreter stem from reading modern conventions about genealogies back into an ancient text which does not work with those conventions. "Genealogies" in the ancient world were not attempts at comprehensive scientific descriptions of legal or biological descent.[1] A single individual could have *more than one legitimate genealogy*. For example, Sheba is both a son of Raamah, the fourth listed son of Cush, and the tenth in a list of the sons of Joktan, a descendant of Shem (vv. 7,28). The modern interpreter tends to assume that Sheba must be two people of the same name. While this is a possibility, only one group of people and their territory are called Sheba in the Bible and the ancient Near East. More likely the original audience (Israel) would assume that the tribal group Sheba is related to both the descendants of Shem and the descendants of Ham. Similarly Havilah is both a descendant of Ham's son Cush and Shem's descendant Joktan (vv. 7,29). The lists of "sons" is *not comprehensive*. Japheth has seven sons but only two of them are noted as having "sons," Gomer and Javan. The other sons must have had descendants or we would be unable to identify any of them today. The genealogy of Japheth goes two generations deep while that of Ham goes three generations deep and Shem up to five generations.

---

[1]Merrill ("Peoples," p. 7) commenting on the genre of Genesis 10: "One thing it clearly is not intended to be is a scientifically constructed analysis of the origin and development of races in the modern sense of that term."

Unlike modern genealogies *sometimes* the names of *individuals* are given; in other instances the *names of tribal groups or lands* are listed (vv. 13-15).[2] Ancient genealogies are *not democratic* in coverage. Japheth has seven "sons" and seven "grandsons" listed which descend from only two of his sons. Ham has four "sons" listed but only three have descendants listed. Of those three sons Cush has five sons and two grandsons listed, but we are then told that Cush was the father of Nimrod who is not listed among the five listed sons. *Numerical patterns* are a characteristic of ancient "genealogies" which are foreign to the modern interpreter. The name lists in chapters 5 and 11 both have ten "generations" and the seventh generation in chapter 5 has special importance (Enoch). A fondness for sevens is evident in chapter 10. Japheth's sons (v. 2) and grandsons (vv. 3-4) are seven, as well as the sons and grandsons of Cush (v. 7) and the sons of Mizraim (Egypt, vv. 13-14). By most reckonings of chapter 10 there are 70 nations listed.[3] This is consistent with the pattern which we have observed of *anticipating the experience of the nation of Israel* on the verge of entering the promised land. Jacob has 70 descendants whom God has promised to use in reaching the world of 70 nations. Israel is a "miniature version" of the world.[4] The number 70 is only

---

[2]Merrill (ibid., p. 19). "It is important to note again that the names in the lists are not to be understood as lineal or even ethnic descendants in any strict sense. Rather, they are indications of geographic contiguity or relationship. The fallacy of attempting to see them otherwise is apparent in the fact that the same names are occasionally linked to different 'ancestors.'" For example Havilah is referred to as a son of Cush (v. 7) but also a descendant of the Semite Joktan (v. 29). Also Sheba is a son of the Hamite Raamah (v. 7) and of Joktan (v. 28). Nimrod the Hamite is credited with carving out powerful city states in Asshur (Assyria, v. 11), but Ashur is a son of Shem (v. 22). Even the table, then, distinguishes between the ethnic and geographic implications of the various names, sometimes emphasizing the one and sometimes the other.

[3]Cassuto (*Genesis: Part One*) omits Nimrod in his count while Wenham (*Genesis 1-15*, p. 213) suggests omitting the Philistines who are included as a sort of parenthetical remark but are not one of the named descendants.

[4]Anderson, *Genesis of Perfection*, p. 13: "The number 70 is important not only because it symbolizes wholeness or completeness — early Jews and Christians believed that there were 70 guardian angels in heaven apportioned over the 70 nations — but because it points to the genealogy of Israel herself. When Jacob and his family descend to Egypt at the close of the book of Genesis, they do so in seventy persons (Genesis 46; Exodus 1). When

achieved by being selective in how exhaustive the genealogy is. There is *no attempt to be comprehensive* as verse 5 makes clear.[5] Further the order is *not chronological*. Ham is the youngest son of Noah, but is listed second while Shem is the second oldest but comes last. Japheth's descendants are those nations which have the least contact with Israel and are considered first and most briefly. The descendants of Ham include the Babylonians, Assyrians, Egyptians, and Canaanites, i.e., those nations who have the most influence on Israel. The Semites, the forefathers of Israel and Israel's nearest neighbors are listed last. The terminology of "sonship" and "brotherhood" were sometimes used in the ancient world to refer to a *treaty relationship* or a blood-based kinship.[6] What the terminology implies in many instances is political or geographical relationship, not lineal, biological descent. Often *generations are skipped* so that "son of" means merely descendant. For all of these reasons and others discussed below it is inappropriate to ask modern genealogical questions of this text.

Israel leaves Sinai, on her way to the holy land, she is made up of 70 families (Numbers 26). Israel is a microcosm of the whole world. God had promised Abraham that he would not only grant his children the land of Canaan, but he added that the whole world would somehow in return derive blessing from this nation-to-be (Gen. 12:1-3). Through a careful calibration of numbers, our biblical writer fastens this theological detail deep into the heart of our text. What God does on behalf of the smaller seventy (Israel) will have enormous ramifications for the larger seventy (the world at large)."

[5]Merrill ("Peoples," p. 5): "Shem's descendants were the Shemites, most notably Hebrews and Arabs. Hamites are associated primarily with Africa, especially Egypt and Nubia, but also with the Canaanites and other non-Africans. The Japhethites consist of all others, including East Asians, Indians, and Aryans. The Japhethites therefore embrace two races as they are normally defined, the Caucasian (or Indo-European) and Oriental. . . . Striking by their omission from the Old Testament record are references to a number of major ethnic or even racial groups. Most remarkable is the lack of any allusion to East Asians such as Chinese, Japanese, and Koreans. Also missing are peoples such as Intuits, native Americans, Polynesians, Australian aboriginals, and others. Even such prominent shapers of ancient civilization as the Sumerians are bypassed in the sacred record. The reason in each case is the fact that the Bible is a theological history oriented to a chosen people, and not a handbook describing ancient racial and ethnic distribution on a global scale."

[6]Wenham, *Genesis 1–15*, p. 215.

The relative amount of "press" given to each of the three sons demonstrates the point of this chapter. Japheth's offspring are described in four verses (vv. 2-5), while Shem's receive eleven (vv. 21-31). Since the proper noun "Shem" means "name" in Hebrew and the theme of the "name" runs throughout the Flood, Babel, and call of Abram sections, this focus of attention on the descendants of Shem is not surprising. But Ham's descendants are surprisingly given fifteen verses (vv. 6-20)! Why? His descendants are treated generally in verses 6-14. But one descendant, Canaan is given five additional verses (vv. 15-19). Since the Pentateuch ends with the children of Israel poised on the edge of the Promised land, where they are about to enter into battle with the descendants of Canaan, the answer is not difficult to discover. This chapter helps Israel to understand herself in light of the other nations with which she is in cultural contact.

1. Introduction (10:1)

10:1 This is the account of Shem, Ham and Japheth, Noah's sons, who themselves had sons after the flood.

This chapter has no parallel outside the Bible.[7] It is marked off as a unit by inclusio. Verse 1 speaks of the account of ("generations of") Noah's sons. It ends (v. 32) with "these are the clans of Noah's sons according to their lines of descent ("generations"). The use of the phrase, "This is the account of" is the structural marker of the introduction of a new section in the book.

The sons of Noah are not listed in the order of their birth. Ham is the youngest (9:24), Shem the middle child, and Japheth the oldest (10:21). But Shem is the most important son for the author's purposes and of most interest to Israel who along with its closest relatives are descended from Shem. The same thing apparently happens in Genesis 11:27 where Abram is not the oldest son of Terah, just the most significant for the narrator. Ham is next in significance since his descendants make up the nations with which Israel is in contact and conflict. Japheth's descendants are the most distant

---

[7]Hess's 1989 critique of VanSeeters' contention of a Greek parallel is sound in my judgment. Richard S. Hess, "The Genealogies of Genesis 1–11 and Comparative Literature," *Biblica* 70 (1989): 241-254.

from Israel and have the least contact with them. He is, therefore, listed last even though he is the firstborn.

Shem's name means "name" and later becomes part of a wordplay which contrasts the desire of the failed builders of Babel to make a "name for" themselves with Abram who responds in faith and obedience to God's promise, "I will make your name great." Ham's name is either related to the Egyptian word for "servant" or a West Semitic word for "paternal kinsman, uncle."[8] Japheth's name is unattested as a personal name. Since his descendants include the inhabitants of Greece and the island nations of the Aegean Sea, a Greek named Ιαπετός[9] has been suggested. The descendants are listed in the reverse order of significance in the ensuing text, beginning with Japheth and concluding with Shem.

2. The Descendants of Japheth (10:2-5)

10:2 The sons of Japheth: Gomer, Magog, Madai, Javan, Tubal, Meshech and Tiras.

Seven sons of Japheth are listed. The proclivity of this text for sets of seven has already been noted. **Gomer** is attested in cuneiform sources as Gimirrai and in Greek sources as the Kimmerioi or Cimmerians. David Baker suggests that they were Indo-Europeans from modern Ukraine who were forced out of their homelands by the Scythians.[10] They eventually settled in Asia Minor. The Assyrians eventually defeated them and they disappeared from history thereafter. **Magog** is of uncertain location, although the association with Gomer, Javan, Tubal, and Meshech would suggest modern Turkey. Ezekiel 38:1-6 speaks of Gog, from the land of Magog as coming from the "far north." Wenham suggests the name may mean "Gog's place." Josephus thought of the Scythians while Jerome suggested the Goths. More recently Skinner suggests the Gagâ(ya) mentioned in the Amarna letters. A common suggestion is that Magog is the

---

[8]Hess, *Studies*, pp. 30-31. He rejects "hot" as a plausible meaning for the name as it does not occur in any known personal name. Merrill ("Peoples," p. 5) debunks the notion that the name means "black."
[9]Hess, *Studies*, p. 31.
[10]David W. Baker, "Gomer," *ABD*, II:1074.

land of Gyges the Lydian king.¹¹ **Madai** is usually assumed to be the ancestor of the Medes from present-day Iran. **Javan** is located around modern-day Greece or a Greek colony in Ionia in Southwest Asia Minor. **Tubal** is again a people in Asia Minor to Israel's north. **Meshech** is linked to Tubal and along with Javan traded slaves and bronze with Tyre (Ezek 27:13). Early Akkadian sources mention the *mushkaya* from *mushku* in Eastern Asia Minor. A later king of Meshech, Midas, was legendary for turning everything he touched to gold.¹² **Tiras** is otherwise unknown from historical and biblical sources. The context would suggest a land in Asia Minor.

10:3 The sons of Gomer: Ashkenaz, Riphath and Togarmah.

The first descendant of Japheth, **Gomer** has three "descendants" listed. Of Japheth's seven sons only two, Gomer and Javan, have descendants listed. This reminds us of the selective nature of this "genealogy." **Ashkenaz** is usually identified as the people Herodotus calls the Scythians who appeared between the Black and Caspian seas by driving out the Cimmerians (Gomer). At present archaeological evidence for a separate Scythian culture begins only in the seventh century B.C. **Ripath** has not yet been identified. Josephus (*Ant.* 1.126) suggests Paphlagonia in Asia Minor although there is no corroborating evidence for this. The association with Ashkenaz (Scythians) and Togarmah makes Asia Minor a likely location. **Togarmah** is probably to be identified with Til-garimmu mentioned in Neo-Assyrian texts on the eastern border with Tubal in eastern Asia Minor. Ezekiel's oracle against Tyre mentions that the "house of Togarmah" traded horses and mules with Tyre. Earlier Hittite sources (c. 1350 B.C.) mention a Tegarama¹³ which is apparently the same site, identified with modern Gurun. All three of the descendants of Gomer are probably to be located to the North of Palestine in eastern Asia Minor.

10:4 The sons of Javan: Elishah, Tarshish, the Kittim and the Rodanim.

Javan (Greece), listed fourth among the descendants of Japheth, has four "descendants" listed. **Elishah** was renowned even in the

---

¹¹Ibid., "Magog," IV:471.
¹²Ibid., "Meshech," IV:711.
¹³*ANET*, p. 318

trade center of Tyre for its high quality purple dyes (Ezek 27:7). Most scholars would identify Elisha with Alashiya mentioned in second millennium texts from Egypt, Amarna, Ugarit, and Mari. Eastern Cyprus (Enkomi?) is the most likely location. Alashiya may derive from the Sumerian word for copper for which Cyprus was famous.[14] **Tarshish** is a place name with a debated identification. Jonah 1:3 requires that it be accessible from the Mediterranean Sea while Ezekiel 27:12 indicates that Tarshish exported iron, tin, and lead. Sarna notes three possibilities: Tarsus, the hometown of the apostle Paul in Cilicia (southwestern Turkey); Tartessus on the Iberian (Spanish) Peninsula west of the Straits of Gibraltar; and Tharros on the western side of the isle of Sardinia.[15] The second of these alternatives is often favored. The **Kittim** are a people group from Kition (Larnaca) on the island of Cyprus and sometimes stand for the entire island nation. The **Rodanim** probably refers to the people of the island nation of Rhodes in the Aegean. The NIV footnote notes that the MT reads "Dodanim," while the parallel text in 1 Chronicles 1:7, the LXX, and the SP read "Rodanim." The "d" and "r" are among the most easily confused letters for a scribe.[16]

10:5 (From these the maritime peoples spread out into their territories by their clans within their nations, each with its own language.)

Only the descendants of Japheth are said to have "spread out" which perhaps hints at their being peoples on the edges of the world known to the original readers. The cause of the spread and the origin of their languages is not mentioned here. The Babel narrative in chapter 11 gives at least one possible answer.[17] If so, this indicates that chapter 10 records events after the time of Babel and is therefore out of chronological sequence. Hebrew narrative, which is typ-

---

[14]See, Paul J. Kissling, "Elishah," *EDOB*, p. 400.

[15]Sarna, *Genesis*, p. 71.

[16]A daleth, ד, is distinguished from a resh, ר, only by a tittle which squares off the daleth. This, of course, presumes the adoption of the square Aramaic script, not the earlier paleo-Hebrew script.

[17]If the Babel narrative is referring to the entire earth rather than the entire land (the Hebrew word, אֶרֶץ, 'ereṣ, can mean either) as having one language, then Babel would be the only explanation for the rise of languages in this text.

ically chronological in arrangement, does, from time to time, depart from chronology for thematic or other reasons.[18]

3. The Descendants of Ham (10:6-20)

The Descendants of Ham (10:6)

10:6 The sons of Ham: Cush, Mizraim, Put and Canaan.

Typically scholars regard Cush as approximately Ethiopia, Mizraim as Egypt, Put as Libya, and Canaan as Palestine. Oded suggests that if Shem represents the nomadic tribes, then Ham represents their natural enemies, the sedentary population living in villages, towns, and cities, and organized in the framework of kingdoms. He notes the rape of Dinah, the abhorrence of shepherds by Egyptians (Gen 46:34), and one interpretation of the Cain and Abel conflict (that between pastoral nomadism and the cultivator) as textual indicators of the tensions. He also notes the appearance in the genealogy of Ham of the words "city" (v. 12) and "kingdom" (v. 10), words appropriate to the sedentary population. Oded says:

> It is my contention that only by a socio-economic and socio-cultural criteria [sic] could a scribe combine in one setting the kingdom of Babylonia and the great cities of Mesopotamia in the north with Egypt and Cush in the south.[19]

Cush, according to Merrill, usually means Ethiopia or Nubia, the land south of Egypt. But there is also a "Cushan" which includes the Midianites and occupants of the great Arabian peninsula such as Sheba. Habakkuk 3:7 is used to argue that Midian and Cush are synonymous. It is true that they are parallel members within a synonymously parallel couplet. Thus Cush, for Merrill, means the Arabian peninsula. But perhaps our problem is regarding Africa as a distinct entity from the Middle East for the original readers. Why Cush cannot include Arabia and the area south of Egypt escapes me. It is only in relatively modern times that the continent of Africa is set apart as

---

[18]W.J. Martin, *"Dis-Chronologized" Narrative in the Old Testament*, VTSup 17 (Leiden: Brill, 1969): 179-186.

[19]B. Oded, "The Table of Nations (Genesis 10) — A Socio-Cultural Approach," *ZAW* 98 (1986): 28.

a distinct entity. There is no evidence that I am aware of that what we call Africa was a category used in the biblical period.

The Descendants of Cush (Ethiopia) (10:7-12)

10:7 The sons of Cush: Seba, Havilah, Sabtah, Raamah and Sabteca. The sons of Raamah: Sheba and Dedan.

Seven descendants of Cush are mentioned, five "sons" and two "grandsons." This is another piece of evidence of the selective nature of this genealogy and the fondness for numerical patterns. **Seba**'s location is not certain although Africa or South Arabia or both[20] seems most likely. **Sheba** here is often assumed to be a northern Arabian location given the association with Dedan here and in Ezekiel 38:13.[21] The Sheba in verse 28 would then be the southern Arabian kingdom whose queen visited Solomon. **Dedan** is a people known for caravan trading in Isaiah 21:13 and Ezekiel 27:15,20. They are associated with Arabia and Edom (Jer 49:8; Ezek 25:13). Dedan is the name given to the Al-'Ula oasis in Northwest Arabi, a major center of the spice trade. **Havilah** is here a son of Cush while in verse 29 he is a son of Joktan. Two tribal groups with the Arabic equivalent to the Hebrew Havilah (*Ḥaulān*) still exist in different parts of Yemen (in southern Arabia). It may be that there was originally one tribe which split into two and that Genesis is reflecting a time when the split had already occurred.[22] **Sabtah** may refer to Shawat, the ancient capital of Hadramaut in southern Arabia, but that region is listed in verse 26 as Semitic. **Raamah** is mentioned together with Sheba in Ezekiel 27:22 as a trading people whose merchandise happens to be characteristic of Arabia, but it is otherwise unknown. **Sabteca**'s locality is unknown, but a Nubian prince

---

[20]Sarna, *Genesis*, p. 72, notes, "It is known that from very early times, the African and Asian shores of the Red Sea, particularly at its southern part, engaged in active and reciprocal sea commerce. South Arabians crossed the Bal el-Mandeb as traders and colonists and greatly influenced the culture on the western side." Genesis's Seba may have been a tribe with people on both the African and South Arabian sides of the Red Sea.

[21]Sarna, ibid., suggests, "In Psalm 72:10 [Seba] is paired with Sheba, which also appears in the present list. It is possible that the two forms, Seba and Sheba, are dialectical variants of the same name and refer to one tribe that split up. Seba would designate the African branch."

[22]W.W. Müller, *ABD*, III:81.

named Shebteko (ca. 700 B.C.) is recorded, whose name may reflect a place name.²³

The relating of Nimrod to Cush is a famous interpretive difficulty. Cush, in the Bible is ordinarily used to refer to an African people to the south of Egypt (Ethiopia). But Nimrod started his kingdom not in Africa, but in the fertile crescent in Babylon. Speiser has attempted to resolve the seeming difficulty by arguing that Cush, here means the Cassites, but most have not been convinced. B. Oded has argued that Egypt and Mesopotamia represented "the settled and organized branch of civilization, in contrast to the nomads and their tribal confederations."²⁴

Nineveh (modern Kuyunjik) and **Calah** (modern Nimrud) are well-known cities which flourished during the Neo-Assyrian empire. Speiser has argued that Nimrod should be identified with the Assyrian king Tukulti-Ninurta I (1243–1207). K. van der Toorn responds:

> Apart from the minor difficulty that the first part of his name would obviously have been dropped, the historical range of the dominion ascribed to Nimrod does not fit this ruler. Though his political influence embraced Babylonia, it cannot be maintained that Babylon, Uruk, and Akkad were "the beginning of his kingdom." Also, the cities mentioned in Gen 10:9-12 are given in a more or less chronological sequence. The list reads as a condensed résumé of Mesopotamian history. Akkad, though still in use as a cult center in the first millennium, had its *floruit* under the Sargonic dynasty. Kalhu had its heyday in the first half of the first millennium B.C.E., some fifteen hundred years later. If Nimrod is not a god, he must at least have enjoyed a divine longevity, his reign embracing both cities.²⁵

Toorn argues that Ninurta was actually the god of hunting and that Nimrod is modeled on that Assyrian god. He says, "The identification of Ninurta with Sirius, the principal star of Canis Maior (referred to as "Bow" by the Mesopotamians), may have facilitated the identification of Nimrod with Orion in late antiquity."²⁶

---

²³Sarna, *Genesis*, p. 73.
²⁴Oded, "Table of Nations," p. 28.
²⁵K. van der Toorn and P.W. van der Horst, "Nimrod before and after the Bible," *HTR* 83 (1990): 10.
²⁶Ibid., p. 11.

10:8 Cush was the father of Nimrod, who grew to be a mighty warrior on the earth.

Cush is usually understood to mean Ethiopia or something similar. What is remarkable about Nimrod is that he is said to descend from Cush in northern Africa and yet to found kingdoms in Mesopotamia. Nimrod is the one name in the genealogies of Japheth and Ham which seems to refer to a person and not a land or people. Nimrod's name means, "we will rebel." While Nimrod has been identified with several ancient kings (e.g., Sargon of Akkad), Von Soden has more plausibly shown parallels with the Sumerian/Babylonian god of war and hunting, Ninurta who was a protector of kings.[27] The author may be inferring that behind the myths is a person. That Nimrod became a **mighty warrior** (גִּבֹּר, *gibbōr*) probably alludes to the "heroes" (הַגִּבֹּרִים, *hĕggibbōrîm*) of Genesis 6:4. Nimrod's violence is thus linked to the violence that brought on the divine judgment of the Flood. That Nimrod is later associated with the founding of the great kingdoms of Israel's experience leads the audience to be reminded of the violence of kingdoms with their secular views of authority (whether it be Egypt who enslaved them or Babylon who exiled them matters little). They start from a man whose name means "we will rebel" and who became a warrior like the warriors destroyed in the Flood.

10:9 He was a mighty hunter before the LORD; that is why it is said, "Like Nimrod, a mighty hunter before the LORD."

One potential problem with assuming that Genesis is affirming the desirability of a vegetarian lifestyle is this text. Humanity is not originally given the animals as a food source at creation, but only as a sort of concession after the Flood (Gen 9:3). This would seem to suggest that in an ideal world we were meant to be vegetarian. However, this text states that Nimrod was a mighty hunter "before the LORD." The phrase does not necessarily imply the LORD's approval[28] although it could be read that way. If so, this implies that hunting is, within the ideology of this text, an acceptable practice. It may, however, be simply a Hebraic way of expressing the superlative, i.e., the

---

[27]Wolfrom Von Soden, *The Ancient Orient*, trans. by Donald G. Schley (Grand Rapids: Eerdmans, 1994), p. 90.

[28]Wenham (*Genesis 1–15,* p. 223) cites Genesis 6:11 which reads literally, "And the earth was corrupt *before God,*" a parallel expression.

greatest hunter. To translate it literally here the NIV (perhaps unintentionally) gives divine sanction to violence against animals. Still the case for vegetarianism has its problems. The acceptance of the animal sacrifices of Abel may imply that there are legitimate exceptions to a generally vegetarian lifestyle.

10:10 The first centers of his kingdom were Babylon, Erech, Akkad and Calneh, in Shinar.

Three of the first centers of Nimrod's kingdom are well known. **Babylon** is the Mesopotamian capital city located on the Euphrates south of Baghdad. **Erech** is the ancient Uruk (Warka), a key Sumerian city. **Akkad** (also spelled Accad and Agade) has not yet been located, but from references in the ancient sources it was located on the Euphrates in northern Babylon. It was the capital city of Sargon's dynasty. **Calneh** is a known city in the ancient Near East, but it is located in northern Syria according to the most natural reading of Amos 6:2, not in **Shinar** in southern Mesopotamia. While some have speculated that there was a southern Calneh, the namesake of the northern Calneh, others have suggested a minor textual emendation supported by Samaritan evidence[29] which would yield "all of them in Shinar." The original readers would perhaps see in the mention of Shinar (the place of the Babel narrative) an implicit critique of the work of Nimrod in building Babylon.

10:11-12 From that land he went to Assyria, where he built Nineveh, Rehoboth Ir, Calah and Resen, which is between Nineveh and Calah; that is the great city.

Assyria was located on the Tigris to the north of Babylon. One of its capital cities was the famous **Nineveh**. It seems likely that the **great city** referred to is Nineveh (Jonah 1:2; 3:2,3) although grammatically it could be **Calah**. Calah is probably the modern city called Nimrod (after this verse) 24 miles south of Nineveh. It became the capital of Assyria in the ninth century B.C. although there is evidence of settlement there from the beginning of the third millennium B.C. **Rehoboth Ir** means "city squares" and may be located near Nineveh, although we are uncertain. The **Resen** (possibly "fountainheads") which lies between Nineveh and Calah has not yet been

---

[29]J.A. Thompson, "Samaritan Evidence for 'All of Them in the Land of Shinar' (Gen 10:10)," *JBL* 90 (1971): 99-102.

identified although there are several places elsewhere in Assyria bearing the name. Nimrod is portrayed as the founder of several great cities in both Babylon and Assyria.

The Descendants of Mizraim (Egypt) (10:13-14)

**10:13 Mizraim was the father of the Ludites, Anamites, Lehabites, Naphtuhites,
10:14 Pathrusites, Casluhites (from whom the Philistines came) and Caphtorites.**

Various theories have been proposed to identify the **Ludites** and the **Anamites**, but at present we simply do not have enough information to be certain. The **Lehabites** are the Libyans, Egypt's neighbors to the west. The three names which follow the Lehabites have a most striking vocalic similarity: CaCCuCim where C = consonant. Of these the **Pathrusites** seem to be a Hebraization of an Egyptian word meaning "the south land," i.e., Upper Egypt.[30] The **Naphtuhites** seems again to be a Hebraization of an Egyptian word meaning "those of Ptah." Since Ptah was the local god of Memphis (the middle Egyptians) Rendsburg, following Jacob, argues that the Memphites are referred to here. The **Casluhites** have defied identification, but Rendsburg argues that since Upper Egyptians and Middle Egyptians are joined to them, the Casluhites must be lower Egyptians, i.e., those inhabiting the Nile Delta. The biblical text therefore, reads that the Philistines came from the Nile Delta. Coupled with the tradition in Amos 9:7, we may assume a two-stage Philistine migration, first from the Delta to Caphtor (Crete) and then from Crete to Palestine. Many recent translations (NAB, NEB, NJPSV) have moved the parenthetical remark about the origin of the Philistines so that it follows the **Caphtorites**, who are usually assumed to be the ancestors of the Philistines (Amos 9:7; Jer 47:4; Deut 2:23). A. Evans, notes that Cretan civilization is obviously dependent on Egyptian culture so much as to make an original migration probable.[31] In fact, it is particularly the Delta people of Egypt who had the most direct influence on the civilization of Crete.

---

[30]Rendsburg, "Gen 10:13-14," p. 91.
[31]A. Evans, *The Palace of Minoa at Knossos* (London: Macmillan, 1921-1936), II:28, 21, 45.

The Descendants of Canaan (10:15-19)

**10:15 Canaan was the father of Sidon his firstborn, and of the Hittites,
10:16 Jebusites, Amorites, Girgashites,
10:17 Hivites, Arkites, Sinites,
10:18a Arvadites, Zemarites and Hamathites.**

The relevance of Canaan to Israel explains the amount of detail included in this passage. **Sidon** was the most ancient of the Phoenician cities. It lay halfway between Tyre and Beirut and regarded itself as Canaanite. That Sidon is described as Canaan's **firstborn** argues that just because a name is listed first does not mean that the person so listed is to be regarded as the firstborn. The **Hittites** in the OT should not be confused with the great Hittite empire in Turkey. The Hittites in the OT refer to original inhabitants of Canaan's hill country. The Hittites mentioned in the OT have Semitic names which makes their relationship to Canaan intelligible. **Jebusites** were probably the original inhabitants of Jebus or Jerusalem. The names of Jebusites recorded in the OT suggest that they were not a Semitic people but of Hurrian origin.[32] The word **Amorites** is used loosely in the OT of the inhabitants of the hill country in contrast to the Canaanites who tended to live in cities nearer the Mediterranean. There was an Amorite kingdom just north of Canaan and several of the great civilizations of the ancient Near East had Amorite dynasties at some point in time. **Girgashites** are sometimes mentioned in lists of the original inhabitants of Canaan (e.g., Genesis 15:21), but little is known about them. They do seem to be mentioned at Ugarit.[33] Although **Hivites** are mentioned numerous times in the Hebrew Bible nothing of substance is known about them other than the fact that they are sometimes listed among the nations to be conquered by Israel in Canaan. The next five peoples beginning with the **Arkites** are all inhabitants of five known Syrian cities, Israel's direct neighbor to the north. The Arkites inhabited Arka, a town about 13 miles northeast of Tripoli in today's Lebanon. The city is mentioned in Egyptian execration (cursing) texts and in the Amarna letters.[34] The **Sinites** hail from the town of Sin, a town bordering

---

[32]Hoffner in *POTT*, p. 225.
[33]David W. Baker, "Girgashite," *ABD*, II:1028.
[34]"Arkite," *EDOB*, p. 103.

Ugarit. **Arvadites** inhabited Arvad the most northern of the main Phoenician cities while **Zemarites** hail from Zemar a town halfway between Arvad and Tripoli. **Hamath** lay on the Orontes river about 50 miles inland from Arvad.

10:18b Later the Canaanite clans scattered
10:19 and the borders of Canaan reached from Sidon toward Gerar as far as Gaza, and then toward Sodom, Gomorrah, Admah and Zeboiim, as far as Lasha.

This note parallels verse 5. Both verses serve to explain later developments deemed especially relevant to the audience. In this case the borders are relevant since Israel inherits Canaan (and only Canaan initially) as part of the promise to Abraham. It is to be noted that the borders of Canaan do not include Sidon but only land to its south and only land west of the Jordan, not to its east. The original audience would be reminded that the transjordanian tribes, Reuben, Gad, and half of Manasseh, are the result of a concession and not part of the original vision of the promised land. Sarna notes that the description of Canaan here corresponds to the Egyptian province of Canaan delineated in a peace treaty between Egyptian king Ramses II and Hittite king Hattusilis III in 1280 B.C.[35] This may hint at the general era from which this information was derived but does little to explain this text's relevance to the original audience. It may have served to give Israel its ideal borders, even though they never conquered as far north as Sidon. The towns of **Sodom, Gomorrah, Admah and Zeboiim** were, prior to their destruction, located on the eastern shores of the Dead Sea thus making the Dead Sea one of Canaan's boundaries. The location of Lasha is unknown, although the context suggests the eastern shore of the Dead Sea also.

Summary Statement (10:20)

10:20 These are the sons of Ham by their clans and languages, in their territories and nations.

This summary statement sets off this section (vv. 6-19) from what precedes and what follows. The "sons" are described in terms of their clans, languages, territories, and nations. The actual physical descendants of Ham are only one of the interests of the author.

---

[35]Sarna, *Genesis*, p. 77.

4. The Descendants of Shem (10:21-31)

Introduction (10:21)

10:21 Sons were also born to Shem, whose older brother was Japheth; Shem was the ancestor of all the sons of Eber.

Oded has argued that Eber is not a proper name, but a social description of nomads or seminomads, such as Abraham is depicted as being. He argues that the Hebrew phrase, אֲבִי כָּל־, (*'ăbî kol-*) means "the progenitor of all who" have some specific trade or function in society or some other recognizable social characteristic. In this case the Hebrew word, עֵבֶר, (*'ēber*) means those who cross over boundaries or wander from one place to another in nomadlike fashion. Whether Eber is to be equated with the Habiru (foreigners, outsiders) is debated. Rashi and Ramban take Eber here not as a name but as meaning "the (region) beyond [the Euphrates]."[36] Joshua 24:2 refers to a region "beyond the river" as the place of Abraham's origin.

Oded suggests that by describing Shem as "whose older brother was Japheth" and not as the brother of Ham shows the enmity between the Semite and Hamite groups as is suggested in the curse on Canaan in chapter 9.[37]

The Descendants of Shem (10:22)

10:22 The sons of Shem: Elam, Asshur, Arphaxad, Lud and Aram.

The five sons of Shem listed here are, with the exception of Lud, probably fertile crescent powers to Israel's north and east. Since Israel itself arose from Shem through Abram, this section of the Table of Nations is especially pertinent to the original audience. **Elam** was in the earliest period of the OT a major power to the east of Mesopotamia in the modern Iraqi province of Fars. The Elamites were famous for battling the Mesopotamian powers in Babylon and Assyria. **Asshur** was the chief city of Assyria and its main religious center throughout most of the OT period until its destruction in 614 B.C. Worship there centered on the god Assur from whom the city's name is derived. **Arphaxad** is apparently a place name given its context with other place names in this passage. Its etymology is unknown although some have attempted to equate the first part of the

---

[36]Sarna, *Genesis*, p. 78.
[37]Oded, "Table of Nations," p. 22.

name with Arrapḫa (modern Kirkuk?) often mentioned in the Hurrian Nuzi texts from northern Iraq and the second part with *kasdîm*, the gentilic for Chaldeans.[38] Arphaxad is mentioned in the genealogy leading from Shem to Abram in chapter 11. **Lud** is listed here as a descendant of Shem while in verse 13 the Ludim (people of Lud) are descendants of Mizraim (Egypt). This may be evidence of genealogical fluidity and the changing history of the Ludim. The Ludim have been identified as a people related to the Libyans by some. Ezekiel 30:5 lists Lud along with Cush, Put, Arabia, and Libya as allies of Egypt. In Jeremiah 46:9 the Ludim (Lydians in NIV) seem to be allies of Egypt, although they could merely be being used as an example of a people especially adept at archery in war. The majority have identified Lud as Lydia in western Turkey. In Isaiah 66:19 they are included in a list of distant nations to whom the survivors of the nation will be sent. Tubal and Greece, mentioned with Lud, would support western Turkey. **Aram** is roughly equivalent to the modern nations of Syria and Lebanon. Its capital was Damascus and its language, Aramaic, became the *lingua franca* of the ancient world in the time of the Persians. Aram was the major power directly to the north of Israel for much of its history as a nation. Its language was adopted by many Jews[39] and was probably the native tongue of Jesus and the earliest churches.

The Descendants of Aram (Syria) (10:23)

10:23 The sons of Aram: Uz, Hul, Gether and Meshech.

Since Aram is the most significant nation to Israel's immediate north and the adopted home of Terah and Abram prior to the latter's migration to Canaan, the Table of Nations lists the "descendants" of Aram in detail. The location of **Uz** is disputed with Edom to the south of Israel and Syria to the north of Israel as the alternatives. Uz is Job's homeland, usually assumed to be near Edom, south of the Dead Sea.[40]

---

[38]Hess, *Studies*, pp. 77-78.

[39]Parts of Daniel and Ezra (along with a few isolated words and verses elsewhere) are actually composed in Aramaic. The Aramaic Targums (second century A.D. and later) are paraphrases of the Bible for those Jews no longer conversant with Hebrew.

[40]The LXX additions to Job 42:17 make this explicit. Cf. Marvin H. Pope, *Job*, AB 15, p. 354.

The name Uz appears in the Edomite genealogy in Genesis 36:28 and the personal names found in the book of Job are probably Edomite. Lamentations 4:21 places "you who live in the land of Uz" in parallel with "O daughter of Edom." Conversely Uz is a son of Nahor and Milcah in Aram whom Josephus contends is known as the founder of Damascus. This dual identity of Uz may reflect genealogical fluidity or there may have been two locations known as Uz. Certainly the Uz mentioned here fits more easily in Syria than in Edom. **Hul** and **Gether** are otherwise unknown. The NIV's **Meshech** is based on the LXX and the parallel genealogy in 1 Chronicles 1:17. The MT reads, "Mash." Mash might be associated with Mount Masius near the headwaters of the Euphrates or with the Akkadian *Mašu*, a name for Lebanon and the anti-Lebanon ranges. The MT seems the more "difficult reading" and should therefore probably be retained. If, however, we read Meshech with the NIV text, the reference is to Meshech in Turkey. Meshech is included among the sons of Javan in 10:2. Again, assuming Meshech should be read here, we have yet another example of genealogical fluidity.

The Descendants of Arphaxad (10:24)

10:24 Arphaxad was the father of Shelah, and Shelah the father of Eber.

Arphaxad, the third in the list of Shem's sons has two generations of descendants listed. The meaning of **Shelah**'s name is related to Methuselah's. The meaning of his name is unknown, although Hess speculates that it was a divine name.[41] Shelah's descendant **Eber** is associated with the Hebrews of the Bible. Some claim that it refers to nomadic groups similar to our modern use of the word Gypsy.[42] The name means, "to cross over (water)."

The Descendants of Eber (10:25-29)

10:25 Two sons were born to Eber: One was named Peleg, because in his time the earth was divided; his brother was named Joktan.

Peleg's name may derive from a Hebrew root which may mean "to divide." There certainly is at least a wordplay between the name Peleg and the Hebrew word "was divided" (A related noun refers to

---

[41]Hess, *Studies*, p. 80.
[42]For other options see commentary on 10:21 above.

the division of the land by irrigation canals. Some think that the division of the land referred to in this verse alludes to an early division between those settled peoples, the descendants of Peleg who used irrigation canals from the nomadic descendants of Joktan. Others think that Peleg is a place name. Certainty is impossible. The division of the earth in Peleg's time is more likely referring to the division of languages at Babel which this chapter assumes has already taken place. **Joktan** seems to mean, "he is small." His descendants are Arabian and South Arabian tribes.

10:26 Joktan was the father of Almodad, Sheleph, Hazarmaveth, Jerah,

Almodad is undoubtedly the name of a South Arabian tribe, but its identification or location is unknown. Müller tentatively suggests a location in South Yemen.[43] **Sheleph** is apparently the name of the Yemenite tribe as-Salif.[44] **Hazarmaveth** is the name of a South Arabian tribe and the land inhabited by it, Hadramaut.[45] The name **Jerah** is undoubtedly another South Arabian tribe. Interestingly the name in Hebrew means "month" or "moon." The moon was the main deity of the South Arabian pantheon.[46]

10:27 Hadoram, Uzal, Diklah,

Hadoram is the ancestor of a South Arabian tribe. Müller argues that Hadoram is the name "Daurum" attested in two votive inscriptions.[47] **Uzal** is the ancestor of an Arabian tribe traditionally located at 'Azal (modern San'a', the capital of modern Yemen). According to Ezekiel 27:19 Uzal was a source of wine.[48] **Diklah** is the ancestor of a South Arabian people or region. Some associate the name with an oasis in Saudi Arabia near Sirwath, west of Marib.[49] The name probably comes from a word meaning "date palm." While these identifications are necessarily tentative, they do suggest that Israel would have been familiar with the places and peoples mentioned.

---

[43]W.W. Müller, "Almodad," *ABD*, I:160-161.
[44]Ibid., "Sheleph," V:1192-1193.
[45]Ibid., "Hazarmaveth," III:85-86.
[46]Ibid., "Jerah," III:683.
[47]"Hadoram," *ABD*, III:16.
[48]Alan Millard, "Ezekiel 27:19: The Wine Trade of Damascus," *JSS* 7 (1962): 201-203, suggests minor emendations to achieve this reading.
[49]See W.W. Müller, "Diklah," *ABD*, II:198-199.

10:28 Obal, Abimael, Sheba,

Obal is called Ebal in 1 Chronicles 1:22 and is to be located somewhere in South Arabia, quite possibly in the highlands of Yemen.[50] **Abimael** is another South Arabian tribe of uncertain location. Müller tentatively suggests that the name means either "(my) father is truly God" or more simply, "Father is God," and comes from the region of Haram in Yemen where a dialectical peculiarity is attested.[51] **Sheba** is in Hebrew spelled and vocalized identically to the Sheba in verse 7, but is to be carefully distinguished from the Seba also mentioned in verse 7. Some suggest that this Sheba is the southern Arabian kingdom whose queen visited Solomon, not the northern Arabian people or kingdom associated with Dedan.

10:29 Ophir, Havilah and Jobab. All these were sons of Joktan.

Ophir is a place famous for its gold[52] as is Havilah in Genesis 2:11,12. Since **Havilah** might be located in either Nubia (south of Egypt in Sudan on the Nile) or Arabia, it is possible that Ophir was in either place. It was accessible by sea from Ezion Geber on the northern edge of the eastern extension of the Red Sea. **Jobab** has so far not been identified as a place or people with any certainty although it is probably Arabian. A Sabaean tribe from Yemen has a similar name and may be being referred to here.[53]

Summary Statement (10:30-31)

10:30 The region where they lived stretched from Mesha toward Sephar, in the eastern hill country.

The importance of the Joktanites ("they") to Israel is demonstrated by the fact that only the Canaanites (extremely relevant to Israel) also receive mention of their borders in this Table of the Nations. Unfortunately, like several of the names in the list, the borders Mesha, Sephar, and the "eastern hill country" are unknown. Commentators often surmise that Mesha is the western and Sephar the eastern border of what we would call southern Arabia.

---

[50]Ibid., "Obal," V:4-5.
[51]Ibid., "Abimael," I:20.
[52]See 1 Kings 9:28; 10:11; 22:49; Isa 13:12; Ps 45:10; Job 28:16; 1 Chr 29:4; 2 Chr 8:18; 9:10.
[53]W.W. Müller, "Jobab," *ABD*, III:871.

10:31 These are the sons of Shem by their clans and languages, in their territories and nations.

This summary statement matches those of verses 5 and 20. Shem is listed last (although first in interest for the author and audience) in order to tie together the theme of "name" (the meaning of the proper noun Shem) with the following narratives.

5. Overall Summary Statement (10:32)

10:32 These are the clans of Noah's sons, according to their lines of descent, within their nations. From these the nations spread out over the earth after the flood.

This overall summary statement recapitulates the entire chapter and as such is typical of the style of Genesis. A first-time reading (without knowledge of the Babel episode) would suggest that the Lord's commission in 9:1, "Be fruitful and increase in number and fill the earth" is fulfilled without complication. It is only after reading the Babel narrative that the audience recognizes that the commission at first met with resistance and it was only the judgment of the confusion of the languages that resulted in its fulfillment.

GENESIS 11

C. THE BABEL EPISODE (11:1-9)

¹Now the whole world had one language and a common speech. ²As men moved eastward,ª they found a plain in Shinar[b] and settled there. ³They said to each other, "Come, let's make bricks and bake them thoroughly." They used brick instead of stone, and tar for mortar. ⁴Then they said, "Come, let us build ourselves a city, with a tower that reaches to the heavens, so that we may make a name for ourselves and not be scattered over the face of the whole earth."

⁵But the LORD came down to see the city and the tower that the men were building. ⁶The LORD said, "If as one people speaking the same language they have begun to do this, then nothing they plan to do will be impossible for them. ⁷Come, let us go down and confuse their language so they will not understand each other."

⁸So the LORD scattered them from there over all the earth, and they stopped building the city. ⁹That is why it was called Babel[c]—because there the LORD confused the language of the whole world. From there the LORD scattered them over the face of the whole earth.

ª2 Or *from the east*; or *in the east*   [b]2 That is, Babylonia   [c]9 That is, Babylon; *Babel* sounds like the Hebrew for *confused*.

According to Harland[1] Christian tradition has interpreted the story of Babel as one of human pride (the vertical view), while Jewish tradition has focused more on the resistance of the builders to God's command to disperse (the horizontal view). Interestingly the putative sources J and P tend to mirror what Harland claims is

---

[1]P.J. Harland, "Vertical or Horizontal: The Sin of Babel," *VT* XLVIII/4 (1998): 515-533.

Christian and Jewish tradition respectively. He argues that a canonical reading gives P, the horizontal view, the last word. But he fails to account for the fact that P, even if we grant its existence, still allowed J to be heard. Therefore a canonical reading requires some sort of merger of the two perspectives; they are not mutually exclusive. For Harland the dispersion is not necessarily a punishment for sin, but the will of God. But something can be both punishment for sin and accomplish the will of God. I suspect that the dichotomous theology (either grace- *or* human-response-based theology) which lies behind Wellhausen's relatively low opinion of P influences such readings. It seems to me that the only text which we have emphasizes that human pride inherent in building great civilizations leads to direct rebellion against God's express will. This is true paradigmatically at Babel, but is a general biblical principle.

Read within the context of the book of Genesis, this narrative explains why a shift in God's strategy from dealing with humanity as a whole to choosing a specific line is necessary: the drastic measure of starting creation over again with the Flood has not solved the fundamental problem of humanity's tendency toward evil and rebellion against God.

Read within the context of the entire canon, Babel is one of the symbolic images used throughout the canon to depict humanity's tendency to build our own autonomous lives on the backs of the weak without regard for God's purpose in creating us. Babel stands for the mighty persecuting Roman empire in the book of Revelation (17:1–18:24) and 1 Peter (5:13), and in Isaiah's oracles against foreign nations stands for both the literal Babylon (ch. 21) and the entire system of world empires which fight against God and his people (chs. 13–14).

1. The Setting for the Episode (11:1-2)

11:1 Now the whole world had one language and a common speech.

Since chapter 10 has already anticipated the results of the confusion of languages at Babel, this section begins by reminding the reader of the state of the world prior to the scattering of the nations after the Flood. This is an example of a phenomenon which is surprisingly frequent in Hebrew narrative, dis-chronologization.² Hebrew narrative sometimes departs from its typical chronological arrangement for thematic or other reasons. Here, one reason seems to be the wordplay on the Hebrew word *shēm* (שֵׁם). This word can either be the common noun "name" or a proper noun for Noah's son Shem. By placing the narrative of Babel after chapter ten, the narrator is able to connect this narrative in which humanity seeks a name for itself, through a genealogy of the person Shem (Name) to the narrative of Abram's call in which God promises to make his name great. At Babel humanity sought to achieve through their own efforts and in rebellion against God's purposes, a great name. The LORD judges that attempt with the confusion of languages. The name they make for themselves at Babel is an ignominious one. In contrast, the LORD seeks out a person and family of faith(fulness) and promises to make his name great for him. Ironically (is it divine irony?) his ancestry is traced through Shem, the person whose name means Name.³ By holding the Babel narrative until after the Table of Nations in chapter 10, the narrator is able to give emphasis to the theme of the "name." The failure to appreciate the technique of dis-chronologization and to notice how the motif of name = Shem structures the narrative results in some rather implausible readings. Yoder, for example, reads the Babel narrative as a purely local affair which follows the general repopulating of the earth recorded in chapter 10.⁴ Others similarly read the dispersion of humankind in this narrative as a positive thing and not at all as a result of God's judgment.

11:2 As men moved eastward, they found a plain in Shinar and settled there.

Moving eastward in this verse seems to echo the eastward move out of Eden when Adam and Eve were expelled from the garden

---

²See Martin *"Dis-Chronologized,"* pp. 179-186.

³Robinson, "Literary Functions," p. 603: "But, even before the people came together to their task, God had already provided a Shem through the orderly process of procreation. The reader is treated to the ironic and even slightly ludicrous spectacle of humanity attempting to create by its own exertions a counterfeit of what God already provided. God responds to the foolishness of the people by coolly scattering them, then order returns in the form God intended, once again through genealogical succession from Shem."

⁴John H. Yoder, *The Jewish-Christian Schism Revisited*, ed. by Michael G. Cartwright and Peter Ochs (Grand Rapids: Eerdmans, 2003), p. 189.

and when Cain settled in the land of Nod, east of Eden. When humanity moves eastward in these chapters, it is a sign of leaving God's presence and thereby being under God's judgment, not his blessing. This is true of Adam and Eve, Cain, and here at Babel. **Shinar** is an alternative name for Babylonia. It is first attested in Egypt in the fifteenth century B.C. and may be derived from the cuneiform *Samharu*, the name of a Kassite tribe which ruled Babylon during that time.[5] This may be an indication of the early date of the traditions on which the text of Genesis is based.

2. The Goals of Babel (11:3-4)

11:3 They said to each other, "Come, let's make bricks and bake them thoroughly." They used brick instead of stone, and tar for mortar.

It seems likely that this verse alludes to Babylonian building techniques where kiln-baked bricks were used for the outer layers of monumental building projects and hot bitumen was used for mortar. But I also suspect that the quality of the materials used to build the city and tower is being critiqued here. **Bricks** and **tar** are second-class substitutes for stone and mortar.[6] The point would seem to be, then, that when you build without God's blessing, what you achieve is of secondary quality at best. But there may well be another reason the readers are given this seemingly incidental detail about the building materials. Perhaps the original readers would have thought of the bricks they were required to make while enslaved in Egypt and God's judgment on that nation.

The NIV's "come let's make" (with the contraction) is inconsistent with verse four where the more formal "come, let us build" is used to translate the same Hebrew form. This phrase may be hinting at the arrogant presumption of the builders of Babel who pridefully echo God's words at creation, "Let us make" (Gen 1:26). The builders are taking upon themselves the prerogative to decide their own purpose in life without regard to the will of the God who cre-

---

[5]James R. Davila, "Shinar," *ABD*, V:1220.

[6]In Isaiah 9:10 bricks are contrasted with dressed stones as being of inferior quality.

ated them. As such this passage is a critique of the desire for autonomy ("being a law to oneself") whether it be ancient or modern.

11:4 Then they said, "Come, let us build ourselves a city, with a tower that reaches to the heavens, so that we may make a name for ourselves and not be scattered over the face of the whole earth."

Often this text is interpreted as though it were focused on the tower and not the city. The NIV shows this tradition by adding the section heading "The Tower of Babel." The focus of interpretation then becomes the tower and possible allusions to the Babylonian ziggurat.[7] A ziggurat was an immense pyramid-like structure with a core of sun-dried brick surrounded by kiln-fired brick to make it waterproof. The foundation was usually square and housed a temple; its elevation was achieved by a series of graduated steps, often seven in number. On top of the ziggurat was a shrine where sacrifices were performed as well as astronomical observations taken. The famous ziggurat temple of Marduk in Babylon, Etemenanki, was about 300 feet tall.[8] Greenspahn argues that this passage speaks of the literal hope of reaching heaven and thus crossing the divine-human barrier.[9] He

---

[7]Byron L. Sherwin, "The Tower of Babel," *TBT* 33 (1995): 104-109. A midrash discusses the motivation for building the tower. According to the rabbis, the king of Babylon who directed the building of the tower was Nimrod. That the name Nimrod is related to the Hebrew word, *mered* ("rebellion") served as an invitation to their interpretation of the building of the tower as having been motivated by a desire to rebel against God. Another Midrash even describes how the tower builders stood on the top of the tower and shot arrows into heaven to kill God, and how the arrows they shot up came down with blood on them, convincing the tower people that they had indeed murdered God.

[8]Holloway ("What Ship Goes There?" p. 330) speaks of the ziggurat:

Physically the ziggurat consisted of an immense solid structure comprised of a core of sun-dried mudbrick surrounded by a water-resistant shell of fired mudbrick and bitumen for mortar. The foundation was either square or rectangular; its conspicuous elevation was achieved by means of a series of graduated stages, usually 3, 5, or 7 in number. Constructed upon the flat alluvial floodplains between the Tigris and Euphrates rivers, the ziggurat symbolized and functioned as an artificial mountain. It is known from textual sources that a shrine or cella of sorts occupied the summit, where sacrifice and various rituals were performed, in addition to routine astronomical observations.

[9]Frederick E. Greenspahn, "A Mesopotamian Proverb and Its Biblical Reverberations," *JAOS* 114 (1994): 33-38.

points to a parallel in the Gilgamesh epic where the hero justifies his quest for immortality with the words:

> I would enter the land
> I would set up my name
> In its places where names have been raised up
> I would raise my name
> In its places where names have not been raised up
> I would raise up the names of the gods

But given the anti-idolatry tone of these chapters, I am skeptical. This passage, as all of Genesis 1–11, is critical of the great polytheistic cultures of the ancient Near East. The literal hope of reaching heaven is just the sort of polytheistic notion Genesis is combating. The God of the Bible, whose handbreadth can measure the heavens (Isa. 40:12) cannot be limited in this way. God has to "come down" to even see the city and the tower. Genesis is not merely critiquing the idea that a tower can be built high enough to reach heaven, but even the idea that God should be conceived of as being limited in spatial terms.

It is interesting that the tower is not mentioned at all in verse 8, only the city. The focus of this narrative is more on the city than on the tower. The obsession of interpreters with the tower/ziggurat parallel may be an example of using a possible explanation based on an observed archaeological parallel instead of allowing the text to interpret itself. Such imposed interpretations are questionable. A tower was a normal part of a city in the ancient Near East. The builders of Babel probably are not being portrayed as building a tower to climb to heaven. Instead they build a city with an impressive tower in order to make a name for themselves[10] and to prevent them being scattered over the face of the earth as directed by God in 9:1 and 1:28. The building of the city is in direct defiance of God's will. Instead of scattering and filling the earth after the Flood, humanity decides to gather together and build a civilization which will make a name for them. With whom? The name that they might make for themselves would only impress themselves! The use of the phrase "make a name for ourselves" in this narrative is contrasted with the call of Abram in

---

[10]Pseudo-Philo preserves a tradition that each builder inscribed his name on one of the bricks (James H. Charlesworth, ed., *The Old Testament Pseudepigrapha* [Garden City, NY: Doubleday, 1983-1985], 2:310).

chapter 12. He obeys the LORD's command to leave and is promised that a great name will be made for him by the gracious God who calls upon him to leave. Having a great name comes from God's gracious promises, not from making a name for ourselves.

Again in this verse we see the evidence of human presumption, "let us." Notice also that their purpose is in direct contravention of the commandments of the Lord. The theme of the "name" which began in the introduction to the Flood narrative ("men of the name") and is followed up on in the call of Abraham ("I will make your name great") is here carried forward to the genealogy of Name (Shem).

3. The Lord's Judgment on Babel (11:5-9)

11:5 But the LORD came down to see the city and the tower that the men were building.

The narrator uses a bit of biting irony here. The great city with a tower that reaches to the heavens is so small that the LORD has to *come down* even to be able to see it. The great name which the building of the city and the tower was to bring is a fantasy. Humanity allied against God's purposes does not achieve very much.

11:6 The LORD said, "If as one people speaking the same language they have begun to do this, then nothing they plan to do will be impossible for them.

This has parallels to Genesis 3:22: "See, the man has become like one of us, knowing good and evil; and now, he might reach out his hand and take also from the tree of life, and eat, and live forever."

At first reading this seems to imply that the Lord is somehow insecure about humanity. It is as though he were afraid of what they might do, if they teamed up. But this statement must be read in light of what God "discovered" about mankind during and after the Flood. Humanity's fundamental tendency toward evil was not wiped out even when the human race was reduced to one righteous man and his immediate family (compare Genesis 6:5 and 8:21). The plans that such people might make, when united in resistance to the will of God is horrifying to contemplate. The scattering at Babel is a sort of preemptive strike against the escalation of evil. It is in fact an act of grace. For if God allowed the evil to escalate once again, his holiness would demand universal judgment, something he had promised not to ever bring upon the cosmos again. By stopping the builders of Babel the LORD avoids the necessity of more severe forms of judgment.

11:7 Come, let us go down and confuse their language so they will not understand each other."

God uses the "let us" form as the builders did and as he did in the creation narrative. The LORD meets their arrogant "let us build" with "let us go down and confuse their language."

11:8 So the LORD scattered them from there over all the earth, and they stopped building the city.

God's will that humankind fill the earth (9:2) is fulfilled despite the rebellious resistance of humankind. Notice it is the city, not the tower, which is in view primarily. The scattering that God commanded the new humanity after the Flood is accomplished with a rebellious humanity despite themselves. The "city" as used in this passage may be being used typologically of any human scheme to attempt to create a life without the Creator of all life. The city stands for the human hubris which produced it.[11] As one of the great cities of the ancient world, the judgment on the city of Babel is a judgment on "civilization" whenever such a civilization is based on its own autonomous values and is sustained by violence and the mistreatment of others. Whatever the original date of Genesis, in the postexilic period when the Pentateuch was canonized, the "canonical audience" would see the fall of Babylon to the Persians in 539 B.C. as another example of divine judgment on human hubris.

11:9 That is why it was called Babel—because there the LORD confused the language of the whole world. From there the LORD scattered them over the face of the whole earth.

Here the narrator, stepping out of usual technique of remaining in the background and merely describing events, uses a Hebrew wordplay. In Akkadian, the language of the Babylonians, Babel meant "Gate of God." But because of the rebellion of humanity it is

---

[11]Sherwin thinks the tower episode is a critique of Babylonian civilization and of the urban life in general. He notes that *Pirke d'Rabbi Eliezer* speaks of when the tower was very high and a brick fell they lamented its loss because of the difficulty of getting a brick to the top. When a human being fell, they didn't lament because he could easily be replaced.

not the gate of God, but confusion. The Hebrew word translated "confused" is pronounced *bālal* (בָּלַל) in contrast to the word Babel (בָּבֶל, *bābel*). What rebellious humanity regards as the doorway to the secret powers of the universe results only in the confusion of disparate and warring factions. It is at Pentecost that the world received a sort of down payment on the reversal of the curse of Babel. One day, in the new creation the world will once again have a common language. Zephaniah 3:9 refers to a time after universal judgment when the LORD will "change the speech of the peoples to a pure speech, that all of them may call on the name of the LORD and serve him with one accord" (NRSV).

The end result of the Babel episode is the scattering of the people over the face of the whole earth. In the end the LORD has his way. He commanded that humanity scatter and fill the earth (Gen 9:1). When they refused to do so and in rebellion tried to do the opposite, in the end they were scattered. We who live among the great urbanized civilizations should take warning from this passage. If the goal of our civilization is human autonomy motivated by exaggerated hubris, we should not be surprised to see it result in confusion.

D. THE FAMILY HISTORY FROM SHEM TO ABRAHAM'S FATHER TERAH (11:10-26)

¹⁰**This is the account of Shem.**

Two years after the flood, when Shem was 100 years old, he became the father[a] of Arphaxad. ¹¹And after he became the father of Arphaxad, Shem lived 500 years and had other sons and daughters.

¹²When Arphaxad had lived 35 years, he became the father of Shelah. ¹³And after he became the father of Shelah, Arphaxad lived 403 years and had other sons and daughters.[b]

¹⁴When Shelah had lived 30 years, he became the father of Eber. ¹⁵And after he became the father of Eber, Shelah lived 403 years and had other sons and daughters.

¹⁶When Eber had lived 34 years, he became the father of Peleg. ¹⁷And after he became the father of Peleg, Eber lived 430 years and had other sons and daughters.

¹⁸When Peleg had lived 30 years, he became the father of Reu.

¹⁹And after he became the father of Reu, Peleg lived 209 years and had other sons and daughters.

²⁰When Reu had lived 32 years, he became the father of Serug. ²¹And after he became the father of Serug, Reu lived 207 years and had other sons and daughters.

²²When Serug had lived 30 years, he became the father of Nahor. ²³And after he became the father of Nahor, Serug lived 200 years and had other sons and daughters.

²⁴When Nahor had lived 29 years, he became the father of Terah. ²⁵And after he became the father of Terah, Nahor lived 119 years and had other sons and daughters.

²⁶When Terah had lived 70 years, he became the father of Abram, Nahor and Haran.

ᵃ*10 Father* may mean *ancestor*; also in verses 11-25.   ᵇ*12,13 Hebrew; Septuagint (see also Luke 3:35, 36 and note at Gen. 10:24) 35 years, he became the father of Cainan. ¹³And after he became the father of Cainan, Arphaxad lived 430 years and had other sons and daughters, and then he died. When Cainan had lived 130 years, he became the father of Shelah. And after he became the father of Shelah, Cainan lived 330 years and had other sons and daughters.*

After mankind has tried and failed to make a name (in Hebrew *Shem*) for themselves at Babel, the theme of the "name" is continued through the genealogy of Shem, the man whose name means "name." This genealogy ends with Abram who receives God's promise that he would make his name great (Gen 12:3). The genealogy thus functions to connect the last episode of the primeval history to the narrative of God's promise to Abram, the focal point of the remainder of the book of Genesis, of the Pentateuch, and even the Bible itself. Like chapter 5 which connects Adam to Noah, this genealogy, which connects Noah's son Shem to Abram, has ten "generations" and ends with a key person who has three sons. The life spans of the individuals in the list reduce significantly from 600 for Shem to 148 for Nahor, a mere eight "generations" later. This is the continuation of the decline in longevity which is begun in the parallel genealogy in chapter 5. There is a dramatic decline in longevity between Shem (600) and Arphaxad (438) and especially between Eber (464) and Peleg (239). One wonders whether this might be a subtle hint that there are gaps in the genealogy at those specific points.

Name	Age at birth of descendant	Years lived after the birth	Age at death
Shem	100	500	600
Arphaxad	35	403	438
Shelah	30	403	433
Eber	34	430	464
Peleg	30	209	239
Reu	32	207	239
Serug	30	200	230
Nahor	29	119	148
Terah	70	135	205
Abram	100	75	175

1. Introduction (11:10a)

11:10a This is the account of Shem.

This is yet another example of the use of the introductory formula which divides Genesis into sections. With the possible exception of Genesis 2:4a each time it introduces the section that is to follow. We have already seen this formula with the name of Shem at 10:1 where he is joined by his brothers Ham and Japheth. Here Shem is mentioned alone because of the meaning of his name (Shem means "Name" in Hebrew) and because his line leads to Abram, the subject of the next section of Genesis.

2. Ten "Generations" between Shem and Abram (11:10b-26)

11:10b Two years after the flood, when Shem was 100 years old, he became the father of Arphaxad.

Since Noah was 500 when he began having children and 600 when the flood began, his oldest child would have turned 100 when the flood began. Shem was 98[12] during the flood so, although he is listed first among Noah's sons in 5:32, he was not the oldest. The fact that Noah was 500 when he began having children and Shem is only 100 shows a rapid escalation in the pattern of decreasing

---
[12]Here I am presuming that we are dealing with exact numbers and not round numbers.

longevity after the Flood compared to the pattern prior to the Flood. Shem's name is the Hebrew word for "name" and his genealogy connects and contrasts two ways of attaining a name, that of Babel (by human effort in direct disobedience to God's will) and Abram (who by God's grace is promised, "I will make your name great"). By placing the Babel narrative first in the chapter even though the account of Shem precedes Babel chronologically, the author gives emphasis to this important theme. Humanity on its own will never achieve anything more than the confusion and injustice which great civilizations seem to inevitably produce.

11:11 And after he became the father of Arphaxad, Shem lived 500 years and had other sons and daughters.

While Shem's longevity after the Flood is substantially more than the next generations, it is substantially less than those of the pre-Flood generations. The pattern of reduction of ages down to something like that familiar to the audience's own experience continues. The fact that Shem had other sons and daughters indicates that the "genealogy" is deliberately selective. Shem's descendants through Arphaxad lead to Abram, the next major character in the book. There is no attempt to provide anything like an exhaustive genealogy in the modern sense.

11:12 When Arphaxad had lived 35 years, he became the father of Shelah.

The steep decline (from 100 to 35) in the number of years between generations beginning with Arphaxad is striking. This may be an indication that at particularly this point the genealogy is skipping over multiple generations in order to preserve the ten generations in the genealogy. This would be consistent with the theory that the name lists are especially concerned about the individuals at the beginning and end of the lists and less concerned about the generations which fill out the list. Arphaxad is listed third among the descendants of Shem in Genesis 10:22. This does not necessarily imply that he was not the eldest as the order given in Hebrew name lists is not always oldest to youngest as we have seen. The meaning of Arphaxad's name is not clear. Since Arphaxad's "siblings" in Genesis 10 are place names, it seems likely that Arphaxad refers to a land named after a descendant of Shem. The last part of the name in Hebrew, אַרְפַּכְשַׁד, (*'arpakšad*) has been equated with the *kaśdîm*, the gentilic for Chaldeans, i.e., Babylonians. The first part of the name *'arpakšad* has been related to the city Arrapḫa frequently mentioned in the Nuzi texts.[13]

11:13 And after he became the father of Shelah, Arphaxad lived 403 years and had other sons and daughters.

The fact that Arphaxad had other sons and daughters indicates that the "genealogy" is deliberately selective. Shem's descendants through Arphaxad lead to Abram, the next major character in the book.

11:14 When Shelah had lived 30 years, he became the father of Eber.

The age at which Shelah became the father of Eber (30) continues the pattern of declining numbers of years between "generations" which began with Arphaxad. The LXX as well as the Pseudepigrapha (Jubilees 8:1) and the New Testament (Luke 3:36) list a Cainan as the direct descendant of Arphaxad with Shelah being listed next. Cainan is not listed in the genealogy in the Table of Nations in Genesis 10. It seems most likely that Luke and Jubilees follow the LXX in this case. The LXX does not preserve the ten generation parallel between the genealogies in chapters 5 and 11 and this could explain the lack of Cainan in the Hebrew text. The name Shelah[14] is unattested elsewhere other than in the final part of Methu**selah**'s name. There is no known person, place, or deity of that name in the ancient Near East.[15]

11:15 And after he became the father of Eber, Shelah lived 403 years and had other sons and daughters.

Shelah's longevity after beginning the next generation is identical to his predecessor, Arphaxad, 403 years. Shem's descendants through Shelah lead to Abram, the next major character in the book. There is no attempt to provide anything like an exhaustive genealogy in the modern sense.

11:16 When Eber had lived 34 years, he became the father of Peleg.

The age at which Eber became the father of Peleg (34) continues the pattern of declining numbers of years between "generations" which began with Arphaxad.

---

[13]Hess, *Studies,* pp. 77-78

[14]Another Shelah (Genesis 38:5) occurs, but the name is spelled differently in Hebrew.

[15]Hess, *Studies,* p. 79.

11:17 And after he became the father of Peleg, Eber lived 430 years and had other sons and daughters.
11:18 When Peleg had lived 30 years, he became the father of Reu.
11:19 And after he became the father of Reu, Peleg lived 209 years and had other sons and daughters.

Shem's descendants through Eber lead to Abram, the next major character in the book. Peleg's name could reflect a Hebrew root which can mean "to divide." With Reu the number of years after fathering the next generation dramatically declines (from 430 to 209). The fact that Peleg had other sons and daughters indicates that the "genealogy" is deliberately selective. Shem's descendants through Peleg lead to Abram, the next major character in the book. There is no attempt to provide anything like an exhaustive genealogy in the modern sense.

11:20 When Reu had lived 32 years, he became the father of Serug.

The age at which Reu became the father of Serug (32) continues the pattern of declining numbers of years between "generations" which began with Arphaxad. The name Reu may be a shortened form of Reuel "friend of God"[16] or "God is a friend."[17]

11:21 And after he became the father of Serug, Reu lived 207 years and had other sons and daughters.

Reu's longevity after the birth of Serug (207 years) continues the pattern which began with Peleg. Shem's descendants through Reu lead to Abram, the next major character in the book.

11:22 When Serug had lived 30 years, he became the father of Nahor.

The age at which Serug became the father of Nahor (30) continues the pattern of declining numbers of years between "generations" which began with Arphaxad. The name Serug is commonly related to a place name in northern Mesopotamia near Haran. If so, the text is hinting by wordplay at the movement of Terah with Abram, Sarai, and Lot recorded in 11:31 from Ur to Haran.

11:23 And after he became the father of Nahor, Serug lived 200 years and had other sons and daughters.

Serug's longevity after the birth of Nahor (200 years) continues

---

[16]Sarna, *Genesis*, p. 85.
[17]Hess, *Studies*, pp. 83-85.

the pattern which began with Peleg. Shem's descendants through Serug lead to Abram, the next major character in the book.

11:24 When Nahor had lived 29 years, he became the father of Terah.

The age at which Nahor became the father of Terah (29) continues the pattern of declining numbers of years between "generations" which began with Arphaxad. Nahor's name may derive from an Akkadian root meaning "to help."[18] Similar names are found at Mari and elsewhere. There is a place east of Haran spelled similarly attested in Babylonian sources.[19]

11:25 And after he became the father of Terah, Nahor lived 119 years and had other sons and daughters.

Nahor's age at death, 148 begins to approach the life spans with which Israel was familiar. This may continue the theme of the reduction of life spans that was announced at the time of the Flood in Genesis 6:3.[20] While we have not arrived at 120, Nahor's age at death is approaching it. Shem's descendants through Nahor lead to Abram, the next major character in the book.

11:26 After Terah had lived 70 years, he became the father of Abram, Nahor and Haran.

Joshua 24:2 informs us that Terah along with his sons Abram and Nahor lived beyond (east of) the Euphrates and worshiped other gods. Genesis 31:53 refers to Laban and Jacob swearing by the God of Abraham and the gods of Nahor, their respective ancestors. The names of Terah's sons are evidently not given in chronological sequence but in order of their significance for the continuing narrative. If Abram was born when Terah was 70, he did not leave for Canaan until he was 130, not the 75 years indicated in the Hebrew text (Gen 12:4).

This last section of the Primeval History prepares the reader for the next major section of Genesis which begins in 11:27. While detailed consideration of that text must await the next volume in this commentary, here the reader is prepared for what is to follow.

---

[18]Ibid., pp. 86-87.

[19]Ibid., p. 87.

[20]Assuming, of course, that the reduction in human life spans to no more than 120 is the correct way to interpret, "[Humanity's] days will be one hundred and twenty years" (Gen. 6:3).

The genealogy of Noah's son Shem ("Name") leads to Abram. God promises him, "I will make your name great." With him God's strategy becomes focused primarily on a single man and his descendants. Ultimately it is one particular descendant of Abram, a completely faithful boy named Joshua who grew up to become Jesus the messiah, through whom God's ultimate purposes in creating have been and will be fulfilled. He is the final new Adam, the new Israel, the one descendant of Abram through whom all the nations of the earth will be blessed. Genesis 1-11 closes pointing to him.

222.1107
K619
v.1

LINCOLN CHRISTIAN UNIVERSITY

131611